*Punk was like we didn't have a map and we
didn't have an address. It was like someone
nicking a car and saying, 'Who's coming?'*

Jimmy Pursey, Sham 69

About the author

Escaping Blackpool suburbia care of punk rock, John Robb formed the Membranes in the punk wars. Fired by the DIY ethic of punk, he also edited his own fanzine, *The Rox*. He toured the world with the Membranes and put out several critically acclaimed albums. In the late Eighties he wrote for *Sounds*, the sadly defunct music paper, and was first to write about Nirvana and the upcoming Manchester scene, as well as inventing the word Britpop (sorry!). In the Nineties he put together Goldblade, who have toured the world several times with their incendiary live show and released yet more critically acclaimed albums. He has also appeared countless times on TV and films and has written bestselling books on the Stone Roses and Nineties' pop culture.

About the editor

Oliver Craske is a writer and editor specialising in music, photography and other illustrated books. He is the author of *Rock Faces*, a survey of rock music photography.

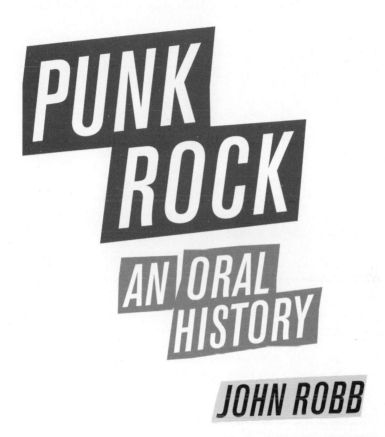

PUNK ROCK

AN ORAL HISTORY

JOHN ROBB

Edited by Oliver Craske

PM

Punk Rock: An Oral History
John Robb
© PM Press 2012

ISBN: 978–1–60486–005–4
LCCN: 2011939680

First published by Ebury Press in Great Britain 2006
Text © John Robb 2006

Interviews with John Lydon, Mark Perry, and Nils Stevenson conducted by John
Robb and reproduced by kind permission of UKTV and free@last TV. Siouxsie Sioux
interviews conducted by Michael Bracewell and reproduced by kind permission.
Keith Levene interview reproduced by kind permission of Perfect Sound Forever
online music magazine (www.perfectsoundforever.com). Chrissie Hynde interviews
reproduced by kind permission of Simon Price. All other interviews by John Robb.

PM Press
PO Box 23912
Oakland, CA 94623
www.pmpress.org

Cover by John Yates/stealworks.com

10 9 8 7 6 5 4 3 2 1

Printed in the USA on recycled paper, by the Employee Owners of Thomson-Shore
in Dexter, Michigan.
www.thomsonshore.com

CONTENTS

EDITORIAL NOTE

Selected footnotes have been added throughout, where it was felt they would add to the overall picture without interrupting the flow of the text. This has necessarily been an arbitrary process – it would be impractical to footnote everything – but we considered that the book might be impenetrable without them.

All views expressed are those of the respective speaker. The author and editor have checked facts as much as possible, but all memories are subjective and fallible and time plays strange tricks, so it is to be expected that some readers may disagree with the accounts of certain incidents. As you'll see, some contributors disagree about them too.

THE CONTRIBUTORS

A brief description appears for each contributor the first time he or she appears in the book. Where the contributor appears again later in the book, it may help you to refer to the following list, which, for ease of use, provides the same information in alphabetical form. Most contributors have had long and complex careers and these descriptions do not purport to be comprehensive profiles, but rather attempt to present the most relevant information, such as the bands and instruments with which a musician is most closely associated or those most directly relevant to the period covered in this book.

Colin Abrahall (GBH: vocals)
Gaye Advert (The Adverts: bass guitar)
Chris Bailey (The Saints: vocals)
Arturo Bassick (The Lurkers: bass)
John Bentham (Film-maker, manager of Outl4w)
Beki Bondage (Vice Squad: vocals)
Clint Boon (Inspiral Carpets: keyboards)
Billy Bragg (Riff Raff, then solo: vocals and guitar)
Michelle Brigandage (Brigandage: vocals)
Ian Brown (Stone Roses and solo: vocals)
Budgie (Big in Japan, the Slits, Siouxsie and the Banshees, the
    Creatures: drums)
J. J. Burnel (The Stranglers: bass and vocals)
Jake Burns (Stiff Little Fingers: vocals)
Garry Bushell (Journalist. The Gonads: lead vocals)
J. C. Carroll (The Members: guitar)
Nick Cash (Kilburn and the High Roads, 999: guitar and vocals)
Robin Chapekar (Bazooka Joe)
Jaz Coleman (Killing Joke: vocals)

Pat Collier (The Vibrators: bass)

Hugh Cornwell (The Stranglers: lead vocals and guitar)

Mick Crudge (The Fits: vocals)

Jeremy Cunningham (The Levellers: bass)

Andy Czezowski (Managed the Damned and Generation X. Ran
the Roxy club)

Tony D (Editor, *Ripped And Torn* and *Kill Your Pet Puppy*
fanzines)

Eric Debris (Metal Urbaine: vocals)

Deko (Dublin punk. Paranoid Visions: vocals)

Howard Devoto (Buzzcocks, Magazine: vocals)

Bob Dickinson (Journalist)

Jeremy Diggle (Student at St Martin's College, London)

Steve Diggle (Buzzcocks: guitar)

Eddie (Real name Jonathan Edwards. Bazooka Joe roadie. The
Vibrators: drums)

John Ellis (Bazooka Joe, the Vibrators and the Stranglers)

Micky Fitz (The Business: vocals)

Gavin Friday (Virgin Prunes: vocals)

David Gedge (Wedding Present: vocals)

Micky Geggus (Cockney Rejects: guitar)

Geordie (Real name Kevin Walker. Killing Joke: guitar)

Vic Godard (Subway Sect: vocals)

Charlie Harper (UK Subs: vocals)

Mark Helford (Clash fan club)

Paolo Hewitt (Writer, journalist)

Al Hillier (Punk fan; member of the 'Finchley Boys')

Peter Hook (Joy Division, New Order: bass)

Mick Hucknall (Simply Red and solo: vocals)

Kevin Hunter (Epileptics, Flux of Pink Indians: guitar)

Chrissie Hynde (The Pretenders: vocals)

Brian James (London SS, the Damned, Tanz Der Youth, Lords of
the New Church: guitar)

Tony James (London SS, Chelsea, Generation X, Sigue Sigue
Sputnik: bass)

Richard Jobson (The Skids: vocals)

Watford John (Argy Bargy: vocals)

Wilko Johnson (Dr Feelgood, Ian Dury and the Blockheads: guitar)

Mick Jones (London SS, the Clash, Big Audio Dynamite: guitar and vocals)

Andy Kanonik (Demob: vocals)

Steve Kent (The Business: guitar)

Knox (The Vibrators: guitar and vocals)

Lemmy (Motörhead: bass and lead vocals)

Don Letts (Filmmaker, DJ at the Roxy. Big Audio Dynamite: effects and vocals)

Keith Levene (The Clash, Public Image Limited: guitar)

Rob Lloyd (The Prefects, the Nightingales: vocals)

John Lydon (The Sex Pistols, Public Image Limited: vocals)

Malcolm McLaren (Manager of the Sex Pistols)

Paul Madden (Photographer)

Noel Martin (Menace: drums)

Glen Matlock (The Sex Pistols: bass. Rich Kids: bass and vocals.)

Mensi (Real name Thomas Mensforth. Angelic Upstarts: vocals)

Pauline Murray (Penetration, the Invisible Girls: vocals)

Colin Newman (Wire: vocals)

Gene October (Chelsea: vocals)

Damian O'Neill (The Undertones: guitar)

John O'Neill (The Undertones: guitar)

Mark Perry (Editor, *Sniffin' Glue* fanzine. Alternative TV: vocals)

Marco Pirroni (Siouxsie and the Banshees, the Models, Rema Rema, Adam and the Ants: guitar)

Tessa Pollitt (The Slits: bass)

Jimmy Pursey (Sham 69: vocals)

Aki Qureshi (Southern Death Cult, Fun-Da-Mental: drums and producer)

Ranking Roger (The Beat: vocals)

Paul Research (The Scars: guitar)

Eugene Reynolds (The Rezillos: vocals)

Marc Riley (The Fall; BBC Radio 1 DJ 'Lard')

Penny Rimbaud (Crass: drums and ideology)

Richie Rocker (MDM: bass)

Henry Rollins (Black Flag, the Henry Rollins Band: vocals)

Mick Rossi (Slaughter and the Dogs: guitar)

Rat Scabies (London SS, the Damned, the White Cats: drums)

Segs (Real name Vince Segs. The Ruts: bass)

Captain Sensible (The Damned: bass and lead guitar. Also solo: vocals)

Steve Severin (Siouxsie and the Banshees: bass)

Pete Shelley (Buzzcocks: Guitar and vocals)

Adrian Sherwood (Producer)

Siouxsie Sioux (Siouxsie and the Banshees, the Creatures: vocals)

T. V. Smith (The Adverts: lead vocals)

Neville Staple (The Specials, Fun Boy Three: vocals)

Linder Sterling (Artist and photographer. Ludus: vocals)

Nils Stevenson (Early co-manager of the Sex Pistols; manager of
    Siouxsie and the Banshees)

Mark Stewart (The Pop Group: vocals)

Paul Stolper (Art dealer and punk collector)

Poly Styrene (X-Ray Spex: lead vocals)

Justin Sullivan, aka Slade the Leveller (New Model Army: vocals)

Barney Sumner (Joy Division: guitar. New Order: vocals and guitar)

Terrie (The Ex: guitar)

Nicky Tesco (The Members: vocals)

Mike Thorne (A&R at EMI; producer of Wire)

Tom (Punk fan from Middlesborough)

Guy Trelford (Punk fan, writer from Northern Ireland)

Ari Up (The Slits: vocals)

Tom Vague (Editor of *Vague* fanzine)

Gee Vaucher (Artwork for Crass)

Nick Wells (Student at St Martin's College, London)

Tony Wilson (Broadcaster. Founder of Factory Records)

Jah Wobble (Public Image Limited: bass)

Brian X (London punk)

Brian Young (Rudi: vocals and guitar)

FOREWORD
BY MICHAEL BRACEWELL

In the 30 years since the first rumblings of punk occurred in the UK, the movement – such as it was – has become a cultural industry to rival those around Andy Warhol's Factory, the Beatles or the Bloomsbury Group. There is an unintentional irony, therefore, in Malcolm McLaren's pronouncement, back on the barricades of 1976, that 'history is for pissing on'. As it transpires, many of the people who were responsible for creating punk have become either conscientious archivists and careful caretakers of their own memories, or at least profoundly aware that they were briefly a part of something extraordinary.

There have been any number of books concerning British punk – most famously Jon Savage's *England's Dreaming: Sex Pistols and Punk Rock*, which in many ways has become the magnetic north by which other histories of the period have taken their bearings. But where many books have sought to survey punk or champion its mythology, John Robb's *Punk Rock: An Oral History* is the first detailed study of the period to be based entirely on the recollections and insights of the people who participated in punk and witnessed its rise and change. And herein lies its scope and its intimacy.

Naturally, punk sought to booby trap its own history by making a rhetorical fetish of the slogan 'No Future'. And, equally naturally, many of punk's founding participants are deeply uneasy of enshrining punk's core years (between 1976 and 1978) in any form of sentimental nostalgia for a somehow better time. What is remarkable therefore is the way in which, despite such denials, punk is still

FOREWORD
BY HENRY ROLLINS

Punk rock changed music forever. Punk came at the right time and did the right thing. The better albums from the genre hold up without failure no matter what has happened in the world of music since their release.

Bands like the Damned, the Sex Pistols, the Clash, X-Ray Spex and Generation X are perhaps not iconic in the classic sense as the punk ethos would thankfully preclude such deification. That being said, they all looked really cool, didn't they? Watching old footage of the Clash or another punk band from those early days still can make one pause.

The truth is that these bands were more than good—they were great. They were saying something. Rock'n'roll took a sound thrashing from punk and both were all the better for it.

Punk rock saved a lot of people's sanity, emboldened the timid and gave countless youth all over the world a voice.

It's been many years since the original bands played sometimes brilliantly, sometime raggedly on less than good gear, in front of small and sometimes abusive audiences in adverse conditions. In that time, much has been written. Biographies, historical overviews and the like, often by writers who were not there. It happens.

That's what makes *Punk Rock: An Oral History* such a tremendous document and worthwhile read.

The book is valuable on all levels. To get an understanding of how some of punk rock's most memorable players started, what music they were listening to before they started playing, what alliances they made and the challenges they faced, not only makes listening to the records more interesting but allows one to understand the cause and effect of punk rock.

Decades after the first punk bands hit stage, the genre is here to stay. It's all too easy to take it for granted and to miss out on what is to be learned by getting an understanding of how it all came to be.

It's a great story, too. There's lots of naiveté, ego, guts, talent, all the expected recklessness, excess, and pretenders but also some true visionaries whose contributions deserve mention.

John Robb took on a monumental task in making this book. It was obviously a lot of work and anyone with less knowledge of punk music would have produced a lesser work.

Now that punk rock has been around long enough to become your parents' music, now that it sits quite comfortably in box sets and expanded editions, complete with color photos and liner notes, it is relevant to read the stories from the people who were actually there.

Many of the people interviewed in this book are very close to sixty years old. Here we are, indeed. It is, at this point, completely fine to let the belt out a couple of notches and say that many of them were damn heroic and conclude that their music changed people's lives.

You might as well get it from those who sweated through it the first time.

INTRO

Punk changed everything.

Not just our trousers.

Our lives.

Everyone came into punk with a different agenda, and everyone who left took their own version of events with them. And the rest of us stayed there, still burning with the bright inspiration of the revolution.

Before punk we were a generation waiting for a soundtrack. The Sixties hung over everything, a party that everyone heard about but nobody could get into. The early Seventies had some great music but we wanted something of our own.

Watching, goggle-eyed, the wam-bam-thank-you-glam of the early Seventies on the never-ending freak show *Top of the Pops* was one thing, but making music yourself was a sheer impossibility. Only rock stars from outer space did it, or those funny kids no one ever spoke to who hung out in the music room at school.

Growing up in Blackpool in the Seventies was to grow up on the outside looking in. The tatty seaside town was already rusting away from its glory days of the Fifties. We'd go and watch the mighty Tangerines (Blackpool FC) and come home disappointed. We felt a million miles away from the centre of the world in our windswept, safe European home. And then punk rock came along like a freakin' thunderbolt.

Punk rock was a culture war. You were either on the bus or off the bus.

1975 was boring.

1976 wasn't much better. A life in the civil service stretched out in front of me and I wasn't having that. I had to get out. I didn't want some shitty job. I didn't care about going to university.

I saw photos of punk rockers in the papers, and I knew instantly what they sounded like. Never had a music and its threads been so closely associated. Life is not just about existing, it's about living at 100 miles an hour. But living in the mid-Seventies in a rainswept town was living in the monochrome, and I needed escape and colour.

And then, hanging round the ice rink in Blackpool, where you went when you were fifteen in 1976, I heard 'Anarchy In The UK'. It was a revelation: a lumbering wall-of-sound intro and the most amazing vocal I'd ever heard. Who cares if John Lydon is cynical as fuck about it all now? In 1976 his voice sounded like liberation. He was also funny, sharp and said all the stuff that everyone felt – the skinny punk kid who spat back at the hypocrisy of the establishment.

Why write an oral history of punk? Well, why not get the story from the horses' mouths? Jon Savage has already done the definitive punk history, and *Burning Britain* is a great account of the second wave. I just wanted the story direct from the people who were there, and I wanted their story and not the rubbish theories that were added on afterwards. I wanted the story that didn't stick to the official punk rock party line.

It's a lot more complex than that. It's not just a bunch of Bowie freaks creating punk whilst hanging round the Sex shop. It's not just the Clash's heroic quest. It's also the foot soldiers of the revolution: the smaller groups, the less hip groups. It's Vic Godard's genius eccentricity, J. J. Burnel's supercool karate-kicking bass sound, Adam Ant's charismatic S&M black leather pop for the sexpeople, Linder's stunning artwork, Siouxsie Sioux's iconic style, Jimmy Sham's heartfelt anthems for the kids, Pete Shelley's knack for knocking out saucy pop classics.

It's also the legions of spotty kids up and down the UK, the fresh-faced youth you'd see bouncing up and down in the bruised Victoriana dancehalls, delirious with excitement in their rough-hewn punk rock outfits – inside-out school blazers and home-made badges – climbing through the dressing-room window as Joe Strummer sneaked them in on one of those iconic Clash tours. It's the DIY brigade fumbling with musical instruments, trying to make sense of the world with three chords learned last week on second-hand guitars. It's scruffy nervous bands onstage for the first time in youth clubs and church halls. It's the battered prose bashed out on battered typewriters as the Xerox generation started the insanely-detailed documenting of perhaps the first pop culture to analyse itself to death.

It's all that crazed, bug-eyed energy, the cheap drugs and the crap snogs, and always the amazing music coming at you every week on seven-inch singles, complete with day-glo cut-up artwork and yet another angular band posing on the back.

You could go anywhere in the UK and speak to anyone who had spiky hair. It was a secret society, a world within a world, with the most intense and glorious soundtrack, the best clothes, the fiercest debate, the most idealistic politics. It changed everybody's life who was touched by it.

But the best thing about it was that we were not just passive consumers: we owned it as well. We were all involved. It wasn't just the superstar groups dictating the debate. We all were! Everyone had their own version of punk. Everyone decided what punk was *for them*. There were endless arguments about what we were fighting for, what we should be wearing on our feet, what we should listen to and how we were going to change the fucking world. It was the first pop culture driven by the grassroots, by the kids.

Its energy never dissipated. It goes on forever, worldwide: great gigs, great festivals, great people.

Punk terrified the establishment.

Punk made me get onstage and make music.

Punk made me change my world.

Punk...

Punk saved my life.

And I wanted to know why...

Twist and shout! Iggy Pop bends over backwards and helps to invent punk rock at the Stooges' only UK appearance, in London at the Scala in 1972

CHAPTER 1
1950/69: THE ROOTS OF PUNK

Where does punk rock start? 1976? 1975? Does it start with the Stooges, or can we go back to the Stones, to Elvis or further back to medieval times and beyond? There is no doubt that rebel songs have always been with us, from crazed loons singing anti-imperial songs in Roman times to wild-eyed medieval minstrels enlightening the market place with their toothless anti-authoritarian rants. It's always been with us, that wild spirit, that outsider cry. It's only recently it's been with electricity – and louder and wilder.

Punk rock as we know it was a culmination of everything that had gone on in pop before, from the electric filth of hard rock, the wild abandon of the Stooges, the mass media fuck of Elvis, the pure revolution promised by the hippies, the sharp lines of the mods and the sneering rebel shapes of the rockers, to the stomping pop blitzkrieg of glam rock – even the experimentation of prog rock and Seventies underground art rock. Punk didn't just come from the love of Ziggy Stardust. It came from everywhere: from the Beatles to glam, from Iggy to the Sweet, from pub rock to Captain Beefheart. Punk pulled these strands together and when it all finally coalesced in the UK in 1977 it went straight to the heart of the establishment. The interviews in this book show just how diverse the backgrounds of the key players were. Everything wild and colourful has been referenced.

For the fashionistas it only lasted a few months, but whilst they were squeezing their lardy hipster arses into the trite (and frankly quite rubbish) New Romantic outfits, punk went underground and re-emerged as the second wave, and a plethora of other punk-influenced scenes from goth to psychobilly to anarcho-punk to 2 Tone, and more besides – a whole bunch of vital music scenes that along with punk rock have become the key influence on all the best modern music and the yardstick by which it is measured.

THE MASS MEDIA F.U.C.K. OF ELVIS
Early Rock'n'Roll and the Birth of the Modern Rebel Song

Penny Rimbaud (Crass: drums and ideology)

I listened to Bill Haley before Elvis, but it didn't hit me in the way that rock'n'roll hit me later. 'Rock Around The Clock' and 'See You Later Alligator' seemed like music hall. It didn't knock me in a physical way, it was much more cerebral – if a kid of twelve or thirteen could be cerebral! I remember pedalling home on my bike with a copy of Bill Haley's 'Oh When The Saints'. My brother stopped me by the village pond and he got really cross. He was into jazz. We had a huge row about the fact I was polluting good music.

I went out and bought Elvis the moment it came out. Oddly, all the Teds were really into Bill Haley more than Elvis. Elvis made rock'n'roll sexy and sexual, and it was the first time I realised I was a sexual person.

I was also listening to English jazz, and some American stuff like Gerry Mulligan which was groovy cool stuff. The English stuff like Humphrey Lyttelton was great. Humphrey got a sax and that was considered really wicked and all the trad jazz people ruled him out.

Hugh Cornwell (The Stranglers: lead vocals and guitar)

The first music I liked? I suppose it would have been Cliff Richard.[1]
It was a period of discovery and these artists were appearing out of
nowhere. The English ones were there, but they weren't affecting
me as much as the Everly Brothers or Buddy Holly around at the
same time. So until Cliff came along and had those early hits I don't
think anything touched the American stuff.

I'd already discovered Chuck Berry. I was playing along to his
songs. I discovered Chuck Berry through my other brother who had
a big record collection of jazz stuff as well. He was into jazz and
when he would go out he would tell me not to touch his records,
but I would go through them anyway! I discovered Art Blakey,
Mose Allison – I was very lucky I had these other siblings who liked
these kinds of music I was into at a really early age.

Lemmy (Motörhead: bass and lead vocals)

I saw Little Richard at the Cavern in Liverpool in the Fifties. That
was incredible. I was living on Anglesey at the time, so you can
imagine how mind blowing that was. Pretty soon I was a bit of
a Ted.

Penny Rimbaud

I hung out with some kids at public school. We were the naughty
boys that hung out with the bad boys above Burton's, where the
pool table was in Brentwood. There was a terrific tension there with
the squaddies and the Teds, and we were the poncey public schoolboys trying to get a bit of action between everyone. It all felt so
dangerous and exciting. There was something about the Teds that
was really thrilling. They taught me that the world of my father
wasn't the only world.

---

1. Unlike his later schlocky sentimentality, Cliff's first single 'Move It' was a great slice of
rock'n'roll.

Charlie Harper (UK Subs: vocals)

As a kid my first kind of passion was early rock'n'roll. All the greats: Elvis, Jerry Lee, Chuck Berry, Bo Diddley. In the Fifties there was the Notting Hill riots going on, and some kids at our school became racists and decided to get rid of their black records, and because I loved Chuck Berry I got a lot of their record collections off them for pennies. I got into people like Larry Williams, things I would never have heard of otherwise – Big Bopper, Jerry Lee Lewis – things like that.

One of the earliest things I bought was an album by Cliff Richard and the Drifters, as the Shadows were called then. When I was fifteen I left school. I was still very interested in music. I decided I wanted to be an artist and go to Paris. I went to Montmartre, where all the artists hang out, to find out that everyone painted with paper knives not a brush. I was completely overwhelmed; I had no skill at all. I loafed around Paris and went to this café which had rock'n'roll records. Rock'n'roll was big in France.

Knox (The Vibrators: guitar and vocals)

I saw people like Gene Vincent in Watford – I saw him twice in one of those package shows that go round. I saw Eddie Cochrane when I was about thirteen; that was good. Johnny Kidd and the Pirates were very good.[2] Also Cliff Richard and the Shadows – some of the early stuff was really good. 'Move It' was great. It's a pity they didn't carry on their direction, the Shadows. 'Apache', that's a great song too.

Glen Matlock (The Sex Pistols: bass. Rich Kids: bass and vocals)

The first music I was into when I was a kid was a pile of old rock-

---

2. Links can clearly be traced from Johnny Kidd, arguably the first real hardcore British rock'n'roll act, to punk. Dressed as a rocker pirate, complete with eye patch, Kidd's tough music was a precursor to all British hard rock, along with the late great Vince Taylor. Their debut single, 1959's 'Please Don't Touch', and 1960's 'Shakin' All Over' are two of the greatest British rock'n'roll records ever. Kidd died in a car crash in 1966. Mick Green, guitar player in the later Pirates line-up, was a big influence on Wilko Johnson (see chapter 2), who in turn was a key influence on punk and post-punk guitarists.

'n'roll 78s from my uncle – like Little Richard, Jerry Lee Lewis, some raunchy stuff that sunk in at an early age, and then a couple of years later it was the beat boom, the Kinks, Small Faces and Yardbirds, and that was what really sunk in, that mad over-the-top guitar sound thundering out of the radio really got me.

Everything seemed to revolve round the Small Faces, the moddish kind of thing. I had my moments but I was too young to be a mod – I dabbled with that kind of look, I suppose. To me, the mods were very much a Sixties thing. They were the real thing. When I met Steve and Paul they seemed to be from a very similar kind of background. They were into bands like the Faces and the Who. This was 1973 when I met Steve, Paul and Wally.[3]

Growing up in the Sixties, everything was looking to the future. I'm still waiting for my jet pack and flying cars! It was all *Tomorrow's World* back then. There was always that element of modernism. So the songs don't sound 25 or 30 years old now.

WHEN WE WAS FAB
Beatles, Stones, Mods and More

Kevin Hunter (Epileptics, Flux of Pink Indians: guitar)

At school I was always into pop stuff. My parents took me to see the Beatles but I don't remember much about it. I was knee high. It was at Margate Winter Gardens early in '63 – the gig was arranged before they made it big. I remember two shows, including one in the early evening for parents and kids, when the hall wasn't very full.

I always liked chart singles. The first one I bought was a Hollies single, but I was always getting into stuff with a harsher edge, and I remember getting into Kinks stuff then. I couldn't tell you what I liked about it.

---

3. Steve Jones, Paul Cook and Wally Nightingale, who in 1973, along with Matlock, formed the first incarnation of the band that would become the Sex Pistols, called the Strand.

Lemmy

In 1964 I was in Manchester, dossing around in Stockport and Cheetham Hill. I joined this band called the Rockin' Vicars.[4] We played all over town – Oldham, Ashton. We used to go to the Twisted Wheel but never played there. We played the Cavern as well, the Manchester one that's now buried underneath that fucking horrible shopping centre they put there. Manchester was great. It was like Liverpool: there were lots of bands. We knew the Hollies and Herman's Hermits. We all used to hang around in that guitar shop on Oxford Street, Barretts. We played with Manfred Mann. The Rockin' Vicars always topped the bill, except once when we played the Free Trade Hall with the Hollies – it's a long story but our drummer succeeded in being a complete cunt and destroyed the stage under himself and fell into a hole! [laughs] It was a lesson you would have thought he would have profited from but I'm afraid not!

Al Hillier (Punk fan. Member of the 'Finchley Boys')

The Beatles had an enormous effect on most people in the mid-Sixties, and they certainly did on me. My mum would religiously drag me down to Jones Bros on the Holloway Road, and after a quick listen on the headphones or snuggle together in a sound booth she would rush to the counter and buy it.

When the Beatles films were released, and in particular *Help!*, the Beatles suddenly seemed magical to me. Their antics opened up a whole new world for madcap pop performers and without doubt made it possible for zany bands like the Monkees to exist. At primary school I invented a 'band' of my own called the Tigers. The thrill of running about the playground being chased by all the girls because I was a 'pop star' lives with me to this day.

The Rolling Stones were the accepted antidote to the Beatles and I also really liked them. Even as a youngster I liked the more

---

4. Rockin' Vicars were a wild proto-punk band who were based in Manchester and then Blackpool in the late Sixties. Lemmy was in the band for the last couple of years of their existence. Oh, and they wore vicar outfits onstage sometimes.

aggressive risk-taking, law-breaking, drug-using image that surrounded the Stones. Images of Hell's Angels at Altamont cemented this and placed them in my young mind alongside the likes of Jimi Hendrix, who always looked so totally different and cool. When he appeared on TV he never looked like he could give a fuck about anything, an aura that J. J. Burnel was to try and recreate to some degree a few years later.

My interest in the Doors came later, even though I was in Paris on a school trip not more than a few hundred yards from the building in the rue Beautreillis where Jim Morrison died on 3 July 1971 – literally a stone's throw from our Parisian hotel.

Penny Rimbaud

What the Beatles did was to confirm the political element. John Lennon made me realise you could be a voice in your own right. Up till then you had to have a university degree or have studied philosophy to have an opinion, and I always had opinions and had been shouted down. What Lennon helped me to do was to realise that my own opinions were as valid as anyone else's.

Steve Diggle (Buzzcocks: guitar)

We had loads of records: Elvis' 'Wooden Heart', all that Charlie Drake stuff, and Bernard Cribbins![5] I grew up with the Beatles, Stones, early Who and Bob Dylan. There was a girl across the road who had the first Dylan album, a friend of mine had the first Beatles album, and those was the first real things I heard. A couple of doors down my cousin was a Teddy boy and he was playing Little Richard and Elvis, really good rock'n'roll. I got into the Velvet Underground when I was fourteen, the psychedelic thing.

I was a bit of a mod. I remember going to Belle Vue in Manchester and seeing people with 'The Who' on their parkas in

---

5. Charlie Drake and Bernard Cribbins were both well known in the Fifties and Sixties for novelty records such as 'My Boomerang Won't Come Back' (Drake) and 'Right Said Fred' (Cribbins).

1965. That seemed amazing, and I always wanted a scooter. Townshend was smashing the guitars, and the Stones and the Beatles were telling you things that your mum and dad couldn't tell you – that subculture was there.

I thought it was too complicated being in a band. I was enjoying being in street gangs and getting into trouble round Rusholme and Bradford in Manchester, and then Ardwick, and that was the real thing for me. I remember walking down the street in a suede jacket and people shouting stuff. If you dressed weirdly in those terraced streets in those days you would get a lot of hassle. That kind of thing toughens you up. It was like *Coronation Street*: proper northern, where you knew all the neighbours and you got into trouble breaking windows – and that all made me politically aware of things, the environment and your frustrations.

Charlie Harper

When I went back home to London, after living in Paris, the Sixties were happening. I was going to clubs and the Rolling Stones were happening at the time. I fell in love with them and followed them everywhere – my nickname was Charlie Stones. I got to know Brian Jones a little bit; he liked my clothes and shoes. I was wearing more of a beatnik kind of look. I had these kind of sandals painted green that I dyed with leather dye and he loved them.

The Stones played down Ken Colyer's 51 Club. They had an r'n'b night every week – Friday, I think. On Sunday they played the Richmond Railway Hotel, then they would play youth clubs round London. I saw them when I could – quite often that was three times a week. When they made it I saw them at Tooting Granada, a seated cinema. Me and my mate got seats near the front. They came on and three quarters of the audience were young girls screaming, and everyone stood up jigging round. These girls got so excited they would swing down the front over the seats, and my mate got trapped and broke his leg.

After the Stones I got into the Pretty Things. All these clubs had at least one resident band, like John Mayall at the Marquee – that was still jazz-orientated. I'll never forget being down the 100 Club when the Kinks had just been on tour. 'You Really Got Me' had just jumped into the charts and they were the normal residency band down there. A hundred of us would turn up and suddenly 300 girls are down there, just like that.

I was a busker and I would play folk music in summer. I would go to the south of France or Spain with my guitars, and play on the champagne cruise boats going between Spain and the south of France. I'd go to St Tropez and drink Spanish champagne at four bob a bottle. We used to play anything. I never forget the first time I busked in Nice. You'd have your hat destroyed by the end of the evening, there was so much money in it.

Hugh Cornwell

It was an amazing period. We were discovering stuff all the time: it was a really amazing moment listening to the Stones' 'Not Fade Away' for the first time. God, that was electric! When I was fifteen I was going to the Marquee and I saw everybody: the Yardbirds, the Who, Steve Winwood's band before Traffic.[6] And I really loved the Graham Bond Organisation. It was so different, and a bit jazzy as well – it didn't have a guitar in it, mainly organ. Brilliant.

I just went down there on my own. I became a member. It was very civilised. I never used to drink or take drugs. I'd just stand there and watch the music. I never talked to anyone. I was really young. When the Who played there I wore a black roll-necked sweater and made their motif out of felt and stuck it on.

Brian James (London SS, the Damned, Tanz Der Youth, Lords of the New Church: guitar)

As a kid, I was into people like the Stones and the Yardbirds and then the Who, but there was also a blues thing I was into as well – John

---

6. The Spencer Davis Group.

Mayall, Peter Green. That made me check out the American guys, great artists, and think, 'Who writes this? Where did it come from?'

I saw a lot of people play live. I saw John Lee Hooker at the Starlight Ballroom during the late Sixties. He was backed up by the Savoy Blues Band, who did their own set first, then Hooker came on and took the place apart. And B. B. King at the Albert Hall, with amazing support – it might even have been Peter Green's Fleetwood Mac.[7]

Mick Jones (London SS, the Clash, Big Audio Dynamite: guitar and vocals)

I was in the Animals' fan club and the Kinks' fan club when I was really young. I would spend Saturdays going to Cheyne Walk and standing outside where Mick Jagger and Keith Richards used to live. We stood there early one Saturday evening looking down the railings – this was Mick Jagger's house – and he came up to the window and someone pulled the blinds down. We went along to the next window and they shut the window. And then we would go along to Keith's house. That was what we'd do on Saturdays, and then we would go down Carnaby Street.

Knox

I had bands at school. I had a band called Knox and the Nightriders, and the Renegades, when I was fourteen or fifteen – we played r'n'b covers. I was little bit of a Teddy boy at school. I had a bit of a quiff. I saw the Beatles at least once, the Stones a couple of times – I saw them in the Gaumont in Watford. There would be these package tours with six or eight bands on, and we'd go and see all the bands – there were thousands of people in the place.

We used to go and see Screaming Lord Sutch come out of his coffin. I even saw Jimi Hendrix when he played upstairs in the Manor House in London. We thought it wouldn't be that good and

---

7. Fleetwood Mac backed B. B. King at the Albert Hall on 22 April 1969.

hesitated, and it was like, my God! It was really loud, he was doing stuff like 'Hey Joe' and Bob Dylan's 'Like A Rolling Stone'.

In the mid-Sixties we were playing youth clubs, 21sts, weddings and things. I was the singer and guitar player, and it was a four-piece band with another guitar player. We were only little kids and we got all this work. We used to play tons of stuff, mainly what you heard in the charts at the time. We stopped playing to concentrate on A-levels, then I went to art school and I started doing r'n'b bands. There were so many guitar players I switched to keyboards for a few months, as there were not many keyboard players. Then I moved to Bristol in 1965. I didn't really like the music in these r'n'b bands.

I was then in Edinburgh for a few years. For some of the time I was living off my paintings – I was broke, but making some money off them. Edinburgh was good: I worked in fringe theatre as a waiter there, cooking. You would meet everybody there. I met Michael Elphick, Stephen Rea, and later I met Robbie Coltrane, some of the Scaffold, and Mike Radford the film director.

Rat Scabies (London SS, the Damned, the White Cats: drums)

The Who on *Top of the Pops*, Rolling Stones and Beatles stuff – they were the first bands I liked. I was born in Kingston near London. The first records I had were the Dave Clark Five, Sandy Nelson and a few jazz things as well.[8] There was a lot of jazz around in those days on the radio – that was the commercial norm then, crooners or jazz stuff. There wasn't a Radio One or a Radio Two then. There wasn't very much going on. I remember watching the mods and rockers in the newspapers. I remember going down the local fairground and hundreds of kids turning up on scooters. It wasn't something that affected me; I was too young for that. I watched it happen without really understanding it.

---

8. Nelson was a popular American rock'n'roll drummer in the late Fifties and early Sixties, who had hits like 'Teen Beat'. He specialised in instrumental records containing drum solos.

I always had a deep love for the drums anyway; it was just there, an inborn thing really. That's why I liked the Dave Clark Five, and that's why I liked the jazz thing – they always had a drum solo. I remember watching Eric Delaney, the Big Band drummer, at the London Palladium and he had two bass drums. He was the star drummer of the day – they put light bulbs in his drums. He was a terribly innovative bloke, with big tympanis. I saw him on TV once and I got a kid's kit off my parents. They were just toys. Much later I got a proper kit, in the late Sixties when I was ten or eleven.

In the late Sixties I listened to the Who. They had Keith Moon and they used to smash up the gear. I liked groups with a lot of attitude and there were not many. I didn't like the Stones very much because they were weird and scruffy. I didn't like the Beatles that much either; they were clean and tidy. The Kinks were around too, but they didn't smash up the gear. I liked anything that had a lot of drums in.

John O'Neill (The Undertones: guitar)

My first recollection was my big brother Jim's records. He was three years older than me, a Beatles collector. *Sgt Pepper* was the first record I listened to. In our whole house we were all big Beatles fans, avidly waiting for Boxing Day for the Beatles film. We never missed that. It was the best part of Christmas.

Budgie (Big in Japan, the Slits, Siouxsie and the Banshees, the Creatures: drums)

I grew up in St Helens. I've got a distant memory of Pilkingtons Glassworks. Not a lot of prospects. It was like an overspill from Liverpool. Now there are no St Helens accents in the town any more – it's all Scouse accents! It was a kind of older brother/older sister syndrome: they had the rock collections and the Dansette record players. It was the Beatles and then my sister got into the Walker Brothers and P. J. Proby. My brother was into the Animals, Pretty Things. Beyond the Beatles and Stones there was like a Kinks compilation. Ray Davies was a real pioneer.

T. V. Smith (The Adverts: lead vocals)

The Beatles was the first pop that meant something to me, and the Rolling Stones represented the alternative – when I was about six!

Gaye Advert (The Adverts: bass guitar)

The Monkees and the Beatles were mad fixations for me. Later there was Black Sabbath and Led Zeppelin. There must have been something in between, but I don't know what. Some older friends had the Black Sabbath album and thought it was great and that's how I got into it. Then Frank Zappa, Captain Beefheart and all that related stuff, Alice Cooper. Then the New York Dolls – and Iggy. I was at art college at the time – Nick, my boyfriend, he'd got it. I thought it was brilliant and I got everything related to it.

There was a record shop in Torquay where you could get these records. Living in Bideford in Devon, I relied on Virgin mail order, which was brilliant – you could send off for something before release date. And they often used to send the wrong record, or send more than one copy. I got three copies of Pink Floyd's *Ummagumma*! I sent off for Can's *Monster Movie* but I got the *Midnight Cowboy* soundtrack sent instead! It was exciting to get these records down there. There were only four or five of us into that kind of stuff. But you didn't have a chance in hell of *seeing* any of these bands. I only saw the Dolls for the first time last year at Reading Festival!

Wilko Johnson (Dr Feelgood, Ian Dury and the Blockheads: guitar)

I didn't know much about music. The Rolling Stones, I suppose, when they came round, and then when I was sixteen I saw the Beatles. Listening to the Stones got me into American rhythm and blues, and that's what got me into music. I just fancied myself with a guitar! I'm talking about Sixties r'n'b, Stax, the Chess label – the Chicago blues people. I never tried to play blues. But everyone was in a band, and you always played the same r'n'b type of songs.

I had been playing in a band in school in the mid-Sixties, and when I went to university in 1967 I took my guitar with me. But I couldn't find a band so I left it at home under the bed. I didn't think about playing again. I just left it for three years of university and travelling.

Siouxsie Sioux (Siouxsie and the Banshees, the Creatures: vocals)

Being slightly disturbed by visual imagery was always more important to me than seeing a Doris Day movie. That said, my mum used to take me to see Elvis and Doris Day films, and I recognised them for what they were. But the Wicked Queen in *Snow White*, when she appears in the storm as a hag, was much more what I liked. At the same time, I loved Busby Berkeley and *42nd Street*.[9] I like playing with contrast; having a balance and a flatness to something has never attracted me. And so I can see why I'm attracted to certain styles – to the 1920s, for example, or to the early Op Art of Bridget Riley.[10]

I suppose that the suburbs inspired intense hatred. And I think that the lure of London was always there. I remember my sister taking me to Biba on Kensington High Street; I bought a coat, and used to gravitate towards going there on my own later. But the suburbs were a yardstick for measuring how much you didn't fit in, as well. Where we lived was very residential, with neighbours all around, and our house seemed different. It wasn't red brick, to begin with – it was white stucco with a flat roof, and with trees. Everyone else had gardens with patios and neatly cut lawns, and we had these massive copper beech trees at the front, and a huge privet hedge. You could not look into our house! All the others were almost inviting you to look in at the neat net curtains – life in all its normality was being paraded. Which probably wasn't the case behind closed doors, but that was the perception.

---

9. Berkeley was a great Hollywood choreographer of the Thirties, who created spectacular and sometimes surreal fantasy dance sequences in films including *42nd Street* (1933) and *Gold Diggers of 1935* (1935).

10. British artist who emerged in the Sixties as a leader of the Op Art movement, best known for her optically vibrant paintings employing black and white lines or curves.

I think that just because of the kind of family we were, there was definitely a sense of not feeling a part of the community, or of being neighbourly. I was very aware of us being very different. My father had a drink problem, which also sensitised that feeling. I would definitely say that our early material, for at least the first two albums, was suburbia – where I grew up, and the circumstances.

Certainly music was the one big thing that made everything seem OK. So long as the music was playing, it was definitely a time of forgetting differences and problems. It was a cause of happiness within the family, and laughter, and fun. My first love affair with a record was with John Leyton's 'Johnny Remember Me' – which I have since found out was produced by Joe Meek, who was a real character himself.[11] It had these amazing, ghostly backing vocals, a great melody, and it was about a dead girlfriend, basically. I was obsessed by it. I was probably about three or four when it came out, in 1961, and I used to have to get somebody to put it on the record player for me.

As I got older I loved a lot of the Tamla Motown and a lot of r'n'b: Aretha Franklin, the Temptations. And then there was the usual Beatles and Stones. I really got into the 'White Album'. I'd loved the pop Beatles – 'Love Me Do' and so on – but the 'White Album' really meant a lot. I think that pop music for me was definitely escapist, but never studious. I was never attracted to being a very proficient singer or player. I suppose I was interested in creating a vision; in the same way that I was very drawn to tension within cinema. Hitchcock was my other early obsession – *Psycho*, and its score. I loved the almost unbearable tension of, 'What's going to happen?' Joe Meek, if you like, was using the studio in a similar kind of way, as a laboratory in which to experiment with sound. So there was the sense of trying to create an atmosphere: how a sound resonates and makes an effect. And that has always been very important for me.

---

11. Joe Meek was a British pop genius, producing amazing pop soundscapes in a tiny bedsit flat in Islington, London. A true innovator, he developed key studio equipment like compressors. His most famous production was the Tornados' 'Telstar'. He committed suicide in 1967.

Steve Severin (Siouxsie and the Banshees: bass)

The first music I was into was the Beatles. The time my parents bought the 'Twist And Shout' EP for me was the first time any kind of pop music got into my consciousness. After that it was the Stones and then the floodgates opened! Music was my passion from then on, and I had an alphabetical knowledge of records. I was like a complete nerd about it! I knew who played bass, who played drums, which studio it was recorded in on every record. The first album I bought was Cream's *Disraeli Gears*. I remember when we were at school the Beatles' 'White Album' came out and how excited everybody was. It was like a major event. That sort of weirder stuff got in the charts then, mixing it up with the schmaltzy ballads, the older crooners – that's what made it more exciting.

Noel Martin (Menace: drums)

When I was younger I was into the Beatles and the Stones. The first album I bought was *Abbey Road*. I remember sitting down with speakers at either side of my head marvelling at the way the sound jumped around from side to side. I wasn't so much into the music as the production. How did they do that? From there I was a Deep Purple kind of guy. It was about the musicianship – Ian Paice was great on the drums – and then it was pretty much Thin Lizzy because of the Irish connection and then into punk.

ROOTS RADICALS
Dread Meets the Punk Rockers Uptown

Neville Staple (The Specials, Fun Boy Three: vocals)

The first music I got into was reggae, ska and bluebeat – Prince Buster, I Roy, Duke Reid, people like that. I was in Jamaica, then in 1960 I came over to the UK to grow up in Rugby, then I came to Coventry. I lived in Manchester, I lived in London, Sheffield, Huddersfield, all over.

With a beef in his heart: the genius Don Van Vliet twisted music into places it had never been before

Don Letts (Filmmaker; DJ at the Roxy. Big Audio Dynamite: effects and vocals)

I am first-generation British Black: that term rolls off the tongue. I was listening to Toots and the Maytals, bluebeat and ska, stuff my dad was playing.

I was hanging out with my white mates, and I became a big Beatles fan. Back in the day the first single I bought was 'Penny Lane' and the first album I bought was Marvin Gaye. I became a massive Beatles fan in the worst sense. I had a collection of the wigs, the cups, the wallpaper. At one time in my life I was the second largest collector of Beatle memorabilia in this country! It wasn't until punk rock came along that I looked again at all this shit I had.

At grammar school I was the only black kid for about three years. I was submerged, drowned in all this other culture at the same time: Tyrannosaurus Rex's *My People Were Fair* – nice. Cream's *Disraeli Gears*, King Crimson, Captain Beefheart – some cool shit.[12] Then the glam thing was happening.

---

12. Captain Beefheart's dislocated take on rock and the blues was a collision between Howlin' Wolf and John Coltrane, a genius take on the world resulting in a series of brilliant albums, especially the cult classic *Trout Mask Replica*.

Cool as fuck. The young Don Letts poses in front of the 'second biggest Beatles collection in Britain'

The social climate was kind of cool before Enoch made his 'Rivers of Blood' speech in 1968 – although kids called me this and that, it didn't have any kind of political grounding. He makes the speech and all of a sudden I'm the 'black bastard'. It made a massive difference – all of a sudden these innocent digs became heavier.

When I was young, I was 'fat, four-eyed and black', and I could deal with most people – what doesn't kill you makes you stronger. About that time we start to get the images of the civil rights movement coming over from America. We saw the Angela Davis badges.[13] I'm getting that kind of political awareness from that angle, and coming from Jamaica – not too long after was Bob Marley and it seemed to come together.

Glen Matlock

Where I lived up in Kensal Green there was a strong West Indian community, and on a hot day everyone's windows were open and there was bluebeat blasting out, so I was aware of other kinds of music. I played football in the streets with one of the guys from the Skatalites. I always had a left-field slant on music. When I got older there was Tamla Motown and stuff like that, but also the Faces, which I followed on from the Small Faces, and Mott the Hoople. I went to Reading Festival at an early age and saw things like the Spencer Davis Group, Alex Harvey Band, and Quo, not your Clodagh Rogers kind of stuff.[14]

Garry Bushell (Journalist. The Gonads: lead vocals)

When I was a kid I was into T. Rex, ska, Desmond Dekker, skinhead reggae. I was too young to be a skinhead; more of a suedehead. I was into black music mostly. Then on *Top of the Pops* I saw Black Sabbath doing 'Paranoid' and Deep Purple doing 'Black Night'. I'd

---

13. Angela Davis was an African-American radical activist and member of the Black Panther Party, primarily working for racial and gender equality.

14. Clodagh Rogers was a pop singer in the Sixties and Seventies, best known for her hit 'Jack In The Box', the UK's Eurovision Song Contest entry in 1971.

never heard music like that, it sounded great and I started getting into rock as well – Thin Lizzy, stuff like that.

Budgie

I went through a reggae patch which was weird as everyone was getting into Tamla with their scooters and Lambrettas, but I was too young. I got into a bit of moonstomping – the Reggae Chartbusters. I really like the Upsetters. I loved the sax and brass sections and stuff like that.[15]

Then I delved into the world of Led Zeppelin and heavy metal as my hair grew longer. I grew more distant from everyone around me and was intent in getting lost in some sort drug culture or something.

Don Letts

People make a lot of the punky reggae connection. 'That's a weird connection,' they say. But let's be honest about this, the mods had a lot of bluebeat records, the first-hand experience of it was through the first skinhead movement, which was a fashion thing, not a fascist thing, and these white working-class kids were presented with this Jamaican music coming out on the Trojan label. I guess the reason they were drawn to it was that it was the only rebel sound around. It was totally anti-establishment. It had these kind of soundbite lyrics and this emphasis on style, with Sta-Prest, trilby hats, mohair – that totally tapped into the currency of being young. I was a black skinhead. I had my black crombie, my folded hanky, my Prince of Wales check, my brogues, my loafers, my Levi's Sta-Prest, the Ben Sherman. I was totally there. If you couldn't afford Ben Sherman it was Brutus. This was 1970–71.

---

15. The Reggae Chartbusters were a series of compilation LPs on Trojan Records, which specialised in ska, rocksteady and dub. The coolest label of the genre, it has an immense catalogue of quality Jamaican music. The label was started in 1968, named after the Leyland trucks, painted with 'Duke Reid – The Trojan King of Sounds' on their sides, which were used to transport heavy sound systems around Jamaica. The Upsetters were Lee 'Scratch' Perry's studio house band. Perry is *the* innovator in reggae, virtually inventing the form, before later virtually inventing dub.

Al Hillier

At comprehensive school at the end of the Sixties I was immediately drawn to the skinhead culture, and by 1970–71 I was listening to people like Dave Barker and Ansel Collins' 'Monkey Spanner', and the classic skinhead anthems from Trojan Records like the *Tighten Up* volumes, 'Liquidator', 'Elizabethan Reggae', 'Return Of The Django' and a succession of brilliant reggae tunes which just blew me away. I would bunk into the Phonograph club, a subterranean skinhead club opposite Golders Green station in London, on a Sunday by getting some of my older mates to cause some commotion on the steep steps as we queued to get in and then dodge the bouncers in all the kerfuffle.

Reggae music was put on this planet to dance to, and I defy anyone to tell me that they can stay sat in their seat when Prince Buster's 'Al Capone' is on the turntable.[16] That particular song still sends shivers up my spine and my whole skinhead experience is totally defined in that one brilliant piece of music. It all made perfect sense to me, I loved the clothes and I loved the whole skinhead ethos – which, incidentally, was completely accepted by our parents. Our mums and dads approved of the clean-cut, short-haired, smart image, which they thought was infinitely preferable to the long-haired, drug-smoking, kaftan-wearing, stinking hippies. On that basis alone, we used to get away with murder.

I never shook off my skinhead experience and until the birth of punk a few short years later my taste in music was governed by a futile search for something to relieve the succession of encounters with mediocrity and survive a mind-numbing period in our musical history that I consider to be one of the most barren and pointless of all time.

Segs (Real name Vince Segs. The Ruts: bass)

Reggae was my first love. My sister was five years older than me.

---

16. Prince Buster was one of the first big names on the Jamaican scene. A series of superb records on the Bluebeat label influenced a whole generation of upcoming musicians.

She was a Doris, a female skinhead, and got me into Prince Buster in the mid-Sixties when I was ten. I liked 'Al Capone', 'Ten Commandments' – great songs. *Tighten Up Volume 2.* Loads of Motown. I grew up with Radio Luxembourg, the Who. I was into the three-minute single.

I grew up with skinheads. I never liked any violence. We went to the football a little bit – I would stand in the back and avoid the violence. I ran down the high street – it was not for me!

I was listening to music, going to clubs, tunes like 'Liquidator' which have become football anthems now.[17] When I went to school everyone was listening to head music like Deep Purple, whilst I was still listening to ska. I then started smoking dope and got into Deep Purple – I did a crash course in rock. Then it went a bit boring. I had long hair and went round to people's houses and smoked dope. I thought, 'Great!' and got well into that, eating hash cake and listening to this stuff.

Adrian Sherwood (Producer)

My family were Northerners. I got moved around a lot from Slough to High Wycombe. When I was young, I was heavily into soul music. I loved that, and at the same time I was getting into early reggae music and ska tunes – the stuff that was pretty eccentric, freaky tunes like U Roy's 'Wear You To The Ball'.[18] When I heard reggae music at the local black clubs I went to, that was when I got really into it. When I was a kid one of my mates ran a reggae club and I knew another fella who ran the Nag's Head in High Wycombe called Ron Watts.

I started working at this record company Carib Gems and became a junior director for them. I loved roots music and Carib Gems was putting out some great tunes like 'Observe Life' by

---

17. A top ten hit for Harry J Allstars in late 1969.

18. U Roy was King Tubby's DJ. The late King Tubby tore up the rule book along with ...tch Perry to invent dub. U Roy made a series of classic albums that pushed him to the front of the reggae scene.

Michael Rose, and 'Babylon Won't Sleep Tonight'/'Sleepers' by Wayne Jarrett and the Righteous Flames. Lots of really strong tracks.

Colin Newman (Wire: vocals)

I grew up in the Sixties. Me and my mate Declan were complete and utter fashion victims. We read the *NME* every week, and whatever was on the front cover we were into, as all the fashions changed. I was touched by everything – you name it, I was into it. I got as much into Trojan label reggae as prog rock. The first Genesis album was rubbish but the second or third was good, and at the same time I was into the Upsetters and everything in between, from Neil Young or Traffic to Stevie Wonder. Whatever was around that was any good, I was into because I was absolutely mad on music. I didn't have any background in it. My parents were not cultured. I was not exposed to anything like jazz. I was completely self-taught.

PUNK FLOYD
Psychedelia and the Late-Sixties Long Hairs

Hugh Cornwell

When the Summer of Love was happening, I was working in a plant nursery – it was the last summer before I went to university and I was living at home. I didn't know what they were talking about. I was slightly too young to know what was going on.

Charlie Harper

The hippie thing was happening while I was in the south of France. The people I was kind of hanging round with were musicians, and people started to sing more Dylan and Donovan. I remember seeing Paul Simon in the Scotch House on St Giles Circus in the middle of Soho, above a pub at a folk club. I saw these people from the folk scene. I even went to places like Stockholm: the scene out there was

brilliant, everything was with fiddles and they took it years further –
sort of like the Pogues.

I was one of the people at the Isle of Wight festival on 'Desolation
Hill', looking at the Who and Jimi Hendrix. At three in the morning
I got the bus back to London when Joan Baez came on.[19]

Brian James

The hippie thing came along all of a sudden. I was not into that! The
only band I was into in England was the Pink Fairies, who were sort
of more rock'n'roll. They wore leather jackets and didn't give a fuck.
They would be bashing down fences at the Isle of Wight festival,
trying to get in free. I was in there and I left the main festival
because I knew the Fairies had set up an alternative tent down the
road. I was down there for the Fairies and Hawkwind and the
Notting Hill lot.

Mick Jones

There was so much happening in London. There was a feeling that
we were at the centre of the whole thing. It was really exotic to us:
we were young kids, and we saw how the Stones dressed and we
tried to emulate it a little bit, with a kind of tie-dyed T-shirt and a
funny colour, puffy scarf!

I went round London as a youngster on my own from a very
early age. From six or seven I started going to the cinema. I used
to get a 'Red Rover' and go all round London.[20] I didn't have
the same constrictions that a lot of my friends had, like parental
control.

I started going to gigs when I was about twelve. The first gigs
I went to were the free concerts in Hyde Park: the Nice and the
Pretty Things was the first one I attended. There was a few others

---

19. The 1970 Isle of Wight festival was one of the first big festivals in the UK. The festival is famous for the French anarchists trying to smash down the surrounding fence in a
protest against the not-so-free festival vibe.

20. London bus ticket of that time.

Syd Barrett, the charismatic former leader of Pink Floyd who withdrew from life, was an unlikely yet key influence on punk rock

before the Stones played there.[21] I was going all over the place to see bands – that was the main thing.

Captain Sensible (The Damned: bass and lead guitar. Also solo: vocals)

I grew up in the 'Costa del Croydon'. I always wanted to be a biker. I thought Steve Marriott had a great voice, but the problem I had with the Small Faces all through my school years was that I wanted a leather jacket with colours on my back and a motorbike, so although I loved the music of the Who and the Small Faces I had to pretend to listen to Eddie Cochrane and stuff like that when I talked to my fellow biker aspirants.

I was quite normal until I heard 'See Emily Play'.[22] I distinctly remember walking to school one day listening to Tony Blackburn on

21. The original Hyde Park free concerts ran from 1968 to 1971. The first one, on 29 June 1968, featured Pink Floyd and Tyrannosaurus Rex; the Nice and the Pretty Things played at the second, four weeks later; the Stones played at the sixth, on 5 July 1969.

22. Early psychedelic classic from 1967 by the early Pink Floyd, when the band was fronted by visionary songwriter and guitarist Syd Barrett. Their first two albums were driven by Barrett, whose madcap genius was fired by a high ingestion of LSD. This would never last. Barrett left the Floyd in 1968, made two solo albums, and then became a semi-recluse in his home town of Cambridge.

the breakfast show – I had a little transistor radio. I remember I was late for school that morning and I had the radio pressed up to my earhole. And the incredible psychedelia and the beautiful melody and the Englishness of that song! I sat on the wall of someone's front garden, regardless of how late I was and the detention I was going to get, and I was transfixed by this sound. It had a profound effect on me and changed my life forever, that song. I knew at that point that struggling with maths and technical drawing was not for me. I went back home and started nagging my parents to get me a guitar after that.

It's a tragedy what happened to Pink Floyd. I'm almost ashamed to say I liked them, or still like them, but when Syd Barrett was in control it was a totally different band from what it became. No disrespect to estate agents – one day I might have to talk to one – but it became estate agent rock. Syd Barrett never looked like a bank manager! If you went round for a cup of tea at Syd's it would be a life-changing experience!

Mick Jones

I would go and see all the groups. I didn't have any discretion whatsoever. If there was a band, that was enough – we used to go to the Roundhouse, to the big thing on Sundays called Implosion – Hawkwind, a lot of the underground groups. This was 1970. Also we would go to the Marquee to hear Blodwyn Pig, stuff like that.

It was fantastic. I always remember how loud it all was, and I would go to school the next day and my ears would be ringing. I couldn't hear nothing. My hearing has gone now!

I suppose I was a hip kid, but I didn't see myself like that. There was another young kid who was around as well called Nick Laird-Clowes, who formed that band Dream Academy. He was Jeff Dexter's little friend. He was about my age and we used to see each other around those times, around the Roundhouse, because Jeff Dexter was one of the DJs. Andy Dunkley was the other one. They used to play underground and imported records from the States.

There used to be a few record shops in London, in Berwick Street, where they did import records and you could get the new music from America.

My hair was really long, so long that they used to go on at school, 'Get your hair cut!' It just grew and grew and you don't care when you're that age. 'Little Mick' was what I was known as for a long time. I was hanging out with older guys and they didn't know why this little younger kid was there. I was a total hippie, I had long hair and I used to do idiot dancing and everything! It was so great.

Tony James (London SS, Chelsea, Generation X, Sigue Sigue Sputnik: bass)

I went off the rails for a bit when I joined a group at seventeen that only played Mahavishnu Orchestra numbers![23] I found myself playing in 13/8 time. My biggest influence at the time was listening to the John Peel show, hearing groups like East of Eden, Family, Blodwyn Pig, all those kind of classic English underground bands at that time. Mick Jones relates to the same music. He knows all the groups. I go, 'What about Blodwyn Pig?' and he will go, 'Brilliant! Jack Lancaster, two saxes at once.' We both come from the same era.[24]

I was digging Zeppelin and the Stones, and Frank Zappa's *Hot Rats* was one of first records I ever bought. This is when I'm like sixteen, in the late Sixties. The first live music I saw was Deep Purple and Taste at Eel Pie Island, and it totally blew me away. It was that moment you go through, an epiphany, and you go and look at those groups and think, 'I want to be up there and not in the crowd.' You see your destiny. I learned to play on a ukelele because it was the only thing with strings I could find in the house.

---

23. In the early Seventies the Mahavishnu Orchestra was an improvisatory jazz-rock band led by the innovative fusion guitarist John McLaughlin.

24. Formed in November 1968 by Mick Abrahams after he left Jethro Tull, Blodwyn Pig released two underground rock albums. Their first album had a pig's head on the front cover, with a ring through its nose, a fag in its mouth, sunglasses and headphones. In September 1970, Pete Banks joined from Yes but the band split up at the end of 1970. Mick Abrahams formed his own band.

Then I had an old cheap acoustic with only four strings on it because I was going to be the bass player – we immediately had a group at school.

Captain Sensible

I honestly think that, with everyone, what they were into when they were a kid stays with them. I was spoiled with the Move, the Kinks, the Who and the Small Faces.[25] They were pop music, but bloody hell, they wrote their own tunes, they were raunchy, and they could cut it live. And they were not pretty boys – a lot of them were dangerous lunatics. Where are these people going to come from, one asks oneself, in the current regime of TV *X-Factors* and record companies? We are never going to get a Crazy World of Arthur Brown! No one is going to go on with their hair on fire singing, 'I am the god of hellfire!' It's a tragedy for any young music lover. It's not going to be the real deal.

Hitler only started his political party because no one accepted him as a painter. 'I'm a genius. No, fuck off, I'll show you...' This is where the nutters go.

I grew my hair as long as possible, and I had a leather jacket, and eventually I got a motorbike and we used to get involved in some scraps with mods at the time. One in Dreamland in Margate on a run was particularly traumatic.[26] I'm not a big fan of fisticuffs myself, and I wasn't very good with getting the cylinder head off the motorbike either! There was oil all over the place... Help!

Glen Matlock

I was sixteen when I started seeing bands. One of the first gigs I went to was the free concert in Hyde Park when Grand Funk Railroad were headlining, but I didn't go to see them. I went to see Humble Pie, who were supporting, along with most of the 100,000

---

25. The Move was the underrated Roy Wood's great bubblegum pop outfit from the late Sixties.
26. Dreamland was a famous Margate amusement park.

crowd. Everyone left after two or three numbers of Grand Funk Railroad. They were getting really hyped.[27]

Tony James

I was going to free festivals in Hyde Park. I saw bands like Grand Funk Railroad, Canned Heat. Mick went to all of those gigs as well, although we didn't know each other at the time. Mick and I can both remember seeing Nick Kent at one of those gigs and thinking he was an icon because we were reading *Sounds* and the *NME* at the time. There was a great culture around these papers. I was reading journalists like Nick Kent and Pete Erskine, all these great writers that absolutely shaped a generation. The cult of the *NME* became massive in our lives.

Mick Jones

It was great days. When the bands would go on to Tramp nightclub or somewhere in the West End, we would wait outside and when the band arrived we would all try and slip in with the party. Often we were frogmarched out, but we got in with the Stones once, just behind Billy Preston. I got to know the Stones a bit later. I used to love them.

When the Stones played at Hyde Park, there's a photo where I could point myself out in the crowd in a magazine that the *Daily Mirror* or someone else did. Guy Stevens was on stage.[28] I spent all day slowly working my way to the front, till I got right up to the fence. I'm two feet from the front, and I was hit by loads of the butterflies that didn't make it.[29] All the African drummers came on for 'Sympathy For The Devil'. It was pretty amazing.

---

27. This Hyde Park concert took place on 3 July 1971.

28. The legendary Guy Stevens, who ended up 'producing' the Clash's *London Calling*, was a DJ, A&R man, producer and maverick genius whose fingerprints are all over rock'n'roll, from naming Procol Harum, through coming up with the *Sticky Fingers* album title for the Stones, to helping to mastermind (and name) the ultimate precursors to punk, Mott the Hoople. Stevens died in 1980 but somehow his wild genius still resonates around punk rock.

29. Mick Jagger read a Shelley poem and arranged to release thousands of butterflies as a eulogy to former Stones guitar player Brian Jones who had died two days before. But by the time he opened the box and launched them into the air during the concert, many of them were dead and landed inert on the crowd.

Gene October (Chelsea: vocals)

When I was seventeen I would go to the all-night clubs in the West End, doing the black bombers and the blues.[30] There would be just a jukebox in the corner – the only thing that was on them was Tamla Motown. I saw the Stones in Hyde Park – we'd been up all night dancing and someone said, 'The Stones are playing for free.' There was a really big crowd. We walked down there. It was great. They had just released 'Honky Tonk Woman'. I remember hearing a few days before that poor Brian had died, which was a shame as Brian *was* the Stones.

Charlie Harper

We formed our first rock band around 1970 – we played rock and r'n'b. I always liked the West Coast thing – I know Captain Sensible is really into the *Nuggets* scene.[31] I was in lots of different bands then. Some were quite strange. I was even in a band with horns in it. We kind of got discovered down the Old Kent Road. We were going great guns but the horn-blowers went to university, the singer got signed up, and that was it. I was playing the bass in this band.

I had this other band called Charlie Harper's Free Press. That was almost a hippie band, and a bit r'n'b. The drummer had a girlfriend who played violin. We did a show-stopping number called 'Willie The Pimp', and we did a few Beefheart tunes like 'Electricity'. The UK Subs song, 'I Live In A Car' comes from the mid-Seventies. When the Subs got it together in the punk era someone from the *NME* said, 'This comes from the Sex Pistols,' when in actual fact our stuff came from Kinks, Zappa and Beefheart. That was the attitude – the real punk attitude.

Penny Rimbaud

Initially, in the Sixties, I wasn't that aware of the hippie movement. To me there is a huge difference between the English and American hippie

---

30. Nicknames for amphetamine pills particularly popular among mods.

31. *Nuggets: Original Artyfacts From The First Psychedelic Era* was a highly influential compilation of obscure mid-Sixties American garage rock bands that dipped just below the Sixties radar, first issued in 1972.

movements. The American thing was very much about getting out onto the land. I visited Mendocino, which was a big hippie centre, in 1972. It was very much about organic food growing and self-sufficiency. The English thing tended to be more urban, people meandering around smoking too much dope and taking acid. The element I became interested in was what I got from America: self-sufficiency.

I moved into Dial House in 1967. No one wanted a house in the country then. It evolved very quickly. I was still teaching part-time two or three days a week. People would come and go. The idea of having an open house came from watching the film *The Inn of the Sixth Happiness*: all these Chinese travellers would stop off at places and not have to pay to be there. They would have a meal and tell stories. I liked the idea of having a youth hostel where you could turn up and stay. I was living here with two other art school lecturers but they didn't like the idea of opening doors to anyone so they left. I was on my own for two weeks and then it just blew up.

It was quite strange how people just turned up. Wally Hope was one, and he would be an important person in our story. He was a friend of some of the young kids from the local villages who thought the house would be a good place to come to and smoke dope – which of course they couldn't do, as we actually had an absolute no drugs and no alcohol and no coffee rule at the time! We were hardcore at that period, partly for very sensible legal reasons. We wouldn't survive ten minutes otherwise. The cops would visit regularly to see how we were behaving, then have a cup of tea and leave.

Whilst we were sitting in the garden in 1974 Wally came up with the idea for the Stonehenge free festival.[32]

---

32. Phil 'Wally Hope' Russell was one of the instigators of the 1974 Stonehenge festival, a small-scale event with a band called Zorch playing. After the gig a group of hippie revellers stayed behind in a makeshift camp. When they were eventually busted and taken to court they all claimed they were called Wally – part joke and part cloak of anonymity. Their wild hippie attire and piss-taking approach to the court saw them grab tabloid action. Wally Hope, being the ringleader and with an obvious disdain for the ways of court, was already marking himself out for attention. Within a year the authorities had him in their clutches: he was arrested for possession of three acid tabs, and it made front page news at the time. Wally Hope died a broken man and in mysterious circumstances a year later. As a neighbour he had already befriended Penny and the Dial House people the year before, and his demise agitated Penny into action. The booklet that comes with Crass's *Christ The Album* details the whole story, as does *Shibboleth*, Penny's excellent autobiography.

Wally got arrested at the festival. His court case became a cause célèbre. By the time we managed to get to him it was considerably after he had been arrested and he was almost inarticulate, so we never managed to articulate to what extent he'd been fixed up. He was also arrested by the military police and not by the civil police, and that's just unheard of. So the whole thing was ambiguous and inaccurate. We couldn't get any facts and details as there wasn't any available.

I worked for a year after his death investigating it, trying to come to terms with it all. And I don't suppose I'll ever understand what happened. I concluded he was possibly murdered – he was certainly killed by the state: either straightforward murder, or he died because of the medical treatment. It was the state that did it to him, and it made me realise that what I was doing wasn't enough and that I had to get up there and fight for it. Wally was the person who was crucial in my life, in that his death knocked on the head any idea that I'd found this beautiful place to exist and share my life, the naive belief if we were good people and lived a good life then that would be enough. Wally was part of that, and what his death showed me was that actually it wasn't enough and that we were very vulnerable. It seems strange looking back now to think that I wasn't aware that the state could be that vicious against someone who was a really innocent person. He wouldn't have squashed a worm.

Gee Vaucher (Artwork for Crass)

For me in the beginning, I just loved the music and it was all part of growing up and getting a voice. Maybe without meaning to, the Beatles were part of a huge youth voice that was confronting society. In the end, of course, they knew what they were doing. Especially John, Yoko and George. And it was the later stuff that made a deeper impression on me. Of course you have to remember what else was in the air in the arts: Warhol, Rauschenberg, Hockney, Schönberg, Britten, Dylan, Sartre. It must be hard for someone born sometime after '68 to imagine a world where the young had no voice.

Then the hippie thing came along. The hippie movement meant self-empowerment. Taking back your own autonomy, whether learning how to heal yourself, how to eat and stay healthy, how to speak up and express what you feel, how to lose the gender roles that were you were forced into, all the things and more that go with self-empowerment. Of course we all know the story of how the hippie movement went up its own arse and into self-destruct. But people forget or do not grasp how it opened up a whole generation. It was a powerful voice that got destroyed by heavy drugs deliberately supplied by the US government – that's how effective the movement was.

Poly Styrene (X-Ray Spex: lead vocals)

I was totally a hippie. The hippie movement may have been dead but a lot of kids my age were post-hippies, like post-punks now. I went to see Allen Ginsberg in Bath. I did that whole hippie thing for some time, and I did it for real: bathing in streams, living on ferns. I lived on the land for one year until the winter. I met lots of creative people, then I settled in Bath for a bit. I got involved with the Bath Arts Workshop, who were more arty than hippie. There were a lot of public schoolboys going to the Himalayas and coming back to Bath, with their chillums and massive long dreadlocks, trying to imitate the yogis.

Don Letts

All counterculture becomes appropriated and the next movement comes along to react against it. The hippies, give them their due, they had a long run, much longer than punk rock, but it had become this other thing when people who get into it don't understand the original idea. They wear the bell-bottom jeans and smoke a spliff – and that's part of their fucking dynamic, but only *part* of it. It becomes this thing that the next lot have to rebel against; you almost *need* it to happen. You need to get ill before you take the medicine to get the cure.

The glam triumvirate Bowie, Iggy and Lou Reed reinvent rock'n'roll for the Seventies

CHAPTER 2

1970/74: GLAM ROCK AND OTHER
EARLY SEVENTIES REVOLUTIONS

Contrary to received rock history, the early Seventies was a fertile time for music, perhaps even more fertile than the hallowed Sixties. Growing up in that period was a real buzz: every week Top of the Pops *had a great bunch of glam rock droogs stomping their way to the top of the charts. Purists looked on in disdain as first Marc Bolan, then David Bowie and then Slade and lesser lights joined the glitterati. The mid-Seventies was also great for art school rock, with the likes of Roxy Music and the German outfit Can (leading lights in the Krautrock scene) providing fertile inspiration for the upcoming generation. Combine this with pub rock, some of the more bearable acts from prog rock, and the rising reggae scene, and it's easy to see that the early Seventies were far from being the barren period that experts like to paint them as.*

And it was into this period that the New York Dolls made their legendary Old Grey Whistle Test *appearance, leaving the programme presenter Whispering Bob Harris looking bemused in one of those generation-gap moments. The Dolls, along with the Stooges, had pushed the barriers further, making music louder, lewder and cruder than anyone ever before. The Dolls were the gum-chewing, trashed-up, stack-heeled New York super tarts with too much make-up and bad attitude.*

Iggy Pop was the fucked-up kid from Detroit who had single-handedly in the late Sixties pushed rock'n'roll further and deeper into the nihilistic canyon that would eventually yield punk rock. Without Iggy's superhuman performances and the Stooges' two-chord über-grunt rock-'n'roll, punk would never have existed. Iggy Pop is easily the godfather of punk. Bizarrely, in the early Seventies he was treated as a washed-up loser, the Stooges were ignored, and his star was quite definitely not in the ascendancy.

Back in the UK the punk-generation-to-be were getting off on glam rock neo-punk bands and coming to terms with the death of the Sixties, the decade that promised so much but had crashed in a morass of drugs and flared denim. If punk was to be the revenge of the hippies (giving them the revolution they wanted, albeit in a twisted form), then in the early Seventies there was the gradual sound of muttering and plotting as a generation looked for a way into the pop mainstream. And gradually it began to coalesce, on the Kings Road or in small towns up and down the UK, where mad-eyed dreamers pushed the glam thing that bit further, spliced it with Iggy, and started to melt down rock'n'roll. By 1974 all the key players were beginning to pick up instruments or look a bit further than merely collecting records or being bystanders.

TEARING DOWN THE FENCES
The Seventies Underground

The pre-punk underground was a mesh of festivals, post-hippie and neo-prog. It was the fallout from the Sixties, an underrated period of experimenting, idealism and freaked-out rock'n'roll. Revolutionary ideas were in the air as a generation tried to fumble its way out from the Sixties hangover and make its own noise in a tangle of long hair and flares.

Rat Scabies

I used to go to festivals – the Reading jazz and blues festival, when no one used to go – or go to the Lyceum and see stuff like Family. Roger Chapman – he was brilliant. He used to have a lot of anger. Caravan were a good band as well. They were always really clever, playing everything in odd times. To be a musician then, you had to do that kind of stuff.[1]

I went to the Isle of Wight festival on my own in 1970. I was fourteen. I saw Ten Years After, Miles Davis, the Doors, Tiny Tim and Jimi Hendrix. It was quite a weekend. The Woodstock thing had happened, and everyone was dying for the same thing to happen in Europe to show that the love, long hair and flared-trouser thing could work over here. It was a very formative time. There was a political awareness going on with Vietnam. At the festival I remember a group of French anarchists with leather jackets and wraparound sunglasses knocking down the perimeter fence in a protest at the festival not being free. The backdrop was all these legendary bands from the Sixties. I didn't realise till quite recently what a formative thing for punk this tearing down of the fences was!

Captain Sensible

I started trying to hitch to see Jimi Hendrix at the Isle of Wight festival when I was on one of those awful family holidays in Herne Bay. When you're a teenager you don't want to be on holiday with your parents! The Isle of Wight festival was going on, and I got as far as Canterbury and it rained and rained and rained. Nobody would give me a lift. I suppose I must have looked a bit bedraggled with long hair and a leather jacket with made-up biker colours on my back. It was about nine in the morning and I got no lifts so I hitched back to Herne Bay and continued my rancid holiday. I never saw Hendrix play. Which was a tragedy.

---

1. Hailing from Leicester, Family were a prog rock outfit famed for frontman Roger Chapman's manic stage presence. They split up in 1973. Caravan, part of the Canterbury scene which also included the Soft Machine, plied a complex jazz/rock hybrid in the late Sixties and early Seventies.

Once the Seventies started and I was old enough to get into licensed premises the sky was the limit. I saw everything that was going, from Blodwyn Pig to the Keef Hartley Band, to Status Quo. Even the Quo were good in the early Seventies.

I used to go the Fairfield Halls occasionally. They were more cultured there. Bands like Pentangle and the Nice played there. But I preferred the Greyhound over the road. I knew a way through the kitchens so I didn't have to pay. Occasionally I got a punch in the mouth from the bouncers and thrown through the back door!

The bands that really impressed me were the ones that had a bit of spirit on stage, a bit of naughtiness to them. I particularly remember a gig with the Pink Fairies. They had two drummers, Twink and Russell Hunter.[2] Twink must have been on one of his benders at the time because he was all over the place. The two of them couldn't lock in and keep time so Russ jumped off his kit and whacked Twink in the mouth. I thought, fucking hell, I would have *paid* to see that! [laughs] I thought that was magnificent. A lot of pop or rock music is kind of glossy and showbizzy – they try to gloss it over. When I saw that they were real people with crises and onstage nervous breakdowns, I thought that was brilliant. Every time I saw a band obviously displaying signs of personality defects I used to follow them. I even liked Alvin Stardust – he was mad as a hatter![3]

Prog rock was really my thing. The tragedy is you can't say you like prog! Everyone thinks you like Rick Wakeman, Phil Collins, Yes and Genesis and shit like that, the overblown dinosaur bollocks where they were playing 20-minute drum solos and singing songs

---

2. The Pink Fairies were, along with Hawkwind, one of the two key British underground bands in the early Seventies, and both had a far bigger influence on the punk scene than is generally acknowledged. A 'musical terrorist organisation', the Pink Fairies took rock'n'roll idealism to its logical limit, playing free gigs for the people. Their drummer Twink had been a Sixties face. He played for the In Crowd, who became psychedelic band Tomorrow – the latter had an off-the-wall hit with 'My White Bicycle'. He also played on the Pretty Things' *S. F. Sorrow*, arguably the first-ever concept album. After that he joined the Pink Fairies. In 1972 he attempted to salvage the reclusive Syd Barrett's career in the ill-fated band Stars, which fell apart after five gigs around Cambridge. A pretty impressive CV of British underground rock.

3. Stardust was the ultimate footnote in the glam rock scene, arriving towards the end of the era dressed as a black leather Gene Vincent, singing the fantastic 'My Coo Ca Choo'.

about elves and pixies, Arthur's Round Table and all that shit, which didn't really relate to anyone in the real world walking down the road. There was a lot of unemployment in the Seventies and putting out a record going on about pixies and listening to 20-minute drum solos was not that satisfying.

But there were some marvellous prog rock bands around that deserve to get rediscovered, like the Groundhogs. They were raw and telling it like it was. It was angst-ridden! The bloke, Tony McPhee, was extremely passionate about it. It came out in his lyrics and the guitar playing. He was the British Hendrix. When you meet your heroes, some turn out to be arseholes, but not him. We go drinking real ale together. He's a fucking great geezer.

Hawkwind were good, but for me it was mainly the Groundhogs – and Egg. They were kind of proggy, very organ-based, fused with pseudo-classical. That's where I got my love of 20-minute-long pieces and expanded riffs. They took you on a little mind trip. They were extremely good at what they did. They were *not* bollocks. It's hard to define what's bollocks and what isn't bollocks, but they weren't.

Rob Lloyd (The Prefects, the Nightingales: vocals)

Hawkwind? I just love them. I still do. Me and Paul had this idea a few years ago to have a Hawkwind tribute band and hold auditions for Stacias![4]

I was brought up by my dad, who was strict. In the early Seventies I wanted to have flared trousers and long hair and he would not let me. At school, when you got older, part of the uniform was white shirts and I always had grey shirts and because people would always take the piss out of me I tried to make out it was my choice – 'I don't want to be just like you', that sort of thing – because I didn't have long hair or way-out clothes. I always looked out of place at a

---

4. Paul Apperley went on to join the Nightingales with Rob Lloyd. Stacia was Hawkwind's regular dancer; an imposing six feet tall, she often performed onstage wearing nothing but luminescent paint.

Hawkwind gig. When I saw these new punk bands I thought I looked like that already. Throughout my teenage years I looked like one of the Subway Sect, but I wanted to look like Lemmy!

Gaye Advert

When I first heard Hawkwind's 'Silver Machine' I thought, 'Wow!' It still sounds great now.

Lemmy

The others in Hawkwind were pissed off because I got to sing 'Silver Machine'. But it was in the wrong key for the rest of them so I got the job. I'd only just joined the band and I was singing their only Number One. That didn't help matters...

Rat Scabies

Listen to King Crimson's '21st Century Schizoid Man' – I hate the album but that one track was fantastic. Every band would have one track with lots of energy that I liked. The odd Status Quo song was OK. Cream had Ginger Baker and I listened to him, and later on he did Ginger Baker's Air Force. A good drum solo is a thing of rare beauty. Not many were that well constructed. That whole self-indulgence thing with Emerson Lake and Palmer lost me.

Linder Sterling (Artist and photographer. Ludus: vocals)

My family moved from Liverpool to Wigan when I was nine years old. The soundtrack of my adolescence was the conflation of Wigan Casino, prog rock and folk, a fertile seedbed for my later years.[5] I've

---

5. Opened in 1973, Wigan Casino was the epicentre of the Northern Soul scene, the specialist phenomenon of soul fanatics collecting and dancing to obscure import soul records from northern American cities like Detroit and Chicago on labels like Okeh. By the early Seventies the mods in the North kept the faith with the original soul-driven mod soundtrack as their counterparts turned to a more psychedelic sound. Early Northern Soul fashion included bowling shirts, button-down collar shirts, blazers with centre vents and unusual numbers of buttons, and baggy trousers. Along with Blackpool's Highland Rooms, Wigan Casino was the pulsebeat of Northern working-class underground culture pre-punk. For a few tense months after the punk explosion Wigan Casino hosted punk gigs. It closed in 1981 and burned down the following year.

always been attracted to the meeting of opposites, and the collision of Joan Baez with Mistura had its own strange perfection. I think that Edgar Broughton loitered briefly in the background for a while: 'Oh, Aphrodite, in your see-through nightie...'[6]

Mick Jones

᷒ also used to go to Parliament Hill Fields where they did all-night shows, free concerts – Soft Machine, Taste, Edgar Broughton Band – I was really into all that. And Yes, when they were still really good before *Tales From Topographic Oceans*.[7] They were a regular band in the early days. These were all representatives of that alternative lifestyle, and the underground press. We were looking at America as well and seeing what was there, and trying to be a bit like that here with your coal fire and cup of tea at twelve o'clock when the telly went off! Those days you could get sent to prison for a joint as well. A lot of people got sent to prison for not that much. You've got to do a lot more now – that's because the standards have dropped so much!

Keith Levene (The Clash, Public Image Limited: guitar)

I've always been into music. When I was eight I was into ska, rock-steady and skinheads. When I was nine or ten, I was into *The White Album*, the beginnings of heavy metal and Led Zeppelin and all that kind of stuff as it was coming hot off the press. This culminated in my absolute godhead band, Yes. I did all sorts of naughty things like not going to school. Instead I used to work in a factory but I shouldn't have had a job it was sort of illegal. They would take the piss out of me, joshing me 'cause I was the youngest. So I would argue with people there that were into Humble Pie and I'd be telling them, 'Yes is it! Steve Howe is the greatest fucking guitarist in the world.' I was so into the band, the music, although I didn't really

---

6. The Edgar Broughton Band, with their anarchist leanings, were one of the true proto-punk bands, founded in 1968 in Warwick. Songs such as 'Out Demons Out' and appearances at 'free concerts' made them a popular band on the radical fringe.

7. A double album which for some epitomises the overblown, self-indulgent side of prog rock. A UK Number One in January 1974.

care for Jon Anderson. It wasn't like I was into Emerson Lake and Palmer and every classico-rock band you could get. I was into Yes! I was into Steve, and also Rick Wakeman because he did *The Six Wives of Henry VIII*.[8]

By the time I was about thirteen, I was quite good at playing guitar. I got a couple of my sister's boyfriends to teach me a few things. I learned in one day: in the morning I couldn't play and by that evening I could play a tune like a fucking guitarist. I made one of the guys leave his acoustic guitar with me. Then I took a rest from it. I was into music but I was just working, being a kid.

I went to these five Yes gigs in a row at the Rainbow in London. It was the English *Tales From Topographic Oceans* tour – one of their worst albums! It was the best Yes band: Alan White, Rick Wakeman, Steve Howe, Chris Squire and Jon Anderson. It was just fucking heaven at these gigs.

I wouldn't go at the end. I'd just be hanging around at the Rainbow and gradually crept up to the stage and starting helping. Then I discovered that the head boy from my old prep school was working for them. He hated me but I asked them if they needed help on the tour. They told me I could work with this guy Nunu who was Alan's drum roadie. My job was to clean the cymbals and change the snare. I would sit behind Alan and watch him drum. He had every possible analogue/acoustic percussion instrument you could imagine, including a Moog drum (you'd plug it into a Minimoog and you didn't know what noise it was going to make). It was just *incredible*, watching your favourite band that got voted best band in the world, that you've been arguing about with people.

Rob Lloyd

The first group I was a really into was T. Rex, but I started listening to other stuff as well. I know it sounds clever after the event, but I got really into Krautrock and the Stooges, and the MC5. Basically I

---

8. Wakeman's concept album about the Tudor king's spouses was a Top Ten hit in 1973.

was the right age as a teenager in the early Seventies: T. Rex, then Bowie, and Bowie would talk about Velvets and Iggy Pop so I investigated them.

You had all that progressive rock sort of thing as well. The absolute honest story is that there was this girl at school that I fancied. I made a move on her but she wasn't interested. She was a trendy type, and she thought I was a Scruffy Herbert, so she said, 'You'd get on well with my brother. He likes the same kind of music as you do. You should come round our house some time.' I thought, 'I will – that's my way in!'

So I went round. She never wanted anything to do with me, but I got to know her brother who was a bit older than me. He used to bring all these records back from Wolverhampton Record Library, which was absolutely superb – Beefheart, Faust, Can, Amon Düül, all that kind of stuff.

We used to sit around as young kids thinking we were pretty far out listening to this weird music. There were very few people into it. Everyone else would be long-haired blokes into the Grateful Dead and Doobie Brothers. Once in a blue moon we would go to parties, and we would look like weirdos because I had strict parents who wouldn't let me have long hair or loons. I used to love it because it looked like we were some kind of subculture. Me and Dave were into this German stuff and more of the weirdo kind of thing. You couldn't buy the records for love nor money – most of them were imports. There must have been a real character who bought the records for Wolverhampton Record Library! I'll always be very grateful to them. It's weird how someone you never met can be a major part of your education. Possibly Peel played that stuff at that time too – I'm not sure.

Steve Severin

I never wanted to be a 'muso' and I still don't. Consequently, my influences stem from all areas of the arts. I am naturally drawn to anyone who has a unique vision and doesn't deviate. William

Burroughs, Paul Schrader, Eno, Francis Bacon, Jean Genet, Glenn Branca, Iggy Pop, Nino Rota, David Lynch and many others have all touched me in ways that have shaped my words and music.

At the time I was into Beefheart, Zappa, the Mothers of Invention – we all got into the Mothers' *Hot Rats* album, we liked the humour. Before Bowie the other music we were really into was the German group Can, someone came back with this record by them and we really got into it.[9] This was just before I got into Bowie. Can opened up a lot of possibilities. I was very fortunate to have witnessed Can play their first UK show at Brunel University back in 1973. They came on and just played non-stop for two hours, each piece merging straight into the next. It had the most mesmerising effect on the audience. It felt like I was party to a strange, unspeakable ritual.

Jake Burns (Stiff Little Fingers: vocals)

I bought my first album, *Led Zeppelin II*, one Christmas. I was given a Taste album, Rory Gallagher's band. That's what started me: BBC Northern Ireland had the foresight to record the final gig by Taste on New Year's Eve 1970 at Royal Ulster Hall, and the only reason I caught it was it was right after the football results. I sat there with my gob round my knees: I was eleven years old and that was what I wanted to do! My dad was bemused. He didn't want me to be a crap footballer and he definitely didn't want me to be a crap guitarist!

Rat Scabies

I was playing in the band Tor, or Rot as I liked to call them, after I had left home. I was living in Caterham and working at Fairfield Halls in Croydon. The Captain worked there too and he was one of the first people I got on with. He was my kind of age and we would sit around and talk about music and the bands they had on there.

---

9. Can are one of the great bands of the period, leading lights from the Krautrock scene. Their hypnotic groove and their multi-rhythmic music was constructed largely through improvisation – it has never dated, and has been a seminal influence on countless bands.

I remember the famous story about how they banned Humble Pie because Steve Marriott gobbed all over the stage, but when he left Humble Pie they put Steve Marriott's All Stars on instead because they didn't realise that he was the same bloke! The stage manager also told Jerry Lee Lewis that he couldn't put his feet on the piano! And when John McLaughlin's Mahavishnu Orchestra played, the bloke that worked there thought it was a 130-piece orchestra. Officially I was a porter and it was my job to move pianos – and move 130 music stands for the Mahavishnu Orchestra!

We had Roy Castle and Mike and Bernie Winters' show and, I always say this, but Mrs Mills! I thought she was fucking brilliant. The best musical education you could have. She used to have this amazing thing going on – it was really surreal. She only had a piano and yet she got the whole place rocking by playing the right tunes. After the show she would be all sweating. She put in her work. It was a valuable thing to see: it's down to the artist to get the audience going – that's what I learned from Mrs Mills.[10]

Captain Sensible

I had a rotten old Spanish acoustic guitar which was pretty ropey. As soon as I started earning some dosh cleaning toilets, I went out and got a nice proper guitar. It was a revelation. Most people's first guitar is a piece of shit, so difficult to play that even a good guitarist would not be able to get a tune out of it because the strings are so high up off the frets. This one was so easy to play and I found myself rapidly progressing to the high standard I am at now! [laughs]

We had a constant little circle of people playing music. We changed the name of the band all the time. We had names like Black Witch Climax Blues Band and Five Arrogant Superstars. Me, my brother Phil, Johnny Moped, Dave Berk on drums, and this bloke

---

10. Forty-year-old Civil Service typing-pool superintendent Mrs Mills from Loughton, Essex hit the UK Top Twenty in 1961, and for many years maintained a following with her collection of party favourites and standards that she sang at the piano, such as 'Knees Up Mother Brown' and 'We'll Meet Again'. An unlikely influence on punk, but there you go.

called Fred Berk – they were not brothers but we gave them the same name because we thought it was amusing, and Fred didn't! Johnny Moped was enamoured with the biker thing. He wanted to be Johnny Harley, Johnny Vincent, Johnny Norton – some powerful bike name – but we wouldn't let him, so we called him Johnny Moped all the time! He said, 'Guys, a moped is a really feeble 50cc bike, know what I mean? It's not putting across what I want.' We were a bit mean, weren't we?

Saying that, I didn't want to be called Captain Sensible. I fucking hated it. My chosen name was Dwayne Zenith! Mind you, Dwayne Zenith is a bit naff, isn't it? [laughs]

Rat Scabies

Captain's band was all right. They were a bit cruel to Moped. There was this cruel sense of humour they had. Captain and Dave Berk were into Soft Machine and Ornette Coleman, and they would go and kidnap Johnny and do a few gigs and take the piss out of him.

If you were unpopular at Fairfield Halls they put you on bog patrol, which is one of the jobs the Captain would get constantly. He was winding them up all the time. There was a radio in the tea room where you had a break. He connected its speakers to a cassette player, and played a live cassette of Johnny Moped doing 'Johnny B. Goode' through them. The blokes in the room tried to tune the radio, saying, 'What's this horrible racket?'

Captain Sensible

We used to play in the drummer's garage, which had no sound-proofing. The neighbours didn't like it and then we progressed to the garden! I remember once when we were playing these two kids who must have been nine years old were there and we gave them six pence each to come and watch us, and a copper stuck his head over the wall and shouted, 'All right! The Beatles over there, knock it on the head.' The first gig we did was at the Brigstock Arms. There was a talent contest, and we did two songs. After the first song they threw us of the stage! [laughs]

We were influenced by Soft Machine. Soft Machine were quite wacky for lyrics – one of their songs that amused me greatly was called 'A Concise British Alphabet' and the lyrics went 'a, b, c, d, e, f, g, h, i, j...' I thought, 'That's great.' There's a lot of boy/girl songs about and that showed you could throw out the rule book. The punk groups didn't invent it there and then – they were influenced by what went before. Soft Machine broke all the fucking rules, which has to be first thing to do when you start a punk group, throw away the rule book. So we got Moped to count backwards from 20 to 1 over the drums. By the time he got to nought everyone was looking at their watches, and then he took it down to minus 1, minus 2!

WE'RE GOING DOWN THE PUB
The Pub Rock Scene

The much-maligned pub rock scene was pretty much the grounding for the upcoming punk explosion. As a reaction to the glam stardust of the Top of the Pops *world and the stadium prog rock scene, pub rock took rock'n'roll back to its roots in London venues like the Hope and Anchor, the Kensington, the Cock Tavern, the Lord Nelson and the Tally Ho in Kentish Town. In 1972 the bands initially included Bees Make Honey, Ducks Deluxe, Kilburn And the High Roads, Roogalator, Help Yourself, Clancy, Chilli Willi and the Red Hot Peppers, Ace, and the Winkies, and they varied in style. But the key bands in this story appeared a couple of years later, playing stripped-down rock'n'roll: Dr Feelgood and Eddie and the Hot Rods are names that crop up consistently in the testimonies of early punk fans. Joe Strummer's 101ers and the Stranglers also cut their teeth on the pub rock scene, along with a whole host of other eventual key players in punk rock.*

Wilko Johnson

After my travels in India I got back to Canvey. It was bumping into Lee Brilleaux one day that got me back into playing again. I knew he had a band, we were talking in the street and he was telling me his band had lost a guitar player, and I was thinking, 'Mmm...' We didn't actually say anything to each other but then a bit later that evening Sparko the bass player came knocking on the door and said, 'Do you want to join this band?' and I said, 'Well, yeah.' I hadn't even played or thought about guitar for four or five years.

We started the band about the beginning of 1972. We were into r'n'b music, which wasn't dreadfully fashionable at that time, but I liked that idea because that's what I used to play. We had some rehearsals and I was saying, 'We've just got to be like Johnny Kidd and the Pirates.' My whole style was based on the Pirates' guitar player, Mick Green. He was my hero and my main influence. When I saw them on the television on *Thank Your Lucky Stars* I thought, 'Obviously the lead guitarist has failed to turn up. There's only one guitar player and he's obviously not playing all that,' because it sounded like two guitars going on. Then I found out that Mick Green had this fabulous attack, this great guitar technique. I devoted myself to trying to play like that. I was playing Johnny Kidd and the Pirates at 33 rpm to try to work out how he was doing it. I groped towards it and I suppose I found my own way of doing it.

I got all the groovy Johnny Kidd B-sides and we learnt them all. One of those songs was 'Dr Feelgood', and again Sparko came round and said, 'We have decided to call the band Dr Feelgood.' I said, 'It's been used before, but no one on Canvey is going to know!'

For eighteen months we played little local pub gigs. We learned some pop songs to get some gigs, but I said, 'Fuck this pop stuff, let's do r'n'b.' Everyone liked that idea so we were just doing that for a year until somebody told us about this pub rock thing that was happening in London. So we went up there and got these gigs in these venues, starting at the bottom.

Hugh Cornwell

I was in Lund doing my PhD. Lund is the ancient university town, like the Oxbridge of Sweden, and it was here that I drifted into a band. I met these people one by one. The first one was a Swedish nurse, Hans Warmling, who had written hundreds of songs. We started hanging out together. Then we found these two draft dodgers, Gyrth Godwin and Chicago Mike, who was a poet and drummer. Hans was the most creative and I was writing a few songs which we played. I started smoking with this other guitar player who turned up – that was Jan Knutsson, who ended becoming bass player in the band, Johnny Sox.

Johnny Sox were very, very rockabilly, very fast. Two and a half minute songs with lyrics about riding on freight trains and sweet little sisters. It was very high-energy rock'n'roll, a precursor to punk. Very rock'n'roll, very enjoyable. We played around the area and we went down well wherever we played. We didn't make any records, even though we had 50 songs – and no covers. It was all our own stuff.

Hans left Johnny Sox. He just didn't get on with Gyrth, the singer. So I ended up by default as the only guitarist – I was playing rhythm then. Gyrth wanted us to go to the States. I said it would be easier, if we were penniless, to go to the UK. So in late 1973 we came to London and they squatted in Camden Town, Maitland Park Road, while I reintroduced myself to my parents. I went off to see Paul Kennerley, who was managing the Winkies at the time and putting bands into Fullers pubs in London. I convinced Paul to give us some gigs. The one gig when he did come to see us play, Gyrth had an argument with the publican and Paul arrived to see Gyrth waving his studded belt and having a fight outside with the landlord, who had a chair in his hand. That didn't help things.

We played the Brecknock a few times. The pub rock scene was booming: Dr Feelgood, Eddie and the Hot Rods, Scarecrow, Kilburn and the High Roads, Ducks Deluxe, Brinsley Schwarz – these bands were packing houses. We were just starting on that circuit. The pub rock scene was very important and Kennerley was booking all these venues. The Winkies, who he managed, were just about to be signed.

Mick Jones

The Winkies were a really good group. The singer was Philip Rambow.[11] He was Canadian and came over here. They were really Stonesy and Guy Stevens produced them.

The bands in the mainstream were getting a bit more brazen. Slade were good. After Small Faces there was Rod Stewart and the Faces, and another one was Humble Pie – that was Steve Marriott from the Small Faces and Peter Frampton from the Herd. We used to go and see all those types of groups.

Vic Godard (Subway Sect: vocals)

We used to go and see r'n'b bands playing in pubs, like Dr Feelgood and the Count Bishops.[12] The Count Bishops were our favourites. Rob Simmons was more into that than me.[13] He was going to see very obscure ones. Wilko Johnson was the first person to have a punk attitude. He could have gone straight into a punk band. He's still great now.

Wilko Johnson

A lot of the bands building up on the pub rock circuit actually had a past; they were like known musicians, with people like Nick Lowe in Brinsley Schwarz's line-up. There was all sorts of things going on in the pub scene, all types of music. It was more like a type of venue

---

11. One of the nearly men of the pre-punk scene. His band the Winkies played the pub circuit with a glam attitude, they briefly backed up the post-Roxy Music Brian Eno and recorded an album with producer Guy Stevens before crashing back down to earth. His songs include 'There's A Guy Works Down The Chip Shop Swears He's Elvis', which he co-wrote with Kirsty MacColl.

12. The Count Bishops were one of the great bands of the period. Like the Hammersmith Gorillas, they have remained relatively undiscovered. The mean, stripped-down rock'n'roll of both bands was too far ahead of its time, landing somewhere between Dr Feelgood and the upcoming punk rock explosion.

13. Rob Simmons was later the guitar player in Subway Sect.

Phil Rambow, of the Winkies, one of the many aspiring rockers from the pub loved by that erstwhile young dude, Mick Jones

than a type of music. It went from Brinsley Schwarz doing country-rocky stuff to a funk band like Gonzalez. There was rock'n'roll bands and sub-Rolling Stones bands like the Winkies with Phil Rambow. We were completely unknown but we had those couple of years playing round Southend – so although we were unknown we were pretty good.

We were from out of town and whenever we knew we were going to be gigging in London we went up town to check out what was happening. Everyone was talking about this band Ducks Deluxe, so we went along to see them. I was with my brother and I remember saying, 'If these are the top band in London we've fucking got it made.' Which was a fair assessment actually.

We started attracting big audiences right away. Journalists were coming to see us – particularly the *NME* people – and we were in the music papers. It took a while before we got a deal. The thing was, back then people weren't going out to find local bands and signing them. It was all like big techno-flash-type groups put together by managers, supergroups, stuff like that, and to actually go and sign a band from the club level was unusual. Nobody really wanted to make the move, and in the end Andrew Lauder at United Artists went for it and signed us.

Nick Cash (Kilburn and the High Roads, 999: guitar and vocals)

I was at Canterbury College of Art. I started playing in a band called called Frosty Jodhpur, a three-piece art school band. Some of it was a bit blues-influenced, some a bit odd and a bit punk as well. We did a few gigs round the area, then Ian Dury came down to teach at Canterbury. He was my tutor. We formed this band Kilburn and the High Roads to play the end of art-school dance sort of thing. I was the more rock'n'roll Chuck Berry/Eddie Cochrane side of things, and we had other people in the band who were more into the jazz thing – Thelonious Monk, Albert Ayler and John Coltrane.

I played about a hundred gigs with Ian Dury and the Kilburns. We were a good band – Madness paid tribute to us, they copied a lot of our style in their photographs and their music. We played on the pub rock circuit with Dr Feelgood and all those bands like Brinsley Schwarz, Graham Parker and the Rumour, the 101ers. It was the good end of the pub rock scene.

John Lydon would come down to the gigs and look at Kilburn and the High Roads. At the time it was the most happening sort of scene in London. Glen Matlock would go to our gigs. I just think punk rock came out of the pub rock thing really. We used to go and play Biba's; I saw the New York Dolls play there once – it very much crossed over.

Garry Bushell

I loved Dr Feelgood and Eddie and the Hot Rods. Slade as well – that was the mid-Seventies I saw them play. The first band I saw, funnily enough, was Hawkwind. I was on an CND Aldermaston march and Hawkwind played at the end. I also saw Cockney Rebel. It was a fantastic time.

DOWN IN THE SEWER
The Stranglers' Early Days

The Stranglers were one of the key bands of the punk era. Their malevolent bass-driven punk psychedelia came in classic pop songs, and they would be welcomed with open arms by the punk generation. Their surly, tough attitude and outsider status helped as well.

Hugh Cornwell

Chicago Mike decided that he wanted out of Johnny Sox so we suddenly needed a drummer. We advertised and Jet Black turned up at the squat with his Beatles haircut, a suit and a beard. He was portly and a little bit older than us. He was about 35, maybe, and he said, 'Come on boys, come and live in my off-licence in Guildford. We can rehearse there.' This was the spring of '74 and we thought, 'Sounds all right!' All we had to do was a bit of work for Jet and we could live there for free.

We never did any gigs with Jet Black as Johnny Sox; we just rehearsed. We didn't do much work either, and while Jet was work-ing Gyrth was drinking the stock. I was playing piano and stuff. There was not much going on. Gyrth and Jan had a bit of a fall-out one evening in a club. Gyrth got drunk and unmanageable and Jet laid into him for not doing any work and not being committed enough. Gyrth decided to leave and go back to Sweden where his wife and child were. Jan decided to go as well. They left next day leaving us as a duo – a bit like the White Stripes!

Before Gyrth and Jan fell out, Gyrth, on one of his many trips to London, got a lift in a paint truck that John Burnel was driving. Gyrth invited him in for a few drinks as a thank you, and we met up a few times after that and found out that he lived in Guildford. After Gyrth and Jan left I borrowed a bottle of wine from Jet's shop and went round to see John. I needed to be with someone about my own age and John was the only person I knew in Guildford. It might have been in the back of my mind when I went round that I knew he could play and that he had written a couple of songs and that he wasn't scared of singing. Two singers was what I wanted and he was perfect. I talked him round. I had to persuade him to give up his job as a driver and join up. We needed a bass player and even if he was a brilliant classical guitar player he was quite happy to do that, and that's how he joined. We didn't have a name for the band then. It was just after that we were called the Guildford Stranglers, and then the Stranglers.

J. J. Burnel (The Stranglers: bass and vocals)

I don't think we played as a trio, because shortly after Hans Warmling, who had played with Hugh in Sweden, joined. He was a fancy lead guitarist and a handy piano player. We had some songs like

'Strange Little Girl' and 'My Young Dream' which I wrote when I was twelve or thirteen – Hans wrote the music for that.

We had decided, like the Sex Pistols would do when they played loads of Monkees or Dave Berry songs, just to pad out our set with covers, rock'n'roll songs – standards. We found out really early on that we could insert a couple of our own songs in there, and then play a familiar one. We had to, or we would lose the gig, and we were starving then. Really hungry. In fact one time with Hugh we were eating at Jet's place and Hugh ended up with the parson's nose from the chicken – that was all there was to eat! I would walk five miles from the Chiddingfold squat to the nearest sewerage farm to pick tomatoes. There was loads of tomatoes there because the seeds don't get processed in your system, so they grow in all the fields around sewage farms! There was acres of them down there, and that's what we lived on!

We worked with Hans for a year or so till there was a falling out between me and Hans. Either Hans or me had to go – there was a personality clash. One day we were going to play at an East End wedding and he couldn't take it any more. We stopped the ice cream van and kicked him out and that was goodbye Hans. He didn't want to play songs with a lot of chords in like 'Tie a Yellow Ribbon'.

Hugh Cornwell

After a year Hans left because we learnt these standards to put in our set, to make us palatable to audiences, stuff like 'Tie A Yellow Ribbon'. Hans said, 'What the fuck are we learning all this crap for? Our songs are much better!' He was right! But we said, 'Look, it's a means to an end,' and he got fed up with it. It was very hard. He suddenly stopped the truck and got out one day. It was on the way to a gig at a Jewish wedding – he left and said, 'I'm off.' We carried on and did the gig as a trio. Where he was supposed to do a lead break I just carried on playing rhythm, and everyone loved it. So we carried on as a trio for a bit.

ALL THE YOUNG DUDES
Bolan, Bowie and the Glam Rock Droogs
Make the World Technicolour

Growing up in the early Seventies was growing up in the gloom of a grey country. That was until you put on Top of the Pops, *which was a riotous carnival of make-up, platform boots and hairy madness. Cross-dressing quickly turned into brickies with too much slap, but this didn't matter: glam revelled in its dumbness and made the tutting critics sound like yer parents. Glam rock is much maligned, but is perhaps one of the golden eras of British pop. The single was the king and there was an endless supply of great ones. Bowie and Bolan may pick up the critical bouquets from the period, but Slade (Noddy Holder is one of the great British vocalists), the Sweet, Mott the Hoople, the Arrows, Mud and a thousand others were loved just as much, and in their own way their stomping songs with big fuck-off choruses would have a strong influence on punk. It was always anthemic and outrageous, just like pop music should be. This truly was a people's music.*

J. C. Carroll (The Members: guitar)

Well before punk, when I was sixteen, I was into Led Zep, Black Sabbath. Then I graduated onto harder stuff like the Velvet Underground, the Stooges – all different kinds of music around before punk. I used to go and see T. Rex, David Bowie. That was quite exciting. I saw T. Rex when I was fifteen – they were very, very good.

John O'Neill

When the Beatles broke up, we were looking for something contemporary and T. Rex was the next big thing. They were my favourite of all the glam bands. As I got older I got into David Bowie. When the Undertones started, we always did covers of T. Rex, the Glitter Band and Slade.

Brian Young (Rudi: vocals and guitar)

I was just one of a zillion spotty teens growing up in East Belfast in the early Seventies who wanted to be the next George Best. I didn't pay much attention to music, though I did buy the 'Belfast Boy' 45 by Don Fardon about our Georgie! Altogether we must have had about ten singles in the house and even fewer LPs!

So that's how it was, until one fateful weekday, when after trudging home from school I turned on our new rented colour TV and sprawled out on the floor to watch the drivel that passed for children's TV in those days. As fate would have it, *Lift Off With Ayshea* was on. I was blown away when they showed film of T. Rex playing 'Jeepster'. I was mesmerised and raced out to buy it at Graham's Record Shop on the Albertbridge Road that Saturday, soon as I'd got my pocket money. It's still my all-time fave 45! I guess I was hooked and from then on it was downhill all the way! Within a matter or weeks Mr Best and football were a fleeting memory.

Kevin Hunter

When I was at college there were two camps, the T. Rex camp and the Slade camp. I was into the Slade camp. Some of the Sweet stuff I liked as well – more their albums.

Marc Riley (The Fall; BBC Radio 1 DJ 'Lard')

T. Rex's 'Ride A White Swan' on *Top of the Pops* was really important. The next pivotal moment was seeing David Bowie do 'Starman' on *Lift Off with Ayshea*, which was two weeks before the pivotal moment for a lot of people – seeing 'Starman' on *Top of the Pops*.

Like a lot of people, through Bowie I traced back to Iggy and the Velvets. I went out and bought *Raw Power, Berlin, Max's Kansas City*, so I found myself immediately at the age of thirteen pretty well listening to what I listen to now – which is a great thing to be able to say. It was the right music at the right time, and has stuck to me all these years.

On the other hand I also liked Genesis! I saw them doing 'I Know What I Like (In Your Wardrobe)' and I got sucked into the prog rock thing as well. The two extremes were the prog thing and glam. I hated Yes and Emerson Lake and Palmer, but I liked some of Genesis. It was a bit theatrical, you know! [laughs] People who had flared jeans and desert boots and army coats with Led Zeppelin written on the back had their one scene, and we would be into Bowie and Genesis and never the twain shall meet.

Mark Perry (Editor, *Sniffin' Glue* fanzine. Alternative TV: vocals)

Before punk I was into everything really. I started listening to music in 1970–71, to David Bowie and the glam thing – I thought that was really exciting. A lot of American stuff too, like Neil Young, Little Feet. I was a big Frank Zappa fan. Pink Floyd. I am just a big music fan. Which is basically how I found out about punk.

Mick Jones

In the early Seventies David Bowie came out with *Ziggy Stardust and the Spiders from Mars* and they were like a proper band. It wasn't like the David Bowie we all knew about, the 'Space Oddity' David Bowie. This was different. We took that seriously.

We also used to go and see the Faces – Rod Stewart and the Faces, not the Small Faces. We were into Rod Stewart and Ronnie Wood and we used to follow them around as well. I didn't see Mott the Hoople till later.

Steve Severin

To be honest at the beginning I was not that much of a Bowie fan; it was only after *Ziggy Stardust* and 'John I'm Only Dancing' came out that I got really into Bowie.

Brian Young

I experimented spiking and dying bits of my hair, trying to copy

Bowie's spike top, and nicking my Mum's setting lotion! I'd got my ear pierced too, much to the amusement of the old dear in the jewellers we went to. I even pulled out my eyebrows with pliers to get that Ziggy look off pat, but when I went into school the next day my brows had swollen up!

T. V. Smith

I was always into David Bowie. I was interested in the pre-'Space Oddity' stuff. *Man of Words/Man of Music* – I was knocked out with his songwriting on that. The whole idea was brilliant, the way it was all tied up together. Roxy Music were doing the same trick on their first album, a classic: great songs, great lyrics, interesting arrangements. You open up that gatefold sleeve and see them in all those great clothes. I really liked the way it was packaged. The whole thing was better than the normal pap.

I was not interested in the rest of glam rock. I don't know why they were lumped together with these Chinnichap bands that may have got respect now but they were at the opposite end – they were completely manufactured rubbish.[14] They were so calculated, going for the teen market.

Colin Newman

I was a big, big Bowie fan. There was a sense that Bowie was art, that was really permeated by *Hunky Dory* and *Ziggy Stardust*. There was no other music about other than that. There was nothing else to talk about at the time. The fact that people were still talking about Bowie during punk shows how important he was to that generation and not to be slagged in any way, although I think he kind of lost it later.

---

14. Chinnichap were the most successful songwriters in Britain in the early Seventies, a genius glam songwriting team who helped to soundtrack my generation's youth with songs for the likes of Sweet, Mud, Suzi Quatro, and even the country rock-flavoured pop of the later Smokie. Mike Chapman from Australia hooked up with lyric writer Nicky Chinn to create a hit factory at Mickey Most's RAK label. Their glam-tinged stomping pop was perfect for the times, but their pop genius has never been acknowledged. While in America in the Eighties, the inspired Chapman either wrote or produced Exile's 'Kiss You All Over', the Knack's mega-hit 'My Sharona', Pat Benatar's 'Love Is A Battlefield' and Tina Turner's phenomenally successful song, 'The Best', and also produced Blondie.

Getting ready for year zero! Mark Perry at work!

I tended to like the people who couldn't technically sing. I have big problems with that pop star proper singing, that 'Wooohaahoo!' voice that's meant to be proper singing – that's the thing that makes it sound like shit. There's something pure about the way it just comes out of someone's mouth. When I was younger, I very much admired people like Eno and Robert Wyatt. I always liked Eno's singing more than Ferry's. I understood what Ferry was doing. Ferry was very mannered, a very English style. I do love early Roxy Music but there was something ultimately very empty and sterile, too mannered, about them.

John Lydon (The Sex Pistols, Public Image Limited: vocals)

That T. Rex/Bowie period was for very young kids. Pop with lipstick. They got bored when they grew up a little and realised what a bunch of very, very poor transvestites they were worshipping, and were desperate to look into anything else. And then Roxy Music came along and that made dinner jackets become fashionable. Bryan Ferry's depravity introduced a decadent aspect to life that was definitely interesting. St Moritz cigarettes with cheap wine led, quite naturally for me, to other things.

Marco Pirroni (Siouxsie and the Banshees, the Models, Rema Rema, Adam and the Ants: guitar)

The first music that affected me was *Ziggy Stardust*, and Roxy Music's 'Virginia Plain', which is one of my favourite singles of all time. The first record I remember really, really liking was 'Maggie May' by Rod Stewart. Then I liked the Faces for a while, but there was something about them that I couldn't identify with. I wasn't 100 per cent with Bowie till *Ziggy Stardust*. I don't understand the Bowie-as-an-alien thing to this day, but aesthetically I thought it looked amazing.

I went to see Roxy Music at their Rainbow gigs. A lot of people had the clothes on. Because there were five of them there were a lot of disparate elements and you could hear all these influences in their music.

For a kid, seeing Roxy Music was the height of heights. Later on when you do it yourself, and you're sitting backstage drinking cans of Coke and eating crisps, you realise for them it's just another gig, that they get back on the coach and go to Sheffield or somewhere. But I didn't know that then, and Roxy Music could project this sophisticated image. They came from a slightly different scene. They were older. Bryan Ferry was quite old. He was 27! He was an old mod.

Siouxsie Sioux

At a Roxy Music gig I went to, I remember having this black taffeta skirt, which I wore with black high-heeled shoes in a Forties style, and a black double V-necked jumper with white sequins. That was my first look, which I wore with an angora-type bolero jacket that my mum had. Once I started going to Biba on my own, and discovered rust colours for the eyes, I really got quite heavily into wearing red eye-shadow, which used to make the blue in my eyes really stand out.

Poly Styrene

As well as the 'post-hippie' scene, there was this more arty thing, like Roxy Music, going on as well. I was in the Johnny Rondo Trio, a jazz quartet in Bath, Somerset. I used to DJ there as well in the local hippie pub, the Hat and Feather. I'd play stuff like 'Wild Thing' by the Troggs, or 'Diamond Dogs'. I was very much into Roxy Music. Roxy played Bath Arts Festival so I got to see these bands very early, before they were famous. They were sort of a combination of fringe theatre and music. The musicianship side was more like Brian Eno and Andy Mackay, and obviously Bryan Ferry was like a debonair actor with his image.

Nils Stevenson (Early co-manager of the Sex Pistols; manager of Siouxsie and the Banshees)

Pre-punk, I was into disco and electronic stuff – my favourite record was George McCrae's 'Rock Your Baby'. I also loved Kraftwerk. I was a Bowie fanatic. Bowie was a lot of people's role model, the tastemaker of the time. He dictated how you dressed, the books you read, clubs you went to – from Sombreros on Kensington High Street, to Rods in Fulham. I was always after a new experience, any fantasy made reality. The gay scene got Bowie into disco music; from that he got into electronic.

Bowie turned people onto Iggy. Originally Bowie was a folk singer/mime artist. It was after a trip to New York in 1969 that he saw Iggy. He changed, became aware of the New York Dolls and the Velvet Underground, got involved in the Warhol scene – that's when he changed into the fabulous Ziggy Stardust. He made one aware of American acts. Bowie was the only English person who saw what was going on in America and did a version of it. Marc Bolan is credited with being the creator of glam but his was a very cuddly thing. Bowie's glam was dangerous and intellectually challenging.

Roxy Music were very heterosexual. They were big guys dressing up in glam suits, playing with supermodels like Jerry Hall. They did not have the dangerous sexual politics like Bowie had. He created a real fuss. He responded to the feminism of the day: Germaine Greer's *Female Eunuch* had not long been out.[15] The glam androgenous thing was a reaction to that, like stealing the feminist thunder for men.

I went to see Iggy at King's Cross Cinema in 1972. That was a major eye-opener. He wasn't even top of the bill. He ran across the audience's laps, grabbed a girl out of the audience, spat in her face. The band was playing repetitive riffs whilst he was jumping off stage. It was the most extraordinary thing I've ever seen. I wasn't aware of anyone there at the Iggy show who was around later. Most people

15. Greer's landmark feminist work was published in 1970.

were there to see the headline band, the Flamin' Groovies.[16] There were a few who were Bowie acolytes. No one who was involved in punk was there. Malcolm McLaren wasn't there. Johnny Rotten was too young. He claimed he was there. Maybe they were...

Mick Jones

I went to see Iggy at the Scala, the King's Cross Cinema all-nighter. The full-on quality of the Stooges was great, like flame-throwers! It was really early in the morning. Lou Reed played as well. We were doing speed and we would be speeding off our nuts all night. King's Cross looked like a fairy-tale castle at dawn; it looked fantastic high on purple hearts! There was a horrible come-down: it was always really bad, you would feel like shit. We didn't even smoke then. I didn't start smoking till I went on tour! It drives you to it.

Chrissie Hynde (The Pretenders: vocals)

I thought that in London everyone was gonna be into Iggy Pop, because I had some back issues of the *NME*. And then I came here, and no one had heard of Iggy Pop, so I was really bummed. But I did eventually bump into a guy at a party who wrote the article on Iggy which I cut out... and it was Nick Kent.

John Lydon

Iggy has done more than a few excellent records. For me the thing that matters the most is the lyrics, and there are all too few really good writers out there.

Jimmy Pursey (Sham 69: vocals)

I was really into David Bowie, although I never got to see him play.

---

16. The Flamin' Groovies made a habit of being the wrong band at the wrong time. They formed in San Francisco in 1965, playing rock'n'roll and British beat, completely out of sync with the emerging hippie scene. They were overlooked, consigned to the underground where hipsters like Mick Jones discovered them. Moving to England in 1971, they recorded the classic *Teenage Head* album with Dave Edmunds producing. Punk threatened to resurrect their career when they released their best two albums, *Shake Some Action* and *Flamin' Groovies Now*, but they still missed out. Their songs, though, stand the test of time.

Glam was about the music, the sexuality, the clothes – anything goes, and that's why I became a punk rocker.

I liked the Velvet Underground, the Stooges – that type of music. And the Small Faces and the Who for their grit. I wasn't into Slade. They were a knees-up kind of band. In one respect, bands at that time were more showmanlike. The Sweet were good. 'Ballroom Blitz' is still one of the great rock'n'roll songs.

Damian O'Neill (The Undertones: guitar)

In the early Seventies Gary Glitter was my first hero. I don't like to admit that these days! But he made brilliant records. I was really into drums at the time, so I really loved that fact they had two drummers.[17]

During the glam thing I loved T. Rex, the Sweet – 'Ballroom Blitz' was an ace single. Roxy Music – I appreciated them later. I remember thinking 'Virginia Plain' was brilliant. David Bowie was a bit weird for me; I was a bit too young for him. I was influenced by my older brother, John. I loved Slade's 'Cum On Feel The Noize' and 'Coz I Luv You'. Being from Ireland the first LP I bought was by Horslips.

I also loved Status Quo. I'm not ashamed to admit it! 'Down Down' – great single, they were at their peak – and 'Caroline'. When I was learning to play guitar, Quo were kings. They were so simple.

Jake Burns

Status Quo had a sound that was pretty easy to play and learn, so you could make something that sounded like a proper band. That's a huge step forward when you start.

---

17. The later squalid revelations about Glitter don't take away from some of the brilliant records he sang on in the early Seventies. The real genius, though, was Mike Leander, who produced the records and came up with the tribal beast, slowing down the Burundi drummers' amazing beats and making all the instruments play tuned to the same string to create that bizarre drone. Gary Glitter was just asked to grunt over the top. The Glitter Band have also been tainted by association with their former singer, but their post-Glitter career had some great pop moments.

Colin Newman

The Stooges were really funny. I was at school with a guy who actually had his picture on the back of *Raw Power*. He was this guy you see in glasses and he's got his leg halfway over the crash barrier. He was this huge Iggy fan, and he was the person that got me into Iggy. Funnily enough, I never loved the MC5. I remember buying *Kick Out The Jams* at Woolworth's even though I was very young – this was back in the Sixties – and getting it home and it didn't sound very exciting. I guess the production values hadn't moved on enough to capture their live sound.

Mick Jones

We went to Phun City festival at Worthing to see the MC5, and the Pink Fairies played too. That was the first time the MC5 had played.[18] My overriding memory was falling into a ditch! That was a great festival.[19]

Lemmy

The MC5 were a great band. That's what I was trying to do with the original Motörhead.

Mensi (Real name Thomas Mensforth. Angelic Upstarts: vocals)

I was into Slade, Glitter and Bowie but I was more into football. I dressed in Levi's Sta-Prest and brogues – that was the order of the day. Music was in the background, never that important. What was important to me was football. I was a Sunderland fan. I didn't get to the 1973 Cup Final, though. I didn't get a ticket, and I was gutted that I missed that one.

---

18. The MC5 have become one of the key influences on any guitar rock'n'roll hustlers, their hyper-amplified revolutionary sound a highly influential staple of the scene for years after they burst out of Detroit in the late Sixties.

19. Phun City was a three-day people's festival in July 1970. Other acts included the Pretty Things and Edgar Broughton. The Pink Fairies played their set naked. It was organised by Mick Farren, leading light of the anarchist underground, frontman of the Deviants, music journalist and sci-fi author.

Rock'n'roll urban guerrillas with noisy anthems – the Pink Fairies were one of the many proto-punk bands that existed before 1977

Gavin Friday (Virgin Prunes: vocals)

Dublin was very, very repressed. Lots of unemployment, the Troubles – bombs going off in Dublin as well – and a heroin epidemic. It was a pretty fucked-up country. It's turned around in the last ten years. As a kid my only salvation, because I was not into football, was Bowie and Roxy. They were the gods then. I had some idea in my head that you had to be a super genius to be in a band. I was twelve when I got into T. Rex and Bowie in 1972. I never got off on the hippie stuff, you know. Bowie led me into Lou Reed, Velvets, Iggy.

Steve Severin

In 1971–72 I had long hair and went to festivals, but we hated hippies. Lydon had long hair then. After Bowie I cut my hair and started dyeing it.

Terrie (The Ex: guitar)

In 1973 I saw Roxy Music in Amsterdam with Brian Eno, and it was something I'd never seen or heard before in a music venue. I was blown away. When I went to the concert I saw strange people and the music had a weird element for me as well. I also had a bootleg before their first LP came out, when I heard Eno going mad with the synthesisers which was incredible.

I was also into Van Der Graaf Generator, strangely enough, they also had wild live gigs – almost trancey, hypnotic loud music.[20]

Marc Riley

The first band I actually saw was Queen supporting Mott the Hoople in September 1974. Me and Steve Hanley grew up together and we went to the gig.[21] We both had these horrible wire-woollen brown suits. So we saw Queen by default. Mott the Hoople were great, and the rest of the audience looked really cool so we adopted their look within about fifteen minutes! We went straight back home and our parents said, 'Where have those wire-wool suits gone?'

Mott the Hoople were such an important band at the time.[22] Ian Hunter was saying that Mick Jones was a marshall for Mott the Hoople. He was one of the kids that would follow them around, one of the leading fans, like a rock'n'roll prefect.

Mick Jones

Mott were very nice, the way they treated us. We used to go all over. We would sleep on the town hall steps in every town. It was like being on tour without hotel rooms! We used to bunk the trains as well – it used to be easy to do that. It's harder now. One of us used to work for the railway and he would have a special card. We used to hide in the toilets!

---

20. Van Der Graaf Generator were one of the key British underground prog bands.

21. Steve was the rock-solid bass player in the Fall for several years.

22. Mott the Hoople are perhaps the greatest of the British pre-punk bands and their (mad) shadow hangs over the the the Clash and the whole punk scene. Frontman Ian Hunter's bruised voice, brilliant lyrics and tough, working-class, heart-on-his-sleeve, poet stance – like a rainy day Bob Dylan from Shrewsbury – made him at once a charismatic talisman and a street hero. Mott recorded a string of great singles, including their classic version of David Bowie's 'All the Young Dudes', and brilliant albums, all worth checking out. Now!

The poet laureate of glam rock, one of the greatest ever British lyricists and frontman of Mott the Hoople, Ian Hunter was one of the big influences on punk

Mott had brought all these records and stuff from America. In those days you could buy amazing guitars from thrift stores in America, and they did.

Kevin Hunter

I was a fan of Mott the Hoople. Ian Hunter's book *Diary Of A Rock'n'Roll Star* came out in 1974. I've still got the book – it's a bit more dog-eared now.

Mick Jones

Ian Hunter's 1974 book, *Diary Of A Rock'n'Roll Star*, was like the brochure! It was telling you about the world of rock'n'roll. It was like the brochure of being in a band, of what we were going to do, so we lived it. We tried to make it a real thing. More than anybody, we followed Mott. They had their own style but we dressed more like the Faces. Other people that followed them used to work in Kensington Market and had a stall in the basement, these two sisters from Scotland called Anne and Carol. They used to sell the platform shoes and that's where everyone got them from, and the suits. Light-coloured suits with platforms, very long hair, frilly shirts – it was a very cool look for the time; coming out of the hippy thing, it was a bit flash. We were like little kids, fans, really lucky to be around. Seeing it was like, 'Wow, this is what it's like!' We got little titbits from their girlfriends, like, 'Ian likes to have his back washed in the bath,' and we were thinking, 'This is the life!' Just to see these records they had was like the Holy Grail! One was the Crazy Horse album, the Youngbloods one – great records, and Mott had these brought back from America.

Marc Riley

After seeing Mott the Hoople, we used to go to gigs all the time. The second gig I saw was T. Rex, the third was Mick Ronson, the fourth was Lou Reed. It was a great period. If we had managed to start going to gigs four months earlier then I would have got Bowie and Roxy at the Free Trade Hall as well. Along with Lou Reed at the

Palace with his *Berlin* album, they are the three gigs I really wished I had seen. If I could just go back three months and see the gigs I missed, that would be enough – I wouldn't be greedy!

Mick Jones

There was this group over here called Silverhead with Michael des Barres – he was one of those people who would come out in the audience and that used to scare the life out of people. It would scare me! And when I saw Iggy I thought, 'This is so great!' To come out and interact with the audience, that was an amazing thing to see.

Steve Diggle

I used to go to the Stoneground in Gorton. I saw bands like Silverhead – they had an album called *16 And Savaged*. It was a bit like the Dolls and the Stones. The bass player became Blondie's bass player, Nigel Harrison. Michael des Barres was the singer. Initially they were a raw band. I used to go and see stuff like that. I liked Led Zep: they had good dynamics and it was rough. It was really powerful. Even though they were seen as hippies, they were not all peace and love. A mate of mine used to say grammar school boys listen to Deep Purple and comp boys listen to Led Zep.

MOCK ROCK
The New York Dolls and
Rock'n'roll's First Generation Gap

Tony D (Editor, *Ripped And Torn* and *Kill Your Pet Puppy* fanzines)

I was aware of Lou Reed's *Transformer* and *Sally Can't Dance*. I joined the Lou Reed fan club. I was an obsessive. I was pissed off that I never joined the New York Dolls fan club that Morrissey was in. I also joined the Queen fan club. I saw Queen do *A Night At The Opera*. And I liked Mott the Hoople – another great precursor to punk.

Pauline Murray (Penetration, The Invisible Girls: vocals)

New York Dolls, Iggy, Stooges, Roxy Music – all brilliant. I started going to see bands when I was fourteen. I had an older boyfriend. I saw most bands when they came through Newcastle, although I saw the New York Dolls in York. The Dolls were brilliant. It was just students there, and they hated them and threw glasses at the band. It was just great, 1973 – they only did a few gigs in England. It was the classic line-up with Johnny Thunders and Arthur Kane. They looked great, they sounded great and people hated them! It was a forerunner of what was to come.

Mick Jones

Music changed continually. I became more discerning. From glam, I got into American early punk stuff like *Nuggets*, and after that the Dolls came along.

My mum was in America and she was sending me *Creem* and *Rockscene* on a subscription.[23] I was finding out about these groups like the Dolls really early. There wasn't that much you could find out about these groups in England. You might find a record to help fill it in. Rock'n'roll was a lot more unobtainable then. After I'd seen Iggy in *Creem* magazine, standing on people's hands with the audience all holding him, I realised there was something different out there.

When the New York Dolls first came over they played with the Faces at the Wembley Empire in July 1972. The year after they did that classic *Old Grey Whistle Test* appearance. I really went for it once I saw Johnny Thunders. I was looking a bit more airy-fairy till the Dolls came along. I was into the underground thing, quite hippyish, then I got into the more stylish side of things with the Faces and Mott, then I got into the Dolls and that was pretty much it until the Pistols.

---

23. Two key American underground music magazines.

'Mock rock,' sneered presenter Bob Harris after the New York Dolls' classic Old Grey Whistle Test appearance. The band created a rock'n'roll faultline before imploding in a flurry of rock'n'roll behaviour

Tony James

In the early Seventies I was starting to hear about the Dolls and the New York glam scene through *Creem* magazine, which hadn't hit the English scene yet. The music press was totally important then. Mick was the only other person who was buying *Creem*, a magazine I found in the only place in London you could get it.

Gaye Advert

The minute you hear their songs, the Dolls, you still think, 'Wow!' I saw them when they reformed – only two of them left but they still sounded great.

Damian O'Neill

My brother John saw the Dolls on the *Whistle Test*. I was too young – probably in bed! [laughs] John seen them play and afterwards when Whispering Bob called them 'mock rock'. The Dolls and the MC5 were crucial to us.

John was the leader of the early Undertones. He used to read the music press a lot. The *NME* especially was his bible. He was aware of Roxy Music, the Dolls and even more obscure stuff like Argent. For Derry these were weird bands! He was very aware of this stuff – he even bought a Fred Frith/Henry Cow record, stuff like that.[24] He always had his ear to the ground and that helped the Undertones immensely.

John O'Neill

I cannot emphasise how important the *NME* was from 1974 to 1977. It was the highlight of my week. I was buying the *NME* and it was a lifeline. I was checking out who influenced who and where the music came from. It was impossible to hear these groups. I read about the Velvet Underground, and the only Velvet Underground record you could get in Derry was the one after Lou Reed had left.

Howard Devoto (Buzzcocks, Magazine: vocals)

Rock music had been around a long time. It had got very knowing in all kinds of ways. People learned to play with image and media games without thinking about it. The artificiality of glam rubbed off onto punk. 'We're just trash' was now coming through from the New York Dolls. Norman Rockwell, the *New York Times* critic of the time, couldn't connect with glam rock, which he thought of as Elton John, Freddie Mercury and Bowie. To him the Sixties were authentic and these people were more about performance now.

Brian Young

I was about to discover the band that was to change my life: the New York Dolls. I'd bought *Melody Maker*, as Bolan was on the front cover when T. Rex's album *The Slider* came out, and buried in the back was this article on an unsigned group of Big Apple degenerates. Without even hearing them, I knew this was the band for me! From then on I scoured the weekly rags for each and every mention of my

---

24. Henry Cow were an avant-garde band formed at Cambridge University in 1968, featuring Fred Frith on guitar and various other instruments.

The epitome of sex and drugs and rock'n'roll, Dolls
guitarist Johnny Thunders took the guitar hero ideal
to its limit before dying in New Orleans in 1991

heroes, and when they turned up on snorefest *The Old Grey Whistle Test* I was sitting there with my trusty hand-held-mic tape recorder to capture them on cassette. I was floored: they made everything I'd listened to before look and sound kinda tame, and I wanted a skull 'n'bones jacket just like Johnny Thunders! Bob Harris' mocking comments sealed it for me. If he hated them so vehemently they HAD to be the best band on this or any other planet!

STYLE WHORES
Pre-punk Style from Biba to Sta-Prest to Let It Rock

Pauline Murray

We were going to see a lot of upcoming bands for three or four years. I liked to get dressed up and get right to the front where the action was, spray silver stuff into your hair and wear ridiculous platform boots and shiny trousers – that type of thing. Where I lived, to walk down the street dressed like that was a pretty brave thing to do. But you would go to a gig, get on a bus and do it, and you didn't seem to worry.

Charlie Harper

Lots of London clubs that stayed open till 3am were gay clubs, like Chaguaramas which was also a lesbian club. We looked strange. We were into Bowie's *Ziggy Stardust*, with lots of make-up at the time – a street version. We could get into Chaguaramas, no problem: two or three girls, me and a gay guy called Richey got to bop the night away. Every Friday they would have a band on. We went down there to see the band, who were like the Sweet – an ultra glam thing. I also saw the New York Dolls themselves at Biba's – that was a night to remember. I was totally into them when I saw them. I wanted to get a band like that.

Tony James

The most important moment of the week for me was getting the *Melody Maker* and going out to see bands in the Twickenham and Kingston area where I lived. I remember seeing Pink Floyd at the local polytechnic round the corner. What we consider huge bands now were playing local clubs. I'd go and see Soft Machine playing the local club.

In the early Seventies I moved into the *Friends/IT/Oz* magazine world. I've never told anyone about this period of my life, buying those magazines, going to see the Edgar Broughton Band, Pink Fairies and Hawkwind – the anti-establishment Underground. I related to the Pink Fairies and Edgar Broughton. I was into agit prop. People like Mick Farren were around. I was reading him and getting into his band the Deviants. I was digging that whole kind of thing. In Twickenham, much to my parents' distress, there was this huge old factory squatted by long hairs and they had this underground music club. They had a PA and guys living there smoking dope and taking acid.

I was in a kind of sci-fi Hawkwind type of group with two drummers. I liked two drummers because of the Pink Fairies. It was a freaky agit prop/Hawkwind/Pink Fairies type of band. I had very long hair, ripped jeans and a Biba T-shirt. I was already moving slightly towards the Biba era of my life as well! You had to be really thin to wear Biba: they only made small or medium T-shirts. Very tight stripy T-shirts. Biba was a glamorous, hippie, bohemian, Stonesy sort of look.

Garry Bushell

We used to have a lot of skinheads where I came from. Younger kids were into the suedehead look after the skinhead look. The tank tops came a bit later. It seems a bit bizarre now, but there was a Slade gig and everyone was wearing butchers' outfits! It was really stupid! Also flat caps, that kind of look. There was a strange mix of styles – people see it as being very linear but it wasn't really like that. It was all over the place. Black leather jackets were mixed in with Sta-Prest trousers. People wore the Rupert Bear trousers as well, but I hated them, and I never liked those loafers with funny bits on them. I liked brogues. Polo necks were fashionable but that knitwear stuff never really suited me, ha ha!

Mick Jones

We'd go to places like Granny Takes A Trip and Alkasura on the Kings Road.[25] One of these shops had half a car stuck out into the street at the front of it. Alkasura sold dandy gear, lacy and frilly, and we were wearing that kind of thing, a bit like the Faces. For a while we had our hair cut a bit feather-cut style; it looked funny but compared to what else was happening it was not that bad.

Marco Pirroni

People like Bernie Rhodes, Lloyd Johnson, Tommy Roberts, John Pearce – all those old mods who were real clothes obsessives – went on to start all those shops and boutiques on Kings Road. The whole fascination with American clothes, the Levi's stuff like that. There was the shop Paradise Garage, run by Bradley Mendelson. There was the shop before Let It Rock run by Trevor Miles – he was the first person to import old straight-legged Levi's into Britain.[26] In 1971 you'd think you could get them anywhere, but you *couldn't*. Things like a black T-shirt – you couldn't get it. It didn't exist. Sounds odd, but they didn't make them.

It was not mod itself but the old mods that had their influence on punk. They weren't reviving mod, because by being true to the mod ethic they were being modern – not looking back.

---

25. Alkasura was run by John Lloyd, who used to supply Marc Bolan with his stage clothes.
26. Let It Rock was the first shop set up by Malcolm McLaren and Vivienne Westwood at 430 Kings Road when they took over the space from Trevor Miles in late 1971. It specialised in Fifties revival clothing. The shop later became infamous as the fetishware boutique Sex.

Paul Stolper (Art dealer and punk collector)

Malcolm McLaren was into the tribal nature of youth culture. He was very much into the visual side of the partnership, whereas Vivienne Westwood was a haberdasher, tailoring the clothes. I think the conceptual side initially came from McLaren. He was the more interested in the effect the clothes had on people. With Let It Rock he went back to rock'n'roll – that's the music he really liked, early rebel culture.

John Lydon

I remember when it was Let It Rock and it used to sell clothes to Teddy boys. Malcolm and Vivienne were really a pair of shysters: they would sell anything to any trend that they could grab onto.

Marco Pirroni

I started doing the whole Roxy Music in Forties suits thing because of their whole aesthetic. I was into the Roxy Music glamour thing. I then discovered the Sex shop, where they were doing it in a different way. I was looking for a pair of brothel creepers and I heard rumours of a Teddy boy shop in the Kings Road.

The Sex shop was called Too Fast to Live then.[27] It had a big skull-and-crossbones outside. I walked in the first time and I didn't know you were meant to be scared! [laughs] It was all black inside. The imagery they had chosen was pretty out there, pretty scary. There was nothing else like it going on. It was a Tuesday afternoon. Vivienne Westwood was in there and I asked for some brothel creepers. I was thinking, 'Fucking hell, she looks incredible!' She had white hair and she was wearing big leather pegs and purple winklepicker boots. She looked amazing. I *had* to go back again. I would go in every week. I sometimes bought things they were selling: slashed T-shirts, T-shirts that were two bits of cloth sewn

---

27. Too Fast to Live, Too Young to Die was the new name (during 1973–74) for Let It Rock. In late 1974, it was relaunched again as Sex.

together, leather trousers, drapes, leather T-shirts – this was 1973, remember. They had blue winklepicker boots but not in my size so I bought some black ones. Brothel creepers were accepted even before Mud wore them, but winklepickers were really revolting, they made people go, 'Eeeeurgh!'

The jukebox in the shop had things on I'd never heard before. When I put together a compilation album of the Sex shop jukebox last year, one of the reasons I didn't put sleeve notes on the album was that when I heard these records I didn't know who they were or when they were recorded. There was no information, no cover, no internet, no book to look them up in. It was just part of a mish-mash of influences that I was exposed to.

Jordan had only just started working there.[28] It was mostly Vivienne working there with Malcolm, which they hated doing. Later on they got a staff together and then I used to go in all the time. I got chatting to Jordan. I started bunking off school and there came a point I was in there every fucking day, hanging out. They never offered me a job though! It would have been my dream. I was fourteen at the time! The shop was only ever crowded on a Saturday. The people who went were older people who had come from Biba, and kids like me who were indefinable really, Bowie/ Roxy fans.

I went to that big Fifties-revival show at Wembley in 1972.[29] I didn't think the acts were that good. If you look at the crowd you will see people who went to the Sex shop. A lot of Teds used to go to the shop but they tailed off when the shop started getting into the *Scorpio Rising* stuff, all leather hats, jackets and trousers – the whole fetish thing was coming in. Malcolm had gone to see *Scorpio Rising*

28. Jordan was the striking shop assistant in Sex, who would wear the shop's clothes and have her hair in several wild styles, pretty well single-handedly paving the punk look. She went on to dance on stage with the Sex Pistols occasionally, and managed the early Adam and the Ants.

29. The London Rock'n'Roll Show, held in front of 50,000 at Wembley Stadium on 5 August 1972, featured a host of rock'n'roll pioneers including Little Richard, Jerry Lee Lewis, Bo Diddley, Bill Haley and Chuck Berry, plus Screamin' Lord Sutch, Gary Glitter and, incongruously, the MC5. It was filmed as the movie *London Rock and Roll Show* (1973).

at the ICA; he mixed that with the Gene Vincent black leather thing, and it's not far from that to get into the fetish look.[30]

Nick Cash

In Kilburn and the High Roads we had a manager called Tommy Roberts who was a good friend of Malcolm McLaren.[31] Tommy Roberts took us down to Malcolm's shop and Malcolm kitted us out with these outfits, like suits – it was all Teddy boy stuff he had at the time. He was fascinated by the Kilburns and he was into the Jewish tailor thing of zoot suits, general Teddy boy stuff, real drape jackets with velvet collars. We used to go in there and we got all the gear sewn up for us there and then. It was brilliant clobber.

Marco Pirroni

People looking back at Vivienne and Malcolm's clothes will say, 'Why did they do the black leather T shirt? Why chicken bones?'[32] Where did that come from?' Well, it probably doesn't come from anywhere! You know what it's like when you do music, you get something and there is no reason why? I played a twang guitar on a Burundi beat. I suddenly thought this would be good – I can't explain why. It's a random rush of ideas and someone else says, 'That looks great.' They never did things I thought were shit.

I don't think there was a bigger plan. They were doing these clothes, accentuating the revolution in rock'n'roll. Rock'n'roll clothes have always been revolutionary, and they played that bit up. I don't think anyone had done a rock'n'roll shop before. In the Fifties and Sixties if you wanted a drape you had to go to John Dunn & Co and have it made. John Dunn & Co are not a rock'n'roll shop.

---

30. *Scorpio Rising* was a 1964 film about bikers. The director, Kenneth Anger, was also the author of the *Hollywood Babylon* books.

31. The same Tommy Roberts (the former mod) introduced earlier.

32. One of their T-shirts featured dangling chicken bones that spelled out the word 'ROCK' (or, in an alternate design, 'PERV').

There was a political thing going on with the clothes but you couldn't understand it. There was no manifesto. You couldn't tie it down and that's what kept you thinking. It was the first time I'd seen T-shirts with slogans on. Before it was names of bands, and these were random slogans.

Paul Stolper

Malcolm talks a lot about the Paris riots and Situationism.[33] Punk was fairly middle-class and he had an art-school background, so they would have been aware of the Situationists. He was involved with Jamie Reid who already did his own magazine, *Suburban Press*, in the early Seventies and had all the slogans in place. Jamie Reid was already doing the stickers. Helen Wellington-Lloyd did the cut-up lettering.[34] Jamie Reid already had the slogans like 'Demand the Impossible' from the Paris Situationists. He was also aware of Situationist groups like the King Mob, who had all dressed as Santa Claus at Selfridges, grabbing toys and handing them out to kids at Christmas time, before being arrested whilst still being dressed as Santa.[35]

Vic Godard

We went down to the shop and saw all the sex stuff in it. I really liked it, but it was just too dear. There was no way we could afford it. I did have a shirt from there when it was Let It Rock. It was the only place

---

33. The Situationist International (SI) were put together from various splinter groups across Europe in 1957. They continued the tradition of Dadaism and Surrealism, but with a more political edge, rather than creating art. They fermented through the Sixties before petering out in 1970. The key figures in the movement were French.

34. McLaren had met Jamie Reid at Croydon Art School in 1967, and Helen Wellington-Lloyd at Goldsmith's School of Art in 1968. Helen was a close friend and confidante of McLaren, and would be the first to use the cut-up letters that created the classic Sex Pistols logo.

35. In the late Sixties a British group of activists called King Mob were loose affiliates of the SI; they preferred delinquent activity more than their arty-farty continental cousins. (McLaren had apparently been involved in the Selfridges action.) The name King Mob dates back to the Gordon Riots in June 1780, a week of rioting in London – a sort of aborted English revolution, nine years before the French had theirs. In London, law courts were torched and prisons were opened. On the walls of Newgate Prison was daubed the slogan that the prisoners had been freed by 'His Majesty, King Mob'.

that sold original Sixties shirts so I'd already bought stuff there. The jukebox had some great music you never heard anywhere, like Nico.

Nils Stevenson

I had a stall on the Kings Road with Lloyd Johnson, between the Roebuck pub and the Sex shop. I used to see Malcolm and Vivienne in the shop – a friend of mine called Alan Jones used to take me in. He was working there at the time. The first time I went into the shop it was called Let It Rock. An incredibly intimidating shop. The sales staff treated you abysmally – if you were lucky they ignored you! It was like a very exclusive club, almost religious. I was intrigued. I did buy a T-shirt there immediately, which cost £15, a week's wages. It was a grey, oily-looking T-shirt with little soft porn photos. One really struck me: Malcolm had written 'L'Age D'or' and there was a shoe on it. Being into the arty film stuff, I knew *L'Age D'Or* was a Louis Buñuel film and he was a shoe fetishist. Somehow that clicked. We felt this connection: it was the codes that made you feel special and discover people.

Andy Warhol was crucial in the way he enabled freaks to be freaks. We were all very inspired by that. The early days of punk relate very much to the Factory, the fifteen minutes of fame idea. The Sex shop was where the English punk scene would come out: run by Malcolm and Vivienne, it attracted all the lowlifes that Warhol would have attracted in New York, the bottom-of-society people. Malcolm was very aware of the Factory scene. Had he not legitimised who he was by becoming Malcolm McLaren, he would have wanted to become Andy Warhol.

Glen Matlock

I was working in an office where you had to put a document in the system in a tube and whoosh it up to the office. It was like H. G. Wells or something. I'm fifteen years old, I've never done that kind of thing before, and I put the money and not the document in and it fucked the system up. [laughs] No one knew where it had come from! But I was fed up with my job. I had heard about this shop down the road that sold creepers so I walked in there and it was fantastic: it was laid out like a sitting room from the Fifties and it was selling rock'n'roll clothes. I said, 'Do you need anyone to work here?' and they said, 'We do actually!' Just by chance I got the gig there and then. I doubled my money as well and I didn't have to start till eleven in the morning either!

I thought it was cool to be down the Kings Road. But Bryan Ferry would walk past, or one of the Stones, someone like that, and Malcolm thought they were all tossers. They were multi-millionaires and we didn't have a pot to piss in! There was a T-shirt Bernie and Malcolm knocked together saying, 'You're gonna wake up one morning and know what side of the bed you've been lying on!' and it had a list of people who were deemed to be happening and not happening. Mick Jagger came in the shop one day and he went, 'Ooh, I'm on the wrong side!'

Jah Wobble (Public Image Limited: bass)

When I grew up no working-class lad would ever be in a band. It was all middle-class people playing prog rock. It never occurred to us that we could be in bands. It took punk rock to change everything. I was into Trojan stuff, ska, Rod Stewart and the Faces, T. Rex. I was never a massive Bowie fan. I never quite believed him. I was also a big Stevie Wonder fan. *Innervisions* is a great record.

I was at the College of Further Education on the edge of the East End. It was very bohemian and attracted a lot of naughty boys! That's how I ended up there. My first meeting with John Lydon was there. It was a bit of a stand-off – 'You're the nutcase...' 'You're the other nutcase, you'll do!' He was older than me and I was very impressed with him. Sid came the next year.[36] John had fucked off

---

36. The future Sid Vicious was born John Simon Ritchie to Ann and John, a grenadier guard, in 1955. His father left and Ann moved to Ibiza. Returning to the UK, she married Chris Beverley in 1965, resulting in a name change for the confused youth. On meeting John Lydon, John finally acquired his more famous and aptly comical moniker – named after Lydon's pet hamster, Sid the Vicious, which would bite people's fingers (and after his hero Syd Barrett).

by then so I ended up hanging out with Sid a lot. John knew Sid from Hackney College.

Marco Pirroni

Sid Vicious was a tall, geeky kind of bloke into Roxy and Bowie. He was very similar to me and all the other people of that age group who went to the shop. I was two years younger than the rest of them, and at that time two years was a big gap, gigantic.

Honey magazine used to have pictures of Roxy Music fans, and there was a picture of Sid wearing a gold lamé drape in 1975. I think it was the first time he was in the papers, a long time before punk. I saw Vivienne at the Wembley Arena Roxy gig. I was downstairs sitting in the stalls and they were doing 'Every Dream Home A Heartache', a really quiet song, and she walked out shouting, 'You're disgusting!' over and over at the band. She was being ushered out by the bouncers and I thought, 'There's that woman from the shop!'

Glen Matlock

I was working for Malcolm McLaren in the shop. Paul Cook used to come in with Steve Jones. One of them would chat Malcolm up and the other would try and nick stuff, and I would try and keep an eye on them! We started knocking ideas round for a band and having a laugh.

I would say hello to Malcolm. With Vivienne I didn't have much of a rapport going, but then when I was thinking of going to art school and I needed someone to be a referee for me, sign a form, I was speaking to Vivienne and said, 'Do you think Malcolm will sign this?' She said, 'Don't ask him, he's been thrown out of every art school in London.' And because I was thinking of going to art school she started taking a bit more interest in me.

Mick Jones

I definitely wanted to be in a band. I was sixteen before I started guitar. I meant to start earlier but I didn't get round to it! I started on stylophone, to tell the truth. That was my first thing, then it was drums, then I went on to bass and then I thought, 'All right, I can try two more strings here!' I could do a bit of backing vocals as well, but that was enough – I didn't want to be a singer.

Schoolgirl was a band made up of some older kids from the Strand, the school that I was at. These were kids from the year above me. All the people that we knew who went to see Mott were in Schoolgirl. They were a bit like Mott. I started off as their roadie. It was like 'Little Mick' roadying for them. I was always there. I didn't get any lessons, but anyone who played anything, I was always asking how they did it. I must have been embarrassingly naive to the older kids around me. I think they couldn't understand where this kid was coming from. Why can't he just be a lot cooler? Coolness comes with age.

Knox

When I came back from Edinburgh I went to east London. I got really into Jeff Beck. I was in this sort of heavy rock'n'roll band called Heavy Parrot. It wasn't my first band in art school – earlier in Watford I'd been in a psychedelic band. We had supported John Mayall. Heavy Parrot was doing rock'n'roll covers, like a Teddy boy band – that was 1974 or something. It wasn't really my thing. They were nice guys, but they tried to get me to wear the clothes and it wasn't right. I was messing around with these other people in this band called Despair which did a few gigs. We were doing early Vibrators material like 'Whips And Furs' and 'Sweet Sweetheart'.

PUNK ROCK INTERNATIONALE
Far and Wide, Mavericks are Making a Noise

Jake Burns

Belfast was quite cut off because of the Troubles. Bands just didn't come over and play, apart from Rory Gallagher who used to come pretty regularly. Bands in Northern Ireland were like human juke-boxes. The majority played country and western, and the showbands were really good musicians, but it struck me that I would rather have a job on the buses or something – that's just soul destroying. To be fair, it was the only way that they could get a gig. There were a couple of local bands that were playing better stuff. We had the luxury of being so young that we didn't have to work: we could be snotty and play what we wanted to.

T. V. Smith

I was living in mid-Devon, in the middle of nowhere in a village. The nearest gig was Plymouth or Exeter which was a bit of a trip. You had to find someone to drive to take you to a gig, and as often as not it was in a university and you had to blag your way in, get a student to sign you in. It was hard to get to hear music – hardly any bands would come down to Devon. When someone like the Heavy Metal Kids or Stackridge came down, you really latched onto them because you really appreciated the fact they had come down.[37] Most bands you read about never went there; they would never get further than Bristol.

Gaye Advert

Back in the early Seventies I was doing a foundation year at Bideford, and then two years' graphic design at Torquay. I saw Sparks in Torquay. I didn't see Bowie. In Exeter I saw Hawkwind, Cockney Rebel. The Doctors of Madness were great. The first big band I saw was Free: they played a festival in Woolacombe. There were local bands: the Amazing Blondel and Carrion from Ilfracombe. I went on the back of someone's motorbike with a vest on: it was a nice warm night, but coming back was freezing!

We would travel 40 miles to Exeter or go 100 miles to Bristol. We got very loyal to those bands who made the effort to play where we

---

37. Stackridge were a quirky early Seventies folk/rock outfit, who morphed into the Korgis.

lived. We thought about moving to London from 1974 onwards, and it was like getting set loose in a sweet shop when we finally did move.

T. V. Smith

I was totally bowled over by Cockney Rebel: they were one of the bands that came down to the West Country quite a lot. When I first saw them live, they had all the same image thing going on and great songs as well. It was really original, the implied violence, but I was really disappointed in the end.[38]

My band Sleaze were glam rock. We made a record. It was probably pretty shit. We had a cheap studio in Torquay and we put it down live and pressed about 50 copies. We had make-up and loon pants. It was a dangerous combination at the time. The weird thing was that it shocked. All the other bands around at the time did heavy metal covers of Deep Purple. We had make-up on and did strange, self-written songs influenced by Iggy or 'Rebel Rebel' Bowie. A couple of the songs were reworked into Adverts songs, like 'Listen Don't Think'. I did a slow version with different lyrics in Sleaze; it went on for about ten minutes. We didn't do more than ten gigs in total. There was not much in Torquay – it was community halls, that kind of thing. Our first gig was in a village hall in Dartmoor.

Gaye Advert

I met Tim when I was in my third year. He was on foundation year, two years behind me – in the end he only did his foundation year. He had his college band at the time, Sleaze, and I used to enjoy them. They were sort of glammy, good fun. Tim had these amazing masks, like a cast of his face, and he would wear them on stage. It was a bit more interesting than your average covers band.

I always wore jeans and a T-shirt. I never really changed. Other people were into Genesis and Yes and all that sort of stuff. We had

---

38. Briefly Steve Harley's Cockney Rebel looked like they were going to dominate the scene. They arrived between Bowie and punk, and for a series of great singles ('Make Me Smile (Come Up And See Me)' being the most famous) were unstoppable.

reggae as well – I was into Bob Marley. We saw him in Birmingham at the Odeon in 1975. I was nearly nineteen. I read the music press and kept them as well – I had mountains of *Sounds* and *Melody Makers* with pictures cut out!

Tony Wilson (Broadcaster. Founder of Factory Records)

T. Rex had disappeared. It was short-lived, and it was exciting in 1971. In '77, when Granada brought Marc Bolan out of retirement for his TV series, T. Rex had gone. Unfortunately, for me Bowie was kind of some guy from London who was a wanker and that put me off Bowie, and also I never really liked Roxy Music because of Bryan Ferry. He's all about form over substance, so it was a bit boring. When Granada asked me and my mate to start our own music show at that point in time, late autumn 1975, we talked about it and decided that music is so shite we'll do more of a comedy show – which is why Clive James had a spot every week. It was more of a fun show than about music, because music wasn't worth shit – except for a few bits of Americana which were worthwhile.

The one thing Manchester did have was a couple of venues. There was the Hard Rock, which was a fantastic venue, very hi-tech, beautifully done, very expensive. I imagine that's why it must have gone bust – it's where the B&Q in Old Trafford is now. One of the great gigs at the Hard Rock was the Lou Reed concert on the *Rock'n'Roll Animal* tour. We had good venues like that but there was fuck all happening. British music was dull. We knew something was going to happen.

I became obsessed in 1973 with Bruce Springsteen, and my nickname on the Stretford End was Bruce because I kept going on about this unknown American singer-songwriter. Springsteen was unknown for the first two albums – in fact CBS Records' reps in Manchester used to call him 'Loose Windscreen'.

Marc Riley

We would go to lots of gigs. We wouldn't pay to get in. We would go to anything: a load of us would be stood outside a Robin Trower gig desperately trying to get in, and once we got in for free we wished that we hadn't! At that time I'd got to know Mike Rossi from Slaughter and the Dogs – we'd go and see a lot of bands before punk. I seem to remember one night we used him as a battering ram to open the back door at the Manchester Free Trade Hall – probably to get into a Donovan gig! When you broke through the back door at the Free Trade Hall the bouncers would chase you upstairs, right through the bar, right down the front stairs. Fortunately the old guys were not quite with it: they would also do the Hallé Orchestra concerts and were all in their early sixties. You could easily fool them, so we sat at the back watching Back Street Crawler, and I fell asleep immediately! [laughs][39]

Rob Lloyd

I wanted to be in a band although I couldn't play an instrument. I came from Cannock in Staffordshire. The only people who had electric guitars were into Jethro Tull and Cream and stuff like that, which I never liked. I couldn't find people to play with me.

Cannock is a bit of a greaser town and I eventually found this really cool band. This girl who went to our school hung out with these biker types and she had a shed at the back of her house. She used to let these greasers play there. They wanted to be like Black Sabbath, Deep Purple, Led Zeppelin, but they couldn't play. So to my ears they sounded like the Stooges. They were really basic. They had these great Burns guitars that looked like Mosrites. They looked brilliant, scruffy hair and denim waistcoats, leather jackets – you can picture the kind of thing, and all they did was riff away. They would be trying to play like Deep Purple or Sabbath, very primitive. Obviously they didn't give a

---

39. Back Street Crawler were the former Free guitarist Paul Kossof's last band before his untimely death.

fuck about lyrics and singing, so when I joined them I could shout over the top and no one cared. All they wanted to do was rock. I did it with these guys in the shed and I thought, 'Yeah, I'm in a band now.'

The reason I actually left the band was because by the time we were ready to play in public we wanted a name and the three greasers decided that the band was going to be called Witchhazel. I thought that was a really shit name, and we got into a row about it so I quit. Shows what a wanker you can be as a teenager!

Chris Bailey (The Saints: vocals)

I was born in Kenya. We moved back to Belfast when I was young – I still carry the Irish Free State passport – and then we moved to Brisbane. At the end of my teens I came screaming back to the northern hemisphere. When I come back to Oz the customs say, 'Welcome back, mate,' until they look at my passport and then they say, 'I didn't realise you were a foreigner!' Having said that, music is pretty international. Doesn't matter where you come from.

When I was growing up in Brisbane we had access to some great music because of the Vietnam war. American troops would be in town on rest and recreation, and they would come in with their records which they would sell for drink money. The war may have been fairly tragic but for me it was good for getting into great records that I wouldn't have otherwise heard.

In my mind's eye, I see Brisbane in black and white, like an American B-movie. Basically every generation of young people has their notion of rebellion, and in those days it was rock'n'roll. Given that I'm crap at football, being in a band was a good option. We started off playing r'n'b covers, and then Ed and I started writing songs.[40] I met Ed at school. In those days long hair was a bit of a thing and we started chatting to each other. The little gang we hung round with was involved in girls, drinking and rock'n'roll. It was very colourful and entertaining.

---

40. Ed Kuepper, guitarist in the Saints.

SOMETHING BETTER CHANGE
The Mid-Seventies Slump

Al Hillier

The years from 1974 to 1976 were peppered with mostly manufactured futile artists churning out useless meaningless banal shite and it meant absolutely fuck all to me. Apart from the odd notable exception, the music on the radio and in the charts was dominated either by the early Seventies glam rock bands or artificially created dickheads with corporate songs written for them by professional songsmiths with funny names (nothing changes there then, does it?). Even though there were all these massive rock acts like Led Zep, Free, and Pink Floyd lounging in some drug haze somewhere in the background, they were like corporations, performing occasional overblown stage-managed concerts and eventually bowing to record company pressure and releasing self-indulgent albums that seemed to take forever to record. The whole industry stank like a stagnant pond where all life had been suffocated.

After the skinhead thing waned I was constantly searching for something to replace that energy. People like the madcap Alex Harvey and the Heavy Metal Kids instantly attracted me and my interest in music suddenly revolved around the 'live' experience. A few of us used to go and see the Heavy Metal Kids down at the Brecknock up in Camden in '74–75. I loved the antics of Gary Holton and his band.[41] These two bands filled a bit of a gap for me pre-punk and in my opinion they stood out without receiving all due recognition. They were both well ahead of their time musically and in their live performances and I will always cite Alex Harvey as being one of the founding fathers of punk.

---

41. Strangely, the Heavy Metal Kids did not in fact play heavy metal. They took their name direct from William Burroughs, played a variety of rock that was brash and energetic, and didn't take themselves too seriously. Lead singer Gary Holton, formerly a child actor, later had a lead role in the first two series of *Auf Wiedersehen Pet*, before dying from an overdose in 1985.

Rat Scabies

I always wanted to see Alex Harvey. The Heavy Metal Kids were beginning to emerge too. I got fired from a couple of bands because I always wanted to play fast songs and they said, 'You've got to have slow ones for the audience.'

Tony Wilson

Musically it was just dreadful. It was appalling at that point. It was dominated by real second-ratedness. All the great Sixties heroes had disintegrated into drugs or to nothing. I stopped listening to English music, except for John Martyn who would bring out a good album every year in that period. Other than that, I listened to American music, and even that was getting boring.

John Lydon

Early Seventies Britain was a very depressing place. It was completely run-down, there was trash on the streets, total unemployment – just about everybody was on strike. Everybody was brought up with an education system that told you point blank that if you came from the wrong side of the tracks (which of course was of not much use because the trains were on strike) then you had no hope in hell and no career prospects at all. Out of that came pretentious *moi* and the Sex Pistols and then a whole bunch of copycat wankers after us.

The Don holds court in Acme Attractions, the other shop in the pre-punk scene

CHAPTER 3
1975: I'M NOT AN ABORTION: THE BIRTH OF PUNK

Accelerating into the future, the disparate strands of pop culture were coming together. Fast. 1975 saw many of the key players in the punk explosion experimenting with various line-ups, toying with ideas and influences thrown up by the past few years. During this year, whilst much of the music scene was slumbering and England really was dreaming, a disparate mob of pop dissenters were coalescing. The count-down was on.

REVOLT INTO STYLE
The Kings Road Punk Rock Shopping Experience

Punk was more than music. A clutch of clothes stores and stalls were serving as key points of inspiration. The shops served as meeting places, somewhere to exchange influences, and in the case of the Sex shop threw up radical and dangerous new ideas in a series of brilliant clothes designs.

Don Letts

I was into funk and Italian high fashion. I had a right poncey clutch bag! I was very into clothes – that's the currency that young people speak in, as well as music. I dived into the whole thing. I was then into the rude boy thing.

Punk wasn't even in the air then. I was working on the Kings Road in Chelsea at Jean Machine at the time when I discovered Malcolm's shop down at World's End. I walked in and the shop was fucking empty! Malcolm was in the shop and I stumbled into this Aladdin's Den, a kind of subculture of the last 30 years. It was amazing, it has to be said. I was a bit of a mouthy lad back then, so I got friendly with Vivienne and Malcolm. Malcolm went to New York and I now realise that it was to work with the Dolls. Vivienne was still there and I used to hang with Vivienne. I remember her taking me to Lou Reed, pre-the actual punk explosion. I was getting an education in this white culture.

Then I got offered a job by this guy John Krivine who had this other shop down the road, Acme Attractions, which is an important part of the story. He opened this stall selling retro clothing, with a jukebox, and I'm sitting on the scooter in the shop. It's a small stall upstairs at the antique market on Kings Road and I got the jukebox loaded with heavy reggae. It was a really austere place with really old people and our place was pissing them off – they wanted to kick us out and they couldn't. So they pushed me down to the basement, and that was the Acme Attractions that would become semi-legendary.

Andy Czezowski (Managed the Damned and Generation X. Ran the Roxy club)

John Krivine was running a stall at Antiquarias market. They were selling Fifties memorabilia: robots and supermen flasks which they were bringing in from America. They moved into the cellar there in 1975 and opened Acme Attractions. I was doing the books for them. You then started noticing these people hanging around. Dave Vanian came in one day: I remember he smelt of

Ex-mod and natty dresser Czezowski gave punk its first permanent home at the Roxy

embalming fluid! He had a white face and very dark hair and was a gravedigger.

The Sex shop was round the corner. It was much more creative, making clothes, whereas Acme would sell Fifties stuff. The two shops were where everyone would hang out.

Don Letts

I'm doing very nicely in the shop. It was a really cool fucking place. I used to sell weed under the counter and it got around people knew about the weed thing.

Bernie Rhodes had a store in Antiquarias for a while.[1] He sold silkscreen shirts and was playing reggae on a little Dansette. He

---

1. One of the key plotters behind the movement, a punk *agent provocateur*. Rhodes' confrontational style rubbed many people up the wrong way but also pushed the ones that got it into some great work. Before managing the Clash, he was signing T-shirts at the Sex shop and fomenting the punk revolution with Malcolm McLaren.

could have been the man, instead of me. I'm so glad I met those guys when I did, Bernie and Malcolm.

This is happening as the punk rock thing is starting to take root. My white mates are feeling pretty alienated. No jobs. There was a general feeling of no future – the SUS laws, high unemployment, strikes.[2] I was feeling liberated from day one. I had something to alleviate the pressure, which was the music, the reggae. What else is around at the time? Stadium rock shit that's totally removed from the shit on the street. People singing about 'Hotel California', and we don't even know where California is, much less than check into a fucking hotel! My white brethren started creating their own soundtrack *for* the people *by* the people, that would eventually become known as punk rock. This is 1975.

Mark Stewart (The Pop Group: vocals)

I grew up on the outskirts of Bristol. Our mates were running sound systems and knew people in St Paul's, near where I was growing up. You have a top mix in Bristol. We never saw the difference between the styles. Funk was the first thing I got into. I was into reggae. I started the Avon funk army: black kids/white kids. We did this robot monkey dancing to these heavy funk basslines with the older brothers of people who went on to be in Massive Attack.[3] It was a spillover from dressing up. It was a townie sort of thing; some of the lads were hard kids.

When Sex opened in London, everyone rushed up there to get the outrageous clothes. It wasn't the music. No one knew about that. One of my first girlfriends had a rubber dungaree thing – she used to wear it to shock. We were into shock. Through Bowie a lot of the kids were into dressing up and having a laugh. But funk was the soundtrack in Bristol.

---

2. The SUS laws were nineteenth-century statutes against vagrancy, used by the police to stop and search at random. A particular grievance among ethnic minorities, who tended to be targeted.

3. Atmospheric dub dance crew from Bristol who hit the big time in the early Nineties with a series of brilliant moody albums. Key member and rapper 3D was on the Bristol punk scene.

There was a shop called Paradise Garage, which was run by Alan Jones, the sax player from Amen Corner. He was mates with Malcolm McLaren and Lloyd Johnson who had a big Fifties store in Kensington Market. Straight away he was bringing down a lot of the Let It Rock and Sex shop stuff and kids were buying it up – the black kids and the white kids.

Don Letts

People couldn't afford Sex shop clothes. That's why my shop was always full. The staff used to give us it! That's why a lot of people I knew had the Sex stuff. Michael Collins gave me a rubber T-shirt from there once and it nearly fucking killed me. I'm living with my family and I go to the bedroom and put the shirt on. It's a bit hot and sweaty now and I'm thinking it's not really me, and it's stuck halfway round my neck and it's strangling me. Of course I'm not going to call anyone to help me! It was like an auto-erotic asphyxiation. So Vivienne Westwood nearly killed me!

What you can't take away from Vivienne and Malcolm's shop is that they gave the look and identity to punk rock, but as far as social interaction Acme Attractions was it. We sold jelly sandals, plastic see-through macs, fluorescent pink drape peg-leg trousers, and electric blue zoot suits. Also juke boxes and pin machines. Everyone came in there and hung out. Bob Marley came in the shop, trying to pull Jeanette whilst I'm sorting his weed round the back of the counter![4]

Back in those days, shops were the centre of creativity. Before, places like Granny Takes A Trip and Alkasura and Mr Freedom had been the scene, and now it was our shops – they became more like clubs in a way, places where like-minded people could meet.

Gene October

In Acme Attractions they sold second-hand Sixties stuff like Chelsea boots, hipsters and shirts, stuff that was quite cheap. Don Letts worked

---

4. Jeanette Lee, who also worked at the shop.

LONDON SS
Mick Meets Tony

The history of London SS reads like a roll call of punk rock. So many of the key players went through the band's ranks, and in particular it served as a launch pad for both the Damned and the Clash. ('SS', incidentally, stood for 'Social Security', according to Mick Jones, but was also chosen for shock value.)

Mick Jones

I had this band the Delinquents with my best friend John Brown who had been in Schoolgirl. We started planning it in 1973. I started off on bass but moved to guitar. We were doing Flamin' Groovies, Standells and MC5 stuff.[6] We were like a British Dolls and then we come aware of the Hollywood Brats.[7] I'd seen the Dolls on the *Whistle Test* and they blew my mind, the way they looked, their whole attitude.

Another band we were all really into was the Sharks. Andy Fraser, the ex-bass player from Free, formed them. On the first album was Andy Fraser and guitarist Chris Spedding.[8] The lead singer was called Snips and they made two albums with different bass players. The first album had a sort of Batmobile on the cover called the 'Sharkmobile'. The second album was called *Jab It in Yore Eye*. The album cover was very good: they had their eyes shut and someone had painted their eyes in. It looks really weird.

Tony Gordon, who would go on to manage Sham 69, said he might be interested in managing us if we called ourselves Little

---

6. The Standells were an archetypal Sixties garage band from LA. They only had one hit, 'Dirty Water', but it was 'Sometimes Good Guys Don't Wear White' that has become their enduring classic.

7. One of the great lost bands of the pre-punk era, the Hollywood Brats had the swagger, androgyny and nihilism of their heroes the New York Dolls, and their one album (released only after they split up) is a great long-lost artefact of British glam rock'n'roll that lies somewhere between the ubiquitous Mott the Hoople and Johnny Thunders' mob.

8. Session guitar player and songwriter Chris Spedding lurks in the shadows of British music. His name crops up everywhere, from playing guitar with Brian Eno, Roy Harper and, er, the Wombles, to producing the first Sex Pistols demos in May 1976, playing with the Vibrators, and having a mid-Seventies hit with the classic 'Motor Biking'.

Queenie so we changed our name! We did a demo but it wasn't right. So Kelvin rang up Guy Stevens and got him to come down to a rehearsal and maybe manage us. We had two guitars, bass, drums and a singer in our line-up. Guy said if he was going to do something then we needed a keyboard player, to make it more like Mott, and we didn't need the extra guitar player, who was me. He didn't know I wrote the songs! The others were keen to get on so they said all right. John Brown didn't agree but they managed to sway him.

That was the knock-back that made me go to my bedroom and lock myself away for months and learn guitar properly. The lucky thing that happened was that when I started to learn guitar I started writing songs as part of my learning. It helped me because I'd listened to other people's songs and I understood what made these songs work.

Tony James

I was advertising in the music papers, and I was answering ads as well. I was trying to put a band together. Through the ads I was looking for those kind of slightly Stonesy English rock'n'roll glamorous groups. I met Mick for the first time at a Heavy Metal Kids gig at the Fulham Greyhound. I met him through Kelvin Blacklock.

Mick had a group called the Delinquents. Mick was the not-very-good rhythm guitar player! [laughs] And Kelvin was the singer of the group. At the time either Kelvin answered one of my ads or I answered one of his ads in the paper, and I met up with Kelvin in Westbourne Grove and he said, 'I'm going round to see this mate of mine called Mick who lives with his gran.' He took me round to Mick's house, and Mick was reading this book, *The Tale of Willy's Rats*, by Mick Farren and *Diary of a Rock'n'Roll Star*, and I had both of these books as well.

I then went to meet them again at a rehearsal place in Southwark where Kelvin was rehearsing with Mick. We were at the rehearsal and they were sort of firing Mick. They had another guitarist and they were saying Mick was not good enough, so Mick and I went home on the tube together to his gran's house and that how it all started.

Straight away we decided to get a band together. When you're young you go, 'OK, I'll get on with something else.' You don't think your life is in ruins. If it's not working, let's do something else.

Mick Jones

I was on the way out of the band and Tony had sort of just come in. I got the feeling it was kind of Kelvin giving me, as a bit of compensation, an introduction to Tony. We met just at that time; obviously we palled up straight away. We started hanging out together, seriously hanging out. We were into the same things and we talked about it incessantly. We decided to form our own band using a name that Little Queenie had nearly used, London SS.

Tony James

You can see why – London SS/New York Dolls, same sort of thing. It positions you in London, it has that London vibe about it. This is the time in London when you couldn't even buy a pair of dark glasses that looked cool, and you could only get a leather jacket from a second-hand place if you were lucky, or a motorcycle shop. You had to seek this stuff out. We knew what was going on. We were reading about New York, and we knew it was cool and underground – that was the benchmark.

Mick Jones

I actually spent a lot of time in the bedroom playing, about a year, practising along with my records. I actually liked to learn. I listened hard and practised and practised.

Tony James

Mick got a job working in a bookshop in Camden Town to save up to buy a new guitar. After a couple of months I went with him to Denmark Street.[9] He'd seen this guitar, the famous brown Les Paul

---

9. Denmark Street was formerly the heart of London's music publishing business, and became known as Tin Pan Alley. To this day it boasts a number of music shops.

Junior that he used in the Clash. I went with him to buy that guitar. The great symmetry of that is that 30 years later him and I are in a group again and he goes to me, 'You should play guitar and not bass, and I will give you the guitar,' and he gave me the same guitar that he had learned to play on.

THE FINSBURY ANTICHRIST
Enter John Lydon

Glen Matlock

We started rehearsing at Riverside Studios because Wally Nightingale's dad worked there. He got a pair of keys cut so we could get in there. Steve had all this knocked-off equipment which we took advantage of. We slowly started taking it a bit more seriously. Steve was singing at the time.

Malcolm was going backwards and forwards to the States to buy up old clothes and he got involved managing the New York Dolls. When that fell apart he managed to split them up and said he was looking for a band to back Sylvain Sylvain.[10]

Wally Nightingale was like the character in *The Italian Job*, the Noel Coward bloke in the prison telling everyone what to do. He was the ringleader, the godfather! It was hard to get rid of Wally because it was kind of his idea. Steve had started playing guitar good by then, knocking a few ideas around. We were doing Small Faces songs, Ron Wood songs, Love Affair's 'A Day Without Love'. Nick Kent, who was the star writer at the *NME*, was hanging out at another shop called Granny Takes A Trip, where the Rolling Stones would get their stage gear. Nick used to go in there and then into Malcolm's, and I would chat with him. He was an interesting kind of guy and could play guitar.

Also, because he was a journalist, he would get tapes from

---

10. Original member of the New York Dolls. Last spotted as one of the two surviving members of the band, along with frontman David Johansson, in their comeback tour in 2004.

people, and he said he had a copy of an album by this band that we should listen to, an album that John Cale had been producing. This album didn't come out for another year and a half. It was the Modern Lovers album and it had this song 'Roadrunner', so we used to do that.

That came in tandem with us trying out a few singers. What you have to remember was that everyone had long hair then, even the milkman, so what we used to do was if someone had short hair we would stop them in the street and ask them if they fancied themselves as a singer. Once they went up to Glasgow to do something and were in a music shop, and Midge Ure was in there getting the Slik thing together. I spoke to him on the phone and he said, 'Thanks for asking me but I need to do this thing.' And he ended up having a Number One record.[11]

It was about this time that Bernie Rhodes spotted John Lydon. Malcolm takes credit for everything! Bernie said, 'There's this guy that comes in the shop.' At this time everyone would spend their Saturday afternoons on the Kings Road between the two shops. There was the other shop on Kings Road, Acme Attractions, run by John Krivine, where Jeanette Lee and Don Letts worked. John was part of this crowd, and he came into the Sex shop – we knew who to look out for because Bernie had told us.

We used to meet Bernie in the pub. He was older than us and he had loads of ideas and things to say. He was bit of an oddball kind of character and that's what endeared him to us. Malcolm had known him since the Sixties somehow or other, and they had some kind of weird relationship, arguing and being mates, arguing and being mates. They had ideas all the time, the pair of them, and it kind of rubbed off on us a bit.

We didn't yet have that kind of lyrical stance that John would provide. I had a few ideas but I'm not the singer. We needed a focus, someone to put our kind of feelings into practice somehow, and

11. Slik's 'Forever And Ever' hit the top in January 1976.

John fitted the bill exactly. I mean, he could be hard work – he's not exactly conventional, is he! [laughs]

John Lydon

The Sex Pistols were a bunch of dopey boys from Shepherds Bush that needed a singer, because Malcolm told them they did. Bernie, probably as an act of spite, thought I'd be hilarious, and Malcolm thought I was all right. He changed his mind later when he found that I could not be manipulated as easy as the others. No disrespect to them – I like to tell it like it is. Steve, Paul and Glen are notorious for going with the flow and I don't. I care about what I write and this was my first opportunity to get out of the squalor and poverty that is working-class Britain. I don't think I'm a stupid person, so I use it to the best of my ability and the boy did good 30 years later!

The Sex Pistols, when they spotted me on the Kings Road with my 'I Hate Pink Floyd' T-shirt on, thought, 'Oh, he'll do.' I don't think they knew what they were getting hold of. What they really wanted was a kind of upmarket pub band because pub rock was very fashionable at that time: Eddie and the Hot Rods, bands like that. They were all bands that late on in life, like Elvis Costello, claimed to be punks, but they weren't. Neither was Sting. They were pub balladeers.

Glen Matlock

Not many people know this, but Malcolm was going over backwards and forwards to the States and he had met a few people over there, and as well as Sylvain coming over to play with us he suggested this guy Richard Hell. But it was doomed to failure because we had no money and couldn't go over there, and he couldn't come over here – he had no money either.

What you have got to remember is that no one had ever heard anybody's music, and when John came in the shop he looked exactly like Richard Hell. He had the torn T-shirt, the sticky-up hair and all that lark, and it was a total coincidence. To this day Richard Hell thinks Johnny Rotten had nicked his look, and I can understand why, but he didn't, so it was kind of weird. Instead of having Richard Hell over from America we had Johnny Rotten from Finsbury Park.[12]

Late August 1975: Lydon auditioned as the Pistols' singer, miming in spectacular over-the-top fashion to Alice Cooper's 'Eighteen'. Days later, and rechristened Johnny Rotten, he went to the Crunchie Frog pub in Rotherhithe to join Jones, Cook and Matlock for his first rehearsal, but the rest of the band failed to show up and Rotten was pissed off. A couple of weeks later, McLaren persuaded the four of them to start rehearsing in the upstairs room of the Rose and Crown in Wandsworth. By the end of the month, McLaren had guaranteed a £1,000 deposit on a rehearsal space in central London's Denmark Street and the band started playing together daily.

Glen Matlock

I saw an advert in *Melody Maker* for a rehearsal space in Denmark Street. It had been owned by Bill Collins, the manager of Badfinger. His son was Lewis Collins from *The Professionals*. He was a generous, cheery kind of bloke. It was his idea to do 'Without You' as a big ballad, and if you listen to the Badfinger original it was nothing like the Nilsson version which went on to be a massive hit. But anyway that was one of the reasons they split up. There was a lot of money problems and Pete Ham of Badfinger had committed suicide, and he wanted to offload the place. Steve moved in and lived in the room upstairs.

We were rehearsing a lot and listening to a lot of different things. Through Malcolm we got into the Dolls and the Stooges and Sixties punk stuff, but John liked all this kind of hippy shit like

---

12. John Lydon was apparently nicknamed 'Johnny Rotten' by Steve Jones because of his bad teeth, although the exact reason for the nickname is, as ever, blurred by time.

Van Der Graaf Generator, Can – who I quite like as well – and Captain Beefheart. It was like this cross of cultures that made the band interesting.

Marco Pirroni

There was a period when I didn't listen to music at all. I was more into clothes. I thought music was dead – there was nothing happening at all. By the time I saw the Pistols, I hadn't bought a record for a year. The first time I became aware of the Pistols was when I went to Denmark Street. I was looking at guitars in all the guitar shops and I bumped into Vivienne, which was a complete mindfuck because these two scenes – the Kings Road fashion scene and the music scene – did not cross over in any way whatsoever. So I thought, 'What's Vivienne doing in the music biz on Tin Pan Alley?' I thought this was strange. This was not a glamorous place. She had two cups of cappuccino in Styrofoam cups and she said, 'I'm with a band and they are rehearsing.' I said, 'What band?' She said, 'Malcolm's got his new band'– they didn't even have a name then. I went to the rehearsal later on, not that day – she didn't invite me down there.

Nils Stevenson

Malcolm started asking this girl I was going out with called June Bolan about management. She was the common law wife of Marc Bolan and knew a lot about bands. She worked for Blackhill Enterprises, who managed Pink Floyd and Bolan. He was always banging on about this group of teenagers he was managing who were going to be the next Bay City Rollers. Eventually I struck up a relationship with Vivienne because I fancied her like mad. Malcolm sussed and got between me and her. We became good friends.

Malcolm was fascinating. We were drawn to each other because we were both obsessed with art: he went to Goldsmiths and I'd done an environmental design course at Barnet College. We just related. Dragging art out of the gallery – Malcolm had started a shop to do that. He was into the environmental art ideas of the time, as was I. Malcolm is stimulated and excited by everything and interested in everything – always was and still is.

Malcolm thought he was going to manage a band that were far more mainstream pop than the Pistols turned out to be. He's got unusual taste, so he probably didn't realise that Johnny Rotten didn't look like Les McKeown from the Bay City Rollers. Malcolm's ability to get things wrong often makes fabulous things happen.

Malcolm McLaren (Manager of the Sex Pistols)

The band were absolutely out of step with 1975 England. How could they not be, having been born out of the shop, Sex. They were simply young, sexy assassins. That's how I came up with the Sex Pistols' name.

John Lydon

The Sex Pistols, it was implied, got our image from that shop. It's more the other way round, thank you very much.

Glen Matlock

Slowly but surely we were getting something together. The first three Pistols singles date from that kind of period. Everyone is chipping in ideas. The bulk of the lyrics are John's.

In October, the Sex Pistols started writing their own songs, including 'Pretty Vacant' and 'Seventeen', to add to their covers of the Who and Small Faces. On 6 November, the Pistols played their first show at St Martin's College, supporting Bazooka Joe, an art-rock, Fifties-flavoured band featuring a certain Stuart Goddard (soon to become Adam Ant) on bass.

Glen Matlock

I set the gig up. I was at St Martin's doing a foundation course. In the second year, I was going to be the social sec but over the summer holidays I decided to take the band seriously after John had joined that August, so I gave my place to someone else and, as I left, I blagged the gig with Bazooka Joe.

Mark Helford (Early face on punk scene, eventually ran Clash fan club)

I was mates with Glen. I had seen the Pistols rehearsing before the gig quite a few times, before John had joined, when they still had Wally Nightingale on guitar. At that stage it was very rudimentary. How shall I put it? They weren't the best musicians in the world. They were feeling their way. John gave them another dimension when he joined.

John Ellis (Bazooka Joe, the Vibrators and the Stranglers)

I was the founder member of Bazooka Joe with Daniel Kleinman. We started as a rock'n'roll covers band like Sha Na Na. Daniel is one of my best friends and he said, 'This band the Sex Pistols are playing with us; people are making a noise about them.' I'd left the band by then but I went along to the gig.

Paul Madden (Photographer)

I was at London College doing a printing course; a friend in the year below me said he was going to see Bazooka Joe at St Martin's. We went down early at half-seven. It was on the fifth floor in an open common room with no stage. There were no lifts and it was stairs all the way up. It was empty – no tables or anything, pretty dark. There were no more than 40 people there. They were selling cheap white wine at 20p a cup. It was real throw-down-your-neck typical student ruin, really vile.

Jeremy Diggle (Student at St Martin's College, London)

I kind of knew Glen from St Martin's, so I knew about the Pistols anyway. I was switched on to what was going on. I'd seen them hanging round Tin Pan Alley. I knew other people who knew them as well. There were gigs there every second week but it was a fairly shambolic organisation. We'd just set up the bar as a sort of social space. We'd have proper gigs in the basement, bands like Kilburn and the High Roads. Bazooka Joe had a small following so they were in the upstairs room.

Bazooka Joe's gear was set up first and the Pistols dragged their stuff in. I suspect a bit of hassle was going on between the bands, sort of a friendly but sharp atmosphere because bands are sensitive about lending gear.

Robin Chapekar (Bazooka Joe)

We turned up. We had our own PA and backline. We set up and did a soundcheck and in strolled Malcolm McLaren with the boys. He said: 'We've got a problem, our van has broken down with all the gear in it.' They pleaded with us. All they had was their guitars and they wanted to use our amps and drums. We felt sorry for them, we related to them – it had happened to us before – so we said: 'No problem, help yourself, do your soundcheck.' We left a couple of guys, our roadies, there and shot off to the Cambridge Arms for a couple of drinks before we played.

Glen Matlock

What happened was that we were supposed to use their equipment. At the soundcheck, Bazooka Joe, who were a bunch of rich kid rockabilly types, didn't like the cut of our jib and wouldn't lend us their gear.

Malcolm McLaren

The Sex Pistols were never supposed to really play. We just followed from across the road where we had our lair: Denmark Street. I knew clearly that we were going to be obnoxious. It was the nature of the beast. The group were formed not knowing each other, in truth, and certainly not liking each other thereafter.

Glen Matlock

So we had to push our gear through the rush-hour crowd. There was a frosty atmosphere and after four numbers someone pulled the plug on us because we were a horrible din and a bit of a fracas started.

Paul Madden

Before they came on I thought, 'Who's that weird bloke with weird trousers on?' He was wearing peg-leg trousers and it was Malcolm McLaren. The trousers were baggy at the waist and going to nothing at the ankles. Very strange. He stood out a mile. He kept running back and forth. I thought, 'What's he so angry about?' He was trying to start trouble. They had an attitude that was basically, 'Fuck off, we're the Sex Pistols.' They were all going in the same direction at maximum speed.

Malcolm McLaren

I was trying to get them to be wicked and not sound like a band at all.

Eddie (Real name Jonathan Edwards. Bazooka Joe roadie. The Vibrators: drums)

St Martin's is right next to Denmark Street where the Pistols rehearsed. Steve Jones said he couldn't use our Orange amp and went to get his amp with John. While we were waiting we got up and played. I sang 'Bonie Moronie', 'Johnny B. Goode' and some other songs with Paul Cook on drums and Glen on bass. John and Steve came back and they started. John Lydon had a pullover on, full of holes. He was a startling character. I knew him already from when I DJ'd. He would ask if I had anything by the Stooges, like he was the only person to listen to the Stooges!

Paul Madden

My friend went down the Cambridge to meet Bazooka Joe. I waited for the Pistols to come on and went down the front to watch them. I didn't think they were that outrageous. I liked them,. though. I remember feeling jealous: guys my own age who had a good band. I remember Steve Jones had eye make-up on. Being in art college, we all knew about the New York Dolls and Roxy Music. We were inspired by the Dolls visually and David Bowie's *Berlin* album. In a weird way, the Pistols were the ultimate art-school band. I thought they were not that bad. One thing I certainly remember is that there was no riser for the band; they were on the same level as the audience. They played for about five songs and got told to stop. The Sex Pistols were not proficient players at that time. It was their first gig but they had a confidence in what they were doing, a cheeky-chappie confidence.

Glen Matlock

A couple of mates of John's were there. John Grey was there.[13] I don't think Sid was there. Some mate of John's who was always threatening to commit suicide. Also Bill Collins who rented us our rehearsal room was there, with his missus.

We played 'Substitute', 'Stepping Stone' and 'Whatcha Gonna Do About It?' We were going to play 'Pretty Vacant' but the plug got pulled. We were also going to do 'Did You No Wrong' and 'Problems' but that never happened.

Nick Wells (Student at St Martin's College, London)

The Sex Pistols were very loud and grubby. They were extremely unpleasant but you couldn't ignore them. It was a tiny little venue with students milling round the bar, no more than 100 at most. It was also very loud, as loud as Can, who had been the loudest gig I'd ever been to before then.

Pat Collier (The Vibrators: bass)

It didn't seem like a momentous occasion at the time. As I came in I remember them doing a cover of the Small Faces' 'All Or

---

13. One of the 'Four Johns', all friends: John Lydon, John Grey, John Wardle (later known as Jah Wobble) and John Beverley/Ritchie (later Sid Vicious).

Nothing'. From their choice of material they seemed like an average punk rock band but I wasn't really watching. A few months later I saw them and they were unbelievably brilliant, perhaps the best band I have ever seen.

Robin Chapekar

We were sat in the pub and one of our roadies came running in shouting: 'You'd better get back! They're trashing the gear and everyone is leaving in droves.' We shot back. They were making a massive noise. They hadn't got anything worked out at all. It was pure punk but I didn't know that at the time. There we were witnessing the birth of punk. We were pissed off! They were kicking the amps, the drummer was trashing the drums. We went over and said: 'Enough is enough!' Danny took the mic off John and I took the amp off Steve and pulled the plug on him and a brawl ensued, lots of flailing arms and missed punches and stuff. Eventually they stopped playing. They were frightening the audience away.

Paul Madden

Paul Cook put down his sticks and said, 'Now for the real thing,' referring to Bazooka Joe, and the Bazooka Joe singer leapt across the drum kit and it turned into a punch-up.

Glen Matlock

Paul has got a good habit of saying the right thing at the wrong time! We were nervous when we played. Malcolm bought a bottle of vodka and that had kicked in by then as well.

Paul Madden

It was like one of those school playground kind of fights. The antagonism had been building up all afternoon, mainly due to the fact that the Pistols had borrowed Bazooka Joe's backline. Their attitude was so snotty that Bazooka Joe had said, 'Get your own amplifiers.'

Jeremy Diggle

The whole band had a presence. Glen was in a little pink number, I seem to remember, Lydon in a ripped jumper. But enough was enough and I unplugged them. They were bloody awful and untogether. I wasn't expecting anything else. It was something different but they were too loud and the space wasn't big enough. I'm not being wimpish when I say they were over-amplified – that's why I switched them off. It was chaotic and Bazooka Joe wanted to get on and play. It was more a case of, 'You've had your 20 minutes!'

Robin Chapekar

Stuart didn't leave the band the next day, but the gig probably made him decide to get into punk. He went through a big change and eventually embraced punk 100 per cent. He gave all his old clothes away and disassociated himself from his old persona. Good luck to him and he had that tunnel vision of where he wanted to go.

Later on I bumped into Glen Matlock and he said, 'Sorry, mate.' He was the calmest out of the whole lot. I said, 'You can't borrow gear and trash it and scare everyone away!' I then found out through a few mates that they never had a van with gear in it. They had pulled a fast one and gatecrashed the gig. I thought, 'Cheeky bastards but what a brilliant con!' The Pistols were a bunch of chancers really. Nothing made them stand out. No one had an inkling of what was going to happen.

Glen Matlock

We made a horrible racket. Those first few gigs at the end of 1975, people didn't know what to make of it. They would recognise the covers we did of songs like 'Substitute' and get a bit more of an idea of what we were doing. People would recognise the tune and understand what we were trying to do. We were trying our best to make them sound good.

Malcolm McLaren

It was not necessarily a plan to play art colleges first and avoid the pub. I just hated beer. And that's all you got in those stinking pubs in Anglo-Saxon land. Art school preached a noble pursuit of failure. It was part of the legacy laid down by William Morris: art for art's sake, which we attempted to create and indeed succeeded at one level. We made ugliness beautiful.

Gene October

I remember going in Let It Rock one day and Malcolm saying, 'My band is playing in a strip club in Soho tonight.' I couldn't be fucked to go, to be honest. Then somebody said, 'Go to the art college at the back of the Albert Hall,' and the Pistols did a gig there. That was funny. I thought John looked quite funky actually. He had a very sweet little face. He looked great wearing that gear. Malcolm was knocking up all that stuff he was selling in the shop. It was Vivienne that was designing it exclusively for the Pistols to wear, those big baggy shirts. They were not selling them in the shop, just making them for the band to wear. I suppose she had an idea to push it on the band first, and the multitudes around the world would then wear it afterwards because that was what the Pistols were wearing.

9 December 1975: The Sex Pistols played Ravensbourne College in Chislehurst, south-east London. Simon Barker, a friend of Siouxsie Sioux, was there and afterwards told her about the band. They and a number of their friends started seeing the band regularly, becoming known as the Bromley Contingent.

Marco Pirroni

Going into the shop there was no mention of the band. I don't know how much Jordan was involved in it, if at all. It was just a poxy thing that Malcolm was doing. It wasn't very important really. Then these black and white hand-outs started appearing so I went to see them. I couldn't imagine what the fuck they would be like. Jordan said, 'You have to come to the El Paradise. You must go.' It was in a strip club, which I thought was really great as well. I got in for nothing. A Soho strip club as vile as you could imagine, really, with about ten people standing. Some I'd seen before – Jordan, Malcolm, Vivienne, Sid – some of the band, and some people I'd never seen before.

I didn't think the Pistols were shambolic at all. I thought they were really good. They were as good as Supertramp! [laughs] Were they out of tune? No, they weren't. It was pretty fucking tight really. I suddenly thought, 'I could do that' – not because they were shit but because it was easy. I could play guitar by then. I was probably better than Steve at that point, but Steve had done it his way and I was wondering what stance to play in – like Lou Reed or Mick Ronson? Steve had obviously had no dilemmas like that. He was doing the only style he could do. Instead of thinking about it all the time, he went ahead and did it.

LONDON'S BURNING
In Which London SS Meet Bernie Rhodes

Bernard Rhodes was one of the key players in punk rock. As an ideas man, he was unbeatable. He was originally in cahoots with Malcolm McLaren, but the pair would eventually fall out and Rhodes would help to put together the Clash, a band fired by his political agitation, subversive ideas and sharp mod fixation with style. He was also very difficult to work with, but his abrasive persona was perfect for the times and crucial in sharpening the Clash into the awesome band that they became. Rhodes was totally hip to what was going on and fully versed in pop culture. Where his influence begins and ends is difficult to fathom since he rarely does interviews.

Mick Jones

We were at a Deaf School gig. It was the *Melody Maker* Band of the Year competition and the winners were Deaf School, an art school band – Clive Langer was in them. That was the gig where I first met Bernie. He and I had the same T-shirt on. I thought he was a keyboard player because he had a hat on – he looked like one of Gene Vincent's Blue Caps. We were always on the lookout for musicians. We would talk to anyone who looked interesting. We said, 'Are you a piano player?' and he said, 'No… You got one of my T-shirts on, I designed that.' I got the T-shirt from Let It Rock.

Tony James

Then we started talking. We said, 'We got this band, London SS,' and he kind of perked up and looked interested. Obviously at the time this was a name that was quite provocative! Bernie said, 'My mate's got a band called the Sex Pistols. They are these young kids, they are this rock'n'roll band and they live in central London,' and he mythologised them and made it sound more interesting. This was the first time we had heard of them.

Mick Jones

Me and Bernie struck up a friendship straight away. It was like he knew everything and I knew nothing. And he said, 'You don't know nothing,' to me and Tone. He always talked like that. He made you think about things in a different way.

Tony James

Bernie was my worst nightmare. He would ring my house in Twickenham and I would be on the phone for three hours, sitting on the phone freezing whilst Bernie asked me why wasn't I reading Jean-Paul Sartre? What did I know? Why didn't I leave my parents and live with a hooker over Christmas? Toughen up! I was too middle-class and boyish! Bernie would phone me up in my nice semi-detached home in Twickenham and say, 'I need you to go to your local newsagent and buy *Gay News* and *Spare Rib*, the lesbian magazine, please. You need to toughen up.' How great that someone could do that!

Bernie had been to LSE with Malcolm and understood stuff that I didn't know about. What's funny is that I did go and read the books! Bernie gave me a reading list and I would go and get the books from the library and read them all. That's smart managing, not just trooping you down to Johnsons and decking you out in skinny ties. He could have easily told me and Mick, 'You need to write an "Anarchy in the UK", you need to get a political stance, write about what you see in front of your eyes, don't write love songs.' I can still remember standing in the middle of Praed Street with Bernie shouting at us, 'You don't even know what you're about. You haven't told me one clear thing that's new. Wise up!' and we knew he was right. We said we wanted to be the Stones or in the New York Dolls, and he said, 'That's not good enough.'

So I did go to art galleries and I did study modern art and I did read Sartre, because Bernie told me that's what I had to do, and my eyes were opened. I absolutely owe a huge debt to Bernie and Malcolm for making me understand what it had to be all about. Bernie knew that I was intelligent but I'm sure he felt I was too middle-class. I came from a nice home and all that stuff. That's probably why I ended working with Billy – same background.[14] I don't know what Bernie thought of me. I'd hate to ask him. He slags everyone off. Bernie is a nightmare, but I can see why I was dissatisfied with everyone who managed us after that.

Bernie and Malcolm were mates and rivals. Bernie worked for Malcolm. A lot of the ideas were Bernie's. Bernie was certainly creative and very smart. Bernie and Malcolm were not just managers: they were Svengalis, but they were even smarter – they took us to the University of Wising Up and Coolness.

I remember going to a Chinese restaurant with Malcolm and Bernie, and Malcolm saying, 'This is what's going to happen,' and literally telling the story: 'We're going to make this scene and its going to change rock'n'roll, it's going to make all the other groups

---

14. Billy Broad, later better known as Billy Idol.

seem old-fashioned and obsolete.' Malcolm pretty well had it planned out. It freaked me out because in the years to come the story unfolded how Malcolm had predicted it. He'd seen the bigger picture. He'd done it with the Dolls and fucked up, but now he knew what he had to do and he knew how to play the game and work the media.

One evening Bernie said, 'I've got to meet you in this pub in Shepherds Bush, the Bull and Bush,' which in those days was the heaviest pub in west London. So Mick and I nancy-boy into the pub and meet the blue jean/flat cap man sitting in the middle of this crowded, dangerous, scary pub, and Bernie opens his bag and starts slapping Nazi regalia on the bar: swastikas, badges, Nazi flags, the whole lot! We were saying, 'Bernie, we could get killed here,' and he went, 'All right, you want to be called London SS. You're going to have to deal with it, so wise up.' So we went home like, 'Oh fuck, we never thought of that!' What he was saying was, 'You better be able to defend your position.' We were going, 'It means the London Social Security!' We were on the dole queue rock thing already! Mick worked in the dole office at the time, and that's what the name stood for – we never thought any further than that.

By then I had left university, done maths, which I got a first in. Even while I was doing the music I got the degree. Even so I got really ripped off with the money, but I never even care about it. My parents thought I was going to be head of IBM; instead I got a job driving cars. I don't know whether it's Bernie's influence or I had just read *On The Road*, but I got a job delivering and parking cars so I could wear a leather jacket and dark glasses and park cars like Neal Cassady did.[15] I walked away from that great education that I had. I wanted to break free and live the life.

---

15. Cassady was a legend of the Beat Generation and the Sixties counterculture, whose travels with his friend Jack Kerouac inspired the latter's *On The Road* – the character Dean Moriarty is based on him. In 1964 he famously drove the day-glo-painted bus for Ken Kesey's Merry Pranksters, as recorded in Tom Wolfe's *The Electric Kool-Aid Acid Test*.

WANTED: MARTIAN
The London SS Auditions

The London SS auditions are the stuff of legend. The fledgling group went through just about everybody on the scene and were equally and fantastically rude to them all! As a way of getting a band together it was a total failure, but as a meeting point and catalyst for the emerging punk scene it was perfect.

Tony James

We got the café in Praed Street as our headquarters. That was the key thing – Mick and I were such pop culture readers – we were sitting in his gran's one night and we said, 'What we need is something like the 2 I's coffee bar,' you know, like Soho in the Sixties, where they had the coffee bar where everybody met. We said we need one of those types of places. So we got on the bus outside Mick's gran's house, the number 16, and we got off at Praed Street, and by the bus stop there is a café on the corner and we said, 'Here is the place!' Like you do when you're young. We walked in and there was a jukebox in the corner. We said, 'Here is our base – we are in!'

Mick Jones

We advertised in the music press. We used to advertise in the *Melody Maker* every week: 'Anybody who's into the New York Dolls, Stooges, MC5'. And that was enough because if you had heard of those people you would be right. We met all the people interested – everyone who was around.

Tony James

We wanted a singer and a drummer into the New York Dolls, Mott the Hoople and the Stooges. That was like asking 'Wanted: Martian'.

Mick Jones

Lots of people came down. They had to go through a café interview first! We put our records on the jukebox of the café – we had a little scene going on there. It was a pre-check out before the rehearsal. It depended on a lot of factors: what they looked like, the whole attitude – that was important. It never put us off if you couldn't play, but it might put us off if you were into funny things that we weren't into! [laughs]

Tony James

We interviewed them in the café. We were mean to them. We learned from Bernie, who would be there. Imagine meeting us and you got Bernie tearing you to bits. There was this drummer who came from Pinner. We thought he was tragic but he was quite a good player. Bernie thought he was good and said, 'No, let's keep him – we will rename him Shane Pain. We will chain him to the drum kit and have two hookers whipping him while playing drums and he will be like sweating like crazy!'

We got a tragic letter from Manchester – from Morrissey! Manchester to us seemed like a million miles away. It would have been really strange if it had happened. Mick's probably still got the letter. He's such a hoarder. People sort of drifted in and out. We were having no joy in finding anyone who really understood the music that we were digging.

Every time we ran an ad we met the people in the café and we always met Bernie there. Somehow Bernie changed the records on the jukebox to all his records: early Chuck Berry and early rock-'n'roll. Suddenly this café had these hip young guys hanging out in it. Even better, a couple of weeks later Bernie said, 'I've found a place for you to rehearse.' We come out the café, walk round the back into the mews, through a door in the basement of the café, and there is a room with nothing in there, like a dungeon – and this is our rehearsal space. Bernie comes in and he's got horror film posters, Nazi war atrocity films, all that genre of posters, and he puts them on the wall. Little did we know but that was a subtle plot of Bernie's to talk us out of using the name London SS. It was not a fascist name – Mick was Jewish! We saw it as when you walked into your home with a T-shirt with it on, your parents fainted. It was like, 'Great, it works!' You didn't think about wider issues of it.

Mick Jones

I also used to spend a lot of the time on the phone talking to people – you had to get past that one first. The auditions happened from November 1975 till January '76. Loads of people came down, like Keith Levene, Terry Chimes, Topper Headon, Brian James – he was probably the first to come down.

Tony James

Most weeks we got no replies. The first week we got one reply from Brian James, who lived in Croydon and was in a group called Bastard.

Brian James

I had been living in Crawley. I'd be calling up people like the Greasy Truckers, who put on free festivals, and the Fairies, and we played gigs with them. Bastard were a rough rock'n'roll band influenced by the Stooges, the MC5, the Pink Fairies. We were a four-piece: there was a geezer called Nobby on drums most of the time, Dez on bass, and Alan who was the vocalist. Then we moved over to Brussels because we couldn't get any work over here, and our singer got a job in a studio.

There was not much of a scene in Brussels but we kind of created one. They were more open to rock'n'roll, the French-speaking Belgians, and definitely in France – when we played gigs there, they knew all about what was going on in the States. Their heroes were people like Iggy Pop and Lou Reed. People in England didn't give a damn about that sort of music; it was like they had never heard of it. They were more into pub-rocky kind of things, dressing up like cowboys and acting like American bar bands. Fucking weird, and really boring for me.

We had a good scene going on there. People would come because we were playing – it was a 24-hour party scene. Brussels was great, like a mini-Paris without the hang-ups: journalists, DJs, film people would all meet in a small place and you're there a couple of months and you've made all these contacts. I always enjoyed Brussels. When I came back from Brussels I more or less moved back to London, and that's when I met Mick and Tony and formed the London SS. I met them through an ad in the *Melody Maker* and I probably met them on the same day as when I rang the ad. It might have been a small scene but at least it was a scene!

Tony James

Brian sounded like he knew what was going on. He came down and met us. We quite liked him. He had the look.

Mick Jones

Brian James was interested and he played furiously. We liked him but he had to go back to Belgium and tie up his band. I think he got exasperated with Tony and me!

Brian James

My first impression was that they were like a couple of long-hairs. Mick had really long hair all the way down to his arse. When he played he sort of pushed it out like Johnny Thunders. They didn't have anything to play me, but they talked about the right people. I had a tape that I had recorded in Brussels. I played it to them and they loved it and they said, 'Oh yeah, you're the guy for us.' They didn't like my drummer though – they didn't think he looked rock-'n'roll enough for them. In fact, they didn't like nobody.

The next time we played together, we fucked around trying to get a drummer and a singer. It became like a weekly thing down at this place called Paddington Kitchen just off Praed Street in Paddington. There was an endless stream of singers and drummers. All sorts of people would come down or be on the phone. You would say that, 'We are into these bands, have you heard of these bands?' Some of them didn't have a clue, they must have been living up a Welsh mountain playing to goats or something like that, or just come off a steamship doing a cruise gig. All kind of weirdoes came down – it was kind of fun in a way. A few people came down who went on to do other things. There was people into rock'n'roll who were not right for us but it was cool that they were doing it. There was a few good guys. But the percentage of good guys to bad guys was about 10 to 90. You're honing it all the time – the three of you, two guitars, one bass.

I had to go and sort things out with the guys in Bastard and tell them what was going on. There was no future in Bastard. It looked like it was falling to bits and we thought, 'Fuck it!' and I couldn't stay over in Belgium. I was fed up with starving really, living on cabbage and eggs if you got lucky. You got all the beer you wanted for nothing, but food? There was none! People would buy you beer all the time. We had a regular gig at a place called Florios, and it became quite a scene because people knew that we were playing and that. But it was time for a change.[16]

Tony James

Brian was in on it now. He was lead guitar. Mick was playing rhythm. Brian had that Keith Richards look. We had this whole look going on and we now had this French drummer called Roland Hot.[17] We had met in some club. He was the stand-in drummer. Lots of people came in and out of those doors.

And the next weird thing was meeting the Sex Pistols. For some reason Mick and I went to Denmark Street to try and meet up with Malcolm, and we walked in to their rehearsal room and there was three kids in there. (We were kids as well.) They had short hair and

16. The rest of Bastard stayed on in Belgium and ended up recording the backing track for Plastic Bertrand's massive hit 'Ça Plane Pour Moi' – ironically covered by Captain Sensible as 'Jet Boy, Jet Girl'.

17. Roland Hot drummed on and off for the London SS and other groups on the fringes of the mid-Seventies scene like the Boys.

we had long hair – we were the New York Dolls and they were short-haired blokes! We had grown up with the English underground scene, the kind of freak-brother scene where long hair was revolutionary. What Malcolm showed us was that the scene had become bloated and it was the norm now. Suddenly it was short hair – not skinhead, but short spiky hair that was revolutionary. Mick was the first to get his hair cut because it was like I'd spent five years growing my hair. All my life at school I had to stand outside the classroom because the maths teachers said, 'You can't come in with long hair. Stand outside the classroom.' I thought, I've wasted all those years growing my hair!

It was one of those meetings, everyone looking moody. We became friends with Glen and Steve because of that, and by then Bernie had said, 'I'll be your manager.' He was working with Malcolm then. They were looking for bands.

Rat Scabies

They were keen on movements. Bernie always said that if you've got three bands then you've got a movement.

Glen Matlock

The first time I met Mick Jones was he came down our rehearsal place with the rest of his band – they were called London SS. They looked like Mott the Hoople. They all had long hair, stack-heeled boots, and snake-skin/tiger-skin trousers. There was a meeting upstairs with Bernie and Malcolm, and Mick Jones picked up this guitar and played, and there was something about him. I got pally with Mick and I guess he realised that the way he looked wasn't the way to go.

Mick Jones

We had long hair. At first I didn't kind of connect with them. It was about the time John Lydon joined. But he wasn't round that day. It was a bit of an eye-opener. I must admit it changed things – from the way they looked different. The shock of the short hair! They were so different. We had long hair, terribly tight trousers from Biba, with ocelot material! We all went to Biba – Tony and me – loads of ocelot and zebra prints.

Tony James

Once Bernie said, 'I've got this bloke coming down with a load of microphones,' and in walks Steve Jones. He'd 'found' them at a Mick Ronson or David Bowie gig at the Hammersmith Odeon. Then Glen Matlock started coming to rehearsals and was jamming with us – we were doing Small Faces. When you look back it looks like a movie script, but it's just the way it happened.

Glen Matlock

I'd see Mick Jones out and about. I remember helping him out– I played bass and Steve played drums while Mick auditioned Chrissie Hynde as a possible singer, long before it was called the Clash, but it was a project he was trying to get together. So there was a bit of hands-across-the-sea, helping people with things, because we wanted there to be more bands like us. So that it wasn't so lonely out there, you know...

Tony James

When you listen to the London SS demo tape, it's all there. There's only one tape of that band. It's even got a cover and the dates on it. It's the rarest tape in the world. And I've lost it recently! [laughs]

We promised each other that we would never release it. It's a magical archive. It's got Brian James and Roland the drummer on it. We recorded it in front of Bernie and Malcolm in the rehearsal room. We ran through our repertoire. We opened with 'Ramblin' Rose' – a heavier, madder, Stoogesy version of 'Ramblin' Rose', if you could Stooge up 'Ramblin' Rose' – and then we did 'Roadrunner' and a track from the *Nuggets* era, early Rolling Stones tracks and 'Protex Blue' – that was Mick's first original.

Brian James

We didn't really do Stooges-type stuff. What we did was old garage stuff I hadn't heard before, that Mick and Tony turned me onto. 'Slow Death' was one that we did by Flamin' Groovies – they turned me onto that song. There was a prototype version of 'Fish' we did. That became a Damned song on the first album. I was always carrying songs around. Some of the stuff I wrote for the Damned came from Bastard. In London SS Mick had a song called 'I'm So Bored of You' before it became The Clash's 'I'm So Bored with the USA'. I preferred it when it was like a little love song.

Tony James says he has tapes but not good quality tapes. Even so, I'd like to hear them! Release them? Nah! Certain things like professional pride would get in the way!

Rat Scabies

I'd seen this ad in *Melody Maker*. I'd already done a couple of auditions for a rock'n'roll band called the Wild Angels. It was 100 drummers in the room. I got up to leave and then they asked for my number. I didn't get the job, but I felt confident about it because they asked my number. I don't like the whole try-out thing. I'd rather hang with people with the same ideas. I'd been playing in bands including Tor (dreadful name). So I was working at the Fairfield Halls with the Captain, hanging out. We figured out a few skives like sleeping under the stage and getting paid overtime.

Captain Sensible

It was like *Sergeant Bilko*. The bosses at Fairfield Hall thought they ran the show, but me and Rat were like Bilko and we did what the fuck we liked!

Rat Scabies

So I went down to meet them in this café in Praed Street in December. They had some kit set up. The first thing was that I rang up Bernie and got in a big argument with him. They had been running this ad for six weeks and because I had decided I wasn't going to do any more auditions I decided not to answer it. Eventually I thought they must be looking for someone absolutely brilliant or someone totally different, in which case that could be me, so I rang up Bernie who immediately started going on about the current New York scene. I pointed out in Caterham you didn't hear much about the New York scene! He was very confrontational about it. In the end I got gobby with him. I'd heard the MC5 by this time – the ad said 'must be aware of current New York scene and the MC5, Stooges'. I knew who the MC5 were, I'd heard them on a compilation album and seen their reviews and they sounded exactly like my kind of band. I saw the Dolls on the *Whistle Test*. I thought the Dolls were OK. The Stooges was much more experimental and much druggier, and I didn't really do drugs. I always thought the Stooges sounded like something only played in a club that people went to who were in the *Performance* film. I didn't know people like that existed, and then I met Brian who was one of those people!

Mick Jones

We gave Rat Scabies his name. He was a great drummer and a nice guy too.

Rat Scabies

I did have scabies at the time and, you know, they said there was a rat in the room as well and Mick gave me the title. I got that name from the London SS and I got Brian.

Tony James

He had scabies when he came down, and there was a rat in the rehearsal room sitting behind the drum stool – I dropped a brick on it. I feel really bad about it now. I hate to hurt animals. So we now had a dead rat in rehearsal, then Rat came down and he had scabies, and I remember Bernie putting newspapers down where he sat 'cause he thought he was going to catch something. So we christened him Rat Scabies, and then we found he was calling himself Rat Scabies! It was a joke name, a name of derision. We were deriding everyone who came down.

Mick Jones

We were terribly rude to people and uncaring about their feelings. Bernie would be in their faces.

Rat Scabies

When I met Brian it clicked. I thought Brian looked fucking great. He had real short hair. The others didn't, they had long hair, like Mott the Hoople. OK, Mott the Hoople were cool then. We went down to the basement to play. They were kind of really arrogant and they had auditioned so many drummers that they had a television there which they put on and watched. While I played, Mick and Tony were there watching an old war movie.

Tony James

See how cool we sound when other people tell it!

Rat Scabies

We played a couple of things they had written which were flying around. I vaguely remember doing 'Fish' and some Stones covers – the one I remember is 'You Can't Always Get What You Want'. That was the point when I got bored of the whole set-up and I just hammered away a lot harder. Brian joined in. At this point on the war film there was this aeroplane dogfight going on, and Brian was playing guitar to go along with the pictures on the telly. He was doing all the *eeeeengh* noises on guitar. I thought that was good. Brian went on one and we decided that we had something going. That was where me and Brian clicked.

Brian James

As much as I enjoyed playing with Mick and Tony and chewing out musicians, I think they were more into the pose of rock'n'roll. I think they were much more influenced by the glam thing in England and I'd been away and not had that rammed down my throat. They were into the image thing. So when Rat came down it just showed the men from the boys. I don't want to knock anyone here, but when Ratty came down and gave it his all and we just sparked, I just looked at the other guys and they were going, 'He doesn't look right,' and I was thinking, 'I don't give a fuck what he looks like, listen to the cunt play!'

Rat Scabies

For a few weeks that December we rehearsed, and the upshot of it was Mick and Tony decided they didn't want me in the band. I was a Croydon doughboy. My hair that was too long, spiky but long, and so they decided they didn't think I was the right person for it.

Tony James

Like Joe said, 'Like trousers, like brain,' and that's as true today! Rat Scabies was a great drummer but he turned up in his denims, and he turned up with Captain Sensible as well – he was well dodgy! [laughs]

Captain Sensible

When Ratty came back from this audition in London, he's had his hair chopped off and I was shocked! Flowing locks was where it was at if you wanted to pull a bird in those days! [laughs] I said, 'Blimey!' and he told me about meeting this bloke. He said it was like talking to a cross between an evangelist and a conman, he was so persuasive. He said that this bloke had a vision of the future and his name was Brian James.

Rat said, 'You know what's more, he's looking for a bass player,' and I said, 'I'm not going anywhere near that if they are going to chop my hair off!' But I did, and Brian really was on it. It was Brian and a few others in London who started that whole scene. It was him and Mick Jones.

Rat Scabies

Brian was slightly older than me and the Captain. He had been in a band for some time. Bastard were massive in Caterham. They were quite a popular band. Although I'd never seen them, I'd heard about them. Brian looked great as well. He commanded a bit of respect. I dunno where the conman part comes from! I don't think he conned us. Brian was very clear about what he wanted to do. He wanted to do what he was already doing anyway with Bastard, but take it onto another sort of level – that was his game plan. He wanted people with attitude and energy.

Captain Sensible

I didn't know an awful lot about anything till I met Brian. I really liked the Pink Fairies – they were the only raunchy British act; maybe the Sweet as well, they always had great B-sides. Brian James agreed: he used to go and see the Fairies all the time. They were rough and ready, punk as anything at the time. When I met Brian he introduced me to a lot of American stuff like the MC5.

Brian was persuasive. He was like everything you would want at that time – he had the records. It must have been a bit like Liverpool when Lennon and McCartney had these great American imports no one else had heard. Brian was like a DJ playing us all these fantastic tracks by New York Dolls, all this fascinating stuff I'd never heard before. It washed a lot of the drivel out of my ears, got me into some really good stuff.

I had to cut my hair off; that was part of it. It was safety in numbers. Everyone in this circle was kind of a different persuasion at the time from what was normal. The cutting-the-hair thing was part of it. I remember years later when we auditioned a keyboard player just after *Machine Gun Etiquette* period and this guy turned up with long hair and we said, 'You can't go on stage with the Dammed with long hair. And Ratty said, 'We'll cut it, because Captain here, he used to work for Vidal Sassoon, he's done a two-year apprenticeship,' and I said, 'Yeah that's right, I'll give you a nice hair cut,' so I gave him this fucking huge bald patch at the back of his head and he looked like a monk. We painted his bald patch green and gave him this nickname, Astro Turf, we were shouting at him, 'Oi Astro, get a round in!' His dad sent us a really nasty letter saying, 'You smooth-talking cockney bastards taking the piss out of my son, I'll have you!' [laughs]

Tony James

Paul Simonon came down. We said, 'He looks good – can you sing?' and he said, 'I dunno,' and he did 'Roadrunner' with us. He just went, 'Roadrunner, Roadrunner,' over and over. He had no idea really, but he looked good.

Mick Jones

Paul came for an audition. He came down with Roland, started hanging out a bit afterwards. He couldn't play much so we borrowed a bass off Tony.

Things were starting to happen, there was a vibe – everybody could feel something was going to happen and people wanted to be part of it. It got bigger and more people got into it.

Keith Levene

I met Mick and we just really liked each other. Everyone was a couple of years old than me – when you're sixteen, that's a big gap when someone's a few years older. What was going on in west London, which I didn't know about then, was this whole scene with Tony James and Mick Jones, and the 101ers were around.

Mick and Tony were doing London SS and it wasn't really working. Mick thought I was a bass player so that's what I played – they already had him and someone else playing guitar. What we did was good. I picked up an acoustic and started playing and Mick went, 'Fucking hell, I never heard a bass player play guitar like that!'

I said, 'No, I'm a guitarist.' He told me to try one of his tunes and I learned it instantly, playing it better than him, and he was really digging it. He said, 'Do you write?' I told him, 'No, I don't, but I guess that's the next thing.'

So he really dug me and we became really fast friends. He thought I was fucking great on guitar. The next week, he invited me down to Portobello Road and he introduced me to this guy called Paul [Simonon]. He told me, 'This guy comes across as a bit thick but he's a really great artist. I think he could be the bass player but he can't play.' I was cool with that. At the same time, we were looking for something. We didn't know what it was. We were just looking to be different.

Don Letts

I was around for the London SS – they would come into the shop. People on Saturdays would go between the two shops on the Kings

Cheeky girls and friends: Chrissie Hynde, Vivienne Westwood and Jordan display a bare-faced cheek in the Sex shop

A goofy-looking Sid fooling around in Acme Attractions

Road. Our shop was a lot more user-friendly. All the tribes from all over London would meet there. It was showing the way that London was heading, this cultural clash. I would be pumping out reggae. Everybody that was anybody in the punk scene in London would be there. Also Patti Smith would be there, stumbling into the shop with Lenny Kaye. They would hear the bass lines pumping out to the Kings Road. Bob Marley would come in, so would the major players and bit players passing through.

I was being interviewed about my Beatles collection just when the punk thing was just starting in mid-'75, and as I'm doing the interview I'm thinking, 'What is all this shit!' It was only ever about the music and everything else is fucking bollocks, so I stopped the interview and the next day I swapped the whole lot for an American car. And then I stupidly got rid of a lot of great music that I was listening to before the ground zero of punk rock: Beatles, Dylan, folk music, which for me is originally punk rock anyway.

CLOSING TIME
The Heyday and the End
of the Pub Rock Scene

The pub rock scene was seeing a new wave of bands. Bands that very much straddled the later days of the pub rock scene and the early days of the punk scene.

Jimmy Pursey

I was born a punk. The thing is if you're going through life like I was, not running with a gang like most kids are, you're a fucking punk. I formed Sham 69 in 1975 and we were freaking people out, playing in colleges round our way. It was a long time before anyone ever mentioned the Sex Pistols to us. We didn't change what we did like Paul Weller did – they were a mod band. The Stranglers were a decent pub rock group, and when punk came along they became more darker and deeper, played Doors-type material, just faster.

Sham had no ideology apart from me. My own being, I am doing it 24/7. We were playing three chords. It was stuff like 'What Have We Got'. We were playing all those kind of songs. No bullshit. Stuff like 'White Light White Heat'.[18] It was whatever we could play. We would play any sort of stuff with three chords. When the Pistols played 'Steppin' Stone' – we played stuff like that.

Charlie Harper

In 1973–74 I had a lovely band called the Marauders. It was kind of r'n'b, but like the Pistols doing 'Stepping Stone' we were doing that kind of thing very seriously, very well. We had a black guitarist called Richey Anderson, who was very Keef Richards-like in his playing. There was a good scene going on in London at time with Kilburn and the High Roads, Dr Feelgood, Kursall Fliers, the 101ers. There was a real big scene with Eddie and the Hot Rods as well. All the bands were writing their own stuff. We were lagging behind a bit, only 25 per cent original.

Tony James

We were going out to see every band we could, hoping we could spot something. We would begrudgingly go and see this group who would play in this pub across the road from Mick's gran's, called the 101ers.[19] We always used to stand at the back but we liked the singer. We also went to see the Winkies, Ducks Deluxe and obviously Dr Feelgood.

Noel Martin

We were into pub rock. At the time I was getting into playing seriously. It was watching Kilburn and the High Roads, and the Feelgoods, and a band called Scarecrow who you don't hear about

---

18. Velvet Underground song from 1967.
19. The 101ers were a pub rock band fronted by Joe Strummer.

– they were local to Islington. I used to go the Lord Nelson to see them. I was certainly impressed by the Feelgoods when they first came out. Wilko Johnson moving all over the stage was fucking great, going back and forward playing the guitar, hitting it with all his fingers at once. I thought, 'Fucking hell, that's really good.' Kilburn and High Roads were Blockheadesque: Ian Dury was the singer and he had a very particular kind of voice. They were quite funky. There was another band called Moon. I did a bit of roadieing for them. The first time I heard the Stranglers was with Moon at some gig right up north.

Billy Bragg (Riff Raff, then solo: vocals and guitar)

Me and my mates, we kind of got into the Stones and the Who in the Seventies. We were big Faces fans. We were playing in a band called Riff Raff, playing back rooms in pubs. I think in '75 we were starting to work our way back to early British r'n'b. We bought one of the first three Stones albums and early Who.

About the same time we saw Dr Feelgood – they really got our attention – and Eddie and the Hot Rods, and that affected us. Although people don't refer back to it now, when you look back to magazines like *Sounds* in '76 it's all Pistols and Eddie and the Hot Rods. The Pistols were bringing one form of punk rock, and Eddie and the Hot Rods were bringing in what was traditionally thought of as punk rock: white garage rock, like Sam the Sham and ? and the Mysterians.[20] These were all American bands who aped the British Invasion bands. There was this weird symbiosis of the early Stones and the Who and early American bands that was picked up by the likes of Feelgoods and Hot Rods. I think that's why it got the name 'punk', not because of the Sex Pistols. The Hot Rods' *Live At Marquee* EP was the first of the ilk. I bought their version of 'Get Out Of Denver' – it was a 100 miles an hour version and it was very

---

20. ? and the Mysterians were another American garage band of the Sixties. They had a US Number One with '96 Tears' in 1966.

influential. We took the early Stones, early Who and the Hot Rods and brought it up to date.

Knox

Heavy Parrot had become Rocking Pneumonia by the time I left. Then I was in another band called Lipstick, which was formed from the remains of Despair. We were on the fringes of the pub circuit. We played the Elgin Arms where the 101ers played. That was in 1975. I knew people from Ducks Deluxe, and Charlie from Kilburn and the High Roads – he played bass with us a few times. I met Joe Strummer and 101ers down there. They actually beat us to the better night: they got the Tuesday because they got there before us, so we got the Monday night. We played on Clapham Common. We had various line-ups before that band folded up in October 1975. Eddie used to drive that band around and just before Christmas '75 we talked about starting another band. I was in a covers band at the time, playing in an Irish show band. And I was the Christmas entertainment in a gay bar in Hammersmith – it's a gig!

J. J. Burnel

We were grateful to the pub rock scene. It was a fantastic scene for young bands to play on and learn how to front people. We came in at the very end of it. Hugh and I saw Dr Feelgood and we suddenly remembered what rock'n'roll, or rhythm'n'blues as it was called in those days, was all about. They had the attitude, the roots, they could play and they looked great. Wilko was fantastic. You realised that rock'n'roll could be exciting at pub level. It inspired us. We couldn't play like them. They were much more rock'n'roll than us. They did really well and they would have done even better if it hadn't been for Wilko freaking out in the States.

Two years later I couldn't believe it: I was living in a flat with him. From being a normal awe-stricken punter, by the time I was living with him he had had to leave the Feelgoods or whatever and his star was declining and my star was rising. I still looked up to him.

Wilko Johnson in full flight, with his choppy, aggressive guitar style and charismatic stage presence. Wilko was reinventing the guitarist's role in rock'n'roll

He's a lovely bloke, very educated, very erudite. I've seen Wilko change his string with one hand: he's taken it out the packet, shaken it, undone the broken string, tune it up and he's back off again – that's what I call a great rocker!

Paolo Hewitt (Writer, journalist)

I came from Woking, like the Jam did. In the early Seventies it was a run-down town, not like it is now. I first saw the Jam in 1975, playing a small gig above a pub, even though they had been around since 1972. They were like any other young band playing covers. Wilko Johnson was a big influence on Paul Weller – you can hear it in the way he plays his guitar.

Wilko Johnson

In 1975 we were touring America. CBS had signed us there. The first thing we did was that we went to their annual convention in San Diego. All the new signings were doing their tour. We did our turn, and it created a sensation. The boss man of CBS flipped. We were their blue-eyed boys and they were going to put their muscle behind it and we would be millionaires now! It didn't work out.

We did two long tours during the spring and summer of that year, and we did *Stupidity* when we got back. In the teeth of opposition from everybody, I wanted to make the album truly live. I didn't know much about recording, but I knew what I wanted. I wanted to leave the bum notes in. Back then you could buy live albums that had the bass and drum track and everything else overdubbed. They wanted us to overdub but I refused, and it was very gratifying when *Stupidity* went to number one.[21]

I know all sorts of stories from people who told me personally that we were an influence. A lot of the guys in punk bands had certainly taken note of Dr Feelgood. What audiences got from the band was complete energy and absolute simplicity. Rock'n'roll played like that wasn't heard very much then. The way the band looked and everything, it appealed to people. All sorts of people on both side of the Atlantic in various ways were touched by Dr Feelgood. But with the whole thing that produced punk, everyone influenced everyone else.

I think anything is as important as it's perceived to be. Back then when we were doing it, we were fucking important and felt like it as well! As time wears on and things panned out the way they did, Dr Feelgood is more or less forgotten. It's not perceived to be that vital a thing now! In the words of Doug Sahm, 'It Just Don't Matter'.

---

21. Dr Feelgood's third album released in the UK, which hit the top in October 1976.

CHAPTER 4
1976 PART I: INTO CHAOS

I USE THE NME!
The Sex Pistols Introduce
Themselves to the World

J. J. Burnel

I think it was at the Red Cow one night in the spring of 1976
that our manager Dai Davies, who had worked with Malcolm
McLaren with the New York Dolls, introduced us to these two
boys and a girl. She sounded American and she said, 'I'm going to
be your new lead singer.' And that was Chrissie Hynde, and she
had come with Steve and Paul from the Pistols. Steve was dressed
like an American college boy with a silk bomber jacket and slicked-
back hair, which was different in those days. He said to me. 'I like
your haircut.' And he said, 'We're going to be famous in a few
months' time.'

*12 February 1976: The first Pistols gig to get any attention was
supporting Eddie and the Hot Rods at the Marquee. Lydon was now
really pushing the barriers of performance, walking off stage, sitting*

with the audience, throwing Jordan across the dancefloor and chucking
chairs around, before smashing some of Eddie and the Hot Rods' gear.
It resulted in the band's first live review in the NME, *the review by Neil*
Spencer that made so many people round the country who read it
suddenly realise that they were not alone. Under the headline, 'Don't
Look Over Your Shoulder But The Sex Pistols Are Coming', the review
also contained a small interview with the classic Steve Jones quote,
'Actually we're not into music. We're into chaos.' The manifesto was
now in place.

Nils Stevenson

One day Malcolm suggested I come and see the band he was managing, the Sex Pistols. I went down with him, Vivienne, Chrissie
Hynde and Jordan, in Viv's puke-green Mini.

I was hooked. They reminded me of Iggy and the Stooges. There
were no more than 100 people there. They were all there for Eddie
and the Hot Rods bar the Sex shop crew: five of us and Steve Severin
and whoever he was with. All together, ten people to see the Pistols.
I saw them play once, and by the next gig I was working for them.
I closed down my stall on the Kings Road, and the following week
we were working from Malcolm and Vivienne's flat, designing
posters, until he had a ruck with Vivienne and moved in with Helen
Wellington-Lloyd, who became our secretary/co-designer. It all
happened really fast.

Glen Matlock

John broke the PA at the Eddie and the Hot Rods gig. He didn't
like the sound of his voice.

Chrissie Hynde

In 1976 I went to every club every night, with my guitar. I just
walked around the streets looking for someone to get a band
together. I was desperate and determined. Everybody I knew had a
band together by now. Even people who I showed how to play a few

chords! And I was like holding out waiting for my band. And I knew when I found my guys they were going to be right.

McLaren, to his credit, didn't want anyone showing his guys how to play. He certainly didn't want me showing Rotten how to play guitar! McLaren didn't know much about music but he was certainly a visionary. He wanted his poet, and his struggling musicians who could just make a sound. And of course, musicianship killed off punk. Because as soon as they learned how to play, they couldn't play punk any more.

Vic Godard

There was no one there at all, about 30 to 40 people. That was for the main band, Eddie and the Hot Rods. The Pistols were the support band. We went by while the PA was getting smashed up – that was what drew us in. We were in the West End looking for gigs to go to. We walked up Wardour Street and we heard a big kerfuffle going. We thought, 'What's going on in there?' We went in. The Sex Pistols had already done a few numbers, so we saw the tail end of it. It looked like they were getting thrown out of the place! We were desperate to find out when they were playing next. We kept going to gigs finding out when the next one was.

After the Pistols at the Marquee, we went to every gig in London. It was very rough-sounding, nothing like what they turned out to be. They made a lot of errors. They did all the Sixties numbers. That's what got Rob Simmons into them. What I liked about them was that they looked nothing like the Sixties. I wasn't into that Sixties thing so much. I liked the sound of it but I didn't want it to be a band doing just Sixties stuff. They had a New York Dolls type of sound. They were the only group that was anything like that at the time.

Rob Lloyd

The first thing I can remember was reading the review in the *NME* where the Sex Pistols had been supporting Eddie and the Hot Rods at the Marquee and they had ended up in some sort of brawl. The *NME* reviewer said, 'It's really primitive music and it all fell apart.' I can remember the final line: 'We're not into music. We're into chaos...' I just thought, when I read that, '*Yeah!*' Even though I was really deeply into music I thought the chaos sounded great. I thought, 'It's arrived!'

Damian O'Neill

It was in the music press – the first review of the Pistols at the Marquee. I remember the Pistols saying, 'We are not into music, we are into chaos.' I got that cutting in my Undertones scrapbook – on the first page! [laughs] We hadn't heard anything by them.

Nils Stevenson

The term 'punk' hadn't been coined at the beginning. We were booked to do the pub rock circuit where everyone was playing r'n'b, and then the Sex Pistols came on and did their own brand of rock-'n'roll – that created friction. Rotten's attitude further infuriated the audience. Obviously it was the complete opposite of what everybody in showbiz had ever done. There were lots of problems, and then bands started coming out really fast.

Keith Levene

The word 'punk' didn't really exist then, but we had a bit of a manifesto. We were trying to tear things down: the Who's Farewell Tour Part III, Led Zeppelin, the likes of Yes, the likes of these bands that were so fucking incredibly musically talented.

Howard Devoto

Quite what punk consisted of at that point wasn't that clear. Malcolm called it 'new wave', like French cinema. The word 'punk' was in the Neil Spencer review. The American magazine, *Punk*, been around a few months.[1]

---

1. *Punk* was a New York-based magazine/fanzine that covered the upcoming CBGBs scene in a witty and acerbic style from January 1976 till 1979, and was the direct source of the name of the movement. The word 'punk' originally meant a prostitute, mouldy wood or fungus. By the time *Punk* magazine took its name it had gone on to mean a person who takes it up the ass in prison, a loser, or a form of Sixties garage rock'n'roll.

Two days later the band played a Valentine's Ball at Andrew Logan's studio in London. When Jordan jumped on stage, Johnny ripped her clothes off and started smashing the band's equipment. When his microphone cut out he started to smash it up. This caused a punch-up between the PA company and the Pistols' crew, while Lydon kept on singing 'No Fun'.

Gene October

Andrew Logan used to have mad parties in London – he would invite the whole mad arts world of London, the underground, all these real nutters all over the place.

Mick Jones

Everyone had been waiting for a band like the Pistols to happen. I first saw them at Andrew Logan's party by Tower Bridge. You knew straight away that was it, and this was what it was going to be like from now on. It was a new scene, new values – so different from what had happened before. A bit dangerous.

Brian James

It was a great feeling when we were in rehearsal in London SS and Bernie took us down to see the Pistols at Andrew Logan's big Valentine's Night warehouse party at Butler's Wharf. Just seeing them playing made me, Mick and Tony aware that there was other people into this kind of music. They were playing the Stooges' 'No Fun'. They weren't the greatest band in the world – but they had an attitude. They were barking up the right tree. It made you think, 'I wasn't wrong – there is people out there into this stuff!' I spoke to John Lydon afterwards, and I was impressed by his attitude.

I moved on from the London SS at that point. Me and Rat started looking for singers and bass players. I moved onto Portobello Road and started hanging out at the Lonsdale pub. There was quite a scene there. A lot of the people into this new scene started going down there.

Tony James

We were doing London SS, still trying to find people, in early '76. This was not working. Me and Mick didn't fall out. It was not a big deal. Somehow it got lost in the ether. Mick was already off talking to Joe Strummer and I was looking at the wanted ads.

Towards the end of London SS there is a classic Bernie moment. He got me, Brian James and Mick into his car, and we drive to Madison Terrace, which is the millionaires' row, one of the poshest streets in London in those days. There's a party going on and we're sat outside in the car, and the Stones arrive and it's all very bohemian. It was like our dream. We were totally on the outside in those days – guest list wasn't in our vocabulary. We couldn't believe it. *We're in!* Bernie gets us outside and he turns around and goes, 'You will be able to go when you get a great idea.' And he drove us away – 'You're not ready for this yet!' he said – and he was right. We were very pissed off at the time but it was true! He was taunting us.

Mick Jones

It wasn't getting anywhere. We couldn't find a singer. So me and Tony went our own ways. Bernie said to me, 'Don't work with Tony, work with Paul Simonon.' I think we felt we weren't getting anywhere at that time. Maybe Bernie pulled me away a little bit. Tony lent Paul a bass and Paul started learning the bass.

Tony James

We just kind of thought, 'We will never find a singer. Let's go our own way.' There was a time when I was living at Mick's gran's flat. Mick was living at the Davis Road squat by then with Sid Vicious and Viv Albertine.[2] And then somehow Brian hooked up with Scabies and formed the Damned and I hooked up with Billy [Idol] in Chelsea.

It's unbelievable, but we never took a picture of the London SS. The door of the Praed Sreet basement, I have a photo of that from

---

2. Vivienne Albertine was later to join the Slits.

1902 with two blokes in stove-pipe top hats by the front door – it's a spooky picture. The two blokes look like me and Mick.

A lot of great people drifted through the London SS and went on to do great stuff. Bernie would be there most of the times and he would bring Malcolm down. Chrissie Hynde would come down as well, and Mick went off to write songs with her. It was Bernie who suggested that Mick should go and write with Chrissie for a bit, and that didn't work out.

Mick Jones

I played with Chrissie Hynde for a bit. Me and Chrissie were playing songs in my bedroom and we sang together: 'Something's Got A Hold On Me' and Aretha Franklin's 'Every Little Bit Hurts'. I was still a kid and she was quite exotic to me, being from America. She was working for the *NME* and going out with Nick Kent, and I was like *wow!* But Bernie pulled me away from her as well! [laughs] He must have had a plan. He didn't think like other people – that was what was interesting about him. He gave me a proper schooling.

Ron Watts, the legendary booker from the Nag's Head in Wycombe and the 100 Club, was impressed enough by a Pistols show there to book them to play the 100 Club for the first time on 30 March 1976. This was their debut at the venue that made their reputation. John was so drunk he forgot the words and argued with Glen, resulting in the singer storming off into the street.

Glen Matlock

It could be chaotic at times. John would be singing the words to the song perfectly but they may not have been the song that the rest of us were playing at the time!

At the 100 Club he got off the stage. He pissed off, left the venue and waited at the bus stop of the number 73 bus to go home. Malcolm went upstairs, bollocked him and said, 'If you don't get

back on the stage now you are out of the band!' He came skulking
back in and glared, but carried on.

Colin Newman

I saw the early Pistols loads of times. I was living in Hendon and
they played the college. There was a complete schism in the audience
between the rugby crowd and the fans. I saw them play around
London. I was at art school in Watford, part of a circle of people
who knew what was happening. I thought the Pistols were fantastic.
I thought they were very funny, really exciting. John Lydon was a
fantastic performer. I loved the whole power of it. I'm sure I saw the
Sex Pistols more than once at the 100 Club.

Brian James

I really liked the Pistols but they happened to have this absolute shit
as a manager. At least you heard some music getting played for a
change – after all those years in the wasteland trying to prove a
point, it was worth it. Then it all kicked off big time and suddenly it
was all over the papers and bands were getting reviewed playing
rock'n'roll – they just called it punk instead. You could feel it in the
air, there was something going on. Bizarre Records in London were
selling the Stooges and Flamin' Groovies, all kinds of things you'd
not see in usual record shops. It was a hang-out. You'd go down the
Nashville and the Pistols or the 101ers, who were basically an r'n'b
band, would be there, but at least they were giving it full throttle. It
was that kind of a thing starting. The first punks were coming
through. There were more and more familiar faces at gigs.

Jimmy Pursey

When I first saw the Sex Pistols it was great. It was like there were
other people around. It wasn't just us on our own must be doing
something. We thought there must be lots of Sex Pistols doing
something like us, other bands on the same wavelength. Punk came
from the gut. The power and the struggle behind it was saying,

'You're not going to like it but we are going to say it anyway.' It was all about telling the truth. We had nothing to lose. I would rather be a dustman and have a job for life than have a false job. I'm not trying to be anyone else, am I? I'm not saying, 'Fucking hell, I'm an architect.' Basically I'll write about any of the shit you don't want to talk about.

Mark Stewart

We saw pictures of the Pistols wearing mohair jumpers and plastic sandals, and we were wearing that to the funk clubs. We couldn't really relate style-wise to Eddie or the Feelgoods, even though we really loved the music. They were a bit pub rock, know what I mean? There was a real crossover. I never divided music. To me Sly Stone and George Clinton are punk.[3] I go to different things on different nights. To me DJ Hell is punk. I can't make the division.

3 April 1976: The Pistols' debut at the other key London pub rock venue, the Nashville, supporting the 101ers. The ever-astute 101ers frontman Joe Strummer checked the Pistols, saw which way the wind was blowing and made a rock'n'roll leap of faith. He decided to quit his band, even though they were fast rising on the London pub circuit.

Vic Godard

The next gig I went to was down the Nashville. That was really fantastic. The night they played with the 101ers – that was the best one. By then the gigs were getting more packed. There was a buzz by then. The one at the Nashville made it into *Melody Maker*. There was a big splash because of a fight. Steve Jones had a thing going on with someone, and there was mayhem!

There were people going to the 101ers who didn't like the

---

3. Sly Stone was a brilliant Sixties psychedelic soul singer. George Clinton is best remembered for his work with Funkadelic and Parliament, turning funk into a weird trip with elongated, hypnotic grooves and lunatic lyrics – amazing songs, amazing imagination, and a huge influence on the hip-hop scene.

Pistols. Sid used to be good at winding people up. He was always getting into scraps. But the Pistols' crowd were not fighting types. A few gigs later there was a load of Teds who were deliberately there to cause trouble, and this was at pub gigs.

Captain Sensible

I saw them down at the 100 Club and the Nashville. It was good fun. I liked what they were doing. I liked the attitude onstage. It was like that Pink Fairies incident. There was plenty of that with the Pistols. I wasn't greatly thrilled with the music. I thought it was a bit stodgy, but there was loads of spirit and that.

Knox

I was very impressed with them. There were no guitar solos or anything. Steve Jones had his twin reverb and with his playing they were very good. Johnny Rotten, when we saw them, had perfected his singing technique. They had the clothes, the entourage – they were very pressworthy. I thought the Pistols were a new kind of band. We were electrified, the music was so aggressive. When we eventually started to play these towns outside London, it was a very powerful thing. We were knocking these songs out – bang, bang, bang! It had a big impact.

The Vibrators had our first gig on 7 March 1976, supporting the Stranglers at Hornsey Art College. The Stranglers were good. There was not a lot of people there; it was just a tiny room. They seemed quite organised. Jet Black had this ice cream van to take the gear round in! They were a really good band.

I don't think anyone could really tell what was going to happen. We played that gig and then got some work. Eddie the drummer and Pat Collier the bass player went around everywhere that did gigs asking if we could play, and through their hard work we got a lot more gigs. We had a residency at the Lord Nelson on Holloway Road and we started playing outside London. We didn't have a manager to get the thing going. Half the set was covers. It had to

Sticking a big 'V' up to
detractors: a glammed-up Knox
sweats it out on the punk circuit

be, otherwise you got to rehearse for months. We were out playing as soon as possible.

Gene October

The Vibrators were in on that pub rock scene with Eddie and the Hot Rods and Kilburn and the High Roads. The Vibrators were a rock'n'roll band before they went punk – it was a sort of naughty side of rock'n'roll. But it wasn't quite punk.

J. J. Burnel

We knew most of the protagonists in the punk thing from previous lives. I saw the Vibrators' very first gig at a students union in 1976 – they supported us. I thought they were great rhythm'n'blues band with a new kind of attitude.

In 1976 the Stranglers played 300 shows and there were 200 punch-ups, by which anyone would consider us hardened veterans. We didn't take any shit. We developed a belligerent stance. You either do that or you get shown the door. We were not going to get bottled off the stage. It got known that we could get provoked and that added entertainment value! [laughs] It wasn't only me. Hugh had a very acidic tongue: he'd say something and we'd get into a punch-up over it. In those days Jet was fantastic – Jet was really fit, very handy, a big boy, and he was belligerent. He's not so handy now, but he's still belligerent! He's the classic grumpy old man now! We worked as a team. We didn't take any shit from anyone and we would play anywhere. We thought that was what it was all about.

Don Letts

There were these different little crowds for the bands. The Stranglers was more jeans and T-shirts than the other bands' crowds. We saw them loads of times, them or the Pistols. It was always one or the other till the other bands came onto the scene.

J. J. Burnel

By 1976 we had developed our own audience. When we played live everything speeded up. I think we were faster before the Ramones came over, and we got more aggressive as people. Our managers in 1976 gave us an album by the Standells, *Good Guys Don't Wear White*, and they said, 'This is the template for you guys.' We said, 'Hmm, maybe...' They saw a link more with the Sixties than the Seventies. Our songs were catchy pop songs, which was our forte. We were also developing some prog rock stuff with long solos.

'Peasant In The Big Shitty' is a psychedelic song. We never made any bones about our frames of reference, which were the Doors, Captain Beefheart, Love, the Who. Someone penned the term 'acid punk', which was great. By then we starting to find our style.

Rob Lloyd

I was going down to London to see what all the fuss was about. I'd seen the Stranglers several times. They obviously had a really good manager or agent because, even prior to the Ramones coming over, they had supported Patti Smith. They had all the the key supports. Certainly when I hitched down to the Roundhouse it was always the Stranglers opening the show. I think it was John Curd who used to book the Roundhouse. I used to think they were great until they actually released a record and it had that fucking organ doodling all over it! I went off them then. When you saw them live you didn't notice so much, but when they brought out '(Get A) Grip (On Yourself)' I couldn't believe how much doodling there was. I found it really disappointing!

In May the Pistols continued their confrontational series of gigs in the London clubs. On 3 May their second gig at the Nashville ended up with a punch-up. On 5 May they played the Babalu Disco on Finchley Road. The following week, on 11 May, they began a four-week residency at the 100 Club. That night Sid Vicious got carried away with the

*music and invented pogoing. All this was interspersed with gigs in
small clubs in unlikely towns like Northallerton – their first gig outside
London and its satellite towns — and Scarborough.*

Marco Pirroni

I went to the Babalu Club in Finchley Road. It was the furthest out
of town I'd been! Even though it was two minutes on the Tube, five
minutes from the West End, it felt like a million miles away, and the
fact that there was no one there didn't help.

Glen Matlock

There was no one there at all, but it it was one of the best gigs we
ever played.

Pauline Murray

We had read about the Sex Pistols. Me and my boyfriend at the time,
we went down to London and went down the Kings Road. Before
we got to Kings Road we got on the Tube and there was this guy on
it and we said, 'That's Johnny Rotten.' He had a drape on and crush-
ers and stuff like that. We followed him down the Kings Road into
Seditionaries.[4] We went in there and it was like nothing we had seen.
We got talking to McLaren and he asked if we knew anyone who
could put them on, but a lot of the gigs round here were just city
halls, big gigs. He ended up putting them on at Northallerton – not
that we suggested it – of all places! In a tiny little club.

The Northallerton club was strange. People were there for their
normal Friday night disco. There were four people there for the
Pistols. There was us and a couple of friends. The rest were on a
night out. It was just hilarious, really funny. They came on and did
their blistering type of stuff through a tiny PA and the people were
gobsmacked. People forget how funny the Pistols were to people

---

4. Yet another new identity for 430 Kings Road – but in fact it was not relaunched as
Seditionaries until the start of 1977, so it would still have been called Sex at the time
Murray first visited.

Skinny, sharp and angular were all punk requisites in full flow onstage at an early Penetration show

who had never seen anything like it. It was fantastic – they blew all the cobwebs off everything. They went back to London after the gig. At the time I never spoke to them. I was so in awe of it.

That was the first time we saw them. They did pubs, weird places. We saw them at the Ford Green pub in Leeds. We saw them supporting Doctors of Madness and they totally blew them off that night.

John Lydon

In the early days we took gigs wherever we could. Many a time we drove all the way to Yorkshire across the bloody moors for twenty quid to play a Teddy boys convention – a frightening prospect, that, but we would do it. Another joyous occasion was the West Ham United social bar where Arsenal lads like me are hardly welcome. I won them over with love and charm.

Keith Levene

The Pistols were the best fucking thing I'd seen in years. The bands that were hot were the Stranglers (yuck!), Eddie and the Hot Rods and this band called the Sex Pistols. I walked into this pub in west London and I saw my first Pistols gig. It was one of the best, maddest things I'd ever seen. That's when I totally knew that I was in the right place at the right time. It was one of the highest points of my life.

Rat Scabies

The Pistols were doing odd residencies at the Nashville and the 100 Club. They were really funny people. They didn't realise how entertaining they were. They were really colourful and raw for the time. Johnny Rotten was great at winding up the hippies. He'd go onstage and all the audience hated him, people booing and throwing stuff. He was an absolute master of the one-liner. They were a really entertaining night out. I didn't see them as being a big serious threat to society. Other people told them they were and then they realised they could be.

I don't know what the band thought they would have got out of being the Pistols. Glen wanted to be in a straightforward kind of group, but I think he got the concept. Steve and Paul wanted to be in a normal band.

Pauline Murray

Gary Chaplin, our guitarist, had gone to a Roxy Music gig, which was a lot earlier than when we had seen the Pistols, and from that gig we decided to get a band together in 1976. He played guitar. I had never sung before and he said, 'Have a go.' We used to do stuff like New York Dolls and Jonathan Richman's 'Roadrunner'.

Nothing would have happened without the Pistols. It was like, 'Wow, I believe in this.' What they were saying was: 'It's a load of shite. I'm going to do what I do and I don't care what people think.' That was the key to it. People forget that, but it was the main ideology for me: we don't care what you think – you're shit anyway. It was the attitude that got people moving, as well as the music. The attitude was shaping the music.

THE NORTH WILL RISE AGAIN
Manchester, the Second City of Punk

The Sex Pistols' legendary gigs at Manchester's Lesser Free Trade Hall took place on 4 June and 20 July 1976. By the simple act of putting the Sex Pistols on in Manchester twice that summer, not only did the barely formed Buzzcocks become one of the great British punk rock pop bands, and a massive influence on bands from that era till Green Day now; they also took punk rock out of London and kickstarted the whole Manchester punk rock generation – alongside London, perhaps the key creative powerhouse in the whole movement.

Howard Devoto

Peter [Shelley] and I were trying, around October/November

1975, to get a band together. I stuck a notice up at Bolton Institute of Technology to see what would happen, and then I got together with Pete. We tried Rolling Stones stuff like 'Come On' and we tried 'Satisfaction' at one point! We had no name for the band. We probably only got together at this guy's house twice in total. We didn't have a direction until we saw the Sex Pistols review in the *NME*. We didn't know what we were doing, there was nothing to aim for. We had been trying to put the band together for three months just doing cover versions. We had no drummer. So when we did see the Sex Pistols it provided a blueprint. That's when my life changed.

We were sat in the refectory at B. I. T. and Pete was reading the *NME* and saw this review of this band who were compared to the Stooges. There was a quote which said, 'We're not into music, we're into chaos.'

Pete Shelley (Buzzcocks: Guitar and vocals)

We had already been writing songs, me and Howard, in a flat in Salford. At weekends we would go there and write. We were trying to get a drummer and they were like gold dust. The idea was there, but no impetus. We read about the Sex Pistols in the *NME* and we thought they seemed to be having fun doing it so they motivated us.

The *NME* used to come out on Thursdays in Bolton. We read it at college. We were reading it in the coffee bar and Howard said, 'Oh look, there's this band that does this version of "No Fun". That looks interesting.' I was vice-president of the students' union. . It sounds grandiose but it isn't. I was also on the National Committee of Part-Time Students. The rest of the time I was unemployed, so I had punk credentials! [laughs] I had plenty of time on my hands. There was this committee meeting down in London, and they said that they would pay the train fare.[5] Instead of getting the train, a friend of mine lent us a car and we used the

---

5. The committee was chaired by the president of the NUS, Charles Clarke – now Home Secretary.

money for petrol, and me and Howard spent the weekend down there looking for the Sex Pistols.

We had no idea where they were! We bought a copy of *Time Out* (and that's where we got the name of the song 'Time's Up' from). It had a review of the *Rock Follies* in it that same week which said, 'It's the buzz, cock,' which sounded a bit like the 'Sex Pistols', so that's where we got the name of the band from.[6] We phoned up the *NME* when we were in London to find out where the Sex Pistols were playing, if anywhere, and they said as far as they knew they were not playing but, 'Their manager is this guy called Malcolm McLaren and he's got this clothes shop on the Kings Road.' So we got the Tube to Sloane Square and walked all the way down the Kings Road and into the shop. It was very early days: late February 1976. Malcolm was there behind the counter and said, 'Oh yeah, we are doing some gigs this weekend: Welwyn Garden City and High Wycombe.'

We went to both the gigs that weekend. There was about half a dozen people in the audience who had seen the band before, and a bit of trouble, I think, at one of them. The Sex Pistols stood out like a sore thumb from all the other bands and that was what made them so exciting. They were also funny as well. It was the opposite of what you expected from a gig. It wasn't about how good they could play, but how good they were!

Howard Devoto

We didn't know what the hell the Sex Pistols would be like. It was probably halfway through, after three or four numbers, that we found a plot. I wouldn't say they felt quite dangerous but there was something about them, particularly John. I'd not seen anybody like him in a band before and the fragments of words that came through sounded intriguing. The most interesting thing was John himself and the fact that there was bit of a scene round them. Also there

---

6. *Rock Follies* was a TV musical drama series about the fortunes of three women who form a band. The soundtrack, written by Roxy Music's Andy Mackay, was the Number One album during April and May 1976.

was the Sex shop and Malcolm McLaren in his leathers – all that added to it.

The audience included the Bromley Contingent, Malcolm, Jordan, Helen Wellington-Lloyd, Nils Stevenson. In their own ways they almost looked more interesting than the band, except that John was so charismatic. The other great thing about him was he, like Morrissey, was very British. There was no attempt to Americanise it. Even his constantly getting out his handkerchief and blowing his nose whilst he was onstage, or going off to be sick in the toilets after a number and returning ten minutes later – very unusual. The lyrics were great in songs like 'Submission'. There were loads of great bits like that. We thought they were great, the look, the attitude and the music. There was lots of aggression. Malcolm told us that the next night the Pistols were playing Welwyn Garden City, so we went to that show, too.

After the Pistols gig we changed our look. I started henna-ing my hair, ordered some blue striped jeans and had them taken in.

Pete Shelley

Malcolm asked us if we could get the Sex Pistols any gigs in Manchester, and we said that we would see what we could do. Originally we tried to get the Sex Pistols to play our college, but it wasn't interested. Howard used to do the pub rock column for the *New Manchester Review* so he had a few contacts on the pub rock circuit. He was running around trying to get the Commercial Hotel in Stalybridge[7] to do something, but they were not interested either. So we went to the Lesser Free Trade Hall and found out that it was £32 to hire, so we thought we could do that. We printed tickets at a pound each. We did actually make money on the first one, even though there was only about 42 people at the gig! It was very hard to convince people that there was a vibrant new form of music – no long guitar solos, no nothing, really.

7. A beat-up town up in hills near Manchester, a very unlikely setting for a Sex Pistols gig.

Howard Devoto

I made sure we got Malcolm to pay up front in case the band never turned up! Pete and I went out fly-posting the gig. It seemed like every other week there was something about the Sex Pistols in the press, and it just got bigger and bigger. Suddenly, I was involved in a real way with this band that were in the music press.

Before we put the Pistols on we played our first Buzzcocks gig at B. I. T. in March 1976. We hadn't even managed to rehearse the whole band for the gig. Peter and I had run over the songs – I guess we hoped the rest of them could play them. We had ten songs, mostly cover versions – 'Diamond Dogs', Eno's 'The True Wheel' – and two of Pete's early songs, 'Get On Our Own' and 'No Reply'. I can't imagine what we had in mind or how prepared we were. We must have tried all those songs in some form. I must have known the words. I had not met Garth Davies, the bass player, before. He and Pete go back a long time. Garth was dressed up in a bow tie and a white frilly shirt and a dark suit, looking like he was playing in a cabaret band! Till he came to the gig we never met the drummer before, a guy called Dennis. We started playing and 'Diamond Dogs' was half the speed it was supposed to be. They pulled the plug on us after three numbers. At the end of the gig we just sat there and the drummer Dennis raised one hand high and said, 'I'm at this level,' and held the other hand low and said, 'You're at this level.'

Even if the gig hadn't felt like a victory, one was going to present it like it was, and I did on a postcard to Richard Boon.[8]

After that we concentrated on trying to organise the Sex Pistols gig. That was going to be our next gig. I was compiling the listings for the *New Manchester Review*, just phoning round the venues, in a sense trying to find out the places to play. I can't remember where the idea came from for trying the Free Trade Hall. The main hall was

---

8. Richard Boon went to school in Leeds with Howard Devoto. He accompanied Devoto and Shelley on the February road trip to see the Sex Pistols, and went on to run the New Hormones record label and eventually manage the Buzzcocks.

at ground level with a balcony. The Lesser Free Trade Hall was upstairs, separate from it. Nobody had ever heard of it. I think the Pistols must have brought a PA. I can't believe we got a PA together.

We advertised in the *New Manchester Review*. I was able to get a little picture of them in and I wrote a review underneath. We took out a little ad in the *Manchester Evening News* and then Malcolm did some A3 posters for the gig.[9] Peter and I went along Oxford Road pasting them up. They were very small compared to the normal posters on the walls. Peter and I gave out leaflets as well at two concerts: one was at the Free Trade Hall and one was at the Palace. One of the gigs was John Miles.

I don't think till that first gig we knew anybody else who knew of the Sex Pistols. I don't know what we did about ticket sales. I'm pretty sure about 100 turned up. The usual number of 30 or 40 comes from somebody who's pretty anxious to present themselves as being really on the ball. [laughs] I think it was about 100. It had to be that amount for the Pistols to feel it was worth it to come back again. There was enough for there for John to be very positive about the gig.

Peter Hook (Joy Division, New Order: bass)

I used to read the *NME*, *Record Mirror*, *Sounds* and *Melody Maker* religiously every week. I worked at the Town Hall so my escape was to read the music press. I devoured it. I knew about everything. In early '76 you started to read about the Sex Pistols. Then I went on holiday. I was reading that while I was away. It looked quite appealing, really rebellious, and the rebellious part was very appealing at that age. When I got back to Manchester from my holidays I read the *Manchester Evening News* and I noticed the advert for the Sex Pistols.

---

9. The photocopier was one of the key armaments of punk rock. In the pre-internet age the photocopier was king, with primitive fanzines, posters and flyers benefiting from the new, fast and furious, cut-up montages of high energy art and stencilled graphics that became a punk rock staple.

Linder Sterling

The Sex Pistols at the Lesser Free Trade Hall were more like a billboard than a road sign. I walked into that concert with Fate by my side and have only ever looked forward since.

Pete Shelley

We didn't play the first gig because we didn't have a drummer! So we got this really odd band to do the support called Solstice.

Howard Devoto

I think it was a week before the gig when we realised that we couldn't play. It was pretty short notice: 'I think we'll have to find somebody else,' thinking, 'Who do we know?' I was working that summer in a mail order warehouse in Bolton and I'd met this guy who said he had a band, so I phoned him. They were the only band I knew – they were very proficient. One of the few memories of the night was that I'd just got the first Ramones album. I discovered there was a record player above the stage. We hadn't thought much about the interval music. I discovered the record player when I was looking round the hall. It was absolutely ancient. So I put the Ramones album on. It wouldn't go very loud but I played the whole album at the beginning of the night and the interval. The Ramones album had an impact. I liked it. It had tunes. It was funny.

I don't remember talking to many people. I think I would have been rushing round a lot. I tend to be like that. I'm only half taking it in really. I tend to be a very focussed person. Pete is relaxed and I tend to be very directive. I was concerned with how the gig was going.

I got Tony Wilson down for that gig, even though I had no idea who he was at the time. At the house we lived in on Lower Broughton Road, one of the people living there that year was a woman called Sheila McKechnie. She would always be on the telly. She was seeing Steve Morrison, who was working on *World In Action*, so he'd come round. He heard that we were doing this gig and he said, 'You ought to tell my colleague Tony Wilson about this.' So I did. At this point Malcolm had sent up a three-track cassette – they had done a demo with Chris Spedding – so I sent that to Tony Wilson.

Peter Hook

The Pistols gig was horrendous. The sound was really terrible. In them days it was just purely the rebellion, the fuck-you attitude that really grabbed you, and after that music went from being this glamorous world to something that you could do as well. It was a total revelation. I went to buy a bass the next day. I borrowed money off my mum. Barney already had a guitar. He could play a little – the odd chord shape.

I didn't know anyone else there apart from Bernard's wife, and we met the first Joy Division drummer there.

Steve Diggle

The Free Trade Hall was the first time I met Pete Shelley. I was going to Cox's Bar round the corner to meet a mate. I didn't know the Pistols were on. I'd heard about them. My mate said, 'I'll meet you outside the Free Trade Hall and we'll go to Cox's round the corner.' He said it was a good pint of Boddingtons in there. I was stood outside and Malcolm McLaren came out and said, 'Have you heard of the Sex Pistols? Come in. You must be the bass player.' I think he thought I must have been in the Buzzcocks! He introduced me to Pete, who was doing the tickets, and Howard, who was doing the lights. Pete and Howard already had something going on – they had already done a little gig at Bolton Institute doing covers. When I met them they were looking for a bass player and a drummer.

I sat at the back with Pete Shelley. It was fantastic. There must have been about ten or fifteen people there. Everyone claims they went! What happened was there another Sex Pistols gig there a few weeks later and I think that's where everyone gets mixed up.

Pete Shelley

It was the gig that condensed the Manchester scene. People saw that there was other people into this kind of music. People were looking at the rest of the audience more than the band! And they became nodding acquaintances, so three weeks later when we put on the second gig there was all of them and all of their friends there.

Steve Diggle

The next day after the Pistols gig we had a rehearsal, plugged through one little amp. We played a Ramones song and 'Boredom' and a few other songs that were on the go by then. Six or seven songs, like 'Breakdown', that sort of stuff. 'Jackie Is A Punk' by the Ramones, whose album had just come out – that was a real milestone, a big change in things. You can hear the Ramones influence on the first Clash album and the first Buzzcocks album.

After the rehearsal we decided to get the band going. I never met my mate in the end that night! I met him a few days later and said, 'I'm doing the Buzzcocks now, let's see how it goes.'

We got John Maher, who had only being playing drums for six weeks. He turned up at rehearsal and he was fantastic. 'Only been playing six weeks,' he said. He must have been joking! We had a great chemistry there. We had three weeks to get a set together for the second Pistols gig. That was where all the press came down big on the Pistols and came down to the Manchester show and saw us there. They were, like, 'Fucking hell, a local band as well.' We got good reviews. The guy from *Sounds* gave us a bad review though, but he took it all back a few weeks later.

There was no punks around when we started. Pete Shelley always tells me we started two days before the Clash. We were in Manchester. Nothing doing. If you went to Pips nightclub you had to have a suit and tie on to get in.[10] Bowie and Roxy had peaked and

---

10. Pips was the key club in Manchester in the late Seventies, with several different rooms supporting several different scenes.

we needed something else. There was a million on the dole. The music getting made wasn't relevant to our generation. You got prog bands who would have one song that would take up the whole side of an album singing about mushrooms in the sky. I was going to start a band like the Who, smashing gear up, but then the Buzzcocks came along.

Howard Devoto

We met Steve Diggle at the first gig. We had also managed to find a drummer, John Maher, through an ad in the *New Manchester Review*. Steve had now seen the Sex Pistols so he had a bit of an idea of what were trying to do. Certainly the songs were starting to come together from Pete and I. 'Breakdown' – I've got a feeling he didn't have any verses for that but he had the chorus. So I built the whole thing round that. I'm not quite sure how it came together. I know that 'Orgasm Addict' was like that. He had the chorus and opening two lines and I did the rest of it.

By the second Pistols gig at the Free Trade Hall, quite a few people understood what punk was about now. Slaughter and the Dogs brought quite a lot of people with them. I'm sure we wanted somebody who would be able to pull some more people in, and that's why we got them. We were trying to find somebody who wouldn't stick out like a sore thumb like the support band at the first Pistols gig.

Slaughter and the Dogs, even though they were really into Bowie, seemed like they could be the right band for the bill. They were passable, probably because they had a following. We were not particularly close to them. When they put that poster together for the gig with their name as the headliners, it kind of showed where they were coming from.

Marc Riley

Our way into the punk rock thing was going to see Slaughter and the Dogs gigs, because we knew Mike Rossi. We saw them play in St Bernadette's Youth Club at Hough End on the Parkway. We went

Devoto and Shelley onstage at an early Buzzcocks gig in their home-made take on the punk rock chic

to see them at the Free Trade Hall when they played the Sex Pistols gig promoted by Pete Shelley. The first punk band I ever saw was the Buzzcocks – they opened on the night. Slaughter's audience was a bit like a Morrissey audience: they had the sensitive ones and the nutcases, mainly nutcases![11] Slaughter and the Dogs pretty well had the rowdy element, rowdy Wythenshawe bootboys singing along to 'Where Have All the Bootboys Gone'. They were a great night out, naïve, very transparent. They did 'White Light White Heat'. Mike Rossi had become pally with Mick Ronson and they were the band to go and see.

So completely by default we saw the Sex Pistols. I'd seen a review in one of the papers, an interview in the *NME*. It was that famous picture of Steve Jones thumping someone, and Lydon bent over in the audience. I was aware of them. I didn't look at them and think, 'Wow, that's for me!'

It was because Slaughter and the Dogs were on the bill that I went to the gig with Craig Scanlon. At that point in time punk didn't exist, so the gig was full of Slaughter fans and people curious about the Pistols. Mark Smith and Martin Bramah were there – they all had long hair and leathers.[12] It was busy – Slaughter and the Dogs brought along 100. I don't remember the Buzzcocks having much impact, and we went to get chips halfway through the Pistols! We came back just in time for the fight at the end. The Lesser Free Trade Hall had a balcony and we were eating our chips upstairs. Downstairs fists and fur were flying. Inevitable that it would happen, between the south Manchester Slaughter lot and the more north Manchester Pistols fans.

---

11. Although not strictly 'punk', Morrissey, who was at the Sex Pistols gig at Manchester's Free Trade Hall, was a face on the early Manchester punk scene. Although he was initially sniffy about punk in a series of letters he wrote to now defunct music paper *Record Mirror*, preferring his beloved New York Dolls, the punk attitude was definitely there as his days as Smiths frontman and his solo career testify – as do the number of times his name crops up in this book. His brilliant 2004 comeback album underlines his continuing cutting-edge relevance whilst still managing to survive and prosper in the mainstream.

12. Smith and Bramah were founder members of the Fall. Riley joined the band in 1978, and Scanlon in 1979 when Bramah left.

Mick Rossi (Slaughter and the Dogs: guitar)

By the time we did the second Pistols gig we already had a following. In early 1976 there wasn't any other bands around doing our kind of stuff. We get overlooked all the time when the history gets told, like in the movie *24 Hour Party People* – we weren't mentioned in there.

Tony Wilson compèred the gig at the Forum. He turned up in clogs and with a handbag! We were trying to be a street glam band. Martin Hannett came down to see us at Stockport Inn and said he wanted to release something. Tosh Ryan came with him.[13] This was a pre-Pistols gig. We were carving out a little bit of a following and had our own direction. You can't in my opinion just wake up and be a punk band – I think we were there anyway. It's defined by who you are: the sound, style and attitude is with you anyway.

After the Pistols gig we felt part of the punk thing. We had the songs. It did change our sound – I remember we went back to rehearse and we changed the songs. It had that effect on everybody, I suppose. But we were already there, really: we were glam with a bit more edge. We always did our own thing.

We'd heard about the Sex Pistols and we'd heard about the Damned. We didn't know about the Buzzcocks till they played the Sex Pistols gig with us at the Lesser Free Trade Hall. We felt it was good there was another band was on the scene. We really had no idea what we were doing business-wise. We were still trying to find our way.

John Lydon

Nothing was really going on anywhere and places like the Free Trade Hall in Manchester were basically lying there rotting. It had a good novel combination of different bands that night – the Buzzcocks were always good – but can you call it punk?

---

13. Tosh Ryan ran Manchester label Rabid Records. Martin 'Zero' Hannett was a maverick Manc producer who would become best known for his atmospheric work with Joy Division, helping to redefine record production.

Pete Shelley

People always tell me that the Free Trade Hall gig started the whole Manchester scene. If only we had known then what we know now! It feels strange that we spawned a monster out of that gig. As our popularity grew in the next twelve months it enabled us to take other bands with us, like Joy Division. I remember they came to us asking for hints on how to do it! [laughs]

It was a combination of people waiting for it and people responding to the call of arms. The idea of punk fired the imagination of people, I think. We got a big buzz out of that. Manchester city centre is very small – there was only about two or three clubs into music you'd go to. People came from a large distance to the Ranch and the Electric Circus and there was nothing else to do when you were there but talk to people.[14] People were starting their own bands. It was like in skiffle or Merseybeat: not since then have so many people wanted to be in bands. Tied into that was the old xerox aspect of making your own music; also the fact it didn't have to be serious – people would have really stupid names for bands, like the Toilets, so there was an implicit humour in it.[15] Even if you never played you could be in a band. Also reinvention was very important. You could change your name and become another person.[16] People became known for what they felt. It was almost like Year Zero.

I suppose it was good for us being in Manchester because we weren't tainted by the rush to sign once record companies thought they'd buy into this music and sign up anyone they could. London was more media-orientated than Manchester. The only journalists we had then were Paul Morley and Tony Wilson off the telly. In many ways it was less competitive and there was less to fight over.

---

14. The two venues that took over as the hub of the Manchester scene, with the Electric Circus becoming *the* Manchester punk venue till it was closed a year later.

15. The Toilets were an early outfit featuring Mike Peters and Nigel Twist, later in the Alarm.

16. Pete Shelley and Howard Devoto were originally called Peter McNeish and Howard Trafford.

Definitely London always got the attention because of the way the whole thing was set up but Manchester with Tony Wilson and New Hormones Records had something going on. People thought, 'It's happening on my doorstep. I don't have to get on the train for four hours and go down to London.' It also helped that because of Manchester's early involvement it was a place where bands from London would want to play. It had got its own scene going: places like the Electric Circus started off as a normal rock venue and became the number one punk venue.

Linder Sterling

There were fantastic early punk women like Denise and Jodi that I photographed, and the rest are now all nameless; but their negatives are safe and tell such a tale of glamour. Howard Devoto and Pete Shelley were my knights in shining disarmour. I have a photograph that I've labelled 'Stiff Kittens', which shows Ian Curtis talking to John the Postman at the Electric Circus; there is a poster for Mott's new album in the background.

Peter Hook

I was going to all the gigs: the Holdsworth Hall with the Buzzcocks and Eater, loads of gigs at places like the Ranch. Everyone suddenly had a band. There was a real outbreak of bands – it was like chickenpox. There was a very small audience and you started seeing the same people at all the gigs and you started talking to them. I always felt it wasn't a middle-class and arty scene. We looked punk with dog collars and ripped clothes – you went for it big time. Barney went for quite a Germanic look. [laughs] We all started out quite punky, then went quite military.

Warsaw played everywhere.[17] Someone would say, 'Got a gig,' and you'd go, 'Is that in two hours? Fucking great, I'll be there!'

---

17. Early names for Hook and Barney Sumner's new band were Warsaw and Stiff Kittens, before they became Joy Division.

I really sort of miss that immediacy – you just don't get that any more. That's really sad.

Howard Devoto

The next gig we played after the Free Trade Hall was at the Ranch. It seemed like the only punk-type place in Manchester. In some ways we were trying to emulate the Pistols playing in El Paradise in Soho.[18] That seemed the only half-appropriate type of place. The Bowie kids would go there. I remember Lou Reed's 'Charlie's Girl' and 'Coney Island Baby' getting played there. We played there once. Not that many people turned up for it, and of course we got stopped when we were playing because Foo Foo was doing his act in the next room, and there was a sort of hatchway between the two rooms.[19] We start playing and after three numbers this heavy bloke started walking towards the 'stage', which was actually the dancefloor. I said, 'Excuse me, can I help you?' and he said, 'Are you the boss?' and asked us to end the set. So we got chucked off.

3 July 1976: the Sex Pistols played Hastings Pier Pavilion. A trip to the seaside on their seemingly endless tour of London's satellite towns.

Poly Styrene

I saw the Sex Pistols at Hastings. I saw them on my birthday on Hastings Pier. They weren't called punk then, and they were not famous then. They were doing covers mainly! The only difference between them and the people I was working with like the Pretty Things, Pink Floyd types, was their age. They were so much younger.

The Pistols didn't have a huge effect on me, but it made me think I'd rather have a live band than just make demos. They were young and that made me realise that I didn't have to work with these

---

18. London strip club which the Pistols played on 4 April 1976.
19. Foo Foo Lamaar was a legendary Mancunian Danny La Rue-type act, who owned his own club Foo Foo's in the city centre.

established musicians, like I was doing. I liked the idea that you could just go out and play. Basically they were not that good! But I realised it didn't have to be so polished. It could be rawer. And I got my band together at that time.

Noel Martin

Johnny Rotten went to the same school as me. He was in the year below me. When I first saw him fronting the Pistols I said, 'What is that fucking wanker doing! How can he be doing that!' I thought, 'Is this a put-up job? How did they find him?' From that we knew there was something dodgy about the Pistols image-wise – not the music, though, that was groundbreaking.

John Lydon

I come from Finsbury Park and there ain't no safety valve there. That was a hard as nails area. You don't survive through that if you're a wanker. You got to mean what you say – if they catch you out you're doomed. I like that. It's not so much physical all the time, getting pummelled. There was mental abuse that can go on. But that's my community, you see, and I can give it back just as good. I give and take. We're a very varied lot where Finsbury Park is concerned, a multiracial, multicultural place and we're not prejudicial.

I GOT A TV EYE ON YOU
The Adverts

Gaye Advert

We were hearing about British punk in the music press and reading about the Sex Pistols. We had always wanted to move to London, so we moved there in 1976. As we moved to London we read about the Sex Pistols in the music press again. We would always scan the music press every week. We read the Pistols' reviews with people comparing them to Iggy and stuff, and that they did a cover version of 'No Fun'.

T. V. Smith

In the early summer of '76 we moved to London. Partly because I wanted to be in a band, and partly because I didn't want to hang around in Devon. I was bored. There was nothing going on down there that was stimulating. It was clear nothing was going to happen in Torquay, and my band Sleaze were pissed off with doing my songs and not getting whatever they wanted out of being in a band. It's hard to sustain if you don't have a concept of what you want to do in your head. The guitarist wanted to do Jimi Hendrix cover versions. They slung me out of my own band! [laughs] I thought, 'What am I going to do now?' In the meantime I had met Gaye and she wanted to play bass and we thought, 'Let's go to London. There's no point in hanging about down here.'

Gaye Advert

Tim had taught me to play bass in Devon as something to do, really. He was still doing Sleaze then – I always fancied doing something to while away the time! He had a short-scale bass to start with. It was £40 in a seconds shop in Exeter. It didn't have a case for it. I carried it up to London and got a big bright red acoustic guitar case for it. When we first started rehearsing in London, our guitarist Howard (Pickup) said, 'You have to get a proper case,' and then when I got the red case he said it looked even worse! [laughs] Led Zeppelin were rehearsing in the same place and he said, 'What if they see us carrying that round?!' Led Zeppelin were OK, actually, seemed like nice people.

T. V. Smith

I was already aware of punk rock. That 12 February article in the *NME* describing the gig and Jordan throwing the chair about – that was the first inkling I got of something going on in Britain that I was interested in. There was also news filtering over from the States about the Dolls and Iggy, and that was the first time that it was happening in Britain as well, and I thought, 'I want to be in there!'

We had been looking to move up to London for some time but we couldn't find anywhere to live, so we went up for the odd day trying to find a flat. We found a one-room flat in Clapham that we could just about afford. It was a big move when you are eighteen/ nineteen. We just took everything that we owned up on the train and the Tube. We survived by doing crappy day jobs.

Gaye Advert

The idea was to start a band, and it just happened and I fell into it. I was thinking it would be quite good to do a gig. When we first moved to London we went to see the Pistols at the Nashville, at the 100 Club, in Hendon, and the Screen on the Green – that one was really good. We didn't know London that well then. We didn't know where Hendon was! At that one we asked Malcolm for a T-shirt, and he said, 'Come and see me in the office,' and he gave me that one I always wore – it was huge! Twenty years later it was still huge!

1, 2, 3, 4!
The Ramones

On 23 April 1976, the Ramones' eponymous debut album was released. It was to have a seismic effect on the music scene and its influence is still as strong to this day. Of course it wasn't a hit. Still, it fired up the underground and its effect on the nascent British punk scene was massive. The album had been recorded at the prestige Plaza Sound Studios in New York City's Radio City Music Hall on a budget of only $6,000. Fourteen songs rush by in 28 minutes, mashed together in a surge of buzzsaw guitars. Drop-dead classics like 'Blitzkrieg Bop' and 'Beat On The Brat' helped to blueprint punk rock as the record slowly seeped its way into the underground.

J. J. Burnel

The Ramones album came out and one of our managers said, 'Listen to this,' and I thought, 'Fuck me, this is really fantastic!' – like most people did. You either liked it or you didn't.

Paul Research (The Scars: guitar)

I went out to buy the Ramones album in middle of '76. It was the first thing I was conscious of up here in Edinburgh. I wasn't sure what they were singing about, but the Ramones came to me at the right time. It's really aged very well – such an accurate sound. Before that I was a teenage prog rocker! [laughs]

Mark Perry

I think the first experience I had of punk was reading the *NME* really. They started writing a lot of live reviews from CBGBs, about Television, the Ramones, Patti Smith and people like that. It just sounded so exciting and that. Then Nick Kent wrote a review of the first Ramones album, and as soon as I read that it sounded so exciting that I just rushed down to the import shop and bought the album on American Import.

Once I got it home that was it – I was completely converted. It was such a breath of fresh air, so exciting. It was like rock taken down to a level it should be at, real street level. Because rock by that time had become terribly overblown, people doing long guitar solos, the gigs were getting bigger. It seemed so distant from the audience, but the Ramones were like saying, 'Enough of that. Let's take rock back.' It was almost like year zero again! Get rid of all that rubbish.

John Lydon

The Ramones to me were more like Status Quo. They were hilarious but you can only go so far with 'duh-dur-dur-duh'. I've heard it. Next. Move on. It was a gimmick for them to fake being mindlessly dumb. That's all very well, but it's a bit like *One Flew Over The*

Cuckoo's Nest, isn't it? You stay at it too long and you become exactly what you think you are imitating.

The New York scene has always been really seedy, tatty, dirty old people. We were 17; they were 25. The New York bands all had wealthy parents who bought them nice shiny guitars and they stuck Rimbaud poetry over everything, and nonsense like that, and wrapped themselves up in it. They pontificated a lot and pretended to be intellectual but they were just damned university students.

Marco Pirroni

I don't think many people knew about the New York scene. No one knew about that stuff till the records came over. Richard Hell probably did invent the punk look, I'm sure he did, you know. Also McLaren did go to New York and see Richard Hell and come back with slashed T-shirts. In New York, the T-shirts looked stressed. Here it was done carefully by Malcolm so your nipples could be seen. It was different. Who knows? They are such nebulous ideas. I remember people wearing safety pins on the soul scene in the Seventies – it was all kind of messed up.

The genius of the Ramones was to take rock'n'roll down to its uber-basics and write so many brilliant songs out of virtually nothing. They remained an unrelenting military rock'n'roll unit till they retired in the mid-Nineties

Rat Scabies

The first thing we heard from New York was the Television single 'Little Johnny Jewel'.[20] I remember listening to it and being blown away. It was everything we had been talking about. They were all really clever musicians with attitude. They turned up, and then Patti Smith, and then the Ramones' first album, which was great, and now everyone wanted to see them. Patti Smith was doing the rounds as well. Our entire knowledge of New York punk had come from *Punk* magazine. No one had seen the Heartbreakers live, but we thought they looked great. We had seen pictures of Television, Richard Hell and Blondie but nobody had heard anything. Because Danny Fields was involved with the MC5 we knew they had to be the right kind of thing.

Keith Levene

The American scene had a big impact at first. I don't know what was happening at Max's Kansas City or CBGBs. I was too young but I knew about it. Before the Clash were being formed and while the Pistols were being formed, you had Patti Smith and that was really fuelling things. You had the Heartbreakers, after the New York Dolls. If anyone should have the finger pointed at them for being junkies, if anyone came and completely brought a plague to London, those fuckers did. Fuck that anyway, because most of them are dead.[21] Strange guys. Thunders had an amazing charisma. Jerry was a great drummer but he was a caricature, like a thing out of Fritz the Cat.

Penny Rimbaud

I caught Patti Smith on some radio show. I thought, *Fucking hell!* I didn't know where it was coming from. I thought it was jazz! My

---

20. Television's hypnotic guitars weaved their way through two great albums of poetic, art-laced, drone rock. The fact that they were embraced by the punk generation showed the open-mindedness of the era that is often overlooked by commentators.

21. At this stage the New York punk scene was a lot more hard drug-driven than the younger, more naive British movement. Heroin had been around in the UK before punk, of course, but when the Heartbreakers came to town for the Anarchy Tour they brought, along with their fantastic rock'n'roll, some heavy duty rock'n'roll lifestyles – lifestyles that would eventually help to kill drummer Jerry Nolan and iconic guitar hero Johnny Thunders.

immediate reaction to it was that it was some sort of new southern black jazz thing – it had a weird feel, like Bessie Smith. Whatever, it really threw me and I was excited.

VILLAGE OF THE DAMNED
Brian James Gets His Band Into Gear

Rat Scabies

Me and Brian had already decided to split off from the London SS and do something. I knew they didn't want me in the band. Brian said to them that if they didn't want to work with me then he was off to do something, and that's what we did.

It was slow finding people. There were not very many people around at the time. Captain came later. He was still doing the Moped thing, wearing velvet jackets and his hair like Marc Bolan. He was very muso in a kind of way. Brian didn't have an immediate thing with him. But the Captain did have a bass guitar and an amp.

Brian James

Rat had a mild flirtation with this thing that Malcolm or Bernie was trying to put together with Chrissie Hynde, called Masters of the Backside, or Mike Hunt's Honourable Discharge – Chrissie liked that joke. We messed about but it wasn't going very far. Just before that we played with Nick Kent in the Subterraneans.

Captain Sensible

We had some fun with Nick Kent. Blimey, he was out there, was Nick. He was really into it. He knew the New York Dolls, the Velvet Underground. He could see there was something happening as well. That would have been really funny if he had cracked it as a punk rocker! Some of them saw it coming and some of them didn't. Bolan saw it, Nick Kent saw it, but Phil Collins and Cliff Richard couldn't, so fuck 'em!

Rat Scabies

Nick Kent had fallen out with Chrissie. They were not going to work together.

Malcolm decided that Chrissie was going to be a boy! Dress her up as a boy – and she would sing and play guitar, even though she had just started playing. We just played covers like the Pistols did. We used to hang out quite a lot with Chrissie Hynde and go shoplifting and that. She did some stuff with Johnny Moped.

Brian James

Then Rat got into this other thing, and that's how he met Dave Vanian, which was cool. They had two singers: a blonde guy called Dave Zero, and Dave Vanian had dark hair – that was the idea. Chrissie just wanted to play guitar. It was a strange thing.

Rat Scabies

I met Dave at this time through Malcolm. Dave had been going to the shop. That band sort of went into the next band, which Dave Vanian was in as well. We also had another bloke who was a singer called Dave White whose stage name was Dave Zero – he was totally the opposite to Vanian. The idea was to have two totally different kinds of singers, one completely macho and dark and the other doing the opposite. Dave Zero was a hairdresser from Bromley, totally effeminate. He was absolutely brilliant, one of the most wonderful witty people I ever met, and I've never seen him since.

We were still looking for singers, and early that April me and Brian were in the Nashville and John Beverley (aka Sid Vicious) walked in with a gold lamé jacket on, looking like the total star. We said, 'He looks good.' Then quarter of an hour later Dave Letts (Vanian) walks in and Brian said, 'There's another one,' and I said I knew him already, so we asked him along for an audition.

We auditioned Dave at the church hall on Lisson Grove, just round the corner from the dole office where everyone seemed to be signing on. I think Sid was meant to come down for an audition as well but never turned up.

We'd had a few rehearsals whilst me and Brian were still looking for singers. Malcolm said, 'We haven't got a bass player.' At the time Jamie Reid was living in Chislehurst, just round corner from Captain. We were on the way to a rehearsal, so we grabbed the Captain. Malcolm's first comment on seeing the Captain was, 'Oh my God, what an unsightly creature!... Never mind, put him in the band.'

Captain Sensible

I didn't know who I was auditioning for because everything was in a flux all the time, and everyone was playing with each other. One minute Tony James was in a band with Brian, then Chrissie Hynde was in a band with me and Rat, and Brian wasn't there. It was really all mixed up. We were just trying each other out, to see who got on with who. It was a very interesting period, all drinking together. It was a funny little community, down the Nashville Rooms, Portobello Road. To be quite honest, music was so bad in the hands of the 20-minute-long drum solo wankers and Whispering Bob Harris types that you thought what you were doing was so exciting – but you never thought it would ever get anywhere. You never thought that the music press would write about you. Record companies would never touch with you with a barge pole. I liked doing it. It was exhilarating and such fun.

I remember particularly playing 'Can't Control Myself', the Troggs song. It was really funny with the two singers – they both stopped singing at the same time. It would have been incredible onstage. Can you imagine! Me, Chrissie and Rat were staring at each other while they were doing it. It was unbelievable, especially when you consider Little Jimmy Osmond and that sort of bollocks was what was going on at the time.

Brian James

Rat lasted one or two rehearsals and he thought, 'Fuck this.' They dallied with it for a week or two, and then me and Rat got onto the serious stuff of recruiting people for the band.

Rat Scabies

I can't remember why it fell to pieces but I had left. It didn't last that long. I had been playing with Brian James, and Chrissie was only just learning how to play guitar so there wasn't very much to play along with. It didn't seem to gel enough.

Captain Sensible

The two-singer line-up lasted two days, I think. Then the Damned started. It was down to Brian. He was looking for his preferred kind of line-up. I think he picked a good one. Mind you, I would say that, wouldn't I? We all added our own thing, not only musically but personality-wise. In terms of everyone being extreme in their own way, in an almost cartoon-character kind of way.

Rat Scabies

There was a feeling that something was going to happen. Brian always said you could see it was coming. I think people wanted bands playing with a bit of energy. You could be very loud and have energy and people would like it – that was what we wanted to do. I always presumed I couldn't have been the only one who wanted this, and when you saw the Pistols and Jonesey there was other people with the same attitude, so you knew you were not the only person who felt like that, who was angry about what was going on, couldn't get a job, didn't have any money.

Brian James

I had the name. I wanted to use it for a long time. It came from a Visconti film called *The Damned*. Dirk Bogarde was in it. I liked it because of the decadent thing, and also there was a couple of British black and white *Village of the Damned* and *Children of the Damned* films about mothers who become pregnant with strange, threatening children – from an old John Wyndham story *The Midwich Cuckoos.*

Some of the songs we were rehearsing go back to Bastard – a riff here and a riff there. 'Fan Club' had a couple of riffs from Bastard. Maybe 'I Fall' as well, I'm not quite sure. But there were plenty of new songs – 'New Rose' and 'Neat Neat Neat'. I was a bit older than the rest of the band and I'd been around a bit. I was writing the songs. I'd been doing it before with Bastard. Rat had been in a punky kind of band called Rot and Captain had been playing in more old-fashioned bands.

Captain Sensible

We rehearsed a set and played our first gig four weeks later, playing with the Sex Pistols at the 100 Club. The set lasted 45 minutes but once we were on stage with the old adrenaline pumping it was about 20/25 minutes! Which was what we wanted. If the promoter booked you for an hour, we'd have to play the set again because it was all so frantic. People never noticed if you played the same songs twice…

Rat Scabies

We'd rehearsed enough. We knew the songs and we were sort of together even if it was a 20-minute set. We got paid £5 and Malcolm demanded £50 for the PA! [laughs] Him and Bernie were talking about movements and blah blah blah, and this was the reality of it! I never gave him the money.

Captain Sensible

Bernie and Malcolm were buddies. Bernie had this thing about needing three bands to start a movement. Bernie was managing Mick, and the third band would have to be the Damned. He said, 'If you guys get it together, then…' I think Bernie might have been into managing us. I think he liked Brian. But we were bit of a loose cannon for them.

Rat Scabies

We played Wycombe Nag's Head in July. Our manager, John Krivine from the Boy shop, wanted to manage us as a rival to Malcolm at Sex and to promote his shop. He wanted us to be part of that war against Malcolm for the trade on the Kings Road. He was terribly mean about it – he didn't give us any of his clothes! [laughs] He would charge us for the clothes. We rehearsed in his warehouse in Bermondsey and he had this guy Andy Czezowski who worked for him. We all liked Andy and when he said, 'John Krivine is no good for you, let me have a go then,' we did!

Andy Czezowski

I bumped into the Damned a couple of times in early summer 1976 when I was helping Acme Attractions move into their new shop in Notting Hill Gate. I think they even did some work for us there for a couple of days. They asked me to be their manager so I said, 'Yes, why not?' and got them some gigs and a rehearsal space at John Krivine's warehouse up in Bermondsey.

Captain Sensible

When we did our first shows, like the one in High Wycombe, we drove most of the audience out. We were left with four people in the audience. It was considered too extreme.

Getting gigs was not that easy. We had to lie a bit. Give you an example: if someone had a reggae night we would say we were a dub reggae band, and we would then play our punk rock set and get the curtains pulled on us. When we played High Wycombe we were taken under the wing of Ron Watts, who ran the 100 Club. He said he could get us plenty of gigs, but it was mainly the 100 Club and the Nag's Head in High Wycombe! [laughs] It was wasn't until we met Jake Riviera that we got more gigs.

Brian James

At first the Captain was pretty quiet but it didn't take him long.

After the first few gigs where he had been quiet, at our third gig at St Albans he poured a pint of beer over himself onstage and started careering all over the place. I'd never seen him do that before! Talk about coming out of your shell! Captain Sensible was hatched during those gigs.

Captain Sensible

Quite often the main band would be so incensed and outraged that they would come on stage as you were playing and try and throw you off! When we played the Nashville Rooms with a band called S.A.L.T., I remember it particularly well – they really did pull the curtain on us. We fucking kept playing! It must have been amusing for the audience: our heads appeared above the curtains, still playing, and Rat threw his drums through the curtain. There's no way we would get booted off stage by a bunch of rancid old blues proggers...

Brian James

There was a place in Maida Vale on Warrington Crescent where Matt from the Boys used to hang out.[22] He was there at the very start of the punk thing. We recorded a demo with the Damned in this small studio up there – we recorded 'See Her Tonight', 'I Fall' and 'Feel The Pain'.

ANOTHER GANG IN TOWN
The Clash

Glen Matlock

At first there wasn't any other bands. And then we heard of a band called the Damned and then the Jam. Before that we had already met people like Mick Jones, but not yet as the Clash.

---

22. Matt Dangerfield was the guitarist and vocalist from the Boys, one of several bands to form out of the ashes of London SS. They also had connections with the Hollywood Brats, care of keyboard player Casino Steel. The Boys were one of the first punk bands to get a record deal, but the late release of their excellent album saw them unfortunately miss the boat.

Marco Pirroni

And then suddenly the Clash appeared. There was all these bands suddenly appearing.

Glen Matlock

Malcolm started looking for a record deal. One of the things I've found out in recent years, that I wasn't aware of at the time, was that one of the reasons that Malcolm and Bernie fell out was that Bernie had been offered this deal by Maurice Oberstein at CBS to set up his own label and a radio station and Malcolm didn't want to know. That's why Bernie went off to form the Clash. He was trying to do the things right that we had done wrong – and they ended up breaking the States and being a huge band.

Keith Levene

Mick knew Bernard Rhodes. Malcolm went away for two weeks and had Bernard look after the Pistols. Bernard had done this thing where he'd spoken to John and questioned his motives and questioned Steve Jones. The band really improved a lot in these two weeks which Malcolm was away. This *really* pissed Malcolm off! They had this real falling out. So Bernard wanted his own band, and he was working with Mick Jones. I was their absolute brightest find since they'd been together. Bernard was saying to me, 'I know you're young and you should be in school but you seem to know about things.' He was just saying, 'You're the one making this work now.' Me and Bernard used to talk all the time, arguing about everything in a positive way to make the band better.

So in early '76 we were getting the Clash together and I was feeling a bit embarrassed about these guys. We had this singer who was this real Mick Jagger imitation and we were trying to get rid of him.

Joe Strummer had so much fucking energy and he was so cool. When he was in the 101ers (which was named after his address), he wore this zoot suit and looked late Fifties. The band would play this acceptable, clangy, Telecaster-type rock, but they'd be quite good. Joe was just fucking mad. He was really, really a great mover! Couldn't sing to save his life, but gave off all this energy and always ended up in a total sweat. He was like *the* turn-on singer. The only other guy was John Lydon but he was in the Pistols.

J. J. Burnel

Joe Strummer was always lovely to me. He did us a few favours actually. He had a residency with the 101ers at the Portobello Road pub, and when they went off on the college circuit he offered it to us. When we played with Patti Smith I remember him crying on our shoulders. He was pissed and said, 'I wish I had a band that was a gang like yours.' He got one in the end and did very well!

Mick Jones

We met Joe Strummer just before he left the 101ers. We had seen him play a few times with them. They were a good band. It certainly took courage for him to leave, but it was the right decision. Sometimes you got to make that leap.

The story about us seeing him down the dole office is true. It was three of us: me, Paul and Vivienne Albertine. I was going out with Viv at the time – it was her squat on Davis Road I was staying at. The art school was just up the road in Shepherds Bush. I was still at my gran's and staying over – I always went back there in the end. We saw Joe at the dole office. We were really in awe of him – we were not looking to do him over. He was over there in the queue, and we were in a queue over here. There was talk of getting him to join the band. We had seen him a few times round about. There wasn't anyone else out there who could do the job. We thought we would ask him. We didn't know what he would say. We just decided to go and ask in the end, take the chance.

Keith Levene

Me and Bernard went off to a 101ers gig one night and talked Joe into coming over to my squat in Shepherd's Bush. I was playing guitar with him and playing some 101ers tunes. He went, 'Hey man, I just love the way you play guitar.' So I said. 'Will you do it?' He said, 'Yeah,' and we got him in the Clash.

Mick Jones

Bernie and Keith went to ask him at the Golden Lion in Fulham where the 101ers were doing a gig. They said, 'Do you want to come and meet these guys?' It's quite an unusual sort of thing to happen. Someone comes to your gig and asks if you want to join another band. Obviously Joe was intuitive enough and already feeling it. He had seen the Pistols and knew something new was happening. He had seen us in the dole office and he had seen us in the street and had seen what we looked like. By that time I didn't have long hair any more. So Bernie gave Joe an ultimatum, 24 hours to make his mind up, but called him after eight hours and Joe said, 'All right, I'm in,' and he come round. We were just waiting there for the call. We knew it was going to work.

We were rehearsing in Davis Street. We had egg boxes all over the room on the walls to keep the sound down! It doubled as Paul's room. It was a little tiny room. Joe comes to the room. It was a really natural thing – straight away we clicked. We started playing one of our tunes and it was just like that. He had little bits to put in. It worked straight away. He's standing here, I'm there, Paul there and Keith there, in a small room and it really worked.

On 4 July the Clash played their debut gig supporting the Sex Pistols at Sheffield's Black Swan pub. The Black Swan was a regular venue on the pub rock circuit (and still is a regular venue – now called the Boardwalk on Snig Hill, Sheffield) with the likes of Brinsley Schwarz, Ducks Deluxe and the ubiquitous Dr Feelgood playing there. There was probably only a handful of people present, although some eyewitnesses reported a sizeable crowd in the sweltering venue in the middle of the 1976 summer heatwave.

The Roxy in Covent Garden, punk's first club

Mick Jones

It was the back room of a pub. There were fifty people there, a couple of punks – it was interesting, wherever you went you would see a couple of them in the early times. Then you would see more all the time – they would tell their friends. It was a big thing.

Very often people got it completely wrong. But in a way you *couldn't* get it wrong; it wasn't formed. We were just starting to find out what it could be. When you are young you think about it after, in the post-match analysis! By the time everyone had sussed it, it was already over.

We were dressed in black and white. A couple of us had ties on, black and white shirts with suity bits. It was punky style – not good suits, a bit ripped, tight, slightly different. We were dressed fairly straight and well-behaved in a way – maybe a rip here and a little splash of colour there. A couple of pin-type things, not safety pins. The look was still formulating.

There was a bit of paint dribbled here and there. It had come off when we had to paint the rehearsal room. We got the paint from the car spray place down the road. Bernie was involved in garages and he used to go down there and get spray. We started painting all the amps pink, and as we were painting everything we were getting covered in paint. I guess that was our first look. Also Glen has a claim to this as well, because he had a pair of trousers that were paint-splattered à la Pollock, so he should take a bit of credit for it. The style thing came naturally through Paul. We were all into the style, especially Paul and I. Joe not so much, but we would always encourage each other.

Keith Levene

At the Black Swan I remember John sitting miles away from the rest of the band members, looking miserable, and there's me sitting in another corner away from all *my* band members, looking miserable. So I walk over to Lydon and talk to him. We know each other, but we don't *know* each other, because we're the rival bands. We were both in the same scene but we knew we were the best bands on the scene at the time. I said, 'I'm out of here after this gig.' (It turned out I was out a few gigs later, after the Roundhouse show.) 'Do you want to get a band together if the Pistols ever end? Though it doesn't look like it at the moment – looks like you could be the next Beatles. But if it ever changes... And there's no way I'm going to be in a band with Steve Jones.'

On 13 August, the Clash played their second gig at their Rehearsal Rehearsals space in Camden Town, a showcase for journalists.

Ari Up (The Slits: vocals)

I saw the Clash first at Rehearsal Rehearsals in Camden. After that, I was never the same. I realised how important it was for them to spray their clothes. I came back and cut up all my clothes and sprayed all my clothes. I had all these hippie schoolgirl clothes. I looked like a tidied-up hippie with long hair and I thought, *Fuck!* I looked really corny, putting on my first set of punk clothes. I made them myself. I didn't do it very sophisticated.

Vic Godard

The Clash looked really good. The first time we saw the Clash was not at a gig but watching the Sex Pistols, and they walked in and looked really good. The only one we knew was Joe, and we knew this was Joe's new band. Paul Simonon didn't have all the painted gear then; he just looked like a really good version of us, the same sort of clothes that we wore. You could tell they were a band from the way they looked. Same with the Pistols – they looked like a band.

Mick Jones

There was never a planned look. It was much more of a natural thing. Bernie gave us the right outlook – that's the best way to describe it. Bernie had a hand in everything. Not the lyrics – he didn't help with the lyrics. He didn't tell us not to write love songs, as the myth goes – that's kind of a simplified version of it. He told us to write about what we knew about. Joe came from a squat background. He was always questioning things anyway. But Bernie helped us put it in the right context. Bernie helped us formulate ourselves.

Don Letts

Bernie is a trip, but hey, you can't take it away from these people, Bernie or Malcolm. Whatever people say about Malcolm, I love the geezer. He's entertaining with all the kind of ups and downs. I take the good and bad and there was plenty of it! It was in that English colonial way of reinterpreting ideas. It's an age-old thing: you guys are good at it. Malcolm could see it coming a mile off. Good guys don't come up with good ideas anyway.

Malcolm and Bernie were both of the same ilk. They had a knowledge of the counterculture – that's why these people are important. They could see the idea manifest itself before its musical expression. That's why you got all this thing with Malcolm and the Situationists – that's where he got a lot of his ideas and sloganeering. You can't just write those people off. They gave punk depth, a bit of bollocks. It wasn't just the rantings and ravings of angry youth. There was a method behind it and it manifested itself in different ways. Whoever said that thing, about the Pistols made you want to smash your head against the wall and the Clash gave you a reason for doing it, was so right.

AFTER THIS EVERYONE SPEEDED UP
The Ramones' UK Live Debut

4 July: The same night as the Clash's debut up in Sheffield, the Ramones played the Roundhouse in Camden, and nearby Dingwall's the following night. Playing to 2,000 people at the Roundhouse was their biggest gig yet, the first time they had played outside small clubs. These were also their first shows in the UK, and proved to be pivotal moments in the early punk scene. Instantly nearly every band speeded up. All the faces from the nascent punk scene were there and it ended up in a brawl outside Dingwall's.

Marco Pirroni

I went to see the Ramones at Dingwall's. I thought they were great. After that, everybody speeded up. Suddenly its '1, 2, 3, 4, duh-duh-duh-duh-duh...' Before that, everyone was quite different.

Rob Lloyd

Before seeing the Pistols I had seen the Ramones play. They came over and played at the Roundhouse supporting the Flamin' Groovies, with the Stranglers third on the bill. Me and Dave Schofield and Graham Blunt, the bass player in the Prefects, hitched down to London to that gig specifically to see the Ramones. When they had finished, the Flamin' Groovies came on – they were OK but this was the time when they were all wearing Beatles suits and sounding bit ropey. We thought they looked shit and went into the bar area, which was empty because, believe it or not, easily the majority of the crowd had gone to see the Flamin' Groovies.

The Ramones and a few hangers-on were in the bar with Danny Fields, who was their legendary manager. He came up to us and started talking, and they couldn't understand that we had actually travelled to see them. They thought that they meant nothing to nobody in the UK, and when we said that we had hitched a few hundred miles to see them they were made up. They said, 'Do you know we are playing Dingwall's tomorrow night?' which was Sunday night. Danny Fields said, 'Are you coming?' We said, 'We got nowhere to stay, we've got to go back to school in Cannock on Monday.' Danny Fields said, 'Do you want to stay at our hotel?' We said, 'Yeah!' and he booked a room in the same hotel as the Ramones.

The next day we went to dinner with the Ramones and their record company in the UK, and we went to the soundcheck at Dingwall's. Outside Dingwall's was the Pistols and the Clash waiting to meet the Ramones. I remember the Clash had the 101ers' 'Keys To Your Heart' to give to the Ramones — they had nothing else to give them.

There was an air of tension at the gig in general. I don't know what the Ramones thought of the Pistols and the Clash but both bands had turned up to pay homage to them. I think the Ramones were a bit frightened of them. The British bands were sitting on the bonnets of cars that were parked outside. They looked liked they were looking for trouble – when you look back on it that was a big pose. Apart from one person who *was* looking for trouble – J. J. Burnel. I think there might have been a bit of bother between the Stranglers and the Clash.

J. J. Burnel

There was that incident with Paul Simonon at Dingwall's, which didn't help with us and the punk elite. The other bands were a bit pissed off that we had been chosen to represent London at the 4 July bicentennial gig.[23] We were the first to play with the Ramones and

---

23. The Dingwall's gig took place on the 200th anniversary of America's Declaration of Independence.

Patti Smith, and that pissed a few people off. We were out of the inner circle after that. That did us immense favours in the long term. We evolved on our own, as if we had been in Australia for millions of years, like weird animals.

Rat Scabies

You *had* to go and see the Ramones. There was no choice. We went to see them at Dingwall's the following night and everyone was there. I remember Paul Simonon fighting with J. J. Burnel. I remember a photograph somewhere of all the bands standing outside with Danny Fields. Chrissie Hynde was there as well. We were all given miniature baseball bats. Mine was a black one with 'The Ramones' on the side of it. I lost it years ago.

Gaye Advert

I saw the Ramones at the Roundhouse. I've still got my toy baseball bat. Joey came down the side at the end and of the gig and was handing them out. I'd never heard of the Flamin' Groovies before. It seemed strange that the Ramones were supporting them. The Ramones were amazing. You wouldn't have known the lyrics from the gigs! Thirty seconds into the track and you would realise which song it was, and then the song was over.

Marco Pirroni

The Ramones were the biggest influence. Suddenly everything became like the Ramones. That became the standard style, but no one did it as well as the Ramones. They also had that pop sensibility as well. They wrote great tunes. They always looked the same. Their clothes were like a Hanna Barbera cartoon – they always wear the same clothes, they never change, and neither did the Ramones. Initially I hated their long hair but I forgave them because they were so good!

Captain Sensible

When the Ramones came over – that was a bit of revelation.

Everyone sped up after that Dingwall's gig. Everyone in the audience – you knew most of them. The funny thing was when you did your first gig in those days, like that Ramones gig at Dingwall's, if there was anyone who walked in there who didn't know what it was, they would walk out again.

Rob Lloyd

All kinds of things happened. Danny Fields wanted me to start up a Ramones UK fan club. Legs McNeil's *Punk* magazine had a photo story of the Ramones' first trip to the UK. There was a couple of photos of me with the Ramones – the caption underneath said, 'Here are the Ramones with Robert Lloyd, Europe's Number One Ramones fan.' Danny was in touch with me for some time trying to get me to start a Ramones fan club. Apart from managing the Doors, the Stooges and Nice, Danny also had a hand in the American magazine *Sixteen*. Danny was an old gay geezer and this *Sixteen* magazine had pictures of Bay City Rollers and David Cassidy – he loved that kind of pop. He wanted the Ramones to be a cartoon pop band rather than an alternative punk group. He was really keen on the idea of having a fan club because he was into pop bands. By that stage I said, 'I love the Ramones, Danny, but the main thing is I want to start my own group now.'

Vic Godard

That was an important gig. I remember Joe Strummer being right down the front. Everyone was there. Talking Heads were the support band and we were there to see them mainly. McLaren came up and said, 'You look like you are in a band.' We were wearing Oxfam clothes dyed all dark grey to make them all look really drab – it was our look. We were into films. The big film influence were these Polish films that had post-war grimy look about them. We were into the East European look. McLaren told us to form a group at that Ramones Roundhouse gig. We were like a group of people who hung about at college. It was this group that ended up in the band. It was similar to people who went to the Pistols. At first when we got the band togther it was like a piss-take. It was like we were doing comedy! The drummer was singing, doing impersonations of Johnny Cash, Elvis and Danny La Rue. He was a real extrovert, and it was unfortunate that he was the only one who could play drums so I ended up being the singer. All I could do was play harmonica, so that was all that I did, and a lot of the songs didn't have harmonica on them at all. I just wanted to be part of it, but not the singer.

CHAPTER 5
1976 PART II: YEAR XEROX

XEROX MACHINE
Sniffin' Glue

13 July: Mark Perry launched Sniffin' Glue, *the seminal punk fanzine. Inspired by the Ramones' debut, Perry had to get involved and printed up his own magazine – a typewritten affair with his own homemade artwork. It's a genius piece of DIY and one of the ultimate punk statements. Within months there were many copycat versions. In its short one-year run,* Sniffin' Glue *became the very soul of the punk rock consciousness, documenting many of the upcoming bands first and generating several heated debates within the scene.*

Mark Perry

I was the only bloke in Deptford that listened to the Ramones album. But when they came over to play some gigs at the end of July, I went there, and you suddenly met all these other people who were into the Ramones. The Pistols were there, the Clash were there – all the people that were in the UK punk bands were at this gig. It was the first time I had ever met Shane MacGowan.[1] Going to that gig and talking to people, you got that feeling that something was going on. It wasn't just that one-off album. Hold on a minute, something is actually happening here...

I was also into other bands like the Flamin' Groovies, other bands that were considered punky, or new wavey, although that wasn't a term then. Rough and ready r'n'b sort of stuff. I used to go to Rock On record shop.[2] I was always asking if they'd got any magazines about punk and the Ramones. They would say, 'No, we haven't,' and as a joke the guy from there said, 'Why don't you just go and start your own one?' So I said, 'Yeah, I will.' So I went home that night and tapped it out. I had this old kid's typewriter that my mother bought me one Christmas and a felt-tip pen and I knocked out the first issue of *Sniffin' Glue*. Basically it was just a bit about the Ramones and the Blue Oyster Cult, another band I considered to be really exciting, a punky type – maybe a metal band. That is what inspired me, just because there was nothing else about punk at the time. It wasn't a scene really, I just felt you've got to get involved somehow, and that was my way of getting involved, because I wasn't a musician at the time.

At first I printed about 50. It was a joke really! I didn't go to a printer's. I just printed it out on a typewriter, and I did the felt-tipped headings'n'that. And my girlfriend took it to work and got it photocopied on a really old photocopier. In those days photocopying was really primitive, on shiny paper. But I took these 50 copies to Rock On and to my surprise they said, 'This is fantastic. We're going to sell these,' and they took every copy. So I went back a week later to check it out, and they had sold them all. So they said, 'Look, we want 200 more. Here's the money.' From just being a fan, after two or three weeks I was a fanzine writer, sold about 300 copies of the first issue, and was writing the second issue!

1. MacGowan first came to attention on the London punk scene before fronting first the Nipple Erectors, and then, with enormous success, the Pogues.
2. In London's Soho district.

SNIFFIN' GLUE...

30p

AND OTHER ROCK 'N' ROLL HABITS
FOR PINHEADS AND SURFERS! ⑦ FEB '77

...Black...White...Black...White...Bl... ...White...Black...White...Black...

Revolutionising print: Sniffin' Glue invented the notion of the fans answering back – no longer passive consumers, everyone could take part in the xerox revolution...

ADVERTS – DON LETTS – GORILLAS

It started selling progressively well, and at its peak for the last issue we sold about 20,000. It went all over the world. That was a year later. Wherever punk records were sold they would sell *Sniffin' Glue* fanzine. I was lucky to be in at the start. It was about 50 per cent luck and probably about 50 per cent inspiration on my part. Some people in retrospect said I decided to start the fanzine movement. Well, I didn't. I just did it 'cause I wanted to get involved myself. I printed up 50 copies and I honestly thought that was it, end of story, just for a laugh. More people got interested in it. Not just people buying it but also the media – within a month anyone who wanted to know about punk, they were ringing me up like a punk spokesman! In one way it was frightening, and in another way it was really exciting. It was very much a time when if you didn't know you were found out very quickly. You just made things up!

To do a fanzine, you didn't even need a typewriter. Shane MacGowan did a fanzine inspired by *Sniffin' Glue*. He called it *Bondage* and he used to have a go at us 'cause we used a typewriter! He just scrawled it in a pen. That was more punk than us. To form a band, you just needed a couple of cheap guitars that you bought out of Woolworths and a couple of chords and you were away. That was very much the feeling of the time.

I think *Punk* magazine came out almost a year before *Sniffin' Glue*. I don't think it was as regular as *Sniffin' Glue* – I think it was about three-monthly. But I thought *Punk* magazine was really funny. If you look at the early issues, they did a lot of interviews in cartoon. It was fun, but it was a typical American sort of thing. It lacked the edge that *Sniffin' Glue* had. I don't know if it influenced *Sniffin' Glue* – it probably did actually. I did read *Punk* magazine before I started writing.

I did *Sniffin' Glue* on my own for a couple of issues, but as it was getting bigger I got other people to help me, a couple of old school mates of mine. One of them was Steve Nick. Then after six or seven issues Danny Baker got on board. Danny told me that his girlfriend was kind of jealous of what was going on and said, 'Why don't you get involved?' So he jumped on board. Danny Baker was never a punk but he had 200 per cent attitude. That's what made it so great for Danny to be involved in it, a great spokesman. By that time, after about six months, every *Sniffin' Glue* meeting was just like a great piss-up and a great laugh. The most exciting part was that if we said anything in *Sniffin' Glue* it would be taken as a punk fact. We were at the heart of something.

I never wanted it to be just a press release for bands. *Sniffin' Glue* was really there just to have a bit of a laugh, to send people up. But then, when needed, to really get behind punk. So I think in the third or fourth issue we had an interview with Johnny Rotten and we accused him of writing 'Anarchy In The UK' just to sell Malcolm McLaren's T-shirts as a promotion. We used to take the piss out of people. When everyone looks back now, they think the Sex Pistols were a great rock'n'roll band. But their audience was so naff in those days, just a bunch of fashion victims standing round like the Bromley Contingent. They were all sort of Bowie fans. They all had dyed hair, all sorts of pretentious nonsense. We just had a laugh. We were working-class kids from Deptford. We weren't middle-class ponces from Bromley or Chelsea. So in a way we knew what was going on in the terraces, on the streets, more than anyone else.

Nils Stevenson

The punk aesthetic was simple. Me and Helen Wellington-Lloyd were doing the handouts for the Pistols, and we ran out of Letraset so we cut up a newspaper and pasted it. If we hadn't run out of the Letraset there wouldn't have been the blackmail lettering. We made things from what was available.

The point about punk rock is you couldn't buy the things you wanted; they weren't available. It was not the commodified culture we live in now. If you wanted a decent look, there were no style magazines. You took inspiration from all sorts of places, like the Bromley Contingent did with *Night Porter*, *Snow White*. Siouxsie's whole look was based on the queen in *Snow White*. Malcolm and Vivienne did the shop where a lot of the clothes were one-offs. There was a sense of individuality, expressing yourself. You didn't think – it was instinctive.

Ari Up

I first saw the Pistols at that time. Automatically I grew up with the punk revolution, because my stepfather for a while was Chris Spedding. Chris Spedding was the first one to discover the Pistols and really give them a chance. He did a demo with them. I lived with him in London at the time he did that. Nora got into the Pistols.[3] She'd started seeing the Pistols gigs in 1975 – I had no clue of course. I eventually went with her.

So I went to a Pistols gig, and there were all these hippies there. The thing that impressed me was that the band was completely different from the audience. So when I saw Steve Jones with the cowboy T-shirt on, I thought that was great. I was fourteen and that was more impressive to me than John wailing around and going crazy. That T-shirt blew my mind. It was so brilliant. It said it all. It stated everything that society was about and what I was against. It was such a sarcastic T-shirt, I can't even describe it. It means a million things in one picture. There was no stopping me then. When I came back home my mum knew that was it.

Tony James

I answered an ad in the *Melody Maker* – 'Wanted: guitarist into Small Faces, early Who, Rolling Stones, Velvet Underground...' It just caught my eye – you never saw ads like this. And so I drove over to Bromley to this house, and this guy with long hair was sitting with this girl, who was Siouxsie Sioux, and Steve Severin. The guy with long hair was Billy Idol to be. He was looking for a guitarist and I was looking for a singer and here was one. I said, 'I'm not really a

---

3. Nora is Ari Up's mother. She later married John Lydon.

guitarist but I really like the ad. I'm actually a bass player.' He said, 'I haven't got a bass player either.'

We were looking for like-minded people. It was like looking for a needle in the haystack – in London you had to go miles to find one person. We jammed a bit, we played records, like you do, and mooched about, looked at the floor... Billy and I kind of hit it off that day.

FRENCH REVOLUTION, LONDON REVELATION
First Punk Festivals

21 August: The Damned's sixth ever show was a bizarre jaunt over to the first punk rock festival, held in a bullring at Mont de Marsan in the South of France. The Sex Pistols had been turned down because of their violent reputation and the Clash withdrew in support. The Damned were the token punk rock band on what was actually a bill of pub rockers including Roogalator, Eddie and the Hot Rods, Nick Lowe, the Count Bishops, the Tyla Gang and the Pink Fairies. Ray Burns earned his 'Captain Sensible' nickname, and the band scored press coverage with their wild behaviour, pretty well setting in stone the creed of the Damned.

Rat Scabies

Mont de Marsan festival came about through a record shop in Paddington which was central to punk. Everyone lived in Notting Hill Gate and signed on at Lisson Grove just round the corner from where we rehearsed. There was a record shop round the corner called Bizarre, run by two French blokes called Marc Zermati and Larry de Bay who ran Skydog records. Marc organised the Mont de Marsan festival. He was a big Stooges fan.

There was not that many people at the gig. It was a bullring. It was a very bizarre place. We didn't have any money and we drank as much as we could. The bill was all pub rock bands. Roogalator, bands like that. The Pistols weren't that popular yet and were not asked to play. There were no punk bands on there. There were some French bands like Little Bob Story. Some of the groups didn't seem like the real thing; they had some kind of leather jacket attitude and that was it.

I remember Roger Armstrong and Ted Carroll from Chiswick Records being around. They took the Hammersmith Gorillas along – they were a great band.[4] Jesse, their frontman, was classic, a case. He gave it up because it was too easy. They were kind of a cool spectacle. They were playing as well.

Andy Czezowski

I got the Damned on at the Mont de Marsan festival in France. The whole thing was a complete disaster. We went on a coach with all these all pub rock bands. I had a bust-up with the Damned. There was too much alcohol and speed. That's when I stopped managing them.

Brian James

Jake Riviera saw us at the festival. He'd sort of taken over running it as it got a bit too much for the organisers. Jake said he'd like to manage us and he'd got a record company. He said, 'The best song you got is "New Rose" and I could have you in the studio next week,' and I said, 'Yeah! That's the sort of person we would like to work with!'

Rat Scabies

The Pistols were waiting to see what happened with record deals. We liked Jake and the whole Stiff Records thing made a lot of sense, so we signed. We had heard about Jake before the Mont de Marsan festival, about this bloke who was really on the case. When we talked

---

4. The Hammersmith Gorillas were the missing link between Dr Feelgood and punk. If history had been kinder, their high energy rock'n'roll would have been embraced by the punk generation.

to him about Wayne Kramer, he knew who we were talking about.[5] He was hip to what was going on – even with his cowboy boots!

Captain Sensible

That's where I got my name. It was either Larry Wallis who gave it to me or that cunt Sean Tyla! [laughs] I was dangerously out of control at the time! I think Sean wanted to get his own back for pub rockers worldwide. Anyway Sean didn't like our bad behaviour, ripping shirts off people's backs and all this kind of thing. I had loads of eggs in my hair as well. I don't know how they got there. I think Rat must have put them in there! After about two or three days they were kind of whiffy. I think Sean expected we would get collared by customs on the way back because of my hair, so he wanted to stick my head down the toilet and wash my hair and he shouted, 'Oi, Captain Sensible! Get that egg out of your hair before customs or I'll stick yer head down the bog and wash it for you.' And I think that's where the name Captain Sensible came from. So it was Sean Tyla, not Larry Wallis who gave me my name. I like Larry – he was one of the good guys.[6] Sean was a bearded plonker. He was pissed off because pub rock was going down the tubes!

Rat Scabies

I was sitting on this bus that we all had to travel on from London Victoria to the south of France thinking, 'What a boring bunch of cunts.' The Pink Fairies were smoking a load of dope. I was thinking, 'Where's the revolution?' Nick Lowe was talking to Caroline Coon.[7] He was saying he was into rock'n'roll, a phrase I've always hated unless it was about Eddie Cochrane – that's the proper use of the word, and he had an Eddie Cochrane T-shirt on. I thought,

---

5. Kramer was the guitarist in the MC5.

6. Larry Wallis was in the Pink Fairies, who were playing the festival. He was also in the original line-up of Motörhead before making a great solo single on Stiff Records called 'Police Car'.

7. Caroline Coon was one of the front-running music journalists of the time, and an early punk supporter.

'Here's the bloke in Brinsley Schwarz thinking he's rock'n'roll and rebellion, and he shouldn't be wearing that T-shirt.' So I took it off him. It was all good-humoured, there wasn't a punch thrown or anything nasty. I'd tried to make that statement at his expense by ripping the shirt off his back.

Hot on the heels of Mont de Marsan came a British punk rock mini-festival, when the Sex Pistols headlined at the Screen on the Green, Islington on 29 August. As a dry run for next month's 100 Club festival, the all-nighter was perfect. Malcolm McLaren organised the gig along with Nils Stevenson. The event was also the Buzzcocks' London debut and the Clash's first public gig in the capital; in addition the Kenneth Anger films Kustom Kar Kommandos *and* Scorpio Rising *were shown. With this neat juxtaposition of bands, cool films and unlikely venue, it was more than a gig, it was an event – and the Sex Pistols showed that they were more than just another band on the pub circuit. The support bill was evidence that Bernie Rhodes' vision of three bands making a movement was coming true, and the gig was a clarion call for the nationwide disparate freaks who were already coalescing as the punk movement.*

Nils Stevenson

Up until then the Pistols were out on our own, on a limb. We became aware of the Clash, Subway Sect, Buzzcocks. We were aware of these people with a similar attitude and then we put on the show at Screen on the Green with the Buzzcocks and the Clash. Malcolm was aware of creating scenes. Very conscious and contrived.

Marco Pirroni

Roger Austin was a friend of Malcolm McLaren who booked the films at the Screen on the Green, and that's why The Pistols played there.

Steve Diggle

We did Screen on the Green. That was the first time where punk crystallised into this kind of movement. The Pistols, Clash and the

Buzzcocks all played there. Siouxsie was in the audience, all dressed in a punk way. It suddenly all started to make sense. It started to take off. You could tell. At Manchester at the time, if you had straight legs on that was enough. When you got to London and saw all the people with coloured hair and the cinema full of these people you knew it was really happening.

Howard Devoto

There was three bands playing so it was not quite a festival! Before we played, we did a warm-up show at the Commercial Hotel in Stalybridge. There seemed to be about eight people in there. We had to play every single number we knew to do the two sets – all numbers that only ever got played publicly once got played at that gig.

I'm not sure if the Screen on the Green gig was much bigger than the Free Trade Hall. Malcolm was very encouraging. He said, 'Your songs have real content, don't they?' The sound was pretty rough. *Sounds* reviewed the gig and said that we sounded 'rougher than a bear's arse'. We played 'Peking Hooligan' that night, which we never recorded. I can't remember what that song was about – there had been reports of hooligans in Peking. [laughs]

When we covered Captain Beefheart's 'I Love You Big Dummy', Pete reduced it to two chords, which suited our style. It was partly the title I liked as well – it just seemed to be something one could bend around a bit punk-wise. One could have done it with a Zappa track as well.

At the beginning of punk rock there was no set lyrical style. There was not that much of a vernacular. I can't think of anybody else who was part of the idiom on the lyrical side that I was particularly drawn to at that time. The Ramones were kind of funny and all that, I'd hardly heard anything by the Clash, and I didn't know much about the Pistols stuff. When we saw the Sex Pistols in February we had secretly taped them so we could kind of study them and suss them out. Within the general subject area there was a certain confined space to work in. The words were going to be tough. If you were going to say anything, you had to say it in an angry, thrusting way. The tone of how you say things is tremendously important to the understood message.

Linder Sterling

At art school there was a tremendous importance placed upon drawing, and by the summer of 1976 I felt that I had temporarily explored that mode of expression. I took photographs at the Screen on the Green concert in London (Sex Pistols, Buzzcocks, the Clash) and made a series of collages and sewn pieces. I then moved into the almost surgical world of photomontage quite naturally; just a scalpel, some glue and found images. It was a beautifully simple, impersonal method of making art. Very democratic. My work showed quite intimate, claustrophobic, domestic worlds, at odds with Jamie Reid's use of monarchical iconography, but still dovetailing neatly with punk's rhetoric of shock and disruption.

Gaye Advert

The Screen on the Green gig was great. Tim was away and I went on my own. Paul Cook was going, 'Are you going to be all right on your own? I'll get my friend to look after you.' The Buzzcocks and the Clash played – what a line-up! It was funny: it was in a cinema, and the best gig I'd been to at the time. I couldn't believe how good it was. It was the first time I'd seen the Buzzcocks.

Marco Pirroni

I thought the Clash were great. Completely different from the Pistols. The Pistols were slower. The '1, 2, 3, 4, ra, ra, ra!' thing hadn't happened yet. They were menacing whilst the Clash were manic. The Pistols were more of a sneer. I think I preferred the sneer really, although I liked both sides – the sneer and the boredom. At that time boredom was the big pose, not being angry. 'Everything is boring, everything is boring!'

Don Letts

I didn't know what the fuck they were saying – the PAs were really bad – but it was this fucking energy. It was a revelation. Hearing the Clash's 'Janie Jones' and all this stuff, I was transfixed. It was looking into the Ark of the Covenant! All these guys I'd seen sloping around in my shop, facing me off, were up there doing it and it don't seem that big a leap.

Vic Godard

Lots of bands worked to a blueprint. I used to like the Clash when they played the same speed as bands on *Nuggets*. When they heard the Ramones their songs speeded up overnight. I got a brilliant tape of them at Screen on the Green with the Pistols on the other side. Both bands sound a lot better. All the Clash songs are so much slower than on the album, and there are some good tunes that never made it onto their album.. Keith Levene in that era was great. When they got rid of him they changed dramatically. I liked that Sixties garage sound they had. They were more like the Seeds and the Shadows of the Night. They got into a heavier sound after that; same with the Pistols, they were much better before they bought their first proper amps – they always had crappy equipment when we used to go and see them.

Keith Levene

It's always said, 'Keith got thrown out of the Clash because of drugs!' That's bollocks! The reason I left the Clash was because I too depressed being in the band. They were just too lame for me. I'd start turning up at rehearsals and I was really being a miserable git. I wasn't saying anything, just playing the numbers fine. When Mick wasn't there, we'd work out something of mine. Then the next rehearsal we'd get there and it would be a completely different version. That different version could have been another song – we could have kept the idea I worked on, kept what they worked on and called it something else. There seemed to be a my way/your way of doing things.

At the same time, they suddenly came up with this idea for 'White Riot'. I said, 'I'm not fucking singing "White Riot". You're joking!' That line, 'No Elvis, Beatles or the Rolling Stones in 1977' was bad enough for me. We were just about to make the first record. There was a rehearsal where they're in one room and I'm sitting on my own in another room. I wasn't on any drugs or anything, I was being real miserable, giving off a bad vibe. They'd say, 'What the fuck is up with you?' I said, 'If you really want to know, it's as simple as this: this band is either Mick's band or my band. You either do it my way or Mick's way. I think I've got to leave this band 'cause you're already doing it Mick's way and that's fine. The band's really getting me down.'

When it came to drugs, yeah, we were doing a bit of speed. I could handle my come-downs. Joe used to have terrible come-downs. But it wasn't about drugs. They weren't the band I wanted them to be. I didn't like the clothes they wore! I liked Bernard. I didn't like any of the tunes on the first album, even the one I wrote, 'What's My Name'. It wasn't hard enough.

So we had this little vote very quickly. Mick said, 'I want him out.' Joe said, 'I want him in.' Paul just went with the flow of the band. So I was out. Terry Chimes, for some reason, didn't get a vote!

On 4 September, the Sex Pistols made their first TV appearance, on Tony Wilson's So It Goes. *The band flew to Paris on the same day for the opening night of a disco called the Chalet du Lac. On the flight over, Lydon wore a bondage suit for the first time. The Bromley Contingent also made the journey and Siouxsie Sioux offended the locals by wearing swastikas, suspenders and a see-through bra.*

The 100 Club festival, the event when punk went overground, took place on 20 and 21 September. With just about enough bands to make a movement now, the festival saw the debut of Siouxsie and the Banshees with an ad hoc line-up, and the Clash's first gig without Keith Levene, as well as the first proper gig by the Subway Sect. The Damned headlined over the Vibrators and the Buzzcocks on the second night. The growing force of punk rock was becoming apparent, but so too was the already fractured nature of the movement, with underlying rivalries exposed by an incident when Sid Vicious threw a glass at the stage, leaving a sordid aftertaste to the whole event. The glass hit a beam and shattered over several people and a girl was hit in the eye by a glass splinter. Sid was arrested, beaten up, and ended up doing time in the Ashford Remand Centre. The Pistols, who were not even playing at the time, got banned from the 100 Club. Another one to add to the list.

Marco Pirroni

I was only going to see the Pistols. None of these other bands that played could pull a crowd on their own. It was Malcolm's idea to get a scene going. He said to everyone, 'Get a band going.' He said it to me. By the time the Sex Pistols were playing the 100 Club, the gigs they played were never packed. It was always the same people every time: fifteen people from around the shop and the rest I don't know. They were just coming to gawp, and there was Lydon's mates and London gig-goers at the time. I'd never been to a little gig before, only to Hammersmith Odeon and Wembley Arena. I didn't know that level existed. It wasn't my dream to play the 100 Club type of gig; it was my dream to play Wembley Arena. I didn't know you had to do the little gigs first.

T. V. Smith

I saw the Pistols for the first time at the 100 Club festival. It was nice to see this band that we had read about and they didn't let me down one bit: a snotty bunch of kids up on stage, giving it some really interesting tunes and lyrics, and 100 per cent energy. This is what I want! *And I could be in that band!* There was no gulf between me and the person up there on the stage. Other bands thought they were special and you could never achieve that, and the thing about punk was that you *could* achieve it. You didn't have to go to music school and play guitar for ten years to get on stage. It was groundbreaking. Better than that, they were really good. The fact they were just like me was a bonus.

John Bentham (Film-maker, manager of Outl4w)

I first saw the *Melody Maker* article in summer 1976 about the Sex Pistols, and was fascinated that a band could call themselves the Sex Pistols. It almost didn't matter if they were any good, it just sounded exciting. I was in a covers band. The pub rock scene had struck, Stiff Records had recently launched with a Nick Lowe seven-inch, selling out of the back of a car.

A friend and I first travelled somewhere inland in the UK to see the Pistols. We eventually got to a dark, desolate site, and found a note on the door saying there was no gig tonight. I later heard they had played the Screen on the Green in London that night.

Keeping an eye on the music press, the 100 Club festival came up, and risking the sack from our family building business I set off to London for Blackpool for a few days on my aunt's couch. I managed to take in a trip to Stiff Records, based in an old shop, where a couple of members of the Damned were hanging out. I bought a couple of copies of 'So It Goes' by Nick Lowe off a guy called Jake, later to be known as Riviera, and also saw Graham Parker and the Rumour at the Roundhouse.

Michelle Brigandage (Brigandage: vocals)

All I can say about seeing the Pistols was that the first time Johnny stepped on stage I practically fell to my knees – it was like a religious experience. Here was someone who understood what I was feeling inside. We no longer felt alone. We were individuals but with others – not some mindless gang, but a group of people who had finally found their way to a home.

I was really interested in the whole punk thing from the Situationism onwards. Guy Debord's theory of the Spectacle is the resonant one. Simply put, the world that we see is not the real world but the world we are conditioned to see, and the Situationist agenda was to explain how the nightmare works so that everyone can wake up. In some ways *The Matrix* uses this premise. We are all trapped by a commodity culture of owning, not being. If you think of Thatcher, she didn't want workers to own property from the goodness of her heart. Anyone tied up in a mortgage has no recourse but to work, whatever the outrageous demands of employers, because there's no choice. Don't work and you lose everything.

Marco Pirroni

I had already started hearing things about the Subway Sect. Malcolm was half-involved, and then he gave them to Bernie. He didn't have the time. I actually think Subway Sect are the ultimate punk rock band. I've never met Vic Godard. I loved their look – grey jumpers with necks cut out, keys on a bit of string round the neck. There was something about them that worked fantastically, the way they were pretty shambolic and didn't care. I thought they were very cool. They had that bored cool thing.

Vic Godard in typical anti-rock pose as the Subway Sect reinvent art rock into the indie template

Vic Godard

The 100 Club was not the first gig we played. We had already played a party with this bloke I worked with at Burton's. We did some songs at some bloke's house in Ealing – we had to get there by bus with our drum kit. A number 9 bus from Mortlake Garage, and then the Underground to Ealing – that was pretty funny carrying all the stuff. We had three songs we had written and some covers: a Ramones number, a New York Dolls number. The songs had hardly any chords! 'Trash' by the Dolls, because it was easy to play. Just after that we played the 100 Club and did all our own songs. We didn't have long to write our set, about a month.

We played on the first night at the 100 Club. We didn't sound-check. It was Siouxsie, then us, then the Clash and the Sex Pistols. The poor old Buzzcocks – we really liked them, but they got stuck on the other night with the Damned, the Vibrators and the Stinky Toys and all them lot.[8] The Stinky Toys wanted to play on our night. She was really in bad mood at that gig – I remember her storming out! I don't know what happened – maybe they told her she wasn't getting paid. Punk was quite big in Paris before London. They had a punk magazine called *Punk*, not the New York one. I only ever saw one issue with Rotten on the front. It was out incredibly early.

Our false names were made up on the spur of the moment. Someone came round asking all our names. We were all on the dole and we thought we had better not say them in case we make money out of this. Make sure the dole doesn't know. So we had to make up false names. Mine was Godard – my real name is Napper. Rob Simmons called himself something different and got stuck with it. Paul, our bass player, called himself Myers. We were getting paid £15 a week. We thought we had hit the jackpot!

---

8. Early French punk band the Stinky Toys were fronted by Uruguayan-born vocalist Elli Medeiros. Apparently they were booked for the first night but told to play the second night. The band made two albums. After they split, she had further hits in France in the 1980s in techno-pop band Elli & Jacno and as a solo artist before becoming an actress.

Marco glares at the camera as the
Banshees make their noisy debut at the 100 Club

Marco Pirroni

At the 100 Club Festival we put together the Banshees. I knew
Siouxsie and Steve, but not that well – enough to say 'hello' to and
that was it. I went to see Queen at Hyde Park, and Billy Idol was
there with Siouxsie and Steve. We saw five minutes of Queen and
then we went back to Billy Idol's house. Billy I'd known on the
scene for a bit. He started telling me that he had these songs and he
wanted to form a band. He wasn't asking me to join – I think he had
Tony James already. He was supposed to do this thing with Siouxsie
and Steve and didn't want to do it. He wanted to do his own songs.
He was being vague, saying, 'You can play guitar, you do it.' He
didn't want to let his mates down and it was a get-out-of-it type of
situation. Later on Siouxsie and Steve said, 'You can play guitar,' and
I said, 'All right,' and that was the extent of it. I was in the band.

Steve Severin

Me, Billy and Siouxsie were working on getting a band together.
Billy could play guitar, I played bass. Siouxsie had been for auditions
for other bands before up in London, and nothing had really
happened and she was depressed about that. Then the 100 Club gig

came up and we decided we would use that as our debut. And right at the last minute Billy couldn't do 100 Club because Tony James wouldn't let him. He reckoned it would really damage Billy's reputation if he was seen with us trendies, instead of Chelsea who they were putting together at the time! I got that phone call from Billy and that didn't exactly help things! It was around this time that Nils was getting to be really good mates with Marco. He asked if Marco wanted to do it and he said, 'Yes'. We got Sid Vicious in to play drums. Sid couldn't play drums perfectly but it fitted with what were doing. We had a quick rehearsal, went to a pub, got pissed and the next day we played the gig.

Marco Pirroni

We had one rehearsal for about an hour. The idea was to do a set full of cover versions of songs we didn't like: Beatles songs, 'Captain Scarlet', 'Goldfinger' – but they were songs I liked! I said. 'We will never learn these songs tonight, it's impossible,' and Sid said, 'Fuck that! Let's make a big row!' Coming from a Velvet Underground background, I thought that would be cool, or maybe an easy thing to do. 'Sister Ray' without even the riff. Sid had played drums before – he was all right, pretty good actually, and that was it.

We did it once. There was no structure to it. We just made it up as we went along. I was quite good at that. I could jam if I had to. And that's what we did: there were four bands on and the place was packed. The cool bands were on the first night and everyone else the other night.

The Stinky Toys played the first night. I'm not sure why. They got the gig through the Mont de Marsan bloke who knew Bernie. Bernie said, 'Let them play,' and Malcolm said, 'All right,' and then they said, 'We want to go on after the Sex Pistols because we are big in France,' and everyone said, 'All right, go on after the Pistols.' What happened was that everyone fucked off and they played to an empty room. They were hardly punk – more like the Rolling Stones. I remember one had Johnny Thunders hair and a leopardskin guitar strap – I thought that was pretty cool. The French have always had their own cool. Keith Richards is a big hero in France. Gene Vincent was bigger than Elvis over there. They have always liked the Velvet Underground. It's all very black and Raybans. Too fast to live, too young to die...

Vic Godard

It gets overlooked that a lot of the bands didn't have a punk look. The only ones that looked like punks were the Banshees. They had dyed hair and looked more outrageous.

Steve Severin

People say that it was an iconic gig, but Marco has always had the right attitude about it. He said it was just a load of racket. We deliberately did that. The whole idea was the DIY aspect of it, just to get up and do it. The next day we thought, 'That was good. Let's continue.' John McKay came up to us after the 100 Club gig and was really into it, so instead of Sid and Marco we got John McKay and Kenny Morris in the band, and that autumn we rehearsed and got the band together.

John Bentham

The first night at the 100 Club was a pretty spectacular affair, Siouxsie and the other girls in particular. The Banshees' performance seemed to go on forever, and I don't remember too much about the Clash, but when the Pistols came on the place seemed electric. I guess most of us didn't know the songs, and it wasn't the greatest of sounds, but it worked a treat. I had my hair cut and bought some new shoes the very next afternoon.

I went early the next day and got in with the bands arriving, and bumped straight into Rat Scabies and Captain Sensible, who were full of themselves having recorded 'New Rose' for Stiff Records earlier that day. Johnny Moped was there looking for a guitarist for his new band, which I plumped for at the time, later to change my mind.

Rat Scabies

Sid threw the glass on the second day. We didn't know what had happened for years. I knew this girl had been blinded in one eye by the glass shattering. We were very pissed off about the whole thing. It seemed quite wrong that one of our crowd should be injured. Nobody then knew who had done it.

I think the glass was aimed at us. I think there was an element of the band being unpopular with other bands. Maybe we were seen as a threat. Also the other thing was we had Jake as manager and Jake and Malcolm clashed from day one. I think Malcolm wanted to stay in control of the scene, and you had Jake who was from pub rock in cowboy boots. But he really knew what he was doing.

Michelle Brigandage

It was an incredible two nights, but it was marred by the glass-throwing incident, which Sid was later blamed for. My cousin and I got small bits of glass showering over us into our face but it was a friend I'd met at the Blitz – Cherry, I think that was her name – who got it straight in the eye. It blinded her in one eye. I think she was going to be an artist and that put paid to that. So obviously the atmosphere changed suddenly. There was blood, screaming, crying and ambulances. It calmed down after she was taken away, but everybody started to leave and Siouxsie stood on the stairs and asked people to stay and watch the Buzzcocks! We couldn't because we had a train to catch to get back home. Should have stayed to see them – it was Howard Devoto.

Marco Pirroni

The second night was shit. Sid threw the glass and the Damned were crap. Captain Sensible wore big white flares, I think. It was either because he was so fucking clueless and didn't know, or to piss everyone off. Sid threw the glass at him. Sid missed because he was useless.

Captain Sensible

Some poor girl lost an eye because of that wanker. It was the people standing either side of him who persuaded him to do it. They were to blame. Sid was impressionable and gullible. 'Gullible' was his middle name. He wanted people to be impressed by what he did. He was quite weak-willed really. He said, 'They are fucking wankers, this lot,' about the Damned, 'they are really corny.' That was his favourite word. I've heard this is how the conversation went. And he then said, 'I'll fucking show them, kick them off, cause some chaos. I'll tell you what, I'll throw this fucking glass.' And they said, 'Yeah, go on then, go on, throw it!'

It was very interesting, just to see what everyone else was doing at the same place at the same time. I jammed with the Vibrators – they had Chris Spedding who did 'Motor Biking'. I had just bought that – it was brilliant. I liked Spedding from when he was a jazz rocker. I followed his career with great interest. I thought, 'I know a couple of lyrics off that,' so I jumped on the stage. I must have ruined the set, but it was a fucking good song!

John Bentham

Chris Spedding arrived after apparently having seen his name on a poster and thought he'd better turn up. He performed a good set with the Vibrators, and of course the Damned set was marred by the glass incident. I remember it happening while the Damned covered the Stooges' '1970' and stopping the show for a while. There definitely seemed a lot more tension in the air that second night.

Knox

Ron Watts, who put the festival on, had advertised Chris Spedding as playing. We were phoned on the day and asked if we could back Chris Spedding as he said he didn't know anything about the gig and didn't have a band. We turned up and he showed us the songs. You can only learn a couple of songs before you play, so we had to play some covers with him to make up a set. Because he was the headline act, we did our set after the Damned.

During the Damned, someone threw a glass at them, probably Sid, and that made it all really nasty for when we were playing – it doesn't make for a very nice atmosphere. It was our PA as well, and Captain Sensible had broken some PA leads but that was his act, that was OK. Before we went on we had to mend all the stuff. I lent my speakers to the opening band from France called the Stinky Toys, and they had blown the horns in the speakers. Because of that I had a pretty horrid guitar sound, and it wasn't my fault. There was all this horrible stuff going on and we had to fix the PA. Soldering wires before you get on the stage.

People said we played this old stuff, but people didn't realise we had to do that so Chris Spedding could play! After that a load of work disappeared because of all the violence at the 100 Club – people thought we were a punk band. The trouble was reported in the press. They like to encourage that sort of stuff because it sells papers. They immediately associated punk with terrible violence.

Vic Godard

Before the 100 Club festival, punk was like a secret society. Afterwards it got hijacked by everybody.

Nils Stevenson

Punk happened incredibly fast. The Bromley Contingent were the first to pick up on it, along with Marco Pirroni. The other place it happened very quickly was in Wales: we'd never seen such people in our lives.[9] People like Steve Strange with safety pins through their cheeks and plastic binliners. We'd drop Steve Strange off in some tip and he'd disappear over the hills in his strange regalia to be beaten up on the other side of the slag heap! [laughs]

The rest of the country was abysmal. A few people picked up on it in Manchester but not for the look, more for the music. I'd have

---

9. The Pistols played gigs in Cardiff, Newport and Swansea on successive nights (21 to 23 September) straight after the 100 Club festival.

Get in the van! The Sex Pistols get ready to play some 'godforsaken northern town'

to call the police quite often to escort us out of these horrid little gigs we were doing round the country. I would always have to get paid upfront. We had to stay in tacky hovels. Rotten was incredibly charming with landladies; he really did have a way with older women.

There were a number of factions in the band. Rotten teamed up with me at the front of the van because I was driving. He'd sit next to me. We'd share rooms. Steve and Paul were old school friends. Glen was always on his own.

GRRRL POWER
The Slits

Ari Up

All these punk people had been coming round our house long before I was in a band. I saw the Pistols people, and people from different punk bands – Joe Strummer would come round with this Fifties guitar. He had a red one. He was really into r'n'b and that Fifties style. That's where I learned my first guitar – I remember the action on the guitar was really difficult.

The Slits were formed at a Patti Smith concert. I met with

Palmolive – she had a pig earring in her ear and that did it for me! We started chatting and she asked me to sing for her band. The next day I was in the Slits and the day after that I was rehearsing. It was all because of the pig in the ear. It was fast.

When we started the Slits we had nothing to go on. We went straight from Abba to Patti Smith. I'm not sure if Patti Smith was that keen on me, though! I was in Patti Smith's dressing room and anyone could see that I was a kid, I was out of control and wild! [laughs] I was a real kiddie, and she comes in as this grown ass woman shouting, 'Get that bitch out of my dressing room!' I wasn't a bitch to her, I admired her, but she must have hated my guts.

The Slits had a very female energy. We were really into reggae already, although we were not playing it – we were playing what our peers were playing. The first time I came to a rehearsal I had a go on the drums. I love the drums. I knew I had a good potential for rhythm. I went on the mike, which I knew I loved anyway, and started singing. And we did 'Blitzkrieg Bop' – that was the first song we rehearsed. It wasn't because I was listening to the Ramones particularily. It was the music we listened to with our peers. We were all punk people, so-called. We had to play some kind of music at first, whatever we could. We listened to the Kinks and Iggy Pop and different rock music, as well as reggae.

Palmolive had already written a few songs. She had been in the Flowers of Romance.[10] Viv Albertine joined a little bit later.

---

10. One of the semi-legendary early bands of the punk era. Named by John Lydon, the Flowers of Romance are another of those ad hoc bands that briefly flickered before punk went mainstream. Like London SS and Masters of the Backside, they remain key because of the future names that passed through their ranks rather than for any music they ever made. Put together in the summer of 1976 by bass player Sarah Hall and guitarist Jo Faull (the then girlfriends of Cook and Jones), they never played any gigs, just rehearsing in squats and at the Clash's Chalk Farm rehearsal space. Joining the line-up were future Slits Viv Albertine and Palmolive, playing Ramones songs in a shambolic garage-band kind of way. To make up for his pal Rotten getting the Pistols post, Sid Vicious was looking for a band, and he joined, first as singer, then bizarrely switched to sax, and then went back to vocals, contributing some of his own songs like future Pistols tune 'Belsen Was A Gas', 'Piece of Garbage' and 'Brains on Vacation'. With Sid running the band, things unsurprisingly got even more unstable. Jo dropped out and Sid sacked first Sarah and then Palmolive. At the tail end of '76 the band was made up of Steve Walsh and former Clash guitar man Keith Levene. Within months it would fizzle out as Sid got the post in the Pistols that he craved.

Palmolive came with 'Number One Enemy', and 'Shoplifting' as well. We started rehearsing. We didn't have a plan. We just went along with the lyrics or a hookline, fitting the music to the lyrics. We were not going to be influenced by anyone – that's when it becomes uniform. If someone says you sound like someone else, for some people this is a compliment but to me it's an insult. I certainly didn't want to sound like anyone else.

We were never really feminists politically, but we did more for females politically than anyone ever could. We took pride in putting ourselves together without men. The Runaways were put together by men and they were holding guitars at the crotch and they had to compete – 'We are heavy metal maaan! We have to be like men!' – that was the old idea.[11] We were not like that. We wanted to be natural and female. We wanted feminine rhythms, and the tribal thing developed, and there was a Celtic thing in there as well. There was the football hooligan chanting in 'Newtown', half football songs mixed with the tribal thing and the drumming of Palmolive.

Tessa Pollitt (The Slits: bass)

It was mixture of all the music we had ever listened to.

Ari Up

I was not allowed to say it in the punk days, but I was fanatical about Cat Stevens! It was the worst thing to say. John Lydon would laugh at me and take this piss, and John, being involved with my mum, saw my record collection. He would take the piss out of the 'Greek boy'. But I was into what I was into. The whole of the Slits liked so much music, and we also liked different things from each other: dub was big, Tessa liked Van Morrison, Viv Albertine liked a lot of Sixties

---

11. The Runaways, an all-female American group heavily hyped by their manager/producer, Kim Fowley, released their first album in 1976. Their sound was loud, guitar-driven hard rock, more heavy metal than punk. The group included Michael Steele, later to join the Bangles, and Joan Jett, who went on to have a huge hit with her cover of 'I Love Rock'n'Roll' (a long-lost B-side by late-period glam band the Arrows) and became an iconic figure to the mid-Nineties Grrrl Power movement.

pop, Sandie Shaw, and we were taking piss out of Palmolive because she was listening to Indian music, which is really trendy now. Now we love Bollywood and Indian music, and she was listening to it then. [laughs] That's what made the Slits. We were very eclectic and very adamant about liking our personal influences. We didn't give a shit about our peers. We were that rebellious, we were rebellious against ourselves!

It wasn't called punk at the time. We didn't have a name for it. We suddenly found out we were punk when the press labelled it as punk. We said, 'Where was that name from?' Then we found out that it was an American expression for jerks! At the time when you are in it and making a revolution you don't think of going around and calling yourself punk...

CAST OF THOUSANDS
The Adverts and Friends

T. V. Smith

We were rehearsing in the summer of '76. I had a few songs that I was teaching Gaye on bass guitar before we moved to London, and then we carried on doing that. We put out ads in the music papers for a guitarist, and found Howard who worked in a rehearsal room, which was well handy because we got cheap rehearsal time. We wanted to get it together quick because we were excited about it, and we wanted to play some gigs. I just wanted to get up there and do it myself.

At first we didn't have a name. We were called the One Chord Wonders and then the Adverts. I had the songs, and the sound of the band came from the way we played together: a bass player that had never played bass before; a drummer, Laurie (Muscat) Driver, who had never played drums before, and a guitarist, Howard (Boak) Pickup, copying my parts so I didn't have to play guitar. That was the sound of the band. It came from the way it was formed.

And what a sound it was. The Adverts' gloriously ramshackle attack that captured exactly the sound of punk rock. Initial rehearsal tapes recorded in late '76 show a band defying their limitations and holding it together as they work their way through Smith's genius songs. Great tunes, brilliant vocal delivery and the sort of amazing lyrics that you expect from someone who had won national poetry awards in his youth.

T. V. Smith

At first we found a few pub rock gigs going on in London. It was better than nothing – at last it was a few bands with a bit of energy. Pretty soon, down the road from where we lived, the Stranglers were playing every week down the Nashville and we thought, 'This is really something!' Get on the Tube for a couple of stops and get this really exciting band playing for nothing. You could definitely feel that there was something going on. We were around Lemmy's flat before we knew it. We got on well with Lemmy. We bumped into him somewhere and a friend of ours knew him. When Hawkwind played, Lemmy was always the one who would be most like a normal bloke and talk to you. He was always pretty cool. There was definitely a scene going on.

Captain Sensible

Lemmy was there, down the Portobello Gold on Portobello Road. He would mix with us and lend us a bass guitar. He was supportive, and so was Phil Lynott.[12] When the Damned played a gig down the Hope and Anchor they would put you up there after the show, and there was Phil Lynott dossing there. Various members of the Stranglers and Damned would doss there as well.

J. J. Burnel

By the autumn of 1976 we even had our own crew following us from gig to gig, the Finchley Boys. They turned up at the beginning

---

12. Charismatic Dublin-born frontman of one of the great Seventies rock'n'roll bands, Thin Lizzy.

of 1976. They had heard this punk thing was going on so they went round and frightened a few bands, and the only band which didn't walk off stage was us. We were adopted after that and they provided us with much needed security.

Al Hillier

The Finchley Boys were a bunch of lads who came predominantly from two council estates in north London. We all went to the same schools, fought over the same birds and as a group of mates, we existed before we ever encountered the Stranglers. By the time we met them at the Torrington in November 1976, the Finchley Boys as a 'group' had already lived through some very interesting youth cultural experiences...

The buzz surrounding this new music called punk was everywhere but up until then it really just seemed more like a rumour emanating from the West End of London. A fashion-led youth thing. Thinking back now, November 1976 really could be considered to be the month that kicked the punk explosion into life. Both the Damned and the Pistols had singles out but neither had done anything at all in the charts.

Bundling through the doors of the back room at the Torrington, I immediately caught sight of Hugh Cornwell and J. J. Burnel, who were standing together to my left as far away from the stage as they could get. They looked a bit nervous and seemed to be staring at the tiny stage area as if working out how the fuck they might escape if need be. There's no doubt that seeing us pile into that small room gave them a few palpitations, and, to be fair to them, they have admitted to that.

I remember the band taking the stage and launching straight into 'Grip'. I had never heard anything like it before: it was perfect and we just instinctively went totally berserk, completely absorbed into the sound. It wasn't long before we were ripping at each other's clothes in a crazy, sweaty explosion of excitement, instinctively pogoing (even though we had never heard the expression before) like crazed Masai tribesmen, and crashing about at the front of the stage. It was totally fucking crazy and I think the Stranglers were crapping themselves at this fanatical uncontrolled force, but to their credit they showed plenty of bottle to ride out the storm.

Without exchanging a single word to each other in that little, noisy arena, we realised, collectively, that we were witnessing one of the greatest live bands of our time. Now they were *our* band. The energy they created reflected our own character, our own passion and emphasised our desire. It was exactly what we had been waiting for.

Towards the end of the gig we just piled onto the stage and joined in the singing with 'Go Buddy Go', something we were to do on a regular basis from then on. When they realised that we weren't going to destroy them and their gear, the band seemed to turn their tension into genuine excitement. I think at that moment they realised that something important had just happened for all concerned. From that moment on we went everywhere with them and were at every gig, totally loving every minute of it.

Captain Sensible

The Stranglers were a funny band, weren't they? The funny thing about it was the Stranglers were fantastic, they had their own take on it entirely, and they weren't like anyone else at all. Why shouldn't you have a Hammond organ in a punk group? Why not a harpsichord or a cello? Who says you should do this or that? That was the great thing about the original punk: you had all the bands who sounded totally different: the Buzzcocks, the Clash, the Saints, the Ramones – everyone had their own thing. There were no rules and I liked that.

WHAT WE NEED ARE MORE BANDS
Some Other New Punks

Mark Stewart

The Cortinas had supported Patti Smith at the Roundhouse and I went with them and we had talked to Patti Smith. We told her there was this London punk thing going on and she didn't even know about it! We took her to the Clash at the ICA for the 'Night of Treason'.[13]

If I was being a sociologist, it was seeing Paul from the Clash with little Letraset stickers on his bass telling him where to put his fingers. 'It's not the arrogance of power, it's the power of arrogance.'

It's the arrogance to think you don't have to stand there and tip your forelock to people in control. It was the arrogance of Paul Simonon doing that, that gave us inspiration, and that inspiration goes down the line.

Noel Martin

My first band was called Stonehenge. We were more of a pub band. We played a few places like the Lord Nelson, the standard pub gigs you did in those days. Menace formed in 1976, probably late summer. We were all from Islington and we met each other after school. We started to write punk stuff. We just made it more basic. We certainly could play a bit. We were not completely rubbish. We didn't have to stretch our imagination that much to write punk music. We were already there with our songs in pub rock with three or four chords. The songs may have had a couple of 'Ooohs' and 'Aaahs' in there, and may have been more about love than politics, but they were rough and ready songs.

Nick Cash

I'd known Guy Days since I was at school, and then we would advertise in *Melody Maker*: 'Wanted: Bass-player and Drummer for Punk Rock Group.' (At the time people used the name 'punk' for music – this was before the Sex Pistols had come out.) Loads of people turned up, like John Moss who was eventually in the Damned and Culture Club. Chrissie Hynde even came down, and Tony James as

---

13. The Cortinas were leading lights of Bristol punk, alongside Mark Stewart and the Pop Group. The Clash's ICA gig was on 28 October 1976.

well. In fact Tony James was the first bass player in 999. He joined for a short while, but he didn't play a gig with us. We had Jon Watson. We thought he was better. Tony James wanted to be seen in the right places, he wanted to go down that route. We wanted to play gigs and play hard and fast. The songs we'd written went down well in front of an audience – it was different from what he wanted to do so we picked Jon Watson.

Pablo LaBrittain went to school with Joe Strummer. He was the first drummer in the Clash. Because Pablo was a friend of Joe's, he used to play with the Clash up at Chalk Farm, the Rehearsal Rehearsals rooms. He fell foul of Bernie Rhodes. He didn't get on with him at all, like everyone else, and he just left. He couldn't be bothered with him. He liked that type of music, so he turned up at one of our auditions up the Kings Road at a rehearsal studio we used to book called Manos Studio, which everybody used to go to – the Damned were down there and so was Chrissie Hynde. It was just round the corner from Let It Rock/Seditionaries. People used it for auditions.

I DON'T WANNA GO TO CHELSEA
Billy Idol, Tony James, Gene October and the Formation of Generation X

Tony James

Both of us, Billy Idol and me, had also answered another ad. John Krivine, who had Acme Attractions, was putting together Chelsea as an Acme Attractions rival to the Pistols and Sex. I went there to audition – Don Letts, the shop assistant, and Jeanette Lee are there; Don's playing reggae – and I met up with Billy again. We had both applied to the same ad!

We had an audition somewhere under a railway arch in south London. Both Billy and I turned up, as well as other people who later on turned up in other bands. Billy and I got the job as bass player and guitarist. Billy could play guitar a bit – he had an Epiphone acoustic. So Billy and I end up being in Chelsea, with Gene October singing – we knew nothing about him.

Gene October

I remember I used to speak to John Krivine a lot at Acme Attractions. Krivine was a bit of an entrepreneur with loads of connections round London. South London especially – most of the sweatshops were down there. He said, 'Can you sing? Wanna do a band? I'll look after it for you and pay the rehearsal space.' I said, 'OK.'

It was very strange, the way it happened. He put an ad in *Melody Maker* – 'Musicians Wanted. Into Television and Rock'n'Roll' – and Billy Idol and Tony James turned up. They didn't know who Television were. Television were quite prevalent in those days – they had made a bit of a name for themselves already on the American scene with the Ramones. I remember Billy coming along first. I thought he looked great. But he didn't have blonde hair yet, and I said, 'You got to get rid of those glasses,' because he'd look like the Milky Bar Kid. He got himself contact lenses and dyed his hair blonde, and he said, 'I got a mate.' So he introduced Tony James to me. Tony turned up in leather trousers and dark glasses, and looked great. Woooo! With his black bass with 'London SS' on it – I didn't know who they were at the time.

It turned out that Tony was a friend of Mick Jones. One night we went to see this reggae band at the Acklam Hall on Ladbroke Grove. I met Mick and Joe there and they said, 'We're doing this band called the Clash,' and we all got to know each other.

I was very much into the arty rock side of things, so I was quite mad. I loved Fassbinder, the German film director – you can tell from the films that I was into that I was already there.[14] I used to

---

14. The late Rainer Werner Fassbinder, director of films such as *The Bitter Tears Of Petra Von Kant*, was the leading light in the New German Cinema.

drop a lot of acid and watch that stuff – puts you on the far side of crazy! [laughs]

Tony James

Billy and I started writing songs together then. We were in the work room where they made the clothes for Acme Attractions, which was an upstairs tenement in Portobello Road, under the Westway. Billy then cut his hair and dyed it blonde, but it was in a side parting. He looked like an accountant! [laughs] I'm going through a Bob Dylan period, so I've got spiky black hair and glasses and skinny trousers, the leather trousers I had bought from Sex. I had the skinny leather trousers and Dylan look going on.

We were writing these songs for Chelsea. 'Ready Steady Go' was quite a mod thing to write – that was one of the first ones. Billy and I wrote it and we played it for Chelsea, and then we wrote 'Too Personal' and a whole bunch of those songs. 'This Heat' was written in the Chelsea period. We played a couple of gigs in Chelsea. Our first gig was with Throbbing Gristle at the ICA.[15]

Gene October

I think you'll find our first gig was at the Chelsea Potter along the Kings Road. We used to rehearse and do Stones numbers, 'Rebel Rebel', covers – just dress up and be all attitude. We had a little bit of a residency for a month, Friday night there. I remember Keith Richards coming to one of them because he only lived down the road. He told someone to tell us it was cool. I felt quite cool about getting Keef's blessing, so it kind of evolved.

The next one we did was at the ICA. The Arts Council put on a thing where Genesis P-Orridge had a grant to do a show an arts show which he called *Music From The Death Factory* – he had these pictures

---

15. Throbbing Gristle's notorious *Prostitution* show, on 18 October 1976, excited the tabloids, who coined the fantastic headline: 'These people are the wreckers of civilisation'. A mini-precursor to the Sex Pistols outrage – there were a few porn pictures stuck on the wall, a couple of used tampons in a glass case, and a stripper. Throbbing Gristle, a music/performance art hybrid, were the brainchild of Genesis P-Orridge.

from Auschwitz, and James Hanratty and all the people hung in jail, all this sort of thing. Krivine managed Genesis P-Orridge at the time as well. I used to meet him a lot at that time. So having bumped into him in the shop, he says, 'We're doing this thing. Would you guys like to play?' and we said, 'Yeah, fucking great!'

We used it as a kind of launch. Tony Parsons from the *NME* came, and he called us the best thing since sliced bread. Great review. Imagine that on your first gig, and you're only doing covers. What a great start, got our pictures in the papers, in the big one, the *NME*. You're strutting around. 'I'm famous now, mate.' You done nowt for it really. You just dared to move your arse a little bit, do something different, and they were all over you. It was crazy. You'd have Japanese film crews, everything.

And then we did one in Manchester. We supported the Buzzcocks at the Electric Circus, with Howard in the band.[16] We were the only ones who had a PA! Krivine bought it for us, a funny old PA – it was hell of a number to get it working. I don't know how John got that gig – it was a bit strange going all the way to Manchester.

Charlie Harper

The UK Subs used to rehearse at the Furniture Cave on Kings Road. Our line-up changed a lot. There were a few other punk bands in there rehearsing as well. Billy Idol was in there when he was still playing guitar with Chelsea. I met Gene October from Chelsea. I thought they sounded great. I was very much into Iggy Pop and the Velvet Underground, and to me Chelsea sounded like the MC5 with a bit of the Dolls thrown in. I thought they were brilliant. I got to know guitarist James Stevenson really well. A little while later, one of his friends joined our band as a drummer. We had a long-haired drummer, a great drummer but not really a punk – but there was only a handful of kids who looked like punks. The rest looked like students.

---

16. This gig on 10 November, promoted by Buzzcocks manager Richard Boon, was the first punk show at the Electric Circus.

Andy Czezowski

Gene October was being managed by Steph Raynor from Acme Attractions. Gene had heard about my bust-up with the Damned and asked me if I could take over, and I said, 'Yes, why not?' and began managing Chelsea.

Gene October

We got a gig supporting the Stranglers at the Nashville, where me and the boys had a little tiff.[17] The stuff they were starting to write was like 'Ready Steady Go' – I might have done it live, I can't remember – and I said, 'Look guys, that's not what I had in mind.' I wanted to go much heavier and naughtier than that. Basically we had a difference of opinion musically and they said, 'We're going to do our own thing.' I said, 'Let Billy do it.' He always wanted to do it anyway. I couldn't be arsed. I thought I could get my idea together and do it with other people. I'd done it once, and it didn't bother me to do it again.

Tony James

We weren't in Chelsea for long. Billy says, 'Why don't I be the singer, and we'll get a guitarist and form a new group.' We already didn't like John Krivine – and Gene October. I can't remember for what reason. He didn't look right. Or too old? Billy and I just didn't really like him. The breaking point was when we wrote 'Prove It'. We didn't tell Gene about. We did a gig supporting the Stranglers at the Nashville. When we came out to do the encore, Gene said, 'What are we going to do?' and we said, 'We got a new song and you're not on it!' Which was an incredibly cruel thing to do, when you look back on it. We didn't think anything of it. We went back on stage and Billy played guitar and sang the song as well, and Gene is just standing there looking embarrassed. I don't know what his take on it is!

---

17. Chelsea's last gig with the initial line-up, on 21 November.

It's incredible how fast all this happens. We leave Chelsea and the next week we're rehearsing our new band. We thought, 'Let's put an ad in the papers,' but two days later Billy phones me from a call box. He says, 'I'm at this party at this youth club in Fulham, and there is this little band playing.[18] They are kids, the guitarist is seventeen and he's great. He's got long hair but why don't we get him?' I said, 'Go up and ask him and get his number. Get him to come down.' Two days later Billy gets him to come down, he plays and he's in, and the first gig he plays is a week later. So we had found Derwood.[19]

Then I was over at Billy's house and there was a book in the bookcase, and I said, 'That looks interesting.' It was called *Generation X*.[20] It belonged to Billy's mother. I said, 'Let's call the group that.' The book is about mods and rockers, youth culture. I thought, 'That looks really good. I bet there's load of ideas we could nick out of this book for songs.' So we became Generation X. We nicked the book logo as well. See how easy it all is!

---

18. The band was called Paradox.
19. Real name Bob Andrews.
20. Written by Charles Hamblett and Jane Deverson and first published in 1964. Douglas Coupland's better-known book of the same title was not published till 1991.

CHAPTER 6
1976 PART III: PUNK BECOMES A DIRTY WORD

I GOT A NEW ROSE
The First Punk Singles

On 8 October, despite or maybe because of their notorious reputation, the Sex Pistols signed a two-year contract with EMI. A week later punk was fast becoming the most talked-about youth culture in the country when the Sun *ran a two-page spread on this terrifying new cult...*

Mike Thorne (A&R at EMI; producer of Wire)

I was the person who picked up the phone when Malcolm called. I took the tape to my boss. On the afternoon of 27 September, we took the train to Doncaster: the Leeds Pullman, very pleasant. The group played at the Outlook Club, and it was about one third full, audience reaction varying between wild enthusiasm, tepid applause (mostly) and irritation at their interrupted lager consumption. The Sex Pistols did their thing, antagonising the crowd. We enjoyed it, made the formal backstage introductions and agreed to meet back in London the following week. My boss Nick Mobbs signed them and I became the A&R man and worked on the initial demos. The Sex Pistols were just what was needed after a quiet mid-Seventies.

Nils Stevenson

I was kind of Malcolm's assistant and tour manager for the band. I thought I was their co-manager for the first year, but when they had to sign their contracts there was no provision for me. I realised I'd been deluding myself or Malcolm had been deluding me, so I started working with Siouxsie and the Banshees so that I could have a way out of the Pistols.

Rob Lloyd

I saw the Sex Pistols at Bogarts in Birmingham that autumn and I thought they were really great. In all honesty, I had convinced myself they were really great before I even saw them! In retrospect my mate Paul got a bootleg of Bogarts and it don't sound that much, but they just looked absolutely fantastic. I thought, 'This is great, they play the sort of music that I like, the kind of music that people can learn quickly. And they haven't got long hair either.' As soon as I saw they were playing in Birmingham, I had to be there. It just had to be done. It was a little club called Bogarts which was on New Street – it doesn't exist anymore. I got photos of the night. It was a rock club where the disco would have been Deep Purple/Zeppelin sort of stuff. It was not very full – 50 per cent of the crowd were biker types who would have been there any Tuesday anyway. There was a handful of people who were notice-able because they already got the sort of Sex clothes type of stuff on, and there was a bunch of losers like me and the Apperley brothers. The only person that I can think of who was there and would be in a group was Toyah. A lot of people pretend to have been there.

The Damned's 'New Rose' was released on 22 October. The first British punk single and a drop-dead classic. A two-minute rush of glorious riffing and thundering drums, it pipped the Pistols by three weeks and heralded the new scene going public.

Brian James

We decided to put 'New Rose' out as the first single. The Captain wanted 'I Fall' but we went with 'New Rose'. It seems to have become a classic. It still sounds good when I hear it now. I'm kind of prejudiced, though. I do look at my past stuff with a critical ear, but the first album stands up. It doesn't sound dated. There are no gimmicks on it, like on an Eighties album. Nick Lowe did a great job on that album.

Captain Sensible

'New Rose' is a great single. 'I Fall' would have been even more gob-smacking because it's snotty and fast. People, when they heard 'New Rose', said we must have speeded the tapes up, which is ridiculous. People honestly thought we were cheating, and they came to see us live and saw we played the songs twice as fast again! [laughs] 'I Fall' a was a lot faster than 'New Rose'. It would have had more shock value, and it was really good fun for a bass player to play as well.

People say, 'Blimey, you can't hear much production on it,' and that's the fucking point. There *is* no production on it! [laughs] That was the genius of Nick Lowe. He could see that you didn't need to do a big production job on the Damned. On the first album it would have been a tragedy to over-produce it. It sounds raw and rancid and gnarled. To spruce it up would have been a mistake.

ṭat Scabies

We did 'New Rose' in one day. We started in the morning, and by tea-time it was done. I think Nick Lowe might have taken an extra day to mix it. I'm kind of pleased about it. I think it's a lot to do with the studio. Nick left it as it was. I was always a very slow learner.

When we rehearsed I was quite merciless, doing it over and over to get the band to play it around in a loop. Also Captain is a great bass player, even though he hates playing bass – he wanted to be a guitarist. He kind of overplayed on the bass. It was too boring to be normal. He was pushing it. One of the important things about the band was the bass carried the melody – it's kind of because the Captain hated the bass that it was played like that.

Tony D

'New Rose' starts it for me. That's where the whole punk movement really begins. American and British punk are so different. New York stuff is intellectually stimulating but not life-changing. Punk made me leave my job, changed my life. I couldn't live the lie anymore.

Kevin Hunter

The British stuff sounded amazing. The American stuff when you heard it just didn't do that much for me. I remember thinking, 'Not quite what I expected,' after 'New Rose'.

Brian James

We recorded the album in Pathway as well.[1] I went back down there in 1988 for nostalgia's sake. It was exactly the same. They had not swept the place since we were in there. What a fucking shame it was knocked down. Pathway had a really small room and it had a lovely sound to it. You'd have to be a real shit engineer not to capture that sound.

Captain Sensible

Pathway was really kinda basic when you think what they use nowadays. But what do you need to record the Damned? For that album it was all there. Just record it on an eight-track or something. I

---

1. Pathway was a great, tiny studio in London. The control room was the smallest I've ever been in. The drum room was like a cupboard – but it sounded fantastic.

remember we had lolly sticks stuck on the pre-faders, or whatever you call them.

Brian plays some amazing guitar on that album. Really fast stuff. I know – I have to play those bloody things now! [laughs] Brian is a genius. It's a pig playing those solos. On 'See Her Tonight', the guitar-playing is astonishing – you can see why Jimmy Page was so into the Damned.

Marco Pirroni

I thought 'New Rose' was great. I had my doubts about the Damned! [laughs] I didn't like the album that much, but the single was great. 'Neat Neat Neat' was fantastic as well. Half of the album is really good actually. Originally I didn't like their vibe. I didn't think they were very cool, but I always thought that Dave Vanian looked really good. To take that Andy Warhol *Dracula* look and pull it off was cool. I went to see Andy Warhol's *Dracula* – I thought it was really fucking brilliant.[2] Brian James was like Keith Richards. The Damned were not playing by the numbers, there was no '1, 2, 3, 4, ra-ma-la-ma!' They had very well-written songs like the MC5 and the Stooges had. Mind you, I never liked the MC5. I don't know why! [laughs]

Captain Sensible

It was great being the first punk single and typical of the kind of thing that Stiff would do. We were in a punk group and a small independent record label came along and said, 'We got no cash but we got loads of get-up-and-go, and we are trying to kick the major labels in the knackers. Do you want to sign to us?' and we said, 'Yeah, fucking right! The Pistols' whole thing was to go to the biggest label going and do it conventional and that's why they missed the boat, to be honest. Because they were holding out for some big deal. We did it the more independent way.

---

2. 1973 arthouse camp – a faintly amusing Andy Warhol-produced film, directed by Factory stalwart Paul Morrissey, and released in the UK under the title *Blood For Dracula*.

Brian James

If it bothered the Pistols, they didn't let on. Nothing said to our faces. We'd see Steve and Paul in Portobello Road, in a pub now called the Earl of Lonsdale, on Saturday lunchtime when the market was on, or we'd all be in the dole office in Lisson Grove. Steve would say, 'I saw your picture in the paper, you got a good review last week,' or the other way round. It was all very supportive. There was no sense of it being a race really. The Pistols, to start off with, were allies. Any kind of race came from the managements. The Pistols were as happy as we were.

I'm sure that there was other people out there doing it as well. The Pistols would have not gone anywhere without a scene. It would have been a little flash in the pan, a gimmicky thing that would not have happened. The papers would have taken care of that. It needed a few things from all directions, different types of creativity. People wanting to make movies – Don Letts was doing his filming. People wanting to do things artistically and be themselves. The Pistols and the Clash and the Damned were nothing like each other, and then you got the Stranglers who were at least barking up the same tree and had the same attitude.

John Lydon

Most bands did not get it, like Generation X, the Damned. Awful. The Damned's finest achievement, because they were so jealous of the Sex Pistols, was to get the first record released by a punk band – like that matters! Who cares who had the first record? What are you doing this for? Punk was about self-esteem. Winning it back for yourself. Not blowing off somebody else's steam. You know, there are those who fart and those who inhale those farts. I know where I am.

Tony D

I started *Ripped and Torn* fanzine when I saw the Damned in October 1976, before 'New Rose' came out. I went down from

Glasgow to London to see them at the Hope and Anchor. It was pretty incredible seeing the Damned then. I was hoping to see the Pistols as well but they weren't playing when I was there.

I finished work on the Friday night and got the overnight coach to London. I got to London early and got off at King's Cross. I didn't know where the venue was, and I didn't know what it was going to be like. I was expecting Siouxsie Banshee types lining the streets, but it was not like that at all! [laughs] I got to the Hope and Anchor and went in. It was chock-a-block, really busy. There was a great jukebox full of fantastic stuff that you dream of: rock'n'roll, some punk, the Ramones' 'Surfin' Bird'. I met Mark Perry. I recognised him from a picture and introduced myself to him. He said, 'If you can't get *Sniffin' Glue* in Glasgow why don't you start your own fanzine?' So I did. Shane MacGowan was there with Mark Perry as well, doing his own fanzine *Bondage*.

When the Damned came on I had such high expectations I thought it would be disappointing, but it was fantastic. That racket was just incredible, and the speed of the stuff was incredible at the time. Every song seemed to be finished before it started. I was wondering how he could play guitar so fast! I remember Dave Vanian looked great and I remember having my first kebab after I left the gig.

I stayed at Shane's house and slept in his front room. He was on the cover of *Sounds* for biting the ear of that girl. He became a minor celeb because of that. Already there was a scene of people going to every gig. People seemed to know each other.

After staying with Shane I went to Carnaby Street and I bought Iggy's *Metallic KO*.[3] It has that special feeling, it's exciting and dangerous. That was the feeling I got from the Damned. That night I slept on the station and got the first train back to Glasgow.

---

3. The Stooges' final live gig in Detroit on 9 February 1976 saw Iggy take on the local Hell's Angels chapter. You can hear the bottles flying and feel the tension on this official bootleg released in 1976.

Mark Stewart

I remember Shane MacGowan came to a Bristol gig. I said, 'Last time I was stood next to you was at the Clash gig at the ICA when you bit some bird's ear, and there's some photograph of it.'

Brian James

When we supported the Flamin' Groovies they had got it into their heads that they wanted to dress up like the Beatles and do all these Beatles-style songs and wear these collarless Beatle suits. They couldn't have picked a worse time to do that. They were fucking shit-scared of us! But we didn't do anything. They would scarper when we turned up. They had to follow us onto the stage. You can't have a band like the Damned basically at our prime making the racket we made, then follow it with a bunch of Americans dressed like the Beatles with Rickenbacker guitars. OK, the Captain had a violin bass like Paul McCartney, but that was where the comparison stopped.

Captain Sensible

There were bands who came over here who in 1976 who were considered to be kind of raunchy, like the Flamin' Groovies and that lot from New Zealand, Split Enz. They were getting written about in the music papers as being outrageous bands and they came over... [laughs] I remember going to see them and they looked at the audience and it was fucking scaring them because the audience were so upfront and the bands were not. The Groovies ran off back to the States because they were intimidated. Mind you, when me and Rat walked in a room it was was usually the start of something or other! They were terrible, terrible times! [laughs]

The chugging guitars of the Vibrators, whose debut 'We Vibrate' was released on Mickie Most's RAK Records, helped define the sound of what was to come. The B-side, 'Whips And Furs', was a Velvets-influenced sado-masochistic classic. The same month Chris Spedding's single

*'Pogo Dancing', featuring the Vibrators' backing, was also released;
ironically it was more of a punk rock workout.*

*Meanwhile in Manchester the first release on Rabid Records was a
single by Slaughter and the Dogs. The sheer onslaught of punk rock
singles was about to start, coinciding with the appearance of the picture
sleeve. Surely the seven-inch single was the ultimate punk rock statement. Three-minute blasts of inventive fury from all over the UK,
bagged up in garish sleeves of switchblade art – punk rock made the pop
single cool again and the sleeve was the platform for some of the best
artwork ever in rock'n'roll.*

Knox

Because of our involvement with Chris Spedding from the 100 Club
gig, he brought Mickie Most down to the Lord Nelson to see us
play. The Vibrators were playing there on Tuesdays. He liked us and
asked if we wanted to do a single with Chris Spedding and one on
our own. So we recorded with Mickie Most. Some people said, 'You
shouldn't do that, he's a pop producer,' and punk was very anti-pop,
but other companies were not approaching us. Maybe because we
were slightly older than the other bands – and could actually play as
well. [laughs] Anyway we recorded 'Pogo Dancing' with Chris
Spedding and 'We Vibrate' as the Vibrators and they came out in
November '76.

They were some of the earliest punk singles. 'We Vibrate' was a
poppy kind of thing, but it was all right. The Damned's 'New Rose'
was out by then, so we were not the first. We went to tour Holland
and then came back to support Iggy Pop, who had David Bowie
playing keyboards for him – that was fantastic. We did six shows
round the UK. That's probably bigger than the Pistols at the time!
Iggy with David Bowie in the band – we had a 30-second soundcheck in the whole tour! They were very nice guys. It was just the
way it went, we recorded a new single with Mickie Most called 'Bad
Time' but it never got released. Our manager Dave Wernham found
a new deal with Epic, part of CBS. Mickie Most was a bit annoyed,

but it wasn't a very good deal we had with RAK. So we moved across to Epic and started recording our first album, *Pure Mania*.

Mick Rossi

That autumn we recorded 'Cranked Up Really High'. Martin Hannett did a great job of it. We recorded it very quickly – we did Wayne's vocals in the kitchen. It's one of those things where naivety is such a great thing – we didn't have an idea of what we were doing, of how to record. The great thing about naivety is you go off your instincts – that's why a lot of bands lose it in the end. There was no pressure. When you go in a real studio there is a lot more pressure. 'Cranked Up Really High' is about Wayne. He wrote the lyrics and I think they are great. Obviously a drug reference about cocaine... maybe a fantasy. [laughs]

STRANDED FAR FROM HOME
Punk Shockwaves Further Afield

Rat Scabies

One of things that made punk very valid was, when you consider the Saints were doing the same in Australia at the same time and the Ramones in New York, it was obvious that people wanted to do it all over the world. The Saints were totally removed from anything going on anywhere else. They couldn't get *Sounds* or *NME* in Australia. The synchronicity was amazing.[4]

Chris Bailey

The buzz about punk rock bands in those days was getting deafening, and we had stumbled into a scene that we had known absolutely

---

4. The Saints released a cool run of three albums: *I'm Stranded*, *Eternally Yours* and *Prehistoric Sounds* saw the band play blitzkrieg, righteously fast punk rock to buzzsaw guitars laced with Stax horn stompers. The three albums are great, but it is the Saints' three classic songs, '(I'm) Stranded', 'This Perfect Day' and 'Know Your Product', that make their very existence crucial, as they are some of the greatest songs of the punk era.

nothing about! The English record labels all felt that they should have their own punk rock band. Somehow EMI in London had picked up on our single and phoned EMI in Australia and told them to sign this band the Saints. Well, EMI in Australia had never heard of the Saints! And the ones that had heard of us wanted absolutely nothing to do with us! [laughs] We were looked on as some kind of joke band. So EMI in England signed us, which was almost surreal – this unheard-of band from Queensland getting a UK record deal!

Then in November they released '(I'm) Stranded' and sent us a bunch of money to record some demos. So we knocked out the whole album. It took two days to record at Windown Studios in Brisbane. We thought we were doing demos, and I discovered to my sorrow that the label said, 'That's your album,' and promptly put it out!

Eric Debris (Metal Urbaine: vocals)

In France it was pretty grey, nothing happening. People were going to work every day, there were old hippies wearing American gear, green or grey uniforms. It was boring. The whole thing was about who could play as many notes in one second, instead of music with emotion.

When we started in France there wasn't much music. Just music fading away from the Sixties. In France quite a few people were into the MC5, the Stooges and the New York Dolls, and that's why we started to play that kind of music. All these bands played in Paris, to a maximum of 1,000 people. It was the same as in England. Some of the people were into primitive rock music, music to dance to, to get drunk to, to fight to. We were about live music and not something to listen to at home making a joint. Most concerts at the time were people sitting on their asses. We wanted concerts with people standing up. The Velvet Underground started the punk rock scene in Paris. A lot of French people like myself were into raw American rock like them.

There were other bands around. Little Bob Story were more of a pub rock band like Eddie and the Hot Rods. They were rock but not exactly what we wanted to play. There was also the Stinky Toys who started out as a punk rock band, but for some reason said they weren't punk and went more pop. They were more cliquey, playing rich people's parties. Barclay Records was the big indie label at the time. We nearly signed to them, and they signed the Pistols early on as well. We started to rehearse in late '75 and work on the project properly in 1976.

We played a gig in December '76. The early gigs usually ended up with a fight with the audience after a few numbers. Most of the audience had long hair and there was an aggression towards our lifestyle. They wanted to fight with us, running to the back of the club. The funny thing was that the antagonistic people ended up within a month coming to gigs with their hair cut short and suddenly dressed up as a punk! But then punk rock had become more like a uniform.

There was a few bands in Paris like Stinky Toys and Warm Gun. There were maybe ten bands in Paris, but so few musicians that some were playing in three bands at the same time. At the time I was coming to London and it was similar to start with. The scene was small, active and visible. We were really different from other bands. We wanted to play something new and different using electronics and guitars. We were really into electronic music. We thought with synths you can do anything, you could do rock with a synth and a drum machine.

Brian Young

Fortunately for us, Belfast was blessed with Caroline Music in Anne Street, which was staffed by guys who kept the place stocked with all the vinyl you could want. I'd read Nick Kent's Ramones rave in the *NME* and snapped up one of the very first import copies they got in, and it floored us – here, at long last, was a band who wrote killer songs that were simple enough that we could play 'em, but sounded like nothing we had ever heard before! We started to play some of their stuff and it sounded pretty good, and I suppose it made us think about writing our own stuff.

Another big influence too was Eddie and the Hot Rods. Overlooked now by revisionist elitist scum, they were a damn fine band back then – and best of all they came here to play too. They were the first band I saw who wasn't all that much older than us, and again they made us think, 'We can do that.'

As in London, a lot of the early 'punks' were ex-Roxy Music trendy fashion victims who were that little bit older and had been to London and could afford the clothes. I doubt if many of them ever listened to punk music, and a lot of 'em had soon moved onto whatever trend was next off the blocks. Meanwhile the rest of us couldn't have afforded a single Sex/Seditionaries T-shirt between all of us and so it was DIY all the way. Sure, we all got it ever so slightly wrong, but in the process created something kinda unique and very special. Remember the plastic sandals, the cheesy plastic spex, the paint-splattered shirts and school ties, safety pins and paper clips… fun, huh? Oh and one girl here used a kettle as a handbag.

But unlike everywhere else, there was a real war in progress here. As a result, there were no safe city-centre venues as Belfast still closed down at nights. There were curfews in force and people were afraid to travel outside their own areas. Belfast is just so small that everyone knew if someone was an outsider – and if you were in the wrong area at the wrong time it could be very dangerous indeed. To make matters worse, most local clubs and venues were paramilitary-run and dicey at best. And there simply weren't *any* local bands playing anything apart from crappy cabaret covers and hard rock hippy drivel.

But that didn't deter us – and we played anywhere and everywhere we could. As no proper clubs or venues would book us, we hired dodgy function rooms in run-down hotels that sane people generally avoided, and staged our own gigs. We hired amps and tiny PAs, often carrying them to gigs on the bus, and borrowed and stole the rest. Grimmy stole boiler suits from work and we customised 'em ourselves, while two of our mates put together a light show of sorts (again obtained by dubious means). To everyone's surprise (including our own) we packed out these run-down dives and honed our chops in front of hundreds of paralytic teens, leaping about like nutters and employing every means at our disposal to disguise our musical ineptitude (spitting fake blood capsules, talc on the drums). There was no one here doing anything like us and we were the first and only remotely punky-style combo playing in Belfast for a very, very long time. We gradually ditched a lot of the older covers and started writing our own songs too, and as punk started to make real headway elsewhere word soon spread and people started to travel to our gigs from further afield – to get their very own fix of local punky mayhem!

Guy Trelford (Writer from Northern Ireland, author of *It Makes You Want to Spit*)

When punk first started to rear its ugly head in Northern Ireland circa '76, I was living away from Belfast and there was no way of knowing what was going on there, or in Londonderry, or elsewhere at that time. Me and a few mates who were into punk totally depended on the *NME*, *Sounds* and *Record Mirror* for news of what was happening in the punk world; and listening to the John Peel show was a must for keeping up-to-date with all the new sounds.[5]

Damian O'Neill

Feargal Sharkey was Billy Doherty's second cousin. Billy, Feargal, Mickey Bradley and my oldest brother Vincent went to St Vincent's – that's how they hooked up. Mickey and Vincent were best friends at school. John and me went to the grammar school. John quit grammar school after his O levels, and they all met at Tech College in 1976.

I wasn't in the Undertones at first. John and Vincent were at the same school and got a band together. They were playing

---

5. Peel's show on BBC Radio 1 morphed from post-hippie prog to punk rock in 1976/77 and flew the banner for a myriad of bands, giving a vital lifeline to a musical generation. Punk, of course, hardly got a look-in on the rest of radio – in fact most of the punk classics get far more radio and TV now 30 years later than they did at the time!

Beatles/ Creedence Clearwater-type of stuff, a lot of r'n'b – they were learning to play stuff like 'Badge' by Cream.

I came to the band late – the only reason I came in was poor Vincent was told to leave the band because he had not studied for his O levels! I think I was brought in because I had an electric guitar – they all had acoustics and bongos. We were mercenary even then! [laughs]

When I joined them, the first gig we ever did we played this school in front of a few hundred. Dr Feelgood were a huge influence and so were Eddie and the Hot Rods. Once I joined, those bands came along and we suddenly sped up songs we were doing because that was what Eddie and the Hot Rods were doing. They played in Ireland in '76. I was too young to go; my brother and Mickey went. They came back changed. The Feelgoods were on *Supersonic* or something like that in 1976 and they were different, amazing, especially Wilko.[6] He never gets the credit. We were in an r'n'b vein, doing lot of early Stones stuff, standards. Suddenly the Feelgoods came along and it all made sense – and Eddie and the Hot Rods doing 'Get Out Of Denver' and speeding it up – and our lives changed. It all coincided with punk really.

In summer '76 Mickey Bradley got the Ramones' first record as a birthday present. That actually was the first punk record we heard and that really blew us all away. The cover alone was enough! And there were no solos, loads of songs, the sound was amazing – that changed everything. It was, 'Fuck, we've got to sound like this!' It took us a while, though. We started doing Ramones covers.

John O'Neill

You had the pub rock scene in Britain, which was fine for a lot of 30-year-olds, and we were influenced by it – great but nothing new. And then you were reading in the *NME* about the Ramones and

---

6. *Supersonic* was a classic Seventies pop show made by London Weekend Television, showcasing many glam acts. It was produced by Mike Mansfield, whose catchphrase was, 'Cue the music.'

Television and Blondie. I thought, 'I'd love to hear what these bands sound like.' John Peel played the first side of the whole Ramones album all at once, which was unprecedented at the time – he never played a whole record like that on his show. And the whole side lasted about fifteen minutes, which was the same length as a Yes guitar solo! This was great. You wanted to be part of something here, you knew that the lyrics were clever and they acted like they were dumb – they were so perfect. Me, Damian and Mickey were aware when we heard the songs that you could hear a nod to Fifties girl bands and I loved all that. Despite sounding really new, the Ramones had a hint of tradition about them, a hint of classic pop.

The band was getting really good. I wasn't a natural like Damian: I couldn't get my guitar in tune, and my timing was always out. I started to write songs to make sure I wasn't kicked out of the band. The first song we performed live that I'd written was 'I Told You So', which was a pure Dr Feelgood r'n'b-type of song. And then basically we were using the Ramones as a template and their influences like the New York Dolls and the Shirelles, not putting in any fancy chords.[7]

Damian O'Neill

The next punk band we heard was the Damned with 'New Rose', then the Saints' '(I'm) Stranded' came out – that was another major seminal event for us, hearing that record.

Jake Burns

Once we heard punk, we thought we could play it. It was bizarre: one minute we're playing Rory Gallagher stuff and the next we're playing 'New Rose' by the Damned. We were reading about the punk thing and we were all listening to John Peel. We were aware that something was happening. It was a short step from listening to doing it.

---

7. The Shirelles were the first black American girl group to have a Number One in the USA, with 'Will You Still Love Me Tomorrow' in 1960.

We had a band called Highway Star. It formed itself, to be honest. It was myself, Henry, Brian and another guy. We were at school together. At the time I was the one who could play the best so I taught Henry the basics. We only had one original song and it wasn't that original! [laughs] It was a standard boogie thing because we had learned to play along with Status Quo kind of stuff.

We didn't play that many gigs at all. The whole thing was based around covers bands. You were expected to play two sets a night of three hours. We would set up and play a set and the owner would come up and tell us to pack up our gear and fuck off! That's my memory of it. And then Henry came along with the Dr Feelgood album and we started to learn some of their songs, and Eddie and the Hot Rods as well. And of course it's a short step a few months later to, 'Have you heard this group the Damned?' Henry was the first one to have heard any of the new stuff as it came out.

WHAT A FUCKING ROTTER
Anarchy on the TV

Punk was beginning to impinge on the national psyche with a flurry of TV shows. On 12 November Nationwide *showed a clip of the Pistols. A couple of days later they were filmed at their Notre Dame show for Janet Street-Porter's documentary on punk, also featuring the Clash and the Banshees, that was broadcast on the* London Weekend Show *on 28 November. It was pretty clear by now that punk was becoming an unstoppable force and was going to be big news in 1977. And the battering ram would be the Pistols' debut single 'Anarchy in the UK', which also appeared on 28 November, charting at the back end of the Top 30 before all hell broke loose.*

'Anarchy in the UK': the greatest debut single of all time? No contest. How many bands arrive sounding this fully formed, with this much confidence, bravado and sheer inspirational power? From Steve Jones' opening salvo of descending chords, to Johnny Rotten's fantastic

sneering vocals, this song is the perfect statement. Brilliant lyrics, a powerhouse rhythm section and a stunningly powerful piece of punk politics made this more than a normal single. 'Anarchy in the UK' is a lifestyle choice, a manifesto that heralds a new era, and it's a rock'n'roll song that still sends shivers down the spine and inspires revolutionary rock'n'roll fervour.

Colin Newman

I bought 'Anarchy in the UK' the day that it came out in the black bag. I was completely signed up for it. It was the clarion call of a generation. I also went out and bought 'New Rose' by the Damned.

Wilko Johnson

The punk thing emerged while we were in the States. I remember I came back home from America and Eddie And The Hot Rods' guitarist Dave Higgs came round my house and said, 'We did this gig the other night with this band the called the Sex Pistols,' and I said, 'Gosh, that's a fucking good name.' I just remembered the name. Then I was in a hotel room in New York and I bought an English paper. It was that one when they had been swearing on the telly.

Al Hillier

I had heard of the Pistols and the Damned, but in all honesty it wouldn't be till the Pistols appeared live on the Grundy show a few weeks after the Stranglers gig that Britain would be aware of the greater implications of this new phenomenon called punk rock.

That one of the defining moments in rock'n'roll is a bit of swearing on the TV says a lot about how square Britain was in the mid-Seventies. Punk was already doing nicely as a shock-horror cult and it had the talent to back up its sudden intervention in British youth culture. 'Anarchy in the UK' was in the charts and it looked like the movement was going to move quickly but at its own pace into the national pop-cultural zeitgeist. That was until the Pistols and some of the Bromley Contingent appeared live on the Bill Grundy show (actually only shown in London) and changed the course of pop music with a few swear words. Watching it now, 30 years later, one is struck by how tame the interview seems, how innocent the Pistols all look, and how lightweight the swearing seems. In fact the most shocking word is probably Steve Jones' use of 'rotter' – a word not used since then! But this was the moment when punk rock went mainstream and the generation gap widened in rock'n'roll. Up till then the Sex Pistols had been a notorious yet very underground phenomenon, a curio for the music press and bemused inside-page pieces in a curious national press, but now they were front-cover news. For many scene aficionados, this was the moment that punk rock died. For the band themselves, it was the moment they stopped being about music and became a media event.

Glen Matlock

We nearly didn't do it. Queen dropped out at the last minute and we got the slot. The limo came to our rehearsal room and we wouldn't get in. Malcolm said, 'You won't get a tour wage unless you get in.' We were just being stroppy and we didn't like being told what to do. We were rehearsing for the Anarchy tour and wanted to get on with that.

After the Bill Grundy show all hell broke loose, but that was because of the way Bill Grundy reacted to us. I heard that he didn't want us on the show at all and was told, 'If you don't do it you're sacked.' He though he'd be clever and take it out on us.

Steve [Jones] is an uncultured bloke! [laughs] And there he is he is on prime-time TV... I had my moments, but Steve is the main culprit. Steve is embarrassed about it now. He thinks that it was what broke the band up. It wasn't a band after that – it was a media-marketing exercise. It might be good for all you punks out there, a good story, but we wanted to play music and it drove a wedge right down the middle of the band. I thought it was funny, but what came afterwards was The End. We were getting followed by Fleet Street all over the UK.[8]

Steve Severin

Bill Grundy was the one who was really drunk. I don't remember any of us being that drunk – it was a bit of a laugh and didn't seem like a big deal. We went to the Hope and Anchor afterwards, didn't really think about it. My main memory of it was that afterwards Malcolm really panicked and said that the Pistols messed up, made it all look stupid, and I didn't agree. I said it was really good fun, a good laugh. The next morning I woke up and was astonished to see the papers.

Captain Sensible

After the Grundy show, apparently Malcolm McLaren was totally pissed off. Rotten said he was in tears. He said to them, 'That's the end of the band. Thank you for for destroying everything. No one will touch us with a bargepole now. You just fucked it up, thank you very much.' The next day all the newspapers went berserk and he realised he was in charge of the biggest band in Britain.

Marco Pirroni

They didn't ask me to go. I wasn't that in with them. I wasn't that in with the Bromley lot. I knew them and that was it. We were all quite snooty. They had grown up together.

I missed Bill Grundy when it was on television. I was on my way to Sue Catwoman's house in Ealing when it was on.[9] It was a Wednesday night and I didn't know they were going to be on telly. When I got there she was saying the Pistols had been on telly and there had been lots of swearing. Sid was at Sue Catwoman's house

---

8. The *Daily Mirror* led the feeding frenzy with its now classic 'The Filth and the Fury' cover. The punk rock horror cult that had already been covered on the inside pages by Fleet Street was now on the cover, and the confused, garbled message of punk rock was now in every home in the UK – even if most of them had never seen the Bill Grundy show.

9. Sue Catwoman's distinctive hairstyle, cut to look like a cat's ears, made her a punk icon, as did her dress sense. She was one of the very early faces on the punk scene and one of the first Sex Pistols fans, but disappeared to bring up her kids.

too. Sid didn't seem very excited. I think he started saying, 'This is going to be everywhere tomorrow.' He had seen it and sussed out the impact it might have, whereas I hadn't. They don't seem to be that pissed up on it – it all seems very natural when you watch it now. But the next day it was fucking crazy.

Captain Sensible

I'm pretty good at swearing. I could have done the Bill Grundy show on my own! [laughs] I come from Croydon. Me and Rat used to do this thing, especially when we went to the States – speaking in Croydon. When Croydoners speak, they actually talk for minutes without saying anything: 'This fucking cunt... no listen, you cunt...' and you get these Americans gobsmacked. 'What are you talking about?' I could have done that for Bill Grundy if he had asked.

Marco Pirroni

Suddenly punk's gone mainstream. I was a bit confused, then a bit 'What happens now? How do I feel about it now?' I was also happy that everyone knows what I've been going on about. The whole scene was completely underground before, ignored really. There had been a lot in the music press, it was starting to happen but, unlike now, the mainstream papers then wouldn't pick up on an underground scene. They didn't do that then. As an example of how underground it all was, I remember going into Lloyd Johnson's shop. He said, 'Guess what? The woman from *Vogue* came in here and has done a piece. She has also done the Sex shop and she didn't know anything about the scene. She thought the Bay City Rollers was the fashion of the street. She was a bit confused by finding this weird underground scene.' It was ignored. No one was interested, and then all of a sudden, bang! It went crazy.

Howard Devoto

By the end of 1976 punk started to get a strong style, when everyone was piling in after the Grundy thing, I suppose. That really gave it an impetus. That's when it went *wham!* across the tabloids and the lorry driver kicked in the TV.[10]

Tony D

I was talking about punk to mates in Cumbernauld, and most people didn't understand it. And then suddenly after Bill Grundy it's on the front pages. Punk was everywhere, but no one was any the wiser to what it was really about.

Kevin Hunter

Me and my mates saw Billy Grundy with the Pistols on. Two of us in the room were really into it. Everyone else was saying it was really crap. It really did split friends like that.

Don Letts

So punk rock got a reputation now. It's done the Bill Grundy thing, which I must say was detrimental to the whole thing. It created that tabloid punk rocker, which wasn't about punk. Punk would have broken without Bill Grundy. It just got to first base much quicker. I'm there at ground zero and see what's going on.

Rat Scabies

The Bill Grundy show created a lot of problems for the Pistols. First of all the Pistols didn't really know what they had done and everybody was going potty about it. Malcolm was all being very stressed about the whole thing. He didn't have any idea of what was going to happen next. The whole thing could have been bollocksed up. They were lucky to get the slot in the first place. They were meant to get Queen on the Grundy show and they had cancelled. They say you need luck in showbusiness! Then the whole 'Anarchy' tour, which we

---

10. Possibly made-up story in the daily press about a lorry driver who was so incensed by the Sex Pistols' language on the Grundy show that he kicked in his TV set in front of his young child. Strangely inappropriate behaviour in front of a minor, one would have thought.

were booked on as well, went decidedly shitty. All of a sudden the Pistols were front page on every red top, which was kind of fair enough, but what it meant was punk had become a very dirty word.

The notorious Anarchy tour, which was supposed to run from 3 to 26 December, was beset by problems from the start. Put together by Malcolm McLaren very much like a Sixties package tour, with the Clash, the Damned and the Heartbreakers boosting the Sex Pistols on their first major outing, it was an ambitious project. Before Bill Grundy, the Pistols had been playing tiny venues and word-of-mouth gigs. Now they were in the big venues, hoping that their debut single 'Anarchy in the UK' would be a hit.

It nearly was (it reached Number 38), but post-Bill Grundy everything was moving quickly into a very different area. Most of the tour was cancelled by shit-scared local councils and prissy student unions. Out of twenty or so gigs planned, only about seven went ahead, and some of those had been rearranged at short notice at alternative venues following cancellations. Venues they did play included a hastily-rearranged secret show in Norwich on 3 December, Leeds Polytechnic (on the 6th – which proved to be the Damned's only date on the tour proper), Manchester Electric Circus (on the 9th– there was no way Britain's second city of punk would back out), the Castle Cinema in Caerphilly (14th – footage filmed by Welsh TV shows carol singers and Christian pickets outside the gig), Cleethorpes Winter Gardens (20th) and the Woods Centre, Plymouth (21st and 22nd).

Meanwhile, the punk 'movement' was exposed as a sham as the Damned were thrown off the tour. The story went round that they had sold out by doing an audition for Derby Council on the 4th. They were replaced by the Buzzcocks for one show at Manchester's Electric Circus on the 9th.

Mick Jones

All the bands were at Harlesden rehearsing for the tour when the Pistols went off to do Bill Grundy. Then all hell happened. The tour started a couple of days later. All the bands met at Denmark Street and set off. It was meant to be a full tour of the UK, but there were hardly any dates left on it. It seemed like every gig we went to was cancelled! We ended up playing about four gigs altogether. [laughs]

John Lydon

In 1976 we tried to play around the country. That was the go-nowhere-and-do-nothing tour. We were banned from just about everywhere, in places like Huddersfield.

Bob Dickinson (Journalist)

There I was in Norwich, studying English at UEA, about as far away from punk as you could possibly get unless you were a grouse living in the Scottish Highlands. I was desperate to see the Pistols or the Clash or any of the punk bands we were reading about in the *NME*, but they all seemed to come from bigger cities like London, Manchester, Newcastle, Glasgow or Edinburgh. The one thing Norwich did have was a couple of good record shops so you could buy stuff on Stiff, Chiswick, etc., which began to move from pub rock to punk during 1976. And I was able to buy 'Anarchy in the UK' in a black sleeve on EMI the day it came out.

Then the tour was announced, and the posters went up around the university – printed black on fluorescent pink, you couldn't miss them – with the Pistols supported by the Clash, the Damned and 'from the USA, ex-New York Dolls' Johnny Thunders and the Heartbreakers. UEA was the first date. Tabloid headlines about the Pistols' appearance on Bill Grundy's Thames TV show very soon put the dampers on them playing concerts anywhere, however – I think the UEA authorities were the first to ban the band, and in protest a crowd of disgruntled students including me occupied the university admin block. But local councils all over the country mostly followed suit. The only thing left to do was secure some kind of souvenir, a piece of history, so I pulled one of those black and pink posters off a wall. And I've still got it, in a frame.

Not long after, in December '76, the Damned played at a local teacher training college. I was fascinated by how shocked the audience looked – I couldn't stop laughing. It wasn't as good as seeing the Anarchy tour would have been, by a mile, but it was the beginning of something.

Glen Matlock

My memories of the Anarchy tour? We sat in hotels eating fish and chips and not getting paid! Most of the tour was cancelled. We lost money on that tour. The Heartbreakers' phone calls to girlfriends back home cost us a fortune. We had to go through it, but it was a tough time. The band was split into three camps. John thought I was in Steve and Paul's camp, which I wasn't really. John wanted Sid in the band, a friend, because he was last in the band and felt like an outsider. It was all politics.

John was never the most chummy of people. Once Bob Gruen, the New York photographer, was doing a picture of us on Denmark Street and one of the Stranglers – I think it was J. J. Burnel – walked past and I said, 'Hello,' and John said, 'You don't talk to people like that, do you?' There was already that kind of thing going on.

Marco Pirroni

If you're in a band and you're on tour every day and it's a fucking disaster, it must be a total drag. I remember the Pistols going to do the Anarchy tour and it all being cancelled. I didn't go to the gigs after Bill Grundy. I stayed at home. I wasn't annoyed, not angry – I thought, 'I'll have to think of something else to do.' Without Grundy it would have been more musical, less outrage, but maybe it would not have had the impact – but even without Grundy they would have done something.

Rat Scabies

We were invited onto the Anarchy tour. We'd been out touring a lot, playing all these clubs and we had built up quite an audience. The

Pistols hadn't. Johnny Thunders, although people knew who he was, wasn't massive. Malcolm had been trying to put the Pistols' tour together for a long time. He'd been trying to get the Ramones over to tour with them, and then Patti Smith, desperately trying to put a package together. The Pistols were not big enough on their own by this time. The best they could do was with the Clash and the Damned pulling in punters. They never wanted us on. Why would they? The Clash were an unknown quantity at the time, and though the Heartbreakers were kind of heard of they were not that known.

Brian James

I thought the bands got on well. Then it got strange on the tour. There was all this weird stuff going down. Before we went on tour everything was normal. We'd seen everyone a few days before, and then the line checks in King's Cross were on the night the Pistols did the Grundy thing. They come back from doing that all jubilant and having a good time, saying, 'You won't believe just what happened!' They did their line check the next day. They were all big-time news, and Malcolm's keeping them away from the Damned and everyone else. I don't know what happened on the bus. We were all meant to be on the same bus with the Heartbreakers and the Clash and all that, but now there's a funny kind of feeling going on. The guy that was looking after us, Rick Rogers, said he was almost in tears deal-ing with the situation. He was an office boy from Stiff – in fact he later went on to manage Madness. He said, 'You wouldn't believe what was going on. They were having a right go at you when you were on stage.' So I went and saw McLaren, because he had the running order with the Pistols on top. We'd go on before the Pistols, and the Heartbreakers and the Clash would go on first. He was very aloof, and all of a sudden wanted to drop us to bottom of the bill. The only reason he wanted us on that tour was that we had previously played round England and built up a fanbase – Stiff sent us all over the place. The moment the Pistols had become hip and front page news McLaren thought, 'I can do what I want. I don't need the Damned anymore.' So we only did one show. He tried to put us down the bill and I said, 'Fuck you!' I wanted to hit him. If it hadn't been for Steve English and another bodyguard bruiser I would have had hit him. He called Steve over and I knew Steve but he weren't working for me, he was working for Malcolm. He was looking at me like, 'Don't do anything or I'll have to have you.' I had to swallow my words and that was it. Fuck 'em! No more gigs.

Rat Scabies

The other thing was the Pistols, Clash and the Heartbreakers were travelling on one big happy bus and stayed in big hotels. Jake was a bit more astute than that. He said, 'What we will do is go in this transit van and stay in bed and breakfasts and be independent.' Malcolm wanted Jake to pay half of the tour costs. We didn't have the money to do that and why should we? The reason we were on the tour was because we were going to help pull the crowd. Jake said, 'We will not pay half and we will travel separately.' Everywhere we went was journalists and police cars and people wanting to know what was going on and the whole thing turned into a farce really. I remember talking to Steve and Paul and they were genuinely pissed off with it all. The one gig we did was Leeds University and the Pistols were fucking awesome. I'd never seen them that good: Jonesey pulled out all the shots. They were absolutely pucker. The Damned, the Clash and the Heartbreakers, they were all good bands and everybody rose to it. Of course Malcolm turned all the lights on us and gave us half the PA. The problem was we didn't have Jake there with us. No one there to fight for us who knew how to handle those situations. So Malcolm outmanoeuvred us. I think it was at Derby, the second date of the Anarchy tour, where the council wanted the Pistols to audition for them. We were asked to audition and we said no, we wouldn't. They asked if the Pistols didn't play would we play, and we said yes, we would, because people had paid to see the Damned. That became misinterpreted as the Damned having sold out to the council and we hadn't. That's why we were fired.

I never really felt good about it. We used to hang out with the Pistols on Portobello Road. We would all go up there for beer on a Saturday afternoon and then go shoplifting. [laughs] We knew these people. What happened was it got very personal because of Jake and Malcolm. I think what was also going on was Malcolm had EMI behind him saying. 'Make these career moves,' and Malcolm was out of his depth.

Brian James

We got the shitty end of the shadooby for being the one that ain't solid with anyone else. I mean, what the fuck! You think the Damned would play in front of a load of councillors who might deem to allow us to perform?

Mike Thorne

Derby didn't hear music that night. The mayor and council had asked for a private performance so that they could judge whether to grant permission or not. With the tension building, I had to follow the bandwagon to Leeds. Although permission had been debated at length in the mayoral chambers, the first gig of the tour in Leeds had been given the go-ahead, and would be a resounding success. I vaguely remember the Pistols' performance, although it was the Damned who were the standouts that night.

Captain Sensible

I thought it was all going OK. We were all good chums. Steve Jones was a nice enough bloke, so were the Clash. Johnny Thunders and Brian James were getting on. It was the managers who were the problem. The other thing was all these other bands had big labels and the Damned had Stiff who didn't have two pennies to rub together, so we would end up staying in Mrs Bum's B&B. There's nowt wrong with that, but the rest of them were staying in swanky Holiday Inns so they were all together in one group – that was the start of the problem. When they had the meeting about us doing this fucking audition for the council to make sure we weren't punk monsters, decisions were being made in the hotel and we were not party to them. We were in the B&B watching TV at the time, so I really don't know what happened. I do really, though: Malcolm didn't need the Damned any more because he had the front page of all the newspapers, so he chucked us off the bill.

It was annoying because the idea of going up and down the country pissing people off seemed like fun to me... [laughs]

Brian James

So we were not part of the punk inner circle? I mean really! Who cares? I was still seeing Steve and Paul down the pub. The so-called inner circle, that was Malcolm and Vivienne and the posey ones that followed Malcolm.

Steve Diggle

Most gigs on that tour were cancelled. We played Manchester – we did the Electric Circus with them. It was all getting a bit mad. The Pistols were always into us, we always got on well with them. It's a weird thing: we started off with them at the beginning of punk, so there was always that closeness there, that punk rock feeling. The same with the Clash. The Pistols and Clash were maybe too close together in London; they were two sides of the town. They didn't see us a threat. We were from the North, not in their space.

I remember the Pistols at the Electric Circus gig. It was incredible, the electricity of the crowd. The vibe was amazing because it was all new; there was that shock value. They had come from nowhere and were seen as monsters in the press, like a threat to the whole world. Live, they were fantastic, from the first time seeing them at Free Trade Hall gig. They got the dynamic so right, with the massive Steve Jones guitar and a great rhythm section and Rotten sneering. Their attitude was so different from bands before, in that they were not trying to entertain you. They didn't give a fuck about anything. It was very inspiring. They broke down a lot of things, questioned things. They gave you some inner strength about yourself.

I remember Malcolm McLaren saying to us, 'Listen, you've got to sign while the going is good.' But we took our time. It was ages till the record came out. By that time there was Stiff Records and loads of people making their own records.

Clint Boon (Inspiral Carpets: keyboards)

A bunch of us went to Electric Circus on the Anarchy tour. It was amazing, full of punks and hippies. The Electric Circus had been a hippie rock venue up to that point, and started putting punk gigs on weekday nights. We went straight from art college. Thunders was first, then Buzzcocks, Clash and the Pistols, all for a quid. It was one of those moments where your life changes, and I knew that on the night. The only people I knew there, it had the same effect on them – we were friends with Phil Diggle (Steve's brother) – he was at the same college a year above me and he was tipping us to what's going on, telling us about Buzzcocks, his brother's band.

Rob Lloyd

You felt part of something, you know, like something was happening. I started going to London quite a lot then. Just hitching up and down the country to see people play. Somewhere along the line, I'm not sure how, I got a Sex Pistols T-shirt, the one with the naked boys all over it with Sex Pistols written on it. On one of my soirées to Birmingham Town Hall I went to see Ted Nugent, but he wasn't anywhere near as loud as he was meant to be, and his material was really shite. So again, yet another chance thing this is, I left my mate watching Ted Nugent and went to the bar which was completely empty apart for two geezers, normal-looking Brummie blokes, and they came over to me. They were really intrigued, saying, 'You got a Sex Pistols shirt on. What do you know about them?' They were a really unknown band then. They were going, 'We are the agents for the Sex Pistols. We book their gigs,' and I thought, 'You are talking bollocks! You've got a perm and moustache and are wearing glasses, they wouldn't have anything to do with you!' They gave me an address. They were called Endale Associates and they were the promoters in the Midlands area, and Ted Nugent was one of their gigs – the kind of thing they normally did. The Sex Pistols were getting banned from established places, and normal agents wouldn't touch them. They had an out-of-town agent.

When I turned up at Endale's office one day, lo and behold, they had not being lying to me. They were the Sex Pistols' agent! Which is why when you see the early Pistols gigs pre-making records, they were always playing Burton-on-Trent and Birmingham. They were organising the 'Anarchy in the UK' tour at the time. I went with Dave Crook from Endale to some of the gigs. He drove to most of them. So I saw them at Cleethorpes Winter Gardens and the Electric Circus in Manchester. The gigs were fantastic. You got the Clash and the Heartbreakers as well. With all the furore with the gigs being banned, it was very exciting, and because I knew the group I was not having to pay to get in. You could feel part of the whole thing. It was a fabulously exciting time for me. I was still a fifteen-year-old from Cannock.

One thing I remember about Cleethorpes is that I didn't look much different from what I look like now, pretty normal really, and there were these couple of greaser-type characters who tried to pick a fight with me, saying that I was a punk and they were Teds so there was going to be some trouble. I thought it was a fabulous time. The bands were getting better the more they played. Johnny Thunders was a bit of fruit loop, but a decent enough person to get on with. I thought the Heartbreakers were a shit-hot band, certainly live, but they made disappointing records.

Steve Diggle

By the time of the Anarchy tour there were punks everywhere. Because we were from the provinces it made people aware things were happening outside London. It was about Manchester. Later bands came from Liverpool, Sheffield – scenes started everywhere. In every town where there was a run-down club, there would be a punk rock scene. People would be glad you had turned up to places like Sands in Nottingham. All the kids around you were chaotic, people sweating, diving in a small club. It was a really exciting vibe, full of punks and they would all go crazy. For years before you never saw that. Between all those people this sort of dynamic energy appeared. It was phenomenal. It really opened your eyes to things.

Mike Thorne

I was around. It was a lot of fun. What I saw was journalism at its worst. They wanted to stir things up.

Rob Lloyd

It was a brilliant time. I lived the music and the rest of it. Me and a couple of other people, including Joe Crowe, we had a kind of pretend band together.[11] We got some songs. We hadn't got a drummer. We hadn't played a gig apart from playing someone's living room and I bullshitted like I was in a band, and people were interested, which amazed me. That was when I thought, 'This is going to be possible.' It was no longer a daydream to actually do it. There was talk of, 'Come and play with us,' that kind of thing.

Pauline Murray

The Anarchy tour was fantastic. The Pistols had really blossomed. By then they had built them up, they were getting big crowds. They were in the *Daily Mirror*, people had safety pins by then – they had become overground. A lot of the gigs on the tour were banned. We would get to places like Leeds, one of the few places that they

---

11. Joe Crowe met the Prefects on 3 June 1977 when his band the Motivators supported them at Barbarellas in Birmingham. Famous for turning up to rehearsals with his ubiquitous bag of Breaker cans, Crowe contributed to several Prefects tracks including 'Barbarellas', arguably their most enthusiastically received song. He went on to play in the early days of the Nightingales and had a sporadic solo career after.

The pretty boys of punk: Generation X risk critical mauling whilst cutting some classic punk rock anthems

played. We probably saw them two or three times on that tour. I don't think they played many more gigs than that!

Generation X played their first gig on 10 December at the Central College of Art and Design. Their second was on 21 December at the Roxy – the opening night of the soon-to-be-legendary punk club.

Andy Czezowski

Gene October knew this club on Neal Street which was known as Chaguaramas. It was owned by two queens – an early gay club. One of these was a barrister type just trying to make a quick buck. Gene had booked Chelsea to play at Chaguaramas and had mentioned this to me, so we went down to look at the club.

Don Letts

Andy Czezowski is the accountant for Acme Attractions. Punk explodes and the bands have nowhere to play regularly because of their reputation. There are no venues. Andrew sees a gap in the market. He goes to this old gay club called Chaguaramas which wasn't doing too well at the time. He takes it over and has the idea to make the first dedicated UK punk rock venue, the Roxy. Andrew sees the reaction I get from playing music in the shop, because half the reason that people come in the shop is word of mouth or because they would hear the basslines and that would drag them in – or because of Jeanette. Andrew asked if I wanted to DJ at his punk rock club. Luckily for me there are two decks in the Roxy.

Tony James

You can tell how close this was to us being in Chelsea, because it was Gene October who told us about the Roxy. The plan was to find somewhere in London where we could put on a gig, find our own place. We didn't want to play the Red Cow or all those other useless places like the Hope and Anchor. We thought, 'Let's find a place in Central London where we could maybe create our scene.' Gene October had told us about this club and me and Billy checked it out. For some reason Andy Czezowski is in the picture as well – he's managing Generation X. We go down to this club Chaguaramas at the beginning of November. The place is full of gangsters, hookers and gays. We speak to the guy and ask if we can do a gig here on the Friday. Two days later we are building the stage. I remember Barry Jones, who me and Mick had worked with earlier, went down and helped. His girlfriend was in the fashion industry and she lent us a load of material to hang behind the stage. We got Don in to be the DJ and you had a scene in about ten seconds, just like in a Cliff Richard movie! [laughs] We had a club!

Andy Czezowski

The owners at the time were skint so they let us book the weekdays. By the time the gig had come round Chelsea had decided on a name change and became Generation X, as well as kicking out Gene October – they put guitarist Billy Idol on vocals, which made sense as Billy was better-looking and couldn't really play the guitar. So the gig was now Generation X and Chaguaramas had changed its name to the Roxy.

Tony James

We rehearsed at the Roxy Club. We cut Derwood's hair at the Roxy Club as well. Within a week of Derwood joining we wrote 'Your Generation', 'Youth, Youth, Youth', in like a week, and went out and played really fast. John Towe was our drummer who came with us from Chelsea.

Generation X played the first night. The crowd was all punk, queueing round the block the first night. The Clash played there a week later – on 1 January 1977.

CHAPTER 7
1977 PART I: THE EXPLOSION

PUNK'S FIRST CLUB
The Roxy

And now punk had its own club. For 100 nights in the first three months of 1977, one pokey club in Covent Garden was the launchpad for a myriad of weird, wonderful and wild bands.

Andy Czezowski

I didn't manage Generation X for very long, but by then I was more interested in running the club, and for 100 nights the Roxy was *the* place in London. EMI gave us 20 grand and we recorded the *Live at the Roxy* album, which was a Top 20 hit.[1] We were the first club to have colour xerox flyers. I got Don Letts up from Acme to DJ there. It was a happening place. The Buzzcocks, Wire, X-Ray Spex all did important gigs there. The Clash gig on New Year's Day was so packed.

---

1. The *Live at the Roxy* album was the first collection of upcoming punk bands ever to get released and featured Wire, Eater, Slaughter and the Dogs, the Adverts, Johnny Moped, X-Ray Spex, the Unwanted and Eater.

T. V. Smith

The Roxy was like a little club in Covent Garden, nothing special. What was special was the core of 100 people who were down there. Everyone was vibed up, they wanted to do something. They were either in the band that was appearing or starting something. There was a definite feeling of a scene, but apart from that it was a dump with a terrible PA. Behind the bar you had a choice of two kinds of awful beer, Breakers or Colt 45, which was over-priced. You'd forever be trying to blag a free drink or find one that had been left behind.

We played the Roxy in the first couple of weeks it was open. It was open once a week before Christmas 1976, and then it opened regularly in 1977. We played twice in the first week.[2] John Towe, Generation X's drummer, used to work at the same rehearsal space as Howard, and he asked Andy Czezowski to get us a gig supporting them. I phoned Andy Czezowski about the gig and was expecting to have to give him a demo tape. He asked the name of the band and said, 'Yeah,' and gave us our first gig supporting Slaughter and the Dogs.

It moved so quickly: the Roxy club started and by coincidence we were playing the most happening place in the punk scene. It was a great time to be there.

Gaye Advert

The Roxy was great. It was very small. By then there was a crowd who would turn up. At our first gig we were playing to friends. There were lots of bands there. We were certainly watching a lot of bands the first time they got on stage, and when we played we saw all these familiar faces at the front and it was OK. The atmosphere was really good because you knew so many people. And there wasn't much spitting then. That used to piss me off later.

---

2. The Adverts' first gig at the Roxy was on 15 January 1977.

Steve Diggle

The spitting thing was horrible. I got one straight in my mouth doing backing vocals. Joe Strummer got hepatitis at one gig. Also when you were running your hand up your guitar neck and there was phlegm all over it... I always said, 'Save it for the Damned – the Captain will be here next week!' because they loved all that kind of stuff. Later on I hit someone over the head with a guitar. He had a big scar on his head. I saw him a few weeks later and he said, 'It's better than an autograph.'

T. V. Smith

A very mixed bunch of people went down there. There were people who got on with each other and other people who were a bit more aloof. I never once talked to any of the so-called Bromley Contingent. That was interesting, that people were coming from different angles. Punk rock was unformed – there was no name for it. We were not aware that we were actually in a movement. It was just a place that we could go to. Looking back now, Malcolm McLaren claims to have created a movement around his boys! On the other hand they were quite exclusive about keeping the Pistols away from the rest of punk. The Pistols never played down the Roxy. The rest of the bands were the ground over which the Pistols could be moved.

Stiff Records came down to see us. Jake Riviera and Nick Lowe were into the Adverts immediately. They offered to put out a single. Major companies would not go anywhere near it until they knew there was money to be made. It was not a hotbed of record companies down there by any means, till a few months later – and by then it was all over!

Charlie Harper

The whole scene was building up at that time, and the Roxy became the watering hole for all the degenerates, who would be down there shagging at the side of the stage. It was the sort of place where

The iconic Gaye Advert

anything goes. It was something that outside people never see – and never will see!

Ari Up

My mum would take me to the Vortex and the Speakeasy late at night where I'm not supposed to be.[3] I did ended up going to lots of clubs and of course I went to the Roxy.

---

3. The Vortex was the second punk venue, opened on 11 July 1977.

Poly Styrene

I met the journalist Jon Savage and he started taking me to see the Clash.[4] I lived in Fulham then and he took me to the Roxy with Falcon.[5] Jon introduced me and Falcon to the punk world. It certainly wasn't a world that I belonged to. I only went to the Roxy once, then I was playing the next week, I think!

The great thing about punk was that everything was independent. Before that there was only big promoters, there was no room for you. Before punk there was only the bourgeois life of other musicians; it seemed like they were very grand, reminiscent of classical musicians of the aristocracy of the French revolution period. They were getting married into aristocratic families and they were buying stately homes. At the time it was a bit boring. I was more excited to see these slightly wilder shows. I had missed out on Jimi Hendrix and he was already dead.

Noel Martin

When we saw the punk thing happening, and the kids were interested in dressing up and going to gigs, we thought we could be part of one big scene. We didn't need the promoters and the agents that we were kowtowing to. We can do our own thing for people that wanted this kind of music. There were loads of gigs going on and good audiences to play to every night of the week.

Before, you'd turn up at a gig and there would be loads of guys with tight red leotards on stage! Now we were all from the same thing – we could go down to the Roxy and play a half-hour set and be appreciated. It was our scene. It was great, the whole movement: make your own posters, photocopy any old bollocks and give it out to people, make your own music.

---

4. Jon Savage was a key journalist on the punk scene and author of the indispensable punk book *England's Dreaming*.
5. Falcon Stuart was Poly Styrene's manager. In the mid-Seventies he had made high art neo-porn films.

X-Ray Spex live out Poly Styrene's nightmare
vision of a plastic world becoming reality

Pauline Murray

We'd played about three gigs round where we lived, and then we played in London. Our very first London gig was at the Roxy.[6] We got in a furniture van and off we went! We were on with Generation X and the Adverts, and all the punks hung out there. People must have got to know about us because we'd get phone calls. We'd get the Stranglers ringing up saying, 'We're playing the City Hall in Newcastle – do you want to play with us?' Or the Vibrators would play Middlesborough and as there was no one else up here we would get the gig. The Buzzcocks, the Adverts, the Fall and what was to become Joy Division – we would play with them all. We would go to Manchester and play with the Fall. In Liverpool we played at Eric's. And we would go to London regularly.

Tony D

I was going up and down to London. I would finish work in Glasgow on Friday, take some London clothes and get changed at work, and go down to London on the Friday night bus. Get to London at six in the morning, hang around and then go to gigs. Suddenly it was all happening, it was all in technicolour. I'd go to the Roxy. It was all bondage clothes and make-up at a Generation X gig. I was at the Roxy a lot. I saw it change through a variety of owners till it eventually closed down.

Don Letts

I always moaned about having no records to play between the bands at the Roxy. The first thing I got, apart from Iggy, was the first Ramones album. Otherwise the records I could play were things like *Live at CBGBs*, the 101ers' single 'Keys To Your Heart'. Not much. I'd go to the record shop on Praed Street in Paddington. Later they would have all the punk stuff, but it was early in the day and there were no punk rock records yet to play!

---

6. Penetration's first gig at the Roxy was on 29 January 1977.

So I'm slipping in some Velvets, Iggy and the MC5, the Saints' '(I'm) Stranded', Jonathan Richman – all these things that people now know as the lineage of punk – but mostly I played dub reggae, because I couldn't play those punk records all night and I love dub reggae. As the bands started getting signed they did start releasing records – the Damned's 'New Rose', stuff like that – I started slipping them in, and the punks didn't want me to play them! They wanted me to keep playing the reggae. I soon realised that they were turned on by the anti-establishment vibe of the 'Burn Down Babylon' business. Obviously it was the basslines and the lyrical content that was turning them on, and the fact that these songs were about something. It was the ultimate rebel sound around. Some were inspired by it, like the Clash and John Lydon – they were already halfway there without my help, but also bands like the Slits were totally into reggae culture. The ultimate punky-reggae hybrid were the Slits, with their heavy bass, and they were eventually produced by Dennis Bovell of Matumbi.

This was white artists looking to black culture for inspiration. It was like Lennon/McCartney and Jagger/Richards in the Sixties. The difference with the punk lot was before this fascination with black culture was removed from the source – it was some sound coming from the Mississippi Delta. But Joe Strummer and John Lydon were digging sounds they could hear on either side of the River Thames. It was intravenous almost, not this abstract thing, and all this interaction got us to where we are today with multiculturalism. My parents' generation when they moved here tried to be like their hosts, but we were mixing it up and that made us closer. It was a prime example of cultural exchange.

I'd got the rest of my rasta brethren involved. I lived in a house in Forest Hill with five other rasta brethren: Leo Williams, who was later in BAD and Dreadzone, JR, Tony and my brother. We were really the staff, the doormen at the Roxy. Most punks couldn't make spliffs at the Roxy. I realised there was a gap in market, so a couple of us were making ready-rolled spliffs to sell behind the counter. I remember Shane MacGowan one day in the Roxy saying, 'Give me two beers and a spliff.' He paused for one moment, and said, 'Make that two spliffs and one beer.' There was a serious cultural exchange going on here! [laughs]

Punks got the reputation as the bad boys, and because of that the reggae posse can identify with them. The music they don't like, but the anti-establishment attitude strikes a chord. And I would take the punks to their parties in my capacity as reggae ambassador. I became friendly with John and Joe and Ari. And those three I would take them to serious reggae clubs like the 4 Aces in Dalston, where they got respect – 'Here's one of them punk rockers I've heard about.' They could see these guys liked their reggae and they liked that.

The DJ thing was funny.[7] I don't think I realised till years later when Jon Savage told me, that the reggae was a real welcome break from watching the live bands.

I liked the Clash, the Pistols, Subway Sect, Buzzcocks, Slits, Banshees – that's the ones that come to mind. I like bits of other bands, but most of the bands were rubbish. It was absurd. It was an excuse for people who shouldn't have been up there – they should have been in a nuthouse. Johnny Moped, he was straight out of *One Flew Over The Cuckoo's Nest*. Mind you, he was the exception: he was brilliant, there was a mad genius in there. I love Johnny Moped. But there was lots of rubbish up there.

Steve Severin

Everyone kept saying, 'Hurry up, the punk thing is really happening,' but we were not in a rush. We wanted to do it on our terms. The Banshees played our first gig in early '77.[8] We spent the whole of 1977 gigging. We couldn't get signed. There was a campaign to sign the Banshees – it was all hype and half-true. We did have a few offers, but people like EMI wanted to control the lyrics. [laughs] We wanted control.

---

7. It ran in the family: Don Letts's father, Duke Letts, had run a sound system.
8. As support for the Slits at the Roxy.

Nick Cash

Guy and I were working together when I was in Kilburn and the High Roads. We wrote 'I'm Alive' and 'Quite Disappointing', demo'd them and sent the tapes to record companies. The punk rock scene was now happening and all the record companies wanted to sign you, even Mickie Most! It was all the fucking songs that we had written and that they had turned down before! But because it was a happening sort of scene, all of a sudden they reversed their notion and rushed to us with their cheque books.

We played our first 999 gig at Northampton County Cricket Club.[9] We had an agent who used to do Kilburn and the High Roads. I approached him and he said he would work for us. That was the first gig he could get us. We played with this band called Stretch. They had had this hit so were doing all right at the time. We said, 'Can we use your PA?' and they said, 'No, you can't!' We had some speaker boxes and put them onstage and we sang through those, through our own amps, and because the kids were really into our kind of music we went down really well. The time was just right. People were pogoing about, going crazy. Stretch came on like big rock stars and people said, 'Fuck this!' which was good for us. We were a home-made band. We had the clothes and music right and a lot of the songs we still play to this day. As we started touring in places we smacked the audience round the head with our music.

ARE YOU READY
FOR THE 21ST CENTURY?
The Influential Wire

Fast forward to the future: Wire were one of the first bands to seize upon the possibilities of punk and take them somewhere else. They may not have sold millions of records but their influence has been every-

---

9. 21 January 1977.

where, from post-punk through to Britpop and even on American Eighties hardcore.

Colin Newman

It's a bit of weird story, how Wire got together. There was this guy called George Gill in my year at college. I'd been kicked out of home and had moved to Watford to art college and thought there would be loads of girls and I could get into a band. There was talk of this band doing a performance at the end of term. They said, 'We need a singer,' and I said, 'Well, I'm a guitarist and I've never sung in my life.' I got elected to be the singer and Bruce Gilbert was the guitarist beside George. We had a bass player, who was the film director Jack Good's son, John. He was a nice bloke but someone you didn't want to be in a band with. He was in a different place, but he had his own Messerschmitt (the car, not the plane!), which was good for transporting us around.

It was George's band. There were no doubts about it. He was the one who played the guitar solos and did all the shouting. Gradually we acquired a bass player and a drummer and started playing gigs, places like the Nashville and the Roxy, and people said we were rubbish. We were not getting invited back. The material was tedious, to be honest. George fancied himself as a bit of a poet, he drank quite a lot and he had a temper – it was a weird combination. I thought his songs were very average, even though we were putting layers of sound over it.

One day he was pissed and, making his way down the stairs, fell down and broke his leg. We started rehearsals without him and, boy, was that an improvement! Suddenly it was more stretched, more how we wanted it. We were playing the same songs but without the guitar solos, without the interjections and the songs were getting shorter. We did a gig at somewhere like the Roxy, and a friend said, 'You've got to get rid of George. It sounds way better without George.' We said, 'But he writes the songs,' and he said, 'Well, you can write songs.' And I said, 'Of course I can,' and Graham said,

'12XU' sang Wire, as they kissed punk goodbye
and went in search of new soundscapes

'Well, I can write words.'[10] We started playing. Suddenly the band was liberated.

George came back, did a couple of gigs and we sacked him. I had to move. I lived in his house and it was absolutely uncomfortable. I moved to a very rough squat in Stockwell. It was decided it would be better if I sang, rather than played guitar and sang. It would look more cool and I could perform in a more effective kind of way. I taught Bruce all the guitar parts, so I could be free to do the kind of weird jerky movements.[11] I was like the producer and the performer.

The first thing that was recorded was our tracks on the *Live at the Roxy* album at a gig at the Roxy in April 1977. We played half old stuff and half new stuff in the set. There was a very interesting combination of material already. By that point we were playing 'Lowdown' and 'Three Girl Rhumba' – well-known signature Wire pieces – and still doing a couple of George's songs because George had only left days before. So we got half the album there already written.

Every band that was on the *Live at the Roxy* album came in to meet EMI, and some of them were invited in for a further discussion.[12] We were told right at the beginning that we were definitely one of the bands who had been spotted.

The Sex Pistols were a classic generational-signifier band. They were like the Rolling Stones. Those bands are a huge leap in importance – they have a legacy that goes on, but they may not last that long. It's the sound of a generation. Whereas we were not that, perhaps we were where it was all going next. That was what was being said really early on. Maybe like Pink Floyd had come in as weirdo hippies and had turned into the Radiohead of their generation.

---

10. Graham Lewis, bass guitarist for Wire.

11. Bruce Gilbert, Wire guitarist.

12. The two Wire tracks were '12XU' and 'Lowdown', which already showed the band utilising punk for their own ends. Whilst the former is a jerky neo-punk anthem, the latter is a slowed-down darker piece, a very early precursor to the post-punk scene led by the likes of Joy Division.

[laughs] That's why EMI signed us. But times change and I think that was a big miscalculation, and no one understood the change of mentality in the Seventies. Music did not become more experimental and more open and that didn't help us.

The saddest thing from a musical point of view was the lack of individuality. The Pistols' album was an absolute classic rock'n'roll record. Unfortunately the only band who I thought were really doing it were the Buzzcocks – 'Spiral Scratch' was so interesting, it had a completely other kind of feel to it. It didn't sound like a rock record. It wasn't trying to sound like an American band, or the Faces. It wasn't Sixties. It had a hard edge and was really fast and really exciting.

TIME'S UP
Buzzcocks Mark II

The Buzzcocks' 'Spiral Scratch' appeared on 29 January, a four-track seven-inch first released on their own label, New Hormones Records. By the simple act of putting out their own single, the Buzzcocks pretty well inspired the DIY ethic of punk rock record labels, as well as releasing one of the classic punk singles: four sets of great lyrics from Howard Devoto sneered over ramshackle, catchy-as-fuck songs that somehow sounded utterly original, produced by Martin Zero (Hannett). One track, 'Boredom', is an instant punk classic.

Steve Diggle

We wanted to make a record to give out to people who came to our gigs to take home. We wanted to do it ourselves. Imagine going to London cap in hand, tongue hanging out, asking some fucker in an office if they would put your record out? It was all Billy Joel West Coast radio stuff, lots of dead music about – music to pacify people.

When we went in to do the recording, we realised it was only £500 to make a single, not half a million pounds. We could make

1,000 copies – it was an amazing revelation. It seemed so weird at the time. That really opened things up. Our first recording session was at Loft Studios in Manchester in late October 1976. It was an afternoon banging the songs out – we recorded loads of stuff.[13] Andy Macpherson had an eight-track at the top of his house – it was like a sort of do-it-yourself studio. We just played loads of songs one after another. No overdubs. We had to carry all the gear on the bus – it was a nightmare. You wouldn't dream of hiring a van then.

We went back into another studio near Granada TV with Martin Hannett and we did 'Spiral Scratch'.[14] The engineer was getting it right and Martin Hannett was mixing it. We recorded in the corridor, not in the proper area. It was a totally unorthodox approach. It's got that unique sound. It just happened there on that day. When people heard it, they had never heard anything like it, but it was powerful. It had the spirit of punk – it sounded a bit rough, unpolished. It really opened the doors for us and made people aware of what punk was.

Geoff Travis at Rough Trade said he would put it in shops – he said they really liked the record and asked if we needed any help to distribute it.[15] It then started selling. We didn't expect it to take off like it did. We were living for the moment.

Keith Levene

The Buzzcocks were fucking under-rated! Maybe they chose the wrong name or maybe my perception of them is wrong. I think they should have been bigger. I don't get it. All that buzz about the

---

13. The Buzzcocks recorded their whole set in the session at Stockport's Loft Studios. Eleven of the twelve tracks were later released on the semi-official *Time's Up* album.

14. 'Spiral Scratch' was recorded three days after Christmas 1976, at Manchester's Indigo Studios.

15. Geoff Travis is one of the important figures in the UK. His Rough Trade shop was one of the key conduits for the early punk singles; Rough Trade distribution virtually set up the network for the avalanche of post-punk records; and the Rough Trade label released a classic selection of music like Stiff Little Fingers, the Raincoats, the Pop Group, Swell Maps, Pere Ubu, the Smiths and the Fall – a one-label documentation of the punk generation. Currently involved with the Strokes, Travis and his cohorts are still very much hip to what's going on out there.

Manchester scene and everything. Look at Oasis – what did they ever do? Why can't the Buzzcocks be as big as Oasis?

Steve Diggle

When Howard left it was a bit of surprise to me and Pete. We used to rehearse at Howard's house sometimes and we were sat down in his living room and he opened the door and said he was leaving the band – which was a shock! We had only done a few gigs really. He was still doing his degree, it was his last year, and he wanted to finish that off. He said, 'I've done what I wanted to do, which is to make a record. Now I want to leave.'

We looked at each other and said, 'Well, let's carry on.' He was separate from the rest of the band. He never used to go to the pub with us – he was boring like that! [laughs] No disrespect to him, he was great. I'd also just written my first song, 'Fast Cars', for the band. They had 'Orgasm Addict' when I joined. I left the verses of 'Fast Cars' at home, so they re-wrote them. I did that with 'Promises' as well: that was a socio-political song when I wrote it, and it got turned into a fucking love song again! [laughs]

In a way, as much as it was good for Howard to start the band, it was better when he went. If he had carried on I don't think we would have had the Buzzcocks that would have had the hits and had that kind of sound. It meant I could move over to guitar from the bass – that was good for me. It meant that me and Pete could have intertwining guitars, which was important.

Howard Devoto

I announced it on a New Hormones press release dated 21 February 1977, with a headed statement.[16] When I read my leaving statement recently I thought, 'What did I mean by that?'

---

16. The press statement read: 'I don't like most of this "New Wave" music. I don't like movements. Despite all that, things still have to be said. But I am not confident of the Buzzcocks' intention to get out of the dry land of "New Wave-ness" to a place from which these things could be said. What was once unhealthily fresh is now a clean old hat.'

But I didn't regret it for a moment. People still think I temporarily lost my senses. I still sense this 30 years on, that people can't quite accept why I left.

Pete Shelley

Howard goes off and does his stuff and I do mine. It was very simple. It seems strange how we got together and how we thought the impossible was possible.

Steve Diggle

Howard left, so it was up to me and Pete to get on with it. We got Garth Smith in on bass.[17] The standing joke in the band was that we were always trying to find him – we wondered if he would turn up at the gigs. He was a school mate of Pete Shelley's. He was fucking massive, he towered over us! [laughs]

We still rehearsed at Howard's house after he left. I lived in Moston at that time. I would get the bus to Howard's to rehearse and it would take about four days to get back [laughs] – the buses were dreadful. Sometimes me and Garth stayed in the pub and ended up at the Electric Circus instead of going all the way back.

Colin Newman

I remember the day Howard Devoto left the Buzzcocks – in the arrogance of youth I thought, 'That's it! No competition now!'

I still don't get why he left the band. They were so much weaker after he left. Pete Shelley, I can imagine he is a lovely guy, a very likeable kind of person. He's definitely got intent. After Howard left they became so much more lightweight. I think Shelley and Devoto were a really interesting combination.

---

17. Garth was the same ex-school mate of Pete Shelley's who had played the Buzzcocks' debut gig the previous March.

Howard Devoto

Me leaving the Buzzcocks was very liberating for Pete in that he could write much more like that. He's got that fantastic facility with melody.

After I left I was still helping out the Buzzcocks. I still continued to stick the 'Spiral Scratch' sleeves together and get the record ordered. I went down to the Harlesden to see their first gig without me a few weeks later.[18] I was really still quite involved with them, trying to get them a record deal. I can't remember the point at which we started talking to record companies. Maybe they ran into somebody who said something and they decided to get in touch. I would call them up from Manchester thinking, 'OK, they must have heard of us by now! Want to talk about anything?' I was very involved. I was the co-manager.

Even at that early stage, I was interested in management. In a way we were already doing that kind of thing from the start. We'd been promoters, organised the gigs, made the single. In those early stages when you are a band, you can't afford roadies, a manager – you're lucky if you've got anybody. You've got to do everything yourself. Managing yourself is quite counter to what your image is supposed to be, the 'I'm above all this', 'above the practical world' musician attitude – or if you're a punk you're so fucked and anarchic that you can't be bothered with that sort of shit.

PRETTY VACANT
Glen Matlock Leaves the Pistols

The Pistols went back on the road in the New Year after the 'Anarchy' non-tour, travelling to Holland on 4 January. The press reported that the Pistols 'spat, vomited and swore' in the terminal building at Heathrow. It was more sensationalism, but enough to give EMI cold feet and they

---

18. This was at Harlesden Coliseum, supporting the Clash, on 11 March.

*dropped the band, also ordering pressing plants to stop pressing the
'Anarchy' single. Within a couple of weeks A&M had signed them and
EMI had given the band a big pay-off. In February, the gap between John
Lydon and Glen Matlock widened whilst Sid Vicious claimed that he had
been auditioned by the Pistols. On 28 February, Glen left the band and
was replaced by Sid. Musically for the band it was a disaster, but it did
create punk's most enduring icon: Sex Pistol Sid Vicious.*

Glen Matlock

John had become very difficult to deal with. We went to Holland.
We couldn't play anywhere in England. Some of the press was made
up a little bit as well – they would print anything about us. There
was an element of truth in some of it. The song 'EMI' came out of
that period and the 'Rich Kids' song – I wrote that at that time
as well.

Also round about that time I went out to dinner with Mike
Thorne from EMI, who said, 'Look Glen, we know what's going on
with the band.' He knew I did the tunes and he said, 'If the Pistols
doesn't work out we would be more than interested in helping you
out.' In the back of my mind all my arguments were not being
backed up, and I knew I had an escape route. When you're nineteen
years old things seem to be more trouble than they are.

John Lydon

Sid Vicious' name came from Syd Barrett. It came from early Pink
Floyd and a pet hamster – that's not great, is it? Sid Vicious, the
king of the punks, coming in second to a hamster and a Pink Floyd
reject. How come this wasn't noted as being hysterical and funny at
the time? Sid himself got it, and he found it always hysterical.
People would have him down as this violent lunatic – the boy
couldn't fight his way out of a paper crisp bag. The irony of that
was brilliant for a while.

Sid became an icon, and that was delicious. That kept those
arseholes away from me, and I could go on and do what I really

wanted to do, and I didn't have that lot saying 'sell-out', 'cop-out'. That's hilarious to me, really. I still get that from punk imitators. I'll be sat in the pub and one of them walks in and he's wearing £500 bondage pants and a $2,000 leather jacket and he tells me that I'm a sell-out. [sneers]

PLAY IT AT YOUR SISTER
More Firsts for the Damned

18 February 1977: The Damned release Damned Damned Damned *– the first punk album. It's one of the great rock'n'roll records, easily up there with the Stooges and the MC5 as an adrenalised rush of great primal sound that perfectly captures Brian James' much vaunted rock-'n'roll vision. James' guitar playing is phenomenal, whether it's the fast-riffing chords or those furious guitar solos. His songwriting is spot on, and the album is stuffed with great tracks, including two stone-cold classics, the singles 'New Rose' and 'Neat, Neat, Neat'. The rest of the band are bang on as well: Sensible's booming violin bass powers the*

The Damned take punk rock to the street; the next time they would bring their guitars as well

tracks along and Rat Scabies' drums are an incredible barrage of sheer power – it's one of the great drum performances on any British rock-'n'roll record. Frontman Dave Vanian is not slacking. His neo-vampiric Iggy/Jim Morrison croon makes its ghostly mark on the album, proving that punk could be sung with more than a sneer, and opening a door for the goth movement to come. A classic.

Captain Sensible

To be quite honest I was surprised that anyone liked the album! Not that I didn't like what we were doing – I just didn't think anyone else would. The reaction we were getting at the Nag's Head in High Wycombe was not necessarily any indication we were going to make a career out of it! And my picture was not on the back at first. I thought, 'If this is the only album I ever make, I might as well get my picture on it!' I was on the front cover all covered in gunk so you couln't see my face and not on the back cover – I had got my back to the camera. I thought, 'Bollocks to that!' so I went straight to Paddington Station and got some passport photos taken, cut them out, gave them to the bloke who was doing the artwork, and said, 'Stick that on the monitor.' I can't show my auntie Sadie the album and say, 'I'm on this.' She would say [Scottish accent], 'Oh Ray, you can hardly see your face on the picture!'

February 1977: The Damned tour with T. Rex. Marc Bolan was not only one of the key influences on punk rock, but one of the few pre-punk rock stars to champion the new movement. He name-dropped the upcoming bands in interviews, and he also featured several of them on his Marc TV series screened in 1977. Add to this taking the Damned out as support on his tour to promote his final album Dandy in the Underworld *– a risqué move in the context of the furore about punk rock. Unfortunately Bolan's comeback was tragically cut short later in the year, when he was killed in a car crash. It would have been fascinating to see where he would have gone next – one of the great genius talents of British music cut down in his prime.*

Rat Scabies

I liked the idea of doing the Bolan tour. First of all we were competing in the big market, playing with the big boys. I quite liked Marc as well. Me and the Captain reviewed the singles with him at the *Melody Maker* with the journalist Caroline Coon. He was a really sweet nice bloke: 'I am the godfather of punk,' he used to say [laughs] and in some ways he was right. It was nice to do that tour. He let us travel on the bus with him.

Captain Sensible

I was a fan of T. Rex while I was working at Fairfield Halls. T. Rex played and had all these screaming girls. It was 95 per cent birds in the audience. 'Blimey,' I thought, 'I'm only a toilet cleaner. That seems like the kind of job I would like!' [laughs]

Marc Bolan was still getting that audience on the tour we did. He was married by then and the rest of his band were accounted for, so your old mates the Damned did quite well on the bird front! [laughs] The only problem we had on the whole tour was, because Bolan was so nice to us, he let us travel on his bus and all that stuff – there was no starriness, no aloofness – and we'd get these birds on the bus and kiss and cuddle at the back, and Marc said, 'It's great you're pulling these chicks, man, but you know when you're finished with them, no disrespect, but they are using you to get to me.' I said, 'Oi, what you talking about?' but I suppose he had a point. So he told us not to bring any more birds onto the bus.

It was a fantastic tour. One minute I've got a bogbrush in my hand and the next I got a guitar in my hand and I'm tour with Marc Bolan, and your love life improves – put it that way.

Rat Scabies

It was towards the end of his career and there were still hundreds of girls leaving notes for Marc on the windscreen. What happened was a lot of younger fans got into us. Some of the band were quite cute – Brian and Dave were good-looking boys and that helped. I always thought it was a brave step for Marc to put us on. I was homeless at the time as well, so it was great to have hotels to live in – you didn't have to tidy up.

Captain Sensible

T. Rex went through a period of stagnation when Marc was indulging. He went through a creative slump. But by then he was back on form. He used to wear a tracksuit and go jogging. Whilst you were eating egg and chips in Watford Gap services, you would see Marc Bolan jogging round and round past the window every minute and a half – 'Here he comes... there he goes!' He was playing good guitar and playing all these weird electric versions of 'Debra' and 'Get It On'. The band was raunchy, he was sounding good, and the next minute he had a car crash.

The Damned were the band that did everything first. And touring America was no exception. With a handful of dates in April, they took British punk rock to the States. And on their return they immediately set off on a UK tour, starting at the Roundhouse in London on 24 April.

Brian James

America was fun. New York was great – there was a scene with the Ramones being from there. Everyone came down to the gigs. The Dead Boys supported us – that was where I met Stiv Bators.[19] New York went well. Then we went to the Rat Club in Boston, and that was weird. We did one show at about eight and a late one at eleven – we couldn't believe the first lot were sitting there eating pizza, so we took the pizzas up on stage for the second show. We hit a chord or two and grabbed the pizza and chucked it at them and then they got up and got into it a bit. Some walked out, and the ones who stayed had a good time.

---

19. Brian James would later form the Lords of the New Church with Stiv Bators.

Captain Sensible

The first gigs we played were in New York – they got it to a certain extent. When you played out of town a bit, it was a bit more difficult. We gave them the full-on thing – there was a lot of shouting between the audience and the stage and vice versa.

The American scene was different. A lot of the American punk scene was more drug-fuelled. We were very much not into that – maybe a little bit of speed, nothing heavy. People would occasionally give you white powder and it would end up not being sulphate – that happened at that incident at Mont de Marsan festival that August. That was angel dust, your honour... [laughs]

Rat Scabies

With the Damned, the old saying 'The pioneers get the arrows and the settlers get the gold' rings true. We went out there thinking New York was *the* happening place. We got there and didn't realise it was as much of an art scene as it was a music scene. There were a lot of people who wore spandex. When we got to CBGBs they had tables and ate their dinner as they they watched bands.

Captain Sensible

I got on well with all the bands all except for Patti Smith. In those days you get the band on and then the venue would chuck the audience out and get another band. Weird really – that's how they did it in America. We were putting our feet up having a drink after the gig – you'd get a few cases of beer and there is no way you're going to shift me out of dressing room until all the beer has been drunk! [laughs] After the gig Patti Smith comes marching in and goes, 'Get your asses out of here you limey assholes', or something like that, in the spirit of punk rock and all that, and I thought, 'Nice one,' and told her her to fuck off, then her people told us to fuck off as well, and there was a bit of a stand-off. So bollocks to her as well! [laughs]

Brian James

We were not known at all in America. They had 'New Rose' in New York, where it was on the jukebox in Max's Kansas City – it was a bit more hip there. When we got to Los Angeles, where we were meant to be doing a double-head with Television at the the Whiskey, they wouldn't let us play so we had to find another gig. The first time in Los Angeles was like walking into a movie – as a movie fan it was really cool, but there was no scene. It was mostly English people at the gigs – some were Jake's friends – and it was kind of a wasteland on the radio. All the time you would hear the Eagles or Supertramp, all that crap. It was like nothing had been going on in London for the last six months. Then we went to San Francisco which was really good – they were really into it. Mabuhay Gardens was cool – people were obviously well into punk or rock'n'roll.

I think the album was never released properly in America till about two years ago. What we liked about Stiff was the people that worked there and the musicians that were on the label and around, like Lemmy, and Larry from the Pink Fairies. It was like a social club as much as a label. I hated the business side, but Stiff was great. But at the same time there was no money around and you were riding around in shit vans and sleeping in shitty bed and breakfasts, and you saw the record ain't out there and the distribution is not right. But the thought of going from Stiff to a big record company, dealing with suits who might as well have been flogging material – we didn't even consider it. People were always hanging about who wanted to sign us.

Captain Sensible

We played the Roundhouse with Motörhead and the Adverts. To play the Roundhouse meant something to me. I'd seen all my heroes on those stages, the Pink Fairies and all those bands. It's a tragedy what happened to the Roundhouse.[20] I remember this hippie bloke

---

20. It was shut down as a venue in the late Eighties.

The charismatic T.V. Smith in full flight

Jesus always dancing around like a loon. When we played I couldn't believe he was still there – what a great eccentric.

Rat Scabies

The Damned was always the real thing. It was exactly what it said on the tin. We were all genuine, from the psychotic Captain to Dave who would always look like that – no matter what time of day or night, he would always look like Dave Vanian. That was his complete lifestyle.

The Adverts were really great. They had brilliant songs. That was a great tour. It was kind of also the last time the Damned were a proper band. It unravelled after that.

Gaye Advert

It was a very long tour. It zigzagged all over the country and what we referred to as *Sun* readers would turn up to fight. Lincoln was the worst – we had to barricade the door. You could hear them trying to batter the door down. They slashed our tyres – it was all they could do. The idea of something like punk rock coming to their town seemed to annoy them. It was weird, the violence in those days. Tim got beaten up by Teds in Hammersmith when he was on the way home. Out of the blue this guy just jumped him for being a punk. This guy was really young. I bumped into him the next day – he came up to me and said, 'Oi, it was me who beat your friend up.' I said, 'What did you do that for? That was a bit stupid.' He said, 'I'll tell my mates to leave you two alone in the future.' He said, 'Some punks had beaten up my mate.' I always used to wade in. I was harder than my male friends. It was the same back in Bideford. It was skinheads and hippies then – I would have to drag them off.

We were on tour a lot during punk, which seemed a shame! We missed eveything. I was reading the gig guides and there was nothing we could go to because we were always on tour. I was praying nothing important came up during a tour! [laughs] I did enjoy playing, but I was never naturally the sort of person who wanted to be on a stage.

Captain Sensible

The Bolan thing had been marvellous: a lot of his audience went along with the Damned, and a lot of our audience will always love Bolan. The tour worked for some weird reason. But the Adverts thing was the first proper punk tour – we all learned a lot on that.

Brian James

We had a lot of fun with The Adverts. They were great people. It was a shame that Howard passed away, he was a sweet, sweet guy.[21] That was was a fun tour.

22 April: The Adverts release their debut single 'One Chord Wonders', the title being the original name of the band. This classic showcased T. V. Smith's voice, his witty, cynical lyrics, and his knack of writing catchy songs. The Adverts were the one of the first bands to sign with Stiff, following hot on the heels of the Damned; their first recording is now regarded as one of the greatest early UK punk singles.

---

21. Howard Pickup, the Adverts' guitar player, died in 1997.

T. V. Smith

In March 1977, within three months of our first rehearsal, maybe a little bit longer, we were in the studio. That's the way – get on with it! We could play well enough to get the songs over and give it some stick. We were not holding back. We went to Pathway and recorded it there.

There was a very exciting scene round Britain by that point. It was bit corny – people were learning about punk through the media. The first gig with the Damned was in Retford – it was straight into a packed-out club.[22] There was a blistering performance from the Damned. Both bands were trying to outdo each other and the audiences were going wild. All the venues were full every day, the audiences were going nuts. Maybe we were not playing to the technical proficiency of ELP, but the gigs were more than exciting.

Gaye Advert

You forget how completely poor you were in those days. We used to go and see the Stranglers a lot – they played every week at the Nashville. They were great. I wanted my bass to sound like Jean-Jacques Burnel's. He was brilliant. We lived in Hammersmith then. If we walked there we could afford one beer. If we got the Tube we could not afford a beer – that's how it was. We were still poor even after the hit. I had the one pair of jeans, with a monthly trip to the laundrette!

T. V. Smith

Soon after 'One Chord Wonders' came out on Stiff Records, Michael Dempsey started getting involved with the band. He was a book publisher who was interested in what was going on. He was a very creative person, very excited about this music scene that was going down the Roxy and he really got involved with us. He

---

22. 13 May at the Porterhouse, Retford; the two bands toured the UK together till the end of June.

wanted to protect us from getting ripped off but he didn't want the role of being the official manager and he never did. We never had a proper contract with him. He took on the role really to keep us from the sharks, which he knew would be swimming around pretty soon. He took us off Stiff and tried to get us a major deal. We signed to Anchor. They had US backing and could get us into the States, and Michael saw that as something that would have to happen for the band.

Lyrics are one of the main things that inspired me to write. The music gave the lyrics more depth, more emotional charge. Most of the songs were commenting on what was going on round me, and that's what I continue to do. 'Gary Gilmore's Eyes' was the exception. The song was a reaction to the media blitz on him, the tawdry case going on in America. I reacted to it by putting together a horror-comic version of what was going on.

A bit like Morrissey, my lyrics always seem to be miserable till you get inside them, then you realise that they are actually quite funny, trying to criticise what was going on with a twinkle in the eye.

Unfortunately before we had released the album Anchor withdrew funding from us and they decided they didn't like this punk rock thing, and put all the money into the Average White Band, and that left us stranded.

Ian Brown (Stone Roses and solo: vocals)

One of the reasons we got John Leckie to produce the first Stone Roses album was because of the Adverts LP he produced. It still sounds great, doesn't it? It didn't matter that the band could hardly play – it was all about attitude then. I met that T. V. Smith the other week at the airport in New York – really nice guy, still doing it, still out there, still believing. They were great. The first single I bought was 'One Chord Wonders'. I never met Gaye Advert. I asked after her. I had a picture of her on my wall when I was a kid – she always very cool-looking.

AN ALTERNATIVE ULSTER
How Punk Changed Northern Ireland

Very quickly punk took off all over the UK. In some cities the scenes were small, in some really buzzing and in Northern Ireland, with its heavy political situation, all the loose talk of politics took on a whole new edge.

Guy Trelford

Belfast had been a dead city until punk gave it a good kick up the arse. There was little or no entertainment, no rock'n'roll! No bands wanted to come here and who can blame them? So the kids had to do it for themselves. Rudi paved the way and other bands followed by example: the Outcasts, Protex Blue, the Batteries, Victim, while up in Derry the Undertones were doing much the same thing. Word started to spread about these small low-key gigs through early fanzines such as *Private World* and *Alternative Ulster*. Something positive was happening; kids weren't content to sit and wallow in the depths of unemployment, they weren't prepared to let the violence of the Troubles bring them down, they were gonna have some teenage rock'n'roll fun! Nihilistic? Negative? No siree! Ulster punk was creative, positive. Kids were creating their own bands, venues, magazines. They were experimenting with fashion, making records, and kicking down the barriers.

Punk spread like a virus across the six counties. The authorities started to get worried. Punk was corrupting the youth. Ha! Like fuck it was. Other kids were out throwing petrol bombs, joining the youth wings of paramilitary organisations, burning cars and getting sucked into the whole sectarian merry-go-round. Not the punks. Stupid morons couldn't see past the safety pins and zips. Couldn't see the positive things happening under their noses, couldn't see the kids throwing off the shackles of religious intolerance and bigotry, couldn't see them dismantling the barriers of class and sectarianism.

Or maybe they could. Maybe that's what they were scared of. Divide and rule, keep control. Maybe that's why gigs were starting to get cancelled. Maybe that's why when some of the big UK punk bands announced they were coming over (the Stranglers were the first, then the Clash), the authorities made sure they didn't play. Kids were bonding through their love of rock'n'roll, punk rock style. Shit, they couldn't have the kids from the two sides mixing, God forbid even becoming friends! Maybe that's why the paramilitaries and extremists weren't too fond of punk either. Maybe that's why gangs like the Friendly Society started up. They were members of a Loyalist paramilitary organisation whose stated aim was 'to do as much damage to as many punks as possible'.

Brian Young

Our gigs were the only real meeting place for punkers in Belfast. We had gone out and single-handedly discovered and established venues for punk bands to play in, and it's no accident that when Stiff Little Fingers, the Outcasts and a zillion other local acts played their first gigs they held them in the same east Belfast venues we had found.

Now identified as one of 'those filthy punk bands', we lost at least one practice hall and were banned from our regular venues time and time again. Fortunately, a couple of enterprising band members discovered a city centre venue willing to give new punk bands a chance. The Harp Bar gave Belfast a (relatively) safe venue that everyone could get to easily and where people from both sides of the community could come and see local punk bands and hear punk records. Its success was almost immediate. Punk brought together people from all sections of the community, all classes and creeds, and what mattered was not where you were from, or what foot you kicked with (in local parlance), but what music you liked.

Jake Burns

The gigs in Belfast were actually in the city centre. Everyone attributes punk for crossing religious boundaries, bringing kids together from both sides of the divide. The thing was if you went to the Ulster Hall to see Rory Gallagher or Dr Feelgood, everyone in there

Rock the Casbah: The Undertones' very
early days in Derry

was from different parts of the city – you didn't see anyone there with a Union Jack or an Irish tricolour tattooed to their face. Nobody gave a fuck about that stuff. They were there to see a band. I think the one thing that punk did do was it brought kids together on a regular basis and got them to go to backstreet bars that they would never have gone to, to see bands. You were a bit hesitant at first – by going to see one of the bands you had become an outsider by default, so you would bond together anyway.

John O'Neill

The Casbah was the only main type of venue in Derry. Rory Gallagher, because his pa had come from Derry, had a big influence – there was a lot of blues rock getting played. You were judged on how good your guitar solo was. It was crap! We came from the background of loving how T. Rex songs lasted for two minutes, even before the Ramones. Even back then we knew there was different music.

By pure chance we started playing the Casbah on Thursday nights. No one took us seriously because we were not anywhere in the same league as those other bands. We would try and have a new cover version or a new song every week. It was great having that motivation.

Damian O'Neill

We were called the Undertones by early 1977. In Derry when we started off we were loved or hated. We had a good following at the Casbah club. We got abuse in the streets – we used to cower but Feargal would give the shit back. It was another twenty years before Derry accepted us. I never liked the place. The rest of them had a love/hate relationship with Derry and would defend it. I didn't like being there really. We were definitely uncomfortable with being pop stars once we had a few hits.

The Casbah was great. The happiest days of my life! It was a shithole, but it was Derry's equivalent to the Cavern – although much smaller and more dilapidated. It was a pub bombed by the IRA, and they rebuilt it as a prefab Portacabin in 1975. Inside it was a den of iniquity, frequented by hippies who could smoke dope and a lot of ne'er-do-wells, It was a kind of dangerous place to play. Our first show there was April '77. We were the only punk band in town. We did a couple of Stooges songs like 'TV Eye' and at the end of the set Billy kicked the drums over like the Who. We were only sixteen [laughs] and that went down really well with the long-hairs – they loved it. It reminded them of garage bands from the Sixties. The Casbah asked us back to do another show and it stemmed from there. We had a regular gig there once or twice a week and that was how we learned our chops and got our following.

We thought there was nothing going on in Belfast. It was not till 1978 that we found out what was going on in Belfast. It may as well have been Sydney to us. We thought we were out on our own.

IN DUBLIN'S FAIR CITY
Punk in Dublin

John O'Neill

Coming from Derry we didn't know anything about the Belfast scene. Maybe it was the political thing but you felt closer to Dublin. Belfast is a big town but we never went there. It's far more sectarian and there were far more horrific murders in Belfast than in Derry. Our first experience of Dublin was the gig we played there. Most of the set was cover versions at that point.

Deko (Dublin punk. Paranoid Visions: vocals)

I was in reform school, Irish borstal. Until punk there was nothing in my life. It was the soundtrack of the times at borstal. I wasn't into any music at the time until I heard the Adverts and the Pistols. In Dublin there wasn't a real scene here. All the bands like the

Boomtown Rats and the Radiators From Space went away.[23] There was nowhere for the bands to play. Everybody was looking at *Top of the Pops*, looking to England.[24] There was no unity. A lot of punks in Dublin moved to England.

Gavin Friday

The scene in Dublin was a small one. There was one shop, Advance Records, that would get imports, and one shop, No Romance, run by the sister of Johnny Fingers (from the Boomtown Rats) selling clothes. Weirdly enough, McDonalds had just arrived in Dublin. We'd sit in there and eat burgers. I'd get the ferry over to the UK and buy records. I'd say, 'How many people want Pere Ubu?' and I'd go over to Probe Records in Liverpool, where Pete Burns worked, and I'd get fifteen copies.[25] I'd do these shopping runs for singles.

Then Johnny Lydon said, 'Anyone can do it, form a band, scream...' This licence given to us was beautiful – that was the real godsend of punk. I took this DIY thing very seriously: don't try and ape anyone. We just formed a band in '77 – all the influences were coming out. You don't know what you are doing at that age, you are just making it up as you go along. Ireland was very repressed sexually and politically. We were hitting out against a lot of things. We were messing with the androgynous shit as well.

---

23. Fronted by the charismatic Bob Geldof, the Boomtown Rats' energised take on Springsteen and the Stones was punk enough for the kids but has been left out of punk histories. The Rats released some great punky pop singles in 1977–78 and were one of the bestselling bands of the era: both 'Rat Trap' and 'I Don't Like Mondays' hit Number One. They certainly had a punk crowd to start off with.

24. Despite being considered a byword for naff by this time, *Top of the Pops* featured loads of classic punk band perfomances at the time.

25. Pete Burns was the flamboyant frontman of Liverpool's Dead Or Alive who came out of the Merseyside post-punk scene. He also used to work behind the counter at the city's Probe Records, dressed to kill in the most over-the-top freak gear in the UK. Any hassle he got on the streets of Liverpool was returned with a very earthy and cutting wit. Dead Or Alive started as a freaky version of the Doors and hit paydirt in the mid-Eighties with their Pete Waterman-produced disco.

HERE'S THREE CHORDS, NOW GO OUT AND FORM A BAND[26]
DIY and the Punk Look

Don Letts

DIY is the legacy of punk rock. For me as a black man who comes from a third-world background, DIY is intrinsic to the way we lived anyway. Punk showed how to use the DIY ethic to go onto a different level. And as opposed to just surviving, I reinvented myself using the inspiration of punk rock.

When the whole thing kicked off, there was this whole energy kicking around. Everyone was picking up guitars, and very soon the stage was full up. I wanted to get involved. I realised it wasn't a spectator sport. I wanted to be a participant, so I picked up a Super 8 camera and I started filming bands. In the *NME* they said I was making a film and I said, 'That's not a bad idea,' so I started making a film! I was just filming the bands I liked, trying to teach myself the craft of film-making. I called it *The Punk Rock Movie* and in true punk rock style I reinvented myself as Don Letts the film maker that I am today. If I had gone through the the normal route and done the things that school had taught me, I would be a bus driver now. I wasn't told to aspire to anything before punk rock. A lot of aspects of the arts and the media are an old boy network. You couldn't see a way in music and film-making, you wouldn't think about it as an option. Punk come along and the sky's the limit.

Pete Shelley

The good thing about punk was even if you were watching you were part of the whole thing. As well as being in a band you were involved. It wasn't that there was you and there was an us: there was all of us in the room and we are having the party here.

---

26. This classic punk statement is often credited to *Sniffin' Glue* fanzine, but was actually originally in *Strangled* – the in-house 'zine printed by the Stranglers.

Steve Kent (The Business: guitar)

The important message I picked up on was the DIY aspect of punk, the whole attitude which was: form your own group, make your own magazine, create your own lifestyle. You don't need the status quo to make your own way. Also to a certain extent the anti-establishment attitude. Initially all those concepts were part of punk rock and we were interested in that kind of attitude.

I was living in Deptford in the early punk days. Some friends of mine found out that punk groups were playing at the famous Kings Head in Deptford, which later went on to be the subject of a Conflict song. We had a punk gang down there on Friday and Saturday nights, which was the punk night, and there would be bands on in the punk room.

We used to go up the Kings Road. It was the focal point, Mr Strummer sort of leading the punks down the Kings Road! There would be lots of rumours going round about the Clash playing a gig. It was a nice experience going up there, joining a new regime – in our adolescent world this was the new generation having something to say for itself.

I had blond spiky hair, and an actual studded leather jacket. [laughs] Punk was a learning curve. There was a little bit of trouble with Teds. The Teds were stronger and more menacing than the rockers. Usually it went off on the train and at train stations. We would be going to concerts and they would be getting kicked out of pubs at the same time.

Clint Boon

I got battered by Teddy boys with brass knuckledusters in Piccadilly Gardens in Manchester. That was my worst memory of punk. My best memory was the music – I thought the Stranglers were great and then the Fall were amazing – I followed them everywhere. Manchester didn't have the pretentiousness of London.

Punk changed my way of thinking – it affected my way of life through to the Inspirals, which was DIY in the way we operated. My outlook is punk, get out and do it. Can't get a record deal? Make your own record. That's still the way now.

John Lydon

Some great things came from punk. The do-it-yourself aspect – don't rely on others, don't wait for a movement, get out there and start your own! But the trouble is movements require pedestrians and what do pedestrians do? They bloody annoy you, don't they? Oxford Street is full of them.

IDENTITY IS THE CRISIS, CAN'T YOU SEE
Punk Style

Poly Styrene

I ran a clothes stall when I was putting X-Ray Spex together. Before that I was working as a temp, and then in the evening I would go to the studio and make demos. I got fed up with the day job, so I did the fashion thing in Beaufort Market. It worked quite well – not for the money, but it meant I would eventually have a lot of stage clothes to wear. Then I started playing the Man in the Moon on Kings Road, which is next door to the clothes shop. I was with GTO making demos, and I thought it was time to go.[27] I wanted to have a band.

I got the look pretty quickly. We used to wear stuff sort of like that before punk. We used to shop in flea markets and mix it together, creating your own look, not to be like anyone else's. I used to have very long hair so I looked a bit like a little Marc Bolan – that's how it naturally looked. With punk rock I cut all my hair off, before I went to the Roxy. I had it cut at a barber's on the Kings Road.

My look was quite original at the time. I met a fashion student who did my clothes – some I did myself, or I wore her things. Her

---

27. As Mari Elliot, Poly had released a reggae single, 'Silly Billy', for GTO Records in 1976, which didn't chart.

clothes were very different, influenced by Bowie and 'Space Oddity' – she made those weird zipped dresses. I was selling them for her in my shop, so I started wearing them! She'd come to the gigs and would bring me a new outfit to wear. I'm not sure how much money she got paid but we were showcasing stuff for her. She would be at home with her sewing machine, making clothes. I also got her to make things I designed.

T. V. Smith

There was no money, so we got stuff out of charity shops and patched it up and put it together. If you've got an artistic mind I guess it will come out like that. What attracted me to bands was the whole package, the look and everything.

Once 50,000 people get into a scene are there only 50,000 ways to make a jacket original? I guess only one home-made badge is enough. The idea of everyone going down to Sex shop to buy their clothes there was ridiculous. No one could afford it! Everyone would go to Oxfam, get a ripped jacket and pin it up. Find your own style! That's what a lot of people were doing. There were infinite variations of the punk look. I'm still bleaching my trousers. It's always nice to look a bit different. If I go to an airport with a jacket with 'only one flavour' bleached on the back I feel good. Although I get searched every time through the customs!

Gavin Friday

Punk looked like the abortion that Ziggy had.

John Lydon

Clothes do not matter. Clothes to me are a bloody good laugh. I can swap from one extreme to another with a random glee. There is no uniform in it. I'm not a catwalk arsehole. I did what I wanted, plain and simple, and I was not amused to see 100 idiots copying that exact thing. Most of what I would wear would be out of sheer poverty, a sheer lack of money. Safety pins came in because the

fucking arse in my pants fell out. It was just a matter of practical-
ity, but then the likes of Zandra Rhodes at the time would make
her £1,000 dresses out of safety pins, jumping on that like it was a
fashion, a category.

I don't like uniforms. I can't be having that. It isn't like that. If
that's what you want go and join the army where they make really
good uniforms. The leather jacket nonsense that crept in, the studded leather jackets and everybody has a Mohawk, that's unacceptably
third rate. The Exploited were very good when they first started –
Mohawks in Edinburgh, that was hard.[28] I applaud them. What I
don't applaud is the people that jumped on their bandwagon.

The stigma of fashion statement put on everything really
repulses me. It's like my 'I Hate Pink Floyd' T-shirt I wore. My
God, that's become a world-famous cliché! It was just a giggle, you
know. It might mean something but that's all it means.

This icon-building nonsense that goes on: if anything I'm an
icon buster. I don't think I'm the world's most wonderful person.
It's a shame I'm getting handsomer as I'm getting older! [laughs]
That's a fucking problem. We're all spotty pimply arseholes. We all
have armpits from hell. I have never seen a beautiful toenail in my
life! We just settle for what there is. That's how mediocre we are as
a species. We just settle for what there is.

Steve Diggle

London bands were all dressed up; they all had designer gear. My
brother would get shirts and rip a corner of them, paint a Co-op
stamp on them and draw all over them – factory chimneys and stuff
like that.[29] We wore them on that Granada Electric Circus footage.
It's not easy to see with the lights but we looked like orphans!

---

28. Wattie Buchan's Edinburgh crew the Exploited stripped punk down to its very basics
when they emerged in 1980, the end of punk for many of the first wave. The Exploited
instantly became heroes to the new generation of punk kids. Their rebel status sees them
still endorsed today by angry kids the world over. On a recent trip by your author to Russia,
the Exploited was the most popular T-shirt on the streets.

29. Steve's brother is the artist Phil Diggle.

We didn't have a McLaren, Westwood or Bernie Rhodes with connections to get stylish shirts. We had no flash stuff. We thought it was cool to buy a shirt from Oxfam and draw on it. Some people say that we were not really punks, but we would make our own clothes and I made my own speaker cabinet. It was very DIY.

Tony James

We fired John Towe as our drummer in Generation X eventually because we didn't think he was good enough. It sounds fascistic to say that someone doesn't look right, but it's when you look into their eyes – it's not just their shoes. You want to go, 'Why are you wearing those shoes? What are you thinking!?' But it was more than that. Somehow he wasn't right, and then we got Mark Laff who was playing with Subway Sect – he completes the picture.[30] He's got the right hair, the right look. Obviously Generation X looked like it was picked from a pop panel. This is a really cute, great-looking group, and this was by chance. It was a fantastic look. Everyone was the same height. No short fat ones. It was a classic English rock'n'roll band.

SIGNED AND SACKED AGAIN
Further Adventures of the Sex Pistols

March 1977: The Pistols ink their deal with A&M early in the month and sign the contract in the classic shot outside Buckingham Palace. A couple of days later Old Grey Whistle Test *presenter 'Whispering' Bob Harris is involved in an incident with the Pistols' associates. One of his companions needs stitches in his hand. Bob Harris' solicitor sends a letter to the head of A&M who halt the production of the Pistols' upcoming single, 'God Save The Queen', and cancel the band's contract ten days after signing it. Brushing this off, the band play their*

---

30. Real name Mark Laffeoly. John Towe went on to play drums in Alternative TV and then, in 1978, the Adverts.

Johnny as an icon in
full Sex shop regalia

first UK gig of 1977 at the Notre Dame Hall on 21 March. It's also Sid Vicious' debut.

Brian X (London punk)

Jah Wobble was around for the Pistols' ride to the top. One of Lydon's close coterie of friends, he picked up a reputation over the years for being a nutter, one of the psychos hanging out with Lydon who could use his fists. A couple of legendary incidents stand out, including, apparently, the incident with *Old Grey Whistle Test* presenter and media champ of prog, Whisperin' Bob Harris.

Jah Wobble

Those stories have been talked about recently a lot again. Look, I'm a working-class boy and that's the way it is. It's like if you were growing up on any estate, a few boys in gangs will be naughty and ended up in the nick. They know you from other side of the estate and they will fuck with you, maybe throw a brick at you. You can't go to your dad! An ex-army vet, he'd say, 'Sort it out yourself.' You can't go to the police. You got to sort it yourself, and they would know you were not a soft target and it would be best to leave you alone. Speak to any one of my mates, they would tell you – funny geezer, a fucking laugh, a nuisance, but wouldn't say I was psycho. I was considered one of the chaps.

One story I get tied in with is attacking Whispering Bob Harris. Now why the fuck would I attack Whispering Bob Harris!? I wasn't even at the Speakeasy where it happened. I've had a few rows in the past, but that's not the kind of thing I would do. You tell people you were not involved and they ignore it. They want to think of you being a nutcase. I've got mates who are the real deal who are gangsters. I managed to stay away from that somehow.

Steve Severin

I didn't see much of the Pistols after the Grundy show. The last time I saw them was at Sid's first gig.

Don Letts

I used to kick Sid out of the shop all the time, but he was friends with John. He joined the Pistols, and ruined them.

He wasn't dumb – a bit of an oaf, but he was always interested in learning things. He'd hang onto your every word, to anybody with a knowledge of popular subculture. He would be into fashion and put it all together.

I spent a lot of time with Sid. He would hang out with us, and he would always keep doing these things that were that close to getting you into a fight. He would stare into people's faces walking down the street, or if you were on a train he would gob on the window right next to a passenger. We were always frightened because we knew that we would have to get involved.

The Pistols returned to the Screen on the Green on 4 April in very different circumstances. Not only was Sid now in the band, they were now also the most notorious band in the country. The Slits were the support band, and the film Number 1 *was also shown. The Pistols' set was filmed by Don Letts for* The Punk Rock Movie.

Marco Pirroni

I thought the Pistols were rubbish with Sid. I thought he was a cunt. You need a rhythm section to make a good band. When there is only two of you actually playing there is something missing, a big hole in the sound. In Sid's case it was not a big hole but a rumbly, horrible farty bass sound. He was not really in time. When he got the gig I think from what I hear he was very conscientious, trying to learn the bass. Glen could play. You are only as strong as your weakest member, really. I saw that it was fucked up – this was not musically very good. I don't really want to listen to it. He looked good. That was a part of the decision to get Sid in. Malcolm didn't give a toss about the music.

I don't think Malcolm saw how good the band was. Or I reckon he knew why they were good but he didn't want to give them any credit. That's Malcolm – he doesn't want to give anyone any credit.

Tony D

I saw Sid Vicious' second gig with the Pistols at the Screen on the Green. It was fantastic. The build-up was phenomenal. It was a secret gig; there was about 300 there. Luckily I went to Rough Trade that day and saw the flyer – 'The Pistols playing tonight'. We had to wait till the last film was shown at eleven. All these punk rockers were there, people hanging out on the streets. There was a big long anti-Jubilee film on. The Slits played, then the Pistols. It was a bit pompous, the build-up. Rotten had dyed his hair black for this one. Sid and Johnny came down the aisle through the audience; Paul and Steve onstage were playing a riff. Everyone was sat down; there was no room to get up.

Ari Up

I got stabbed at the Screen on the Green gig and what shocked me was at that time was all these different groups – there was the Ted revival, the bad skinheads, the good skinheads, every fucking thing on the earth, and guess who stabbed me? A fucking John Travolta fan, a disco fan! [laughs] Me and Palmolive were walking near the venue. I had this huge mac on, this powerful coat. I wore it to flash at people! Flashing was a big trendy scene at the time – there were loads of dirty flashers with a snake underneath [laughs], and I thought, 'Well, I'm going to rebel against that.' I was taking the power and controlling it and I was saying, 'I'm fourteen or fifteen and not going to be harassed by guys.' They never did try to harass me sexually. That guy with the knife was not harassment, it was a violent outbreak.

For the boys to do punk was just about acceptable, but because we were female it was different. At the time women usually wore mini-skirts with nice tights and high heels, and it was terrible for us to wear them with Doc Martens and torn-up tights and torn-up shirts. We would wear clothes out in the open instead of beneath the clothes where they belonged – I wore the Silver Jubilee underwear over the pants, and the way people reacted! It just became systematically a hunt for the rest of the outside world. It was like they wished it was the Middle Ages so they could have burned us at the stake!

CHAPTER 8
1977 PART II: IN 1977, I HOPE
I GO TO HEAVEN

FIRE AND SKILL
The Jam

Where did the Jam fit into all of this? Were they a punk band? The purists will defiantly say no, but in terms of energy and passion and writing songs that meant something to 'the kids' the Jam certainly were one. They may not have been part of the punk 'elite', but it's difficult to imagine the Jam in any other era apart from punk – they may have been rooted in the Sixties, but Paul Weller's snarling anger and vitriol was very 1977 instead of 1967. Lyrically they were bang on the nail, and if you take punk rock to be a broad church and not a narrow elite the Jam were there.

Paolo Hewitt

When punk came along, the Jam to me were never really part of all that. They seemed separate and they were never accepted by the punk in-crowd. I think that affected Paul Weller. I think he looked up to Joe Strummer. Being from just outside London, they were obsessed by it, romanticised it. The first two Jam albums sounded very like they were influenced by punk – they certainly had that energy, but it wasn't till later on when they branched out that they stood up on their own two feet.

Billy Bragg

We read about the Jam. We could relate to where Weller was coming from, so we went to see them and that transformed us. Whereas the Damned and the Sex Pistols seemed like they were like a parody, taking what the Eddie and the Hot Rods were doing and taking the piss – a bit like the Darkness now. The Jam, when we saw them at the Nashville Rooms, seemed to really mean it. Weller had the words 'Fire and Skill' on his amp. They had skinny ties and suits; they looked good. We thought they were part of that Wilko Johnson/Barry Masters white working-class suburban music scene, compared to the Pistols being art school tossers really. The Pistols' fans also wore swastikas – that really pissed me off as well. I didn't like that idea at all.

So we were happily following the Jam. They were kind of firmly in that mod r'n'b thing. They were getting reviewed in the music papers, 'In The City' had been released. I'd heard the Pistols on John Peel. A mate of mine had the Damned album – I still thought they were taking the piss. The sincerity that Weller had came though in way you didn't get from Captain Sensible. It got to the stage when you couldn't see the Jam any more at the Nashville, and they were going play their first big gig at Finsbury Park Rainbow with the Clash – and we had to be there.

Marco Pirroni

The Jam never sat well with us lot. They looked so smart, they always had those neat ties on. We had the same sort of clothes, but you could tell ours were from Oxfam and didn't quite fit! The Jam had really tight smart suits on. I don't think the Jam ever went to Oxfam! They looked like they had stuff made for them, and had

Paul Weller in classic angry young man pose – a sharp and angular shape still referred to by angry young guitarists to this day

their dad as the manager – that was a total no-no! The idea of having your dad a manager![1]

Mark Perry

To me, the Jam was a fantastic band with a great songwriter. But so pompous. Paul Weller was the easiest person to wind up in punk. We used to always take the piss out of the Jam for tuning up on stage'n'that. You know: 'That's not punk, we don't tune up.' We wanted to wind Paul up. He was playing the Marquee, and I wasn't at the gig, but apparently he got a copy of *Sniffin' Glue* and set light to it on the stage, which was quite an exciting thing to do.[2]

David Gedge (Wedding Present: vocals)

My school friend Dave Fielding turned me on to punk rock.[3] I'd go round to his house to hear whatever seven-inch singles he'd bought that week. So it was stuff like 'In the City' by the Jam, 'White Riot' by the Clash, or the Sex Pistols' 'Anarchy in the UK'. The band names and song titles all sounded so cool to a teenager.

Knox

We used to have these bands supporting us like Sham 69 and the Jam, and they all went on to bigger things – that's the way it is. In some respects our name, the Vibrators, held us back a bit. We couldn't get all the airplay we could have got. If you're called the Jam there is no problem in having airplay. I liked the name Vibrators, though – it looks good written down, and I still think it's slightly sort of subversive. We just carried on touring. It was all pretty full on in those days. Punk was big news. Then Pat Collier left and we got Gary Tibbs in, who later joined Adam and the Ants and Roxy Music – he was very good. We then released our debut album, *Pure Mania*.

---

1. John Weller, father of Paul, managed the Jam.
2. It was actually at the 100 Club, on 25 January 1977.
3. Fielding went on to become the guitarist in the Chameleons.

CITY ROCKERS
The Clash

In March the Clash released their debut single, 'White Riot', an incendi-ary, wiry, speed-driven salvo written in reaction to the riots at the Notting Hill Carnival on 30 August the previous year where black youths had clashed with police, as witnessed by Joe Strummer, Paul Simonon and Bernie Rhodes. In 'White Riot', Strummer expressed his feeling that young white people should vent their outrage over oppressive government just like the black youth, through direct action. This punk rock song was a brusque blast of street poetry and a deceptively brilliant arrangement.

Hot on its heels came the band's self-titled debut album, released on 8 April. Already moving quickly to challenge for the pole position in the punk rock hierarchy amidst the Sex Pistols' inertia in the first half of 1977, the Clash found themselves as the flag-wavers of the punk rock consciousness. There isn't a duff song on the album. It was a rough and ready collection of direct action rock'n'roll street anthems that, perhaps more than any other album of the time, totally connected with the lives of its audience, detailing perfectly the punk rockers' frustration and anger, setting the blueprint for the sound and the soul of what punk rock would be about. Scratchy machine-gun guitars drive along the songs, which have

The Clash tearing it up on stage at the Coliseum, Harlesden. In the audience at bottom right is a young Shane MacGowan

great sing-along choruses. Strummer's lyrics perfectly capture the aspira-
tions and anger of the dolebound generation floundering around in the
shabby UK of the late Seventies. Mick Jones' years studying rock'n'roll
hadn't been wasted: the songwriting is spot on and the arrangements
clever. Their cover of Junior Murvin's 'Police And Thieves' also combines
the two key rebel musics of the late Seventies, punk and reggae, into one
cool whole. The Clash were utterly inspirational, utterly positive, and they
offered a million possibilities. For many they were the ultimate band from
the punk generation – but with this came a lot of pressure and, of course,
many of their peers were quick to sneer at them.

In May the Clash headlined the first big punk package tour to hit
the road since the Anarchy tour the previous December, and it was not
without its own tension.

Mick Jones

We recorded it very fast. They always say I don't remember making
it, but I do. [laughs] We'd play a song, have a quick break, then play
the next one, shout at each other and then do another song. Joe
would give me the words and I would make a song out of them. The
words would have such a great rhythm to them. Everything would
come together really, really fast.

Jake Burns

When I heard the first Clash album, that was when I suddenly
realised, 'Why the fuck are we playing songs about California high-
ways when we could be writing songs about our own lives?'

Colin Newman

I was a bit underwhelmed by them. Their first album was so
abysmally produced, it really put me off them. They did wrong what
Wire eventually did right – they should have debuted with a stronger
album. It would have got them into America quicker. It revealed the
songs in a kind of really annoying way, whereas the Pistols' 'Anarchy
in the UK' sounded chunky and big.

The Clash in punk threads – probably waiting for Mick to turn up!

Mark Perry

I had a run-in with the Clash. I was never one to tow the line for any punk thing, and I was outraged when the Clash signed to CBS. I just thought that this was ridiculous, the most important rock band in the world, as far as I was concerned at the beginning of '77, and they go and sign to CBS. To me that was a complete disaster. The most important thing that punk could have done at that point was to stay independent, because economic independence is the most important thing. To sell out to an American company like that! I did a TV interview and I said that punk died the day that the Clash signed to CBS, and they were like, 'How dare he say that about us? We're still punk.' I went to a gig to see Japan and Ian Hunter at Hammersmith Odeon and Mick Jones was backstage. Sometimes he's a very sweet, gentle guy, but he tried to come on all heavy with me. It was all a bit silly. I think they were just embarrassed really. Well, let's face it, two singles down the line CBS put out a single the Clash didn't want to put out, 'Remote Control'. The Clash soon found out how independent they were.

The Clash could have had money given to them. You had a few bob around the punk scene. You had Jake Riviera, Geoff Travis had just started up Rough Trade, you had the Rock On guys – they were all independent and 100 per cent into it. They would have financed the Clash single. Imagine the first Clash single, or an EP of the best Clash songs, coming out on their own label, like UB40 did a few years later – that would have been amazing. It would have inspired all those other bands to do the same thing. But what happens is the Clash sign up, so all those other bands sign up: the Jam with Polydor, the Buzzcocks with UA, Siouxsie and the Banshees to Polydor.[4]

---

4. In the real world signing to CBS was probably the only option the Clash really had. The Damned were hampered by being on the independent Stiff Records, and setting up your own label and getting your album distributed and promoted worldwide whilst on tour is a ridiculous notion. What the Clash had to say, in retrospect, was far more important than who was distributing their album, and they had to get the records out there. Not everyone was hanging around in the inner circle in London with easy access to the band and their music – try growing up in Blackpool like I did!

John Lydon

I think the Clash swallowed a few books that they didn't understand how to read properly. Most of their stuff struck me as sloganeering. Underlining sentences and reviews of Karl Marx. It's a crappy way out, really. If you're going to rely on bourgeois intellectuals for your political focus you're onto a loser, mate.

The likes of the Clash – those boys took the wimpy route out with their Marxist nonsense. They had a university kind of rocky attitude: what were they challenging? Really when it boils down to it, it was meaningless and nice. The Pistols took the brunt of it, and then they all jumped in on it with no effort at all, and have all gone on to make enormous record sales and have very nice, cosy positions in the record industry for themselves. That's punk rock is it? [sneers] I'm very pleased all these bands found a home – they are all cluttered together in the same dustbin.

Tony Wilson

Independent distribution was available because of Rough Trade. It was wonderful – the independent ethic was so much part of the punk ethic. Punk, though, was never an attack on the corporates: the Pistols signed to EMI, and the first time I heard of the Clash it had a CBS sticker on it. The Buzzcocks signed to United Artists the night Elvis Presley died. It was always about major labels. The indie labels were a way of getting your band signed to a major label.[5]

Rob Lloyd

We had been hanging out on the Anarchy tour pretending to be in a band which was going to be called the Gestapo, which Johnny

---

5. The very backbone of the punk rock underground was the independent labels. A whole army of bedroom labels sprung up in the wake of punk. Homemade record sleeves stuck together with Pritt Stick, a mass of seven-inch singles made free from the fetters of the A&R clowns: for a time it really was a music made by the people for the people. Many of the records were ramshackle, guitar-driven bursts of spontaneous racket with great acerbic lyrics. Nowadays 'indie' (the worst-ever term for a musical form – the very word itself sounds vile) means gutless, Sixties-pastiche guitar music.

Thunders thought was a brilliant name. The Clash hated it and thought we should be called the Blackshirts. They said, 'If you are going to have a fascist name, at least get a British one!' Rotten suggested the Nasty Party. It started out as a pretend band, then we had some songs which ended up early on in the Prefects (the name we ended up with). We put an ad in the *Birmingham Evening Mail* saying, 'Bassist and singer want to form a band.' Lo and behold, I went to meet them, and we got the gig.

We started rehearsing in our school. Having done two rehearsals, we thought we were ready. The first gig we played was at someone's house party in early 1977, and it ended up with the police being called and with the host of the party knocking me out! [laughs] It was a real chaotic affair. Then we played a club called Rebecca's in Birmingham city centre, opposite where Edward's Number 8 was for years. The gig was us and two other Birmingham punk bands – one didn't turn up and other was not really a punk band at all.

Mike Barnet and Dave Cork from Endale, who had booked the Anarchy tour, had become the Clash's agents and they were lining up the White Riot tour for that spring with the Clash, Buzzcocks, Subway Sect and the Slits – and the Jam, who just did the Rainbow gig as special guests. They got in touch with me saying the Slits had refused to play the Rainbow gig because it was a seated venue and they looked on it as some sort of sell-out. Would the Prefects do it? So we said, 'Yeah.' We had only done two gigs before and we got asked to do the Rainbow.[6] We said, 'Yeah.'

Then it suddenly dawned on us: 'Hang on, we are really under-rehearsed. We hardly exist as a band.' So I got in touch with Richard Boon, the Buzzcocks' manager. They were playing in Birmingham and Stafford at this time, and I said, 'We're playing with you and the Clash in a couple of weeks. We've only played a couple of gigs and we are pretty rubbish. Can we do some supports to practise?' One

---

6. The Rainbow gig on 9 May was the Clash's first big headline show.

way or another we got the two other gigs from the Buzzcocks before the Rainbow – so that was our fifth gig.

We were on first and started the set with our seven-second, two-chord number called 'VD' which went: 'Help me please help me I'm so weedy I've got VD please help me I'm so weedy I've got VD.' John Peel was there and booked us for a session. He'd been to a Genesis concert the night before where no song was less than half an hour, and was impressed by the length of our songs. We got invited to go in and did a couple of John Peel sessions. None of us had been in a recording studio before.

Billy Bragg

When we got to the Rainbow we saw the Prefects, the Subway Sect and the Buzzcocks. When the Jam came on, it felt like the place was too big for them. They didn't come over as well as they did at the Red Cow and the Nashville, but the Clash just blew us away. We didn't know their stuff, but to see them play there – they just had everything! We had been to see the Stones at Earls Court in 1975 and the Who at Charlton Football Club the same year, really big venues, but the Clash were our age. To see the Clash on the White Riot tour and realise that they were doing exactly what we loved the Stones for doing, throwing all the same shapes and using the same equipment and making great noises – but they were our generation! It was a great moment for us. It was like discovering how to be a rock star: you just did it yourself. You didn't wait for someone to come and discover you. That was the most important thing that came out of punk. There was something about the Clash that you didn't get from other bands. Also there was a riot at the gig – instead of being on the outside looking in, I was right at the centre of it.

We came home and we cut our hair and bought skinny trousers. It was Year Zero. That was the moment for me.

Vic Godard

We didn't feel that much affinity with anyone. The Prefects looked and sounded like us. They would do a version of whatever was Number One – 'Mull of Kintyre' or 'Bohemian Rhapsody' – and do it as badly as possible. The Buzzcocks were like a Manchester version of us. We really chummed up with them. We swopped lyrics with them – out of all of them they were the ones we liked the most. They had really good tunes and lyrics. The Clash's lyrics were nothing like ours. The Buzzcocks were aiming to do roughly the same sort of thing as us.

Steve Diggle

Joe Strummer liked Garth. On the White Riot tour the Clash had a party in a big concrete hotel. I was stood at the bar with Joe and a few people and we watched as six bouncers carried Garth out of the building. Garth was the hardest, hardest man there. Joe always remembered that.

It was about this time that Garth was kicked out of the band. We went to pick him up one day round his parents' house and they said he was down the pub. We drove down to the pub and he was walking along with six cans in his hand – he had been in the pub for hours. When we got him in the van there was a bit of an argument. We went on and he played one song and threw his bass down, and then came back and started shouting and went berserk. In the van going back we had a ghetto blaster – at this point this was a new thing to have – and we went to a service station and he got the wrong batteries, and an argument started. He's trying to put these massive batteries in it. He blew up. He used to explode now and then. So we had to let him go, really, saying, 'It's no good for you, Garth.'

We had auditions for a new bass player. A few people came down including Steve Garvey. Steve went to the shop and bought John Maher a Mars bar and we thought, 'He's all right, we'll have him over the bloke who came down from the Smirks!' Steve Garvey was the right man. He adapted to it well. With him in the band a lot more girls came to the gigs!

Rob Lloyd

We were only meant to do the one gig on the White Riot tour, and it carried on without us. The three of us went over to Leicester to see them. They only had three or four gigs left on the tour and it was when Garth was in the Buzzcocks – he was a great bloke but a real problem for the Buzzcocks. After they played in Leicester they kicked him out of the band, and because there was three of us from the Prefects at the gig, the guys from Endale said, 'The Buzzcocks are dropping out of the rest of the tour. Will you guys take over?'

And we so we rang up Paul Apperley, who wasn't there, and said, 'We're in this hotel in Leicester and we're on the White Riot tour in Chelmsford tomorrow. Can you get the train and bring the guitars?'

The Clash were already quite a pop band by then. No one was that into the Slits or the Subway Sect or us. We were the fourth on the bill, which meant we got plenty of abuse. We used to rile people on purpose. When we played the Rainbow with the Clash we got treated really shit by them. It was just obvious to me it was the same old cannage being served up – they were the stars. There was a back-stage bar at the Rainbow, a VIP bar. Siouxsie Sioux and Billy Idol walked in there and they were partying, and we were not allowed in it. In Chelmsford, the mayor of Chelmsford came to visit them and they had their photo taken for the local paper. I just thought, 'This is absolutely not what I'm into,' so I went off on one.

The night we got put on the tour was the first night apart from the Ramones that we had stayed in a hotel. Obviously we had raped the mini-bar and we got told off the next morning by Bernie: 'You had £21 of booze and tonight you will have to sleep on the coach.'[7]

I had this naive view that there was something revolutionary going on. It was all smashed to pieces by the Clash. That was fantastic by itself, because otherwise I would have gone on for months

---

7. It's not that customary for the headline band to pay for the support bands' hotel bills and bar bills!

being one of the punk sheep. We were disillusioned by it at an early stage in our 'career'. That's when we started to think punk rock was a load of nonsense and we started playing things like 'Going Through The Motions' and trying to rile the punk crowds and do something different. We started looking at the kind of music we had liked before punk.

You've got to remember we were sixteen or seventeen years old and fairly naive. The Subway Sect and the Slits sort of latched onto us. We really got on with them. The more I look back on it now, I think there was a lot posturing going on in punk rock. We were really bog standard oiks, and I think they liked pretending to be our mates because our working-classness rubbed off on them and made them looked more street. [laughs] I really enjoyed their music. I got on really well with Palmolive and the Subway Sect. The big problem was the Subway Sect's manager was Bernie Rhodes, who was also the Clash's manager, and he hated us. So there was always a bit of tension. They were singing 'No more rock'n'roll' and being so cool and alternative – they used to sneer at the Clash with us – but it always made me think, 'Why have they got the same manager as them?'

Ari Up

Mick Jones was always trying to tame the Slits. He was guiding us for a long time, and Joe was there as well, being sort of secret members from the back. Palmolive was going out with Joe Strummer before the Slits. Joe was really into the idea of a girl band and supported Palmolive in the idea of doing the band. Palmolive had the female vision. And Mick Jones was going out with our guitar player, Viv Albertine. No matter how good Mick thought the Slits were, he was trying to get us to be really straight, ABC-format rock-'n'roll. When 'Typical Girls' was written and we started to play it, Mick Jones tried to change the way we wanted to do it, and if Viv hadn't got the really brilliant weird style she had on the guitar it would have sounded like the straight Clash-style song. I'm not slagging him off, he's very good, but Mick was thinking in terms of a commercial hit record. He wanted it straight, and we were into doing our thing. So no matter what the boys were saying it wasn't going to happen.

Malcolm managed us for two weeks. He was such a clever guy who made the Pistols big and he wanted do it with the Slits. The problem was that he wanted to change us; he wanted to be part of the band! He controlled the sound of the Pistols – maybe they went along with him. He was saying to us the guitar should be upfront – he didn't want the bass heavy. He was saying, 'The bass is not the front instrument. The bass should be not upfront.' What he wanted was a female Pistols, a good selling product, but we were already very bass-orientated. That's what you hear on the John Peel sessions. That's what was so brilliantly unique about the Slits. No one else in punk rock played the bass like that, not even the Clash. They had that trebly sounding punky bass.

We had a reggae bass on top of a punk song. If we had followed Malcolm McLaren, there would have been no Slits sound. So sadly we had to split, not because of business, but we couldn't deal with the interference in our music.

Steve Diggle

Joe Strummer said we were a bunch of nerds from Manchester. At first he didn't like the Buzzcocks, but when we did the White Riot tour Strummer was into us. He came down to the Pistols gig in Manchester. We went to the hotel with the Pistols and all the papers were after them. There was us and the Pistols all sitting in one room with press people outside and Joe Strummer was there as well. We took him to Tommy Ducks and he really liked it.[8] I took him there a few times, from the White Riot tour up to *London's Calling*. 'I like that pub with all the knickers!' he would say.

---

8. Tommy Ducks was a famed city centre Manchester pub, just round the corner from the Free Trade Hall, which had women's knickers hanging from the roof. It was 'accidentally' knocked down by property developers.

Rob Lloyd

Bernie Rhodes was an obnoxious cunt! [laughs] I'm not sure what relationship him and Malcolm had. He obviously wanted to create some sort of movement and wanted the Clash at the front of it, with his other bands the second brigade. The Prefects were not into that. We were not from London. We were not into sucking up to the Clash. We used to take the piss out of them. We were a bit spiky, not too careful with what we would say. We were not particularly political, and there was some sort of agenda. For him it was a revolutionary art movement, whereas we wanted to be a rock band – that made us inferior slobs, so he never liked us. When someone likes you, you tend to like them, so there was always friction. Maybe there was something nice about the feller, but I never saw it.

I've no idea what other people said about him. He soured quite a lot of things for us. It was a good education. On the one hand, I've got to give him credit: we were young and stupid, and we learned things pretty damn quick, even if it was in a negative way. Personally I haven't the time of day for him. He was into the reflected glory. Everyone was pretending to be young and working-class – he didn't like a young working-class band who didn't give a shit.[9]

Vic Godard

It was fantastic. We had a great time. At the big gigs there were loads of bands – the Slits, the Jam, the Buzzcocks – and at smaller venues like Liverpool Eric's it was us and the Clash. Those other bands never came on the bus – they met us there. We also had the Prefects as well. They went on first before us some nights, or the Slits would go on first. We swapped it around. One gig it was us and the Slits together on the same stage – that was amazing. That was the last gig of the tour at Dunstable. Don Letts filmed it. The mic was lost in the crowd at one point – they were shouting anything into the mic. We had an

---

9. Despite his abrasive methods, the very working-class Bernie Rhodes was one of the key ideas men behind punk and his confrontational stance was vital to the movement.

arrangement of the Velvets song, 'Sister Ray', and we had three different bass players and the guitarists were not playing the same chords.

Don Letts

The tabloid thing is now happening and the Roxy closes down.[10] The guys who own Acme Attractions, Steph Rainer and John Rainer, they want to capitalise on the punk thing so they move out of the basement and up onto the Kings Road. They open Boy just as that tabloid thing kicks off. I hated Boy. I can't deny it. It was following, not leading. It was catering to this new breed of tabloid punk. I didn't know anyone who wore a bin liner. The White Riot tour is coming up and the Slits are looking for a manager and I say, 'I'll have a go at this.'

I used to get money out of the till at Boy – it was me redistributing the wealth! Acme funded *The Punk Rock Movie*! I never told anybody that! So the White Riot tour comes up and I give the Slits the money to go on tour in the capacity of being their manager. For six months I was the Slits' manager... [pauses] *Nobody* manages the Slits! I remember standing at the back of the hall with Bernie Rhodes watching the Slits, looking at the stage, thinking, 'Naaah!' They were far too crazy to manage! [laughs]

Ari Up

The first gig we ever played was with the Buzzcocks, Subway Sect and the Clash in this big theatre in Harlesden. It was a pretty stunning place. There was all these people with cameras. I remember it felt like the whole of London is watching us. Shit! The whole of the press was there. I was thinking, 'I'm on stage doing this! The next day it will be all over the papers.' I was thinking like that. I was not even hearing the music – we were tumbling all over the place! [laughs]

---

10. The Roxy closed after being open for exactly 100 days. It soon reopened but under new management.

I remember when Don Letts took off his pants and did a moonie out of the car window. There was fun stuff like that. I remember people were so shocked when they drove past; they looked at us like we were aliens. A car driven by a black man with long dreads with a group of punks – that was too much for people to handle then. So Don took the piss! I've got fond memories of the White Riot tour. We were protected by our peers. I don't think the Slits would have survived without the protection of the boys. It was an unspoken language. They were really great, nothing but fun.

As great as Don was, and as punk as he was, when it came to women and managing us the chauvinism was definitely coming through. [laughs] We were hard to manage, of course. At the same time he was not an experienced manager himself – he was a friend.

There was quite a few people managing us. We had fun with them and we never really fell out with them. My mum managed us for a while. She was the longest really. We never hired her. She helped us a lot: she got us gigs, she helped us with rehearsals. She was the unofficial Slit in a way.

Don Letts

I liked the White Riot tour – that was a crucial tour. A lot of the stuff was just a haze to me. I do remember one time checking out of a hotel with the Clash and everyone else, and the manager totting up the food, the drinks… and the one door that was missing.

I'm with the Slits because I'm managing them – I'm signing the Slits in and Ari is spitting on the floor and we are thrown out of the hotel! The Slits, man, were a trip: not only were they fighting on the stage, they were fighting off the stage! There is nothing like them. It was the girl thing compounded with the punk thing compounded with Arianna being the force that she is – there is nothing else like her.

Mensi

I left school just before punk. There was plenty of work, the coal mines were still thriving, and so were the shipyards. When I left school it was quite shameful if you were on the dole. I was actually working down the pit – Hope Colliery – when I saw two bands that changed my outlook on life. One was the Clash at Newcastle University, and the other was the Jam at Seaburn Hall.[11] Absolutely phenomenal, both of them. With the Clash there were two support bands who at the time I thought were absolute garbage, the Slits and the Subway Sect. I thought, 'If they can be up there playing then there is no reason why I can't.' It was more the Slits and Subway Sect that set us off. I could never aspire to being as good as the Clash – they were phenomenal. The Jam, at the time when I seen them on the In The City tour, were not really punk, but I thought they had all the energy of the punk thing, and that was enough.

After the Clash I formed a band the next day. I knocked on everybody's door. I knew somebody who could play drums, which was Decca. I knew somebody who could play guitar – he wasn't very keen – that was Mond. We hijacked a bass player, Micky, and his ma wouldn't let him play in the band. I was older than everyone else. I was about 20 then.

In April 1977 the Pistols had still been searching for a deal, the band too hot to handle for most labels. CBS was the next label to back out of signing the band, leaving French label Barclay – and Virgin Records, run by Richard Branson. It was not until 12 May that Virgin finally signed the Sex Pistols, giving the band a permanent home after months of hanging about.

The day after, Sid was hospitalised with hepatitis. The only person that bothered to visit him was Nancy Spungen: after hot-footing it over to the UK to hang out with the Heartbreakers, and being turned down by Johnny Rotten, she had hooked up with the Pistols' new bass player, and the ballad of Sid and Nancy started its tragic yet pop-iconic tale.

---

11. The Clash gig was on 20 May 1977. Strummer and Topper Headon were arrested the day after the gig for stealing pillowcases from the hotel room! The Jam played Seaburn Hall, Sunderland, on 17 June.

This also marked the point when punk rock started to lose some of its innocence, and hard drugs crept into the scene.

Mark Perry

The Sex Pistols, for all their talk of revolution and all that, they end up with Virgin. How boring is that! Richard Branson, an old hippie, he's bound to sign them up. That's what made me laugh about the Pistols: they had a go at EMI once they signed to Virgin. What they should have done was set light to the Virgin offices or something like that! That would have been revolutionary, wouldn't it! [laughs] When punk could have taken those chances it just failed miserably. People were like, 'We got a career in this, we better not upset anybody.'

In the early days I got on really well with Mick Jones. We went to parties and gigs, we would be chatting for ages about music. Someone like Mick Jones just wanted to be in a band. If punk hadn't happened for me, I would have just worked in a bank and carried on buying records. Whereas Mick Jones would have been in the music business anyway – that's the difference.

If you're a musician and you've rehearsed for hours and you're into rock, you desperately want to sign a big record deal. I think there was almost too many professional musicians in punk to really make it like revolutionary, like in a streetfighting sense. These guys weren't about to smash their Gibson & Fender guitars all over the stage, were they? They had something to protect so they manipulated punk into, 'OK, we won't have a riot, we will sing about it instead.' Which is cool, at least someone's singing about it – but don't try to make out that you are some hard revolutionary. You're just in a pop band – which the Clash end up being. They were a great pop band, but nothing to do with punk. The real punk bands came a couple of years later, the bands we all hated like the Exploited and all those nasty working-class people [laughs] that have convictions and have been in trouble with the police, and they were from out of London.

Marco Pirroni

The Pistols were their own band: they were supposed to be overblown, supposed to be big, they were supposed to do what they did and affect the rest of the world. This whole Mark P thing that they should sign to Bumhole Records for no money was stupid – that would never work.

TWO SEVENS CLASH
The Floodgates Open

In the wake of the big guns, a whole mass of bands arrived fully formed. Punk, if anything, was a machine-gun attack of great singles, proving the old maxim that everybody has a great song inside them. Each one housed in its own picture bag, the seven-inch single was the king. The avalanche of fantastic bands seemed to pour through, and the arguments over who was and who wasn't punk started as the soul of the movement was quickly up for grabs. All over the country, in every town and city punk scenes sprung up with clubs like Eric's in Liverpool and the Electric Circus in Manchester being regional epicentres.

Chris Bailey

The Saints first came to the UK in the summer of 1977. When I first heard the Sex Pistols I thought, 'This is very well-produced.' I thought it was like the Alex Harvey Band. That was honestly my first reaction – loud pop music! I could relate to that. By the time we got to the UK, punk had become pretty much Kings Road marketing. Even though I never really associated myself with punk rock, I thought it was cool. Like rock'n'roll, OK in the early days. But it was all in the marketing: if you were not a punk rock band, you were dinosaur music. It had all become very trendy very quickly. Having said that, the democratisation of shows I could relate with, and there were still people in the business who had that kind of vibe.

The first gigs we did in the UK was with the Ramones and Talking Heads. It was a bit of shock that we had an audience – the Saints didn't have a hit in Australia till 1984! [laughs] I don't mean this in any bad sense, but I always found the Ramones very cartoon-like. When I first heard them, they were like the Archies, an American comic-book kind of band. The Ramones in fact go directly back to the Shirelles and the Ronettes and that Phil Spector kind of music. For me punk was the wrong kind of tag for the Ramones. I always had a lot of time for them – invigorating pop music.

Rob Lloyd

When the Ramones came back in May 1977, the first gig was up north at Eric's in Liverpool and we went up to that. I travelled round with them on that tour. They did a double bill with Talking Heads. I was really well in with the Ramones camp.

Budgie

In Liverpool there was a heavy cross-fertilisation. I remember going to Manchester as well. The Manc art crowd was far more separate. The Liverpool thing was more interactive, with the theatre, the clubs, the street performance – you were all on the same street. A lot of people came to Liverpool because they were interested in doing things. When I quit college in 1977, a lot of people left at the same time. There was an awareness of what was going on in the clothes, not the rarified atmosphere of normal art colleges. There was some wild ideas during punk – people had ideas of getting rid of all the instruments! Pete Wylie, Julian Cope and Ian McCulloch had this band called the Crucial Three – they never played a gig, maybe had a rehearsal.

The punk thing was starting to happen for me. The first thing I was aware of listening-wise was the Clash album, and then we'd seen a couple of bands at Eric's when it was still the strip joint upstairs – the Saints played there. That was where the early gigs took place that Roger Eagle and Pete Fulwell had promoted.[12] Eventually they got the premises below to make into Eric's.

The first gig we got as the Spitfire Boys was going to be supporting Siouxsie and the Banshees at Eric's, and we never made that. We didn't get there in time. Then we fired the singer and got Paul Rutherford in. We had a couple of rehearsals and started gigging. Paul and Holly and Jayne Casey were the mad trio: they were kind of the trend-setters, the shape-shifters, and first on the Liverpool punk scene.[13]

Liverpool had its scene going. Pete Burns had his own little camp, mostly revolving around the clothes shop at the time. I remember Pete had his own corner of Probe Records eventually. Playing outside Liverpool was scary – when we played further afield, out of town, we had no idea where we were. Leaving your home turf was taking your life into your own hands. Of course you went out to antagonise, and some towns didn't get the punk thing!

In Manchester they already had 'Spiral Scratch' out and the Fall were making noises. People were coming to Liverpool and saying, 'Have you heard Mark Smith?' and, 'My mate's Pete Shelley'. So there's little connections going on. In Liverpool we had Deaf School – they had a Warner Brothers deal and a couple of albums out, and anyone in the art school knew who Deaf School was. A decision for me was that I might secretly get into that band – I thought I could play with Deaf School.

The Spitfire Boys played in London. Paul was a big fan of Patti Smith and Ari Up. Somehow they got in touch with each other. When we played Covent Garden Rock Garden, there was no one there apart from the Slits! We got to know them and went to their

---

12. The late Roger Eagle was a true legend. The DJ at Manchester's mod soul club Twisted Wheel in the early Sixties, he turned the North-West on to underground black music from the States, helping to lay the foundations for the Northern Soul scene. In the late Seventies he was the booker at Eric's in Liverpool and ended up at the Manchester International club in the Eighties and early Nineties, where he booked most of the cool bands that came through Manchester in that period.

13. Paul Rutherford and Holly Johnson would eventually go on to front Frankie Goes To Hollywood.

house on the Kings Road in Chelsea. Linda, the long time partner of John McKay, lived there, and a guy called Steve Strange would always pop in and out. In London everyone knew everyone else. We were hanging out with the Slits. They felt like kindred spirits; they were brilliantly mad.

Chris Bailey

We recorded another batch of stuff, this time properly. Our second single 'This Perfect Day' came out really fast. It's quite funny. It's in a minor key and when you trash open chords in minor keys you get something unique – that's probably part of the charm of 'Perfect Day'. We did an acoustic version of it recently and it's actually quite a pretty song, very similar to 'Paint It Black' in a way.

Arturo Bassick (The Lurkers: bass)

I was actually only in the Lurkers for about six months, I went off to form my own band, Pinpoint. I was on the first two Lurkers singles, 'Shadow' and 'Freak Show'. We were pretty amateurish, sort of like the Ramones but couldn't play as well as them. But Pete Stride could write great tunes. The Lurkers were a real punk band. We didn't hang around in fashion circles. We didn't get our clothes from Boy or Sex shop. We couldn't afford it! We wore homemade clothes.

Tony D

I remember seeing the Lurkers and 999 at the Red Cow in Hammersmith a few stops down the line from where I lived. It was free every Wednesday. The Lurkers were fantastic and 999 turned out to be a better band than I thought. And I saw Slaughter and the Dogs and Eater at the Roxy.

TRY ANOTHER FLAVOUR
Adam and the Ants

The evolution of Adam and the Ants is quite complex. After Bazooka Joe fell apart Adam had got married and dropped out of the scene, but he was soon back in the fray with his own very idiosyncratic take on punk rock. Adam and the Ants were quite unlike any other band. Adam's vision was incredible: mixing sex, bondage and heavy duty themes, he went through several line-ups of the Ants, some of whom ended up in the long-lost Monochrome Set (great band – a much bigger influence on Franz Ferdinand than the Gang Of Four, who are mistakenly credited with being their key influence) and some eventually in Bow Wow Wow.

The original Ants were quick to pick up a core following in the fallout of the initial punk explosion, with heavy duty fans dressing extremely in bondage gear, and some of the first mohicans popped up at Ants gigs. They scored with the punk squat crowd who were looking for something dark and their own in the months that followed punk's explosion into the mainstream – Adam's themes fitted perfectly. This was a very different operation from the one that eventually hit mega-mainstream success with the quite brilliant technicolour tribal pop of Kings of the Wild Frontier, *but one that was equally charismatic – just a more twisted and dangerous charisma.*

Tony D

I was selling my fanzine and it would finance my trips to Compendium Books and Rough Trade. Sex would never have a fanzine in the shop but Boy would. Loads of clothes shops would take them. Poly Styrene would take loads for her stall on Beaufort Market. I was selling a thousand at this point. I used to post fanzines off from work until I got a stern warning from my boss.

The next big thing for me was the Ants kicking off in May/June '77 at the Man in the Moon pub on Kings Road, which was quite heavy at the time with all the Teddy boys. We were living in

Portobello Road at the time, which was much safer and more afford-
able for clothes!

I got really into Adam and the Ants – it was a Damned moment
for me, a Sex Pistols moment. Never seen anything like it. It was what
I hoped punk rock was what going to be: people were getting into
weird S&M stuff and bondage and pornography, wearing rubber-type
gear. The Ants were singing about that side of life – that was not in
other bands' songs. The first time I saw them I was blown away. They
came on in sex gear, leather masks, zipped straitjackets, churning out
these dirty riffs. Adam comes out, sits on this chair and the bass player
opens up the zip on his mouth and he starts to sing 'Plastic Surgery'.
The recorded version just doesn't match it. It took ten minutes till it
started, then he kicked the chair over, writhed on the floor like Iggy
Pop under people's feet. Someone ripped the mask off. People were
kicking him, he was kissing them, causing fights. It was brilliant.

Andy Czezowski was there, Marco was there; there were lots of
people from Sex there, but not Malcolm and Viv. Jordan was there
– she became the manager shortly after the gig. Arturo Bassick was
there. The reason I was there was that Poly Styrene told me I should
check this band out. X-Ray Spex had played with them. The Ants
had played the ICA a few days before.

In *Ripped and Torn* 6 I did the first ever interview with them.
The Ants became a big part of *Ripped and Torn*. I started to see the
Ants all over the place. They started building up a following. They
had this whole 'sexpeople' thing. People wanted a focus, a family.
The Ants suddenly became huge, from the Nashville to the Lyceum,
with no record deal.

A whole new breed of punk rockers were drifting into London
from outside – that was the summer of punk rock, and all these
people were looking for their version of punk rock. There was a
whole new influx with new looks. The tartan and bondage trousers
broke away from the old-school safety pins and paint spray – this was
a new look. Boy were selling cheap bondage trousers. The hair was
starting to go crazy. I remember one huge Teddy boy used to follow

the Ants – he was wearing an Ants jacket and had a mohican. Crazy colour was appearing, and there were loads more records coming out, loads more bands.

Tom Vague (Editor of *Vague* fanzine)

Adam Ant was always mad, bad and dangerous to know. The original Ants were pretty heavy. They played Salisbury while I was at art college: I've got a memory of bikers waving bike chains around and anyone with spiked hair getting walloped. At the time there were so many sub-cults fighting each other.

I did issues of *Vague* about the Ants from then on. *Vague* was bi-monthly. Punk had gone nationwide with the Pistols and the Clash, and now there was an on-the-road sort of scene, hitch-hiking, selling my fanzine while following the Ants up and down the country, and other extreme groups like Throbbing Gristle – and Joy Division, even if they didn't have the same sort of tribal thing.

Liverpool and Manchester were big towns for the Ants. They had these really hardcore fans who would dress extremely – some of these fans were more famous than the band, like Boxhead from Liverpool or the Newcastle lot, or there was Robbo who had one of the first Mohicans, along with Mitch, the Rezillos' roadie.[14] The Newcastle lot were dressed like that, and they lived in Byker and worked on the docks! [laughs] Not all the fans dressed that way. The first time I saw the Ants, the fans were dressed down, almost football/casual, cardigans and kung fu slippers – or it was the other extreme with leather studded belts and kilts as well.

Jaz Coleman (Killing Joke: vocals)

We revered the very early Adam and the Ants. We went to see them a lot. They were really sensational pre-*Kings of the Wild Frontier* stuff.

---

14. The Rezillos, fronted by Fay Fife and Eugene Reynolds, were best known for their hit 'Top of the Pops'. Guitarist Jo Callis went on to huge success with the Human League. After the band split, Fife and Reynolds formed a new line-up using the amended name Revillos. See also chapter 11.

Geordie (Real name Kevin Walker. Killing Joke: guitar)

Adam was a great performer. He would come to our gigs and disguise himself in a fucking trench coat. We were doing 'Wardance' and we would spot him in the venue, that old Virgin venue by Victoria, checking out 'Wardance', before he ever did any of his tribal shit. It was all over with the Ants when Andy Warren left.

NO FUTURE FOR ENGLAND'S DREAMING
The Sex Pistols' 'God Save the Queen' and the Jubilee

Even before Virgin had released the Sex Pistols' second single, 'God Save the Queen', they ran into problems with the pressing plant, who refused to press up the single, and then the sleeve artwork plate makers, who refused to handle the cover. They all had to be coerced into issuing the record. Cheekily enough, Virgin attempted to get a TV ad for the single played during the Bill Grundy Show. Thames TV unsurprisingly didn't let them. On 23 May the Pistols filmed the video for the song at the Marquee club, and finally the single was released on 27 May in its classic Jamie Reid sleeve. It was the biggest promotional campaign in Virgin's history. They needn't have bothered. From its spine-tingling, Steve Jones-riffed intro to its crunching end the record has everything: a brilliant tune, a rousing chorus, incendiary lyrics sung with a magnificent, malicious glee, a genius churning guitar sound and fantastic dynamics. It was a political hand-grenade chucked out in the middle of Jubilee week, and the high watermark of punk rock. Very rarely can a pop record have been so perfectly timed. The BBC inevitably banned it, and many record stores refused to stock it.

7 June was the day of the main Jubilee celebrations in London, and also the day of the Pistols' famous boat trip. As publicity scams go, this was one of the best. The Pistols played on a boat called the Queen

Elizabeth *and set sail down the Thames. It ended perfectly in chaos, as the cops raided the boat and arrests were made.*

Al Hillier

At last it now seemed that the message had started to spread out all over the country and 'real' people from council estates in places like Manchester, Leeds and Birmingham were finally waking up to the music generated by a pop cultural revolution. The excitement on the streets of London was indescribable. Expectations and preparations for the Queen's Silver Jubilee only seemed to add to the carnival-type atmosphere and the planning for these celebrations made it feel like everyone was simply gearing up to take part in one mad fucking party. The Pistols genuinely captured the atmosphere of 1977 and 'God Save the Queen' was its undisputed anthem.

Keith Levene

I know the Sex Pistols get a lot of credit for this 'no future' thing – that's the way Jamie Reid put it, that's the way it was packaged. But we all knew we were fucked. There were no jobs.

John Lydon

I wrote the song 'God Save The Queen' as a laugh. It's a giggle, it's vaudeville, it's burlesque. It's not a rampant anti-royal statement. Far from it. Get with the programme, boys and girls! When I sang 'Pretty Vacant' I was not telling you that I was pretty or vacant. Irony, it was.

The whole idea of the verse/chorus structure was not for me. I don't write like that in any set of lyrics. I write lyrics that you can't fit into that verse/chorus thing. If you really listen to 'God Save the Queen', it's not structured in any normal way at all, as indeed is any Sex Pistols song. We break every rule in the book and we do it without you noticing, and that's a skill, I guess. It was with an absolute pride that we were accused of being poor musicians – that was an achievement, I thought, a major achievement.

The world of music at that time was so pontificating with bands like ELP and Yes and Pink Floyd who brought in this aspect of slow, twaddly self-indulgence, which to me is not what music means. We were against that; at least I thought we were. The reality was, I think, that Steve actually couldn't play, which is why I love his playing the most. Nobody can't play the guitar better than Steve! Paul Cook is basically Charlie Watts of the Rolling Stones, a rock-solid, no-frills-whatsoever drummer, probably one of the best people on stage I've worked with. Paul I could rely on, he had that perfect tempo.

Incompetence is a really, really brilliant thing – don't lose it. You find that way you do things naturally, and you find things that you believe in. You're not trying to fit into a format. You're faking it when the whole purpose of the song is to have structure – that should be the very last thing on your mind. It should have a point and a purpose but not a structure.

We were doing what we wanted to. We were not waving no flag for everyone to go and stand behind. Quite the opposite. We were standing up and shouting what we believed in, and if a few others were like that, that's all well and fine, but you can't have this mass movement nonsense – because you become sheep. You become the problem when you do that.

Ari Up

I was on the boat trip when the Pistols were banned everywhere at that time. They were having a hard time getting gigs. Me and John Grey had a laugh about this the other day. John Grey told me how actually John and them didn't end up getting arrested. John Grey took them sneakily away. John and whoever, Paul Cook, came down the stairways somewhere and they went off to the pub. We were laughing: all the stupid people got arrested and we, all the clever ones, got away because we were in the pub! [laughs]

Marco Pirroni

I wasn't invited to the boat party. They didn't invite me to anything at all.

John Lydon

I'll tell you honestly: on the Jubilee boat trip I didn't even know the Jubilee was going on! I just thought it was a party on the Thames. That's about as much interest as I really had.

On 11 June, 'God Save the Queen' hit Number One despite a blanket TV and radio ban. It was one of the great moments in pop history. The charts tried to pretend it was Number Two but everyone knew who was at the top. It was Jubilee week and whilst half the country was sat there, eating stale sandwiches underneath the bunting, the rest of us had a rallying call. It caused the band some problems and in the next week John Lydon was attacked twice on the streets. Punk was now confrontational and attacking the very heart of the state. Politics, polemic and rowdy tunes were the very soul of punk rock.

Marco Pirroni

I saw the Pistols at Notre Dame Hall. That was the only time I saw them with Sid, and the first time I heard 'God Save the Queen'. They were playing it over and over on the PA and it sounded brilliant. A bit like 'Cum On Feel The Noize – the first chord is the same. It's the greatest pop rock'n'roll single ever. It had everything you need on a record. The fact it got to Not Number One was even better. I see Paul and Steve sometimes and I say to them, 'I know I had loads of Number Ones, but you had a single that got to Not Number One.' I'm not sure if they get the significance of that.

Siouxsie Sioux

Before we were on the Bill Grundy show with the Pistols, and before punk had been seized on by the tabloids, there was a healthy fear of our appearance. And it's funny how that fear turned to hatred once the phenomenon had been identified – or once it was considered to have been identified and contained. When I hired a costume from Berman's & Nathan's to go and see Roxy Music at Wembley Arena in 1975 (it was a cross between a mermaid and a chorus girl – purple sequins with a fish-tail train) I didn't get changed in the toilets at Charing Cross station. I travelled up to town in the outfit. I got odd looks, but more often than not if they saw you looking they'd turn away. I think that people sense that kind of single-mindedness, and don't dare approach you. But all that really did change once punk was picked up on in the media. Then, the public reaction really was abusive.

Mensi

The punk scene was very small at the time in Sunderland. We used to get beat up everywhere. I was beat up in Jarrow one night, beat up in Sunderland one night. The things in the paper about punk outrage were stirring things up. People would just attack you in the streets. We used to get kicked and punched. I had spiky hair and a leather jacket. The thing was, when I started the band it spread like wildfire that I was in a band and people used to take a pop at us for being a punk.

Then punk started to spread and it became acceptable to like us, especially among football fans – they loved that 'Police Oppression' sort of thing – so it went full circle from being beat up to them following us.

The first gig I played was at a youth club in South Shields, then Jarrow – all little venues through 1977. Serious bods came down. All of a sudden we built up a massive following: hooligans, criminals, the whole fraternity. We went from being minute to be being huge. When we first started we had six songs and we had to play them twice. We did have a classic one, straight into the set with 'Police Oppression'. 'Liddle Towers' came soon after, and 'Leave Me Alone' and a couple of covers like Chris Montez's 'Let's Dance'.

Ian Brown

You can't explain to people what those days were like. You used to get chased around town for having your hair spiked and not wearing flared jeans. You used to have to hunt to get the gear. You couldn't just buy punk clothes – that's what doing it yourself was all about.

J. J. Burnel

The Stranglers' song 'Something Better Change' was the zeitgeist of the times. It sums up what was happening. I remember walking down the street to one of the sessions when we were doing the *No More Heroes* album, and there were some Teddy boys on the other side of the road throwing beer bottles at me because I was wearing plastic jeans or something, and they didn't like the way I was dressed. They came over, so I sorted the mouthiest one out. I thought there was things starting to piss people off summer of 1977 and that was what that was about.

Guy Trelford

When the Sex Pistols released 'God Save the Queen', Unionists in general took offence to the song, deeming it a slur on the monarchy, and Loyalists branded us punks as anti-British (which may have been true of some punks, but certainly by no means all). When Rudi played the Strathearn Hotel soon after the single came out, the Holywood UDA (the UDA being the largest Loyalist paramilitary organisation) threatened to go down en masse and kill the punks! Thankfully they didn't carry out the threat, but it was enough to put the wind up the punks and served to highlight just what we were up against.

A couple of years later that song would come back to haunt us. Myself and a couple of mates were on an all-day bender. We ended up in a bar just outside of town. Now it's been the tradition over the years in Northern Ireland that the national anthem, 'God Save the Queen', be played at the end of the night in pubs, clubs and cinemas in predominantly Protestant/Unionist/Loyalist areas and everyone has to stand to attention. And that was the case in this bar. At the end of the night, when the band started to play the national anthem, we were completely wasted. From what I can remember one mate was lying unconscious across the seats, I had my head under the table puking my guts up and the other two started singing the Pistols' 'God Save the Queen'! Unbeknown to us there was a Loyalist paramilitary gang in the bar, and when we left they followed us to the bus stop (stopping at their car on the way to pick up some weapons) and beat the shit clean out of us!

John O'Neill

When the Sex Pistols happened, you could see it was not just a matter of the music, it was the attitude as well – especially their irreverence, that was fantastic. They made great records as well. When you could see what Johnny was saying it made so much sense – they just got up so many people's noses and that made it even better. In Derry most people at the time didn't take it that seriously. We obviously did, and there was 20 or 30 other people who got it. This was our Beatles and Stones, our music for our generation.

Brian Young

Punk was moving overground with the Pistols' media frenzy, and in Belfast things had gotten more dangerous everywhere as the dailies whipped up wholesale punk-bashing. Here too you had an additional implied religious/political spin which added an extra piquancy. Being seen as pro- or anti-monarchy could have a very real impact on your general well-being.

Billy Bragg

I lived through the boring early Seventies, and now my generation was going to take on the things the hippies failed to deliver. We were remaking our culture in a more dynamic way. I don't think we succeeded, though we tried in our own way to stay free, he said, picking up a Clash phrase! [laughs] I'm still engaged in the political process. From '77/78 I got a world view as a result of the feelings of empowerment and anger from punk.

There was a lot of apathy in the UK, and with punk a lot of people wanted to be engaged in the front line, which was more clearly defined in those days. There was none of our music on the TV, none of our music on car adverts. There was just Radio One and that didn't play punk either!

What we had was outrage. People were genuinely, morally offended by what we were doing and that was a great feeling to have. You could offend people by not wearing flares, to the point where you could get beaten up.

Strummer said a great thing: 'Every generation has to find some way of having to deal with the blues,' and when I threw that back to him a few years ago he said, 'Did I say that?' He'd forgotten he said it.

WE TRIED TO TAKE ON EVERYBODY
The Stranglers

They were the nastiest, funniest, darkest, moodiest, weirdest, most glowering bunch of outsider pop stars ever. The most off-the-wall band in the whole punk rock canon – a brutal slab of angry, snarling punk psychedelia served up as three-minute slices of pure pop magic. This surly attitude was combined with killer tunes; their bad attitude and dark charisma was a neat extra. They talked and sang about aliens, karate, motorbikes, Yukio Mishima, Leon Trotsky, heroin, Nostradamus, rats, ravens and alienation... This was no average band.

History has remembered the Clash and pushed the rest of the punk bands away; retro features now rewrite the history of the punk era around the Westway wonders. But as much as anyone who grew up with punk loves the Clash, it is a shame to see the Stranglers pushed aside. Their influence has been enormous and is wrongly overlooked. Their sheer aggression and the utter originality of their music, a dark swirl of keyboards, THAT bass and those guitar hooks, combined with the belligerent vocals of the twin frontmen, J. J. Burnel and Hugh Cornwell, all mashed together into one of the most potent sounds of the period – as reflected in their high record sales. They may have become the critical untouchables from the period, but the people loved them. And that, in punk rock, is what really counts.

J. J. Burnel

In November 1976 we had signed the deal with United Artists and we went straight in the studio. We were signed by Andrew Lauder, who had signed the Feelgoods and wanted to record us live, like on the Feelgoods' *Stupidity*, which had been Number One – probably the last live album to do so well. But we went to the studio in the end, TW studios in Fulham. We recorded most of first two albums in that session. For *No More Heroes*, we added a few more songs over the summer of '77, songs like 'English Towns', 'No More Heroes' and 'Something Better Change'. All the rest were pretty well done during the first session.

When the so-called punk revolution occurred we didn't fit in with the new orthodoxy, which was great. In a way it was better to be yourself, to be your own boss, not to be on a bandwagon, have your identity, your freedom. By the time we released our first album *Rattus Norvegicus* in early 1977, it stayed in the Top 10 for the whole year because we had this grassroots thing going on.

Alan Edwards, our press officer, helped to make us controversial. He had the raw material, though! He didn't have to invent much. Hugh was incredible at winding people up. The sexist thing then got attached to us. Call someone a wimp – just a choice of words – and we would get called fascists or brutes. The so-called right-on people like Rough Trade banned our records for being sexist and male chauvinist – the tag hasn't done us too many favours over the years. It was more a reflection of our detractors than us, because if you looked at it really carefully then you would see that our lyrics were quite journalistic, observations of ourselves

Nice an' sleazy does it! The Stranglers fronting out the audience at one of their hundreds of gigs on punk's frontline

as blokes and also the times that we were living in. I think it's very valid. We were honest; we were not advocating beating women. I don't know how it got from writing a song about a bloke hitting his girlfriend in a certain situation to somehow being reinterpreted as this is what men should do. I suppose people choose to see what they want to see.

There was confrontation all the time. It was a way of life. You've got to realise that when you push someone enough something is going to snap, and I wasn't going to get broken. Pundits would say you're talking intellectually in this song, going on about something genetic or historical, and the next next minute you're brutal and quite violent. They think if you do the intelligent stuff you have to be wimpy and quite sensitive. It was quite violent at the time – a whole bunch of us were fighting for an audience, and you couldn't back down because the credibility would have gone. We married the two and I don't see the contradiction.

We tried to take on everybody. In Glasgow I asked a whole audience out and they shut up pretty quick. [laughs] Someone had thrown beer at me. I made an ostentatious show of cleaning up with my towel, wrung out the towel, and said, 'Who did that? Come up here.' Two thousand people shut up. 'I'm a soft southern bastard. You're tough Glaswegians.' And there was not a peep.

We all took LSD quite a bit in those days. I remember Dave, myself and Hugh taking it one night, and Jet was MCing it for us, letting off indoor fireworks, that kind of thing [laughs], shouting, 'It's the Devil!' Jet did everything else, not the acid. At one point Jet was known as Mr Hoover.

Al Hillier

1977 was almost a blur for me: the Stranglers were like a juggernaut hurtling along, and they must have played well over 150 gigs in that year, as well as recording two albums and releasing four classic singles. The Finchley Boys tried to get to as many of these gigs as possible and I lost count in the end.

During the summer of '77 I was lucky enough to witness the Stranglers recording the album *No More Heroes*. Along with other Finchley Boys we would cram into the tiny TW Studios in Fulham Palace Road and would watch mesmerised as this legendary album was created right in front of us in just a couple of weeks. The spirit and the essence of the time had to be captured and recorded quickly and I really think that the Stranglers could have recorded *No More Heroes* in a dustbin if they had to. What is even more amazing was that the Stranglers were writing all this stuff whilst constantly on the road, and those songs were born out of our experiences at that time.

In the early days the Stranglers were an awesome unit musically as well as in their dealings with the press. John and Hugh would defend each other, the rest of the band or the Finchley Boys against anyone or anything with a single-minded ferocity that is normally reserved only for close family. When shit ever hit fan, it was never about who was right or wrong; it was simply us against them.

Back in '77 there was a relatively good-natured rivalry happening between John and Hugh, and it showed in the quality of their songwriting. They had that essential light and dark which seems to be present in every brilliant writing partnership, and trying to outdo each other by coming up with amazing guitar riffs or stunning bass lines was their driving force. Whatever has been written about them since, John and Hugh respected each other and they trusted each other implicitly. Apart from this dynamic approach to their music they also had interlocking competitive personalities and both of them were up for anything.

The Pistols released their anthemic third single, 'Pretty Vacant', on 1 July. The Glen Matlock-penned tune, while less controversial than its predecessors, still managed to capture the nihilism of the punk generation in a fantastic pop anthem. Boots, Woolworths and W. H. Smith all lifted their bans on Pistols records, and by mid-July the band even managed to get the promo clip for the single screened on Top of the Pops.

On 16 July, Capital Radio broadcast a 90-minute pre-recorded show called A Punk and His Music, *during which Johnny Rotten played some of his favourite tracks. It was a selection that surprised many; instead of the expected punk records, his choices included the Chieftains, Tim Buckley, Neil Young and Captain Beefheart, a good dose of dub reggae and an eighteen-minute Can track, 'Halleluhwah'.*

Tony D

I remember 'Pretty Vacant' standing out. It was too slow on record – live it was really powerful, a real barnstormer. I was thinking for the first time, 'This is a momentous occasion. This is important.' And 'Did You No Wrong' was the best song, although the live version was miles better.

Chris Bailey

We released our third single, 'This Perfect Day' with 'L. I. E. S.', on the same day as the Sex Pistols released 'Pretty Vacant'. It was our hit record: it got to Number 34 in the charts and it got us onto *Top of the Pops* on the same night as 'Pretty Vacant', which I thought was hysterically funny and, well, kind of ironic since we were more punk rock in our attitude than they were.

Even when I was really young I kind of made a concious decision that I never wanted to be a pop star. I loved singing in a band. I loved music. I love being in a recording studio. I don't even mind being on a stage – but being a pop star? I was really not interested in it. The intrusions, and having to live up to what you are, don't interest me at all. But here we are, we had a hit single and I would say we reacted, let's say, unprofessionally. To be on *Top of the Pops* in those days you had to mime to the backing tracks, so I would drop the microphone and sing into the air and get into trouble with the people there.

Don Letts

I remember hanging out with John Lydon, the Slits and the Clash, and no one was sat at home listening to punk. John was looking further afield into stuff like Can. He would be playing songs I had never heard of. He famously did that radio show and championed lots of off-the-wall stuff. John, Joe and Paul were there already with their reggae.

John Lydon

When I played my favourite records on Capital Radio in 1977, it was not important to me. I think it was a laugh. I was asked to go on and play the records that I liked, so I did. Internally, in the Pistols set-up, the management was furious. Malcolm had created this persona without even bothering to speak to me. This personification was that I was going to be a quiet man of mystery. Ha! I'm not quiet and there's certainly no mystery about me. He was barking up the wrong tree clearly.

As a focus of continuing annoyance, Malcolm was superb! Bollocks to all of that. It was a combined effort but, to be absolutely serious with you, how has anybody got anything to do with it if they haven't got the guts to be on the stage actually presenting it? Period. Whenever you hear the likes of managers and hairdressers waffling about, pay no attention.

In July 1977 the Sex Pistols toured Scandinavia. It was not uneventful, as Sid Vicious had to fly home to get fined for carrying a knife at the 100 Club festival. In mid-August the band began a short UK tour of small clubs under assumed names like the Tax Exiles, the Hamsters, and SPOTS (Sex Pistols On Tour Secretly). It was the only way they could avoid the blanket bans and media suffocation imposed on the band. They played off-circuit towns like Wolverhampton, Doncaster, Plymouth and, on 26 August, Middlesborough.

Tom (Punk fan from Middlesborough)

The day before the gig, rumours were rife that the Pistols were playing at the Rock Garden in Middlesborough. I phoned the venue and they told me that 'Acne Rabble' were playing. Bearing in mind that the Pistols had been banned from most venues in the UK and were playing under false names, I took the chance and went.

We got there and there were loads of people hanging around outside without tickets. The atmosphere was pretty heavy and I was nervous but went to the door and told the bouncer I had a ticket. They pulled me through the door and I was in. The atmosphere inside was electric. People had travelled from all over the North of England. In the toilet people were sniffing amyl nitrate. The lights then dimmed and there was an enormous roar. I'm not even sure if half the crowd expected the band to be the Sex Pistols! Cook, Vicious and Jones walked onstage and as they struck the first chords of 'Anarchy', in walked Rotten. The place went mad: bodies flying about, and showers of spit landing on the stage, covering Johnny Rotten and the grim-faced bouncers at the front of the stage. Rotten wiped himself with a towel and said, 'I take it you like us.' Mid-set, Vicious was covered in blood from a self-inflicted wound to his nose and looked totally out of it. The set included all the classics. They encored with 'No Fun'. That night I went from liking prog rock to totally being into punk.

Mark Perry

After a year of doing the fanzine, I got really frustrated with punk, with things like the Clash signing to CBS and the new lot that were coming along, the street punk like the UK Subs. Lovely blokes, but weren't my cup of tea. I thought I could have a go myself. I fancied myself as a bit of a songwriter, and that's why I formed Alternative TV. It was my attempt to try something a little different. I think the biggest difference with ATV was probably Frank Zappa, 'cause we did things like cut-ups, put live stuff with studio stuff, and had four-teen-minute long tracks. I would improvise onstage, have free-form poetry and all that. I wouldn't be considered punk, but I thought we was. Punk was being free to do what you wanted. Not turn into some jazz freak, but being free to explore rock music. I think that ATV could be the hardest-rocking punk band out there, but also we could be the most sensitive punk band, the most interesting.

In the first couple of months when I started *Sniffin' Glue*, I wasn't really aware of any other fanzines at all. But then others started cropping up and we realised that we were probably influencing other people. For the first six months fanzines were definitely important, because punk was not really being written about that in what I considered to be the right way by the major music papers. But after a year, after the Jubilee and that, fanzines had lost their edge. There was almost no need for them, because the press changed so quickly to being punk papers. Incredibly really, within six months to a year you would see the Clash or the Stranglers or the Jam on the front.

Just to add to that – although from my point of view there was no need for fanzines, on a local level fanzines are really important, to tell you what's going on at a local club or local radio station, local bands and all that. The reason I did *Sniffin' Glue* was because there was nothing else about. I finished *Sniffin' Glue* after twelve issues. It could have become a glossy magazine, it could have been quite successful. There was a lot of people at the time offering me money to keep it going as a proper magazine, but I didn't want to keep the magazine going for the sake of it, to make a lot of money like a publishing magnate. When there ceased to be a need for it, I just stopped doing it. What I get now off fanzines is they're just writing so other fanzines can read them. There don't seem any point when you can buy a regular magazine to find out what's going on.

CHAPTER 9
1977 PART III: GENERATION WHY

In the summer of 1977 the punk wars were raging. The big bands were taking the battle to the Establishment. Meanwhile a whole new generation of musicians was coming though.

Barely a week went by without a great punk rock single. From Wire's quirky restructuring of rock to 999's anthemic punchy debut, 'I'm Alive', punk was fracturing pretty quickly into many different interpretations. Everyone came into punk with a different agenda and now everyone was using the tools of punk in very different ways.

Colin Newman

We released our first album, *Pink Flag*, in 1977. Mike Thorne, who produced it, had done the *Live at the Roxy* album. The opening track, 'Reuters', was an attempt to trample unkindly over the Who. (I'm very, very obscure in my references – nobody gets it except for me.) You can go through *Pink Flag* and there's a deconstruction going on, taking rock history apart and putting it back together again. It was like conceptual sampling [laughs]. It wasn't just about destroying rock'n'roll. It was very specific references and being disrespectful in certain kinds of ways to classic rock'n'roll.

Nick Cash

We signed to United Artists. They had done a good job with the Stranglers, and in 999 we had the same managers as the Stranglers. We got a bit overshadowed by them really. The singles sold quite well. We were popular in Japan and in America where we were bigger than the other bands. People were saying, 'I'm So Bored of the USA' – it was a load of bollocks. You should stay in a council flat in Brixton! We were saying to our fans, 'Do you think we should go to America?' and they said, 'If we were in your position then we would go and play there.' People are the same all over the world – America, Brazil and Japan. You got an empathy with young people who passionately cared about things, so why not go there and play music for them?

Aki Qureshi (Southern Death Cult, Fun-Da-Mental: drums and producer)

My elder brother got into punk immediately the whole thing landed, to the total disapproval of my parents, being from Pakistan. It was a shock to my father, as he had sent my brother to private school on the income of a bus conductor, and this was the result! I recall picking up a record – I think it was the Clash – and totally going mad as it blared out of the cheap Waltham hi-fi system, and I was baptised! The day after, I went to school with a baby's dummy hanging from my sad jeans waistcoat, and my hair had been transformed from a John Travolta hairstyle to a scruffy Sid Vicious look. Everyone freaked. Punk and Pakistani? What a combination!

It seemed that all the groups releasing stuff were somehow creating a buzz in some shape or form. The creativity was evangelical – I cannot recall a record being released and me thinking, 'This is crap.' It was all exciting. I loved 999 and Penetration. Adam and the Ants came a bit later, due to the elitist attitude of their followers, but I appreciated their creative edge. Seriously it was a combination of all of them, and also local bands such as the Negatives impacted on me.

The reggae scene also became part of the picture. There were so many things going on.

Pauline Murray

Penetration had started to take off by this time. The Stranglers played at the Newcastle City Hall. They had a record deal and were starting to get into the charts. We did the support which was great.

We recorded the demo in the local youth club on a tape recorder. We set up billiard tables to mask the sound. Proper DIY! We took it into the Virgin record shop in Newcastle, which was then a very small shop, and the manager there then sent it to the London office. They said, 'Do some proper demos,' which we did and they offered us a one-off single deal, which was 'Don't Dictate'. It took a lot longer before they actually signed us.

There was nothing premeditated with our sound. We were very young, about eighteen, and our drummer was sixteen. There was fifteen-year-olds in bands like Eater. Equally you had Jet Black who was ancient! [laughs] A lot of the bands were ten years older than us – Elvis Costello, Joe Strummer, Patti Smith – and really very supportive of all the new bands.[1] It's hard to believe these days, but people did genuinely enjoy and support other bands. All the bands were different. Once the record companies took over that was when it all got fragmented.

The only reason we signed to Virgin was that the Sex Pistols were on Virgin and we wanted to be on the same label as them. Decca were interested. We weren't very sensible about any of that business side. I don't think Virgin were that keen on us. They realised that we were doing well live, that we had a following, but

---

1. One great thing about punk was that there were no rules: a band made up of schoolboys (drummer Dee Generate was actually fourteen when he joined Eater in 1976) could be endorsed alongside a 40-year-old ex-ice-cream salesman. Eater cut some fine singles and frontman Andy Blade's *The Secret Life of a Teenage Punk Rocker* is a great account of the punk years. Meanwhile Jet Black's powerhouse drumming, with its tinge of jazz, was one of the vital contributions to the Stranglers' sound.

we weren't really one of their types of bands. They were more keen on XTC and Devo. XTC were Branson's pet band. We were just on the label and left to get on with it.

Mark Stewart

It was cool, such a mixture of things going on. Punk clubs started opening up in Bristol, putting on Siouxsie and the Banshees and Slaughter and the Dogs. In Bristol we had funk DJs, sound systems – everyone was chipping in. The Cortinas came together, and we hung round them. We started playing school parties, and then we played with Johnny Thunders and the Heartbreakers.

We started off playing what we could, minimal T. Rex things and 'I Wanna Be Your Dog'. Straight away I wanted to play 'Ear' by Edwin Starr and 'Firebird' by the Ohio Players. We ended up with delinquent disco, or whatever you call it. To me the idea of punk was 'cut and paste': if you can cut off the Queen's head and stick it on top of a nude, you can put Norwegian death metal on top of ragga.

The reggae thing was in there as well. The Pop Group were playing mates' parties and school dances. I was a bit of a promoter at school. We had DJs so there was already a vibe with everyone dancing before we played. In two or three days it had taken off, the local press was going mad. In a couple of months the national press was coming down to watch us in churches in Bristol, saying we were cutting edge, avant-garde.

We liked funky Ornette Coleman and Albert Ayler.[2] We weren't trying to be left field, but we were trying to be a pop group. We thought punk had happened and there was no point in doing it all again. We tried to be punk again by mixing punk and funk.

I felt a lot of kinship with James Chance and the Contortions. I was hanging out in New York early on with Keith Leblanc and the

---

2. Ayler was one of the great innovators in free jazz. Ornette Coleman was a revolutionary jazz sax player.

Sugarhill Gang, Doug and the Bambaataa crew, early DNA.[3] We loved 'Little Johnny Jewel' by Television. It blew me and my mates away. It came out in 1975, way before anything else in England. Television played Bristol early on. We were into Patti Smith, who we got to tour with when we were still at school. I knocked off my A levels to play Paris with Pere Ubu!

We were into electronic stuff. We used to play this weird Pierre Henry stuff before gigs to destabilise people.[4] I've just been talking to Richard from Cabaret Voltaire and they were getting into stuff like that in 1974. Genesis P-Orridge was the same. People in isolation were getting into it. Punk gave people the confidence to have a go on their own terms. Before that they had to get dressed in a cape and go to a private school like Charterhouse. The Clash opened up lots of doors to people, broke down the barriers.

Marco Pirroni

The Banshees at the 100 Club was a one-off for me. I didn't want to be in the band. They didn't like me and they didn't like Sid either! I thought it was understood that they could do their own thing, it was their name. I then got together with some old Bowie/Roxy fans, mates from school, and we formed this band the Models and did some gigs, but it was a bit too late. We didn't get it together in time. It took me a long time to decide to actually do it. There is this thing about first and second wave punk, and we were one-and-a-half wave! I was too busy pissing about.

The Models' 'Freeze' is one of the great lost singles of punk. It was released on Step Forward, one of the earliest punk labels, run by Miles

---

3. Hip hop was the next key music scene to emerge after punk. When the black kids in the ghetto first heard Kraftwerk they took it somewhere else, creating electro music. Pretty soon they would rap over the backing tracks at block parties, and a whole new scene, a new way of making music, would emerge.

4. French composer Pierre Henry was, from the late 1940s onwards, one of the founders of *musique concrète*, an avant-garde movement that preferred noise and electronic sound to conventional instrumentation. Far from easy listening but highly influential.

Copeland, which also signed up Chelsea and Sham 69. Its A&R manager was none other than Mark Perry.

Gene October

Punk in '77 changed very quickly, because a lot of very greedy people forced it to change. They all quickly wanted big deals, and forced everyone else who didn't get one to think they were rubbish – if you were any good you got a deal. But I was quite happy for Chelsea to be on Step Forward. There was a nice atmosphere, and the people there were great. If you needed a couple of bob, Miles Copeland gave it to you. I did eat, I did sleep, I got drunk – what more do you want? [laughs]

Our single 'Hi Rise Living' is very street, pushing that thing of living in high-rise blocks, which was a very big thing in London in them days. And in a lot of cities nobody hit that subject.

Marco Pirroni

The Models did the Heartbreakers' tour at the end of 1977.[5]

Damian O'Neill

Me, Vincent and my brother saved up all our dole money and went to see Johnny Thunders play in Manchester Poly. My eldest brother Jim was at university at the time and he put us up. Johnny Thunders was my guitar hero. He was on great form, not smacked up, supported by Siouxsie and the Banshees and the Models – great line-up! I remember Siouxsie Sioux because she was wearing her tits T-shirt. I was like, *wow!* So audacious. Not like a Derry girl at all!

Don Letts

I went off on this tour with Siouxsie and the Banshees and the Heartbreakers, and I'm filming the bands. I was doing *The Punk*

---

5. The Heartbreakers toured all round the UK in October 1977, with the Banshees and the Models as support.

Rock Movie which ended up being screened at the ICA the following year. That's the first film that I made.

Mick Rossi

Slaughter and the Dogs were playing down London a lot. We played the Roxy and the Vortex, we played the Marquee – great gig. Driving down and back in the transit van, freezing in the back with all the gear. We had a bit of following down there. Everyone was trying to sign bands off the punk rock scene. We were in Don Letts' *Punk Rock Movie* – I didn't even know we were in that till five years ago!

Captain Sensible

Two or three things conspired to make us invisible. One, we didn't do the Grundy show. Two, we were banned from TV. At the time we were banned by the technicians' union. I can't remember which show caused it, but on the way to filming the show we stopped off to buy air rifles. We were just shooting them off in the studio! [laughs] We were shooting the cameramen up the arse while they were filming other bands. It didn't go down terribly well and we got banned for six months, and that doesn't help to raise your profile.

The other problem was that people like Don Letts were filming everything that moved on stage at the time, and Jake Riviera, or whoever was looking after us, would go up to them and ask for £500 in the hand and 'I'll let you film the band.' Of course nobody had £500 at the time, so we never got filmed. All these other bands like the Clash, or anyone who played any gigs at the time, were filmed everywhere, but you hardly see any Damned footage at all from that period, and that's why! When people put these films together of old footage, nobody can ever find any of the Damned.[6]

---

6. Not strictly true. There is a great clip of the band playing 'Problem Child', and also their appearance on the *Marc* TV show.

And they just keep coming: another week, another classic single. X-Ray Spex's debut single 'Oh Bondage! Up Yours!' introduced the world to Poly Styrene's fantastic voice, her brilliant day-glo take on the world, and lyrics that hit on many more levels than most people take them for.

John Lydon

I loved Poly Styrene. X-Ray Spex, now there was a tough band. They came out with a sound and an attitude that was just not relating to anything around. It was superb.

Poly Styrene

A lot of people misunderstood 'Oh Bondage!' They thought it was about S&M sex. That was partly my fault for leaving it open to the imagination. I come from a religious background, and it's in the scriptures, the whole idea of being liberated is to come free from the bondage of the material world. At that stage I hadn't gone into the spiritual aspect of bondage. I hadn't gone that far. I certainly had an idea of bondage – those images from history of the suffragettes chaining themselves to walls, or slaves being chained up, were what I was thinking of. When I saw Vivienne Westwood's bondage trousers, I'm not sure what she was trying to do, but it symbolised all the other bondage elements I had grown up with, and somehow that all ended up in the song.

I found consumer bondage too. That's why I became a hippie. I had been working in the fashion industry as a junior buyer before. I'd catch the bus home and everybody seemed to be like wage slaves. In bondage with big business. But you could be a hippie or a dropout – escape the rat race. A lot of heads liked X-Ray Spex.

I did a demo of 'Oh Bondage! Up Yours!' before X-Ray Spex in about 1975. Gary Moore plays on it![7] I don't know what happened to that. Gary was an amazing guitarist. The version was a bit bluesy, not the right sound – it was too sophisticated. When I

---

7. Gary Moore was the guitarist in Skid Row and then, more famously, Thin Lizzy.

formed X-Ray Spex I wanted it more raw. I thought it would be better if it was short and fast.

Budgie

The Spitfire Boys was only going for a few months but it seems like years looking back. We got RKO Records interested – they wanted to put out a single out by a punk band, like everyone did. We had our two minutes of glory. We cut our record, but we couldn't even give it away! At our last gig at Eric's we were throwing them off the stage – 'Take these home! We don't want them any more!' [laughs]

Pretty much after that Big In Japan decided to become a more serious band. Bill Drummond was very ambitious. He wanted to carve a proper band out, a legend!

The Spitfires folded in December 1977 because by that point Pete Griffiths, the bass player, wanted to be a magazine publisher – he wanted to be William Burroughs. I think Holly was himself all wrapped up in homosexual iconography and Burroughs fantasies. I basically joined Big In Japan and that's when we rehearsed properly: me, Ian Broudie and Bill Drummond. We went to Eric's every day and worked songs out, and every now and then we would get Jayne in to work on her songs with us. We worked hard at it for six months. We got knocked back by the labels – it didn't go as we thought it would. We ran out of steam really. Big In Japan had people who went on to do things, it had a lot of drive – it was a good breeding ground if nothing else.[8] We did our EP and decided to call it a day. We played our last gig on Mathew Street. We felt good and said that we were not doing it any more.

---

8. Bill Drummond went on to set up Zoo Records, releasing Echo and the Bunnymen and others, before hitting the big time with his subversive techno-Situationist project KLF (via a Number One hit as the Timelords). Ian Broudie became one of the key guitar pop producers of the Eighties and Nineties, had hits with his band the Lightning Seeds, and wrote the ubiquitous football song 'Three Lions'. Also in Big in Japan were Jayne Casey, who is still a Liverpool face, and Holly Johnson, who went on to front the hugely successful Frankie Goes to Hollywood.

BURNING BABYLON
The Start of the Second Wave

The working-class roots revolution that punk had promised was fast coming to fruition. Inspired by the initial punk explosion and its DIY ethic, a whole new raft of bands had been forming. Punk's second wave, which began to take up the baton in 1977, was generally tougher-sounding and less art school than the first wave. Among its ranks were Sham 69, the UK Subs, the Angelic Upstarts, Menace, the Members, the Cockney Rejects and the Ruts. Arguably, those in the second wave were the true punk bands fulfilling punk's original prophecy. This really was the sound of the streets, and the gigs could get out of hand. A confused, mixed bag of politics was thrown into the pot, creating occasional flashpoints.

Deko

The second wave was much bigger than the first wave. The first wave was a studenty thing, not really punk – rich kids. The second wave was much harder.

Segs

I had met Ruffy, the Ruts' drummer, in a funk import shop near Victoria in 1976. I was buying funk and stuff like Parliament. I still had long hair at that point. He was playing in a band called Hit and Run. I came in one day, and he had a home-made Ramones T-shirt on. I said, 'Who are they?' He played me 'Beat On The Brat' and I thought, 'Fucking hell, brilliant!' Then 'Anarchy in the UK' came out, and we were driving round London listening to 'Spiral Scratch'. I started hanging out with the band, and when they shuffled the line up I joined – although I had to cut my hair! It was round Paul Fox's house – Malcolm made a huge pipe with black hash and we had a beautiful line of coke.[9] They said, 'You passed the audition,' whilst my eyes were spinning around!

---

9. Paul Fox was the Ruts' guitar player. Malcolm Owen was their talismanic vocalist.

We formed as a punk band. Malcolm and Foxy had songs like 'Lobotomy', 'Out Of Order', 'Rich Bitch', 'I Ain't Sofisticated', 'Stepping Bondage' – all primitive punk thrash with some really good playing. Ruffy was a good drummer. It was the real thing. We did the Vortex and the Roxy. It was not the real height of the Roxy. We were looked on as the second wave of punk.

Micky Geggus (Cockney Rejects: guitar)

We were always on the outside looking in at punk gigs. We couldn't stand the punk in-crowd. After the gig we would slope back to the Bridge House in the East End and listen to the home-grown bands like the Tickets. The Bridge House was important – that's where it all started for us.

The punks were totally upper class, the lot of them. The lengths that Bernie Rhodes went to to disguise their middle-class roots was absolutely ridiculous. They made great music and said great stuff, but it was the same with Jagger and 'Street Fighting Man'. I doubt if Jagger has ever had a fight in his life.

The first time I heard 'New Rose' by the Damned it totally blew me away. I thought it was a great rock song. It didn't take too long to get where it was going, which was great when you were seventeen or eighteen. In the early days I went to see the Damned several times. Vince went to see the Sex Pistols on the SPOTS tour.[10] We would also go and see Nazareth, and the Skids when they first started later on – they were a great band, fucking brilliant. They stand up to anyone today.

Jimmy Pursey

Our first Sham 69 gigs were horrendous. I had every fucking lunatic following me about. But it was probably the most exciting time of my life, the early stages when I knocked about with Mark Perry and Danny Baker, Tony Parsons and Julie Burchill and people like that.

---

10. Vince Riordan would play bass in the Cockney Rejects.

Those early days were absolutely awesome, because everybody we were knocking about with was on the same wavelength, and we were all accelerating along at the speed of light.

Mark Perry could see how honest we were. I was not trying to sell myself as a pop star as well. What helped me was that a lot of those people were south London people – Tony Parsons, Mark, Danny Baker – and they influenced the *NME*. Whatever they were saying, the *NME* would let them have it.

At that time you had to have a real hunger for what you were doing because the London audience would eat you alive if you didn't. Within two minutes of having our first record out, 'I Don't Wanna', we were getting told that we had sold out. That went through all of us: the Pistols, the Clash, everyone. That's why the Clash wouldn't do *Top of the Pops*. We said we would do it because

The Hersham boys gatecrash the punk party with their rowdy raucous rabble-rousing anthems

instead of letting them try and get rid of us one of us had to do *Top of the Pops* – there won't be a punk movement without somebody going on TV. Groups won't be seen any more, just disappear.

Terrie

I really liked Sham 69. I like their first LP. All the other punk bands sounded competent, then suddenly these tough cockneys sounded like what I thought punk should sound like. When I saw them live it was a weird gig – all the skinheads beating up everyone. I was really flabbergasted. This didn't happen in Holland! [laughs] Skinheads in Holland were really innocent. When you came to London, Jesus! I remember at an Angelic Upstarts gig I knocked one beer off one skinhead, and it was a bit scary. It was really rough, nothing like Holland. It was fascinating, all these rough guys into music. [laughs]

Noel Martin

In Menace we used to knock about with Crisis, Chelsea, Mark Perry, the Wasps, Cortinas. They were all out the same sort of stable as us. In 1977 we hooked up with an agent who also did Sham 69. We'd played with Sham a couple of times down the Roxy before this, and then we did a lot of gigs with them after that.

We were doing all these little gigs. The first punk festival was going to be at Charlton Athletic Football Club, but there was a great fear about it and it was cancelled by the GLC. So there was a bit of that going on when we wrote 'GLC'. The lyrics don't make sense, but it's kind of about authority. At the time we really didn't know if it was a good song or not. In fact it was Wayne County who said to us, 'You should record that.' Well, we would have anyway – we only ever had eleven songs and we recorded them all! [laughs] How we are still going round playing them is a surprise to me! And how we are an influence on anybody with those songs!

We played as far up as Wolverhampton, as far west as Newport and as far south as Southampton. We basically played around

Embodying the true bohemian spirit of punk rock, Charlie Harper has remained on the road for ever

London and that area, which was a great shame as we were told that people in Ireland really liked us. Even now we are our own worst enemies!

No particular writer liked us at the time, no agent, no record company. The money slowly dwindled away, then Morgan, our singer, one day just didn't turn up. We didn't know he had a drug problem at the time.

Menace's 'GLC' was one of the great anthems of the time. The chorus, 'GLC, you full of shit!', was punk's first real terrace anthem and digs its way into your head. It's still a highpoint of the band's set to this day, with huge crowds of teen punk rockers singing along to a song that wasn't a hit years before they were born!

Nicky Tesco (The Members: vocals)

The Members were influenced by dub and reggae. It was a music that I personally preferred: Marley, Delroy Wilson, Johnny Clarke, Lee Perry was our pop. It was what we listened to. Reggae was our grounding.

J. C. Carroll

Nicky Tesco asked me to join the Members. He was from my home town of Camberley. Punk rock was a very wide spectrum – the difference between the Ramones and Television in America. People seemed to think it was motorcycle jackets doing Ramones-type numbers, but that was not always the case. It gave people a chance.

Our first gig was with the UK Subs. In those days Charlie Harper ran a successful hairdressing business.

Brian X

Charlie Harper, God bless him, still had his hairdressers at the time. The UK Subs are one of the great punk bands, aren't they?

Charlie Harper

I was going to the clubs in London and saw the punk scene happening and wanted to be part of it. Me and Richard started writing numbers that would eventually be Subs numbers, and then I joined a band a friend of mine had. They had a great name, the Subversives, which got shortened down to the Subs, then we heard about the Scottish band called the Subs who had rescued old ladies from snow-drifts in Scotland! So we had to change the name of the band.

I came home one weekend in 1977, and Nicky Garratt was in my sitting room. His mate from his squat had told him about our band, the US Jets! He got the name wrong but the address right! I played him our tapes. He liked them. He wanted immediately to throw away the covers and write his own stuff. He already had his own punk band, the Specimens, and he had some songs written. He got the music from his stuff and gave it to me. In two or three days' writing, we had seven numbers, like 'I Live in a Car' and 'Stranglehold'. We had a set, and played our first gigs in October. Nicky hated all that r'n'b stuff that I'd been doing. [laughs] His idol was Ritchie Blackmore! He was into Deep Purple – you can hear that on early Subs stuff. He plays a Strat, very Ritchie Blackmore. Nicky sounds a bit metal. I don't really like metal, but when you sing over it, it sounds like punk rock.

In 1977 the punk thing exploded. The Pistols went to America, the Clash went to Europe, Siouxsie was touring round the country, the Jam and Stranglers all had hits: all the first wave bands got big tours, and everyone came to London to see what was going on there. We were in the right place at right time. We were a lot of people's idea of what a punk band was all about.

This punk thing sets people on fire. It got radical in those days. We were going places. We were packing out every pub in south London to capacity. We were playing fast and furious. I remember walking down Oxford Street, the four of us, and the Pistols were coming towards us. Punks were everywhere. We were playing Vortex, all the venues. Although there was a lot of it in the papers, we never thought it would get so big. We never thought we would be the vanguard of music. And there were some great bands. The Buzzcocks are still one of the greatest bands in the world.

THE NORTH WILL RISE AGAIN
Manchester and the Buzzcocks

The Buzzcocks released their second single nearly a year after 'Spiral Scratch'. Having just signed to United Artists, they had the extra polish of a Martin Rushent production and 'Orgasm Addict' sets the standard for the new added pop sheen Buzzcocks. The song itself is, of course, a classic. Breathlessly orgasmic, it still cums all over the stereo. And its Linder Sterling-designed sleeve is a punk icon in itself.

Meanwhile the vibrant Manchester scene which they had pioneered was continuing to evolve, producing a number of successful and influential bands in varied styles.

Steve Diggle

We were touring around and there were queues everywhere. We did 'Spiral Scratch' and we had six major labels phoning every day trying to sign us. The bloke from CBS was offering us as much money as we wanted, but we wanted artistic control and knew what we were getting into. We enjoyed our crowd. It wasn't about the fame; it was about the music. 'Spiral Scratch' was a lot for us to do – when you're doing a lot of gigs, it's hard to be a record company on the road. And me and Pete didn't want to run a record label as well as being in a band. But we didn't want to sign a deal and have record companies tell us what to do. The next single was to be 'Orgasm Addict', and we didn't want labels telling us we couldn't release a song with that title.

We would rehearse in Little Peter Street. Joy Division were in one bit and we were in another. We just turned up and blasted through the songs. It was really fast, the way we wrote; it was the magic of the band. Other bands would rehearse the intro for hours and we'd have a couple of songs down! The chemistry between us all was important. We knew what we doing.

We had all these record companies after us, and UA man Andrew Lauder came down to us, and we got to know him chatting to him after the shows. We said we wanted control over the album and put out what we wanted, that we didn't want anyone blanking it if it was outragous. That's why we signed to Lauder. Martin Rushent came with the package of our deal with United Artists. He was kind of the in-house producer. He had already had big success producing the Stranglers.[11] So we went down to the studio that he worked in, TW in Fulham, and started recording the album.

Martin Rushent was a good producer, and the chemistry really worked. We'd run through a song three times, pick the best backing track, put the vocals on and put the overdubs on. From there it was easy to do. We were tight as a band. A lot of people say the first album is the best-produced of all the punk albums. It wasn't polished, it was the *right* production.

---

11. As mentioned above, it was Lauder who had signed Dr Feelgood and the Stranglers to United Artists, and he would go on to sign the Pop Group. A decade later he would sign the Stone Roses.

Linder Sterling

I made the photomontage for 'Orgasm Addict' late in 1976, but it was one of a series. Buzzcocks had asked me to be their designer, but typography never came easily to me at that time. The typography lessons were always on Thursday mornings, and on Wednesday evenings I used to go to the Poly Disco, which was one of the few places in Manchester at that time that played interesting combinations of music. Therefore Thursday I was always a little frayed around the edges, and found it difficult to concentrate on point sizes and typesetting. I asked Malcolm Garrett to help me with the Buzzcocks design.[12] I vaguely remember some democratic process of selection, and my photomontage was the favourite of all. UA paid me £75, with which I bought some bondage trousers. A little known fact is that Anthony Wilson subsequently asked me to design for Factory, but I was moving on by then and passed the job on to the young Peter Saville, who was in the year below me.

Later on I made *The Secret Public* magazine with Jon Savage and it was published by New Hormones. The printers wouldn't give us any kind of receipt because it was seen to be pornographic; interestingly, left-wing bookshops like Grass Roots wouldn't stock it either. Even trying to get the photomontages photocopied in Manchester was almost impossible. I had to go to the one Rank Xerox bureau at Piccadilly and explain myself to the manager. No wonder that there was only ever one issue of *The Secret Public*. My photomontage to illustrate the Buzzcocks' phrase 'TV Sex' was used as the centrefold and adorned many a bed-sit wall.

Clint Boon

The Buzzcocks were crucial. They were the stand-out band, the first band to come out of the local scene. They were the Beatles of the punk scene – all the singles were hits. Also the Drones, Slaughter

---

12. Garrett, Linder and Peter Saville were the three Manchester-educated artists who would go on to help to define the graphics and design of the punk and post-punk periods.

and the Dogs, and the Worst – who were a proper punk band because they said putting a record out was selling out! [laughs]

Marc Riley

The gigs we went to all the time were at Rafters/Jillys. Rob Gretton was the DJ. Alan Wise put the gigs on like the Fall, then Warsaw, the Buzzcocks.[13] We'd go and see the Buzzcocks at small places all the time. Then the floodgates opened and everyone came along – Generation X, all the punk bands. By that time we were following the Fall about.

We really did like the Buzzcocks as well. Pete wrote great love songs – he could have been in any era. Pete's attitude was punk rock, but what he was writing was no different from pure pop like the Rubinoos.[14]

The first time we saw the Fall we were immediately taken with them and we would follow them around. We had our noses rubbed in it and didn't run away. We mainly went to gigs in South Manchester. The Electric Circus was the wrong side of town. The only time I went there was for the last two nights when it got shut down in the autumn of '77.

Rob Lloyd

We played with bands as diverse as you could get. We toured Yorkshire with Sham 69, we played with Ultravox, we played whatever gig we could get. Thankfully, the Buzzcocks and Richard Boon, when they signed to UA, they took us on tour as support with them.

We played in Manchester quite a lot, and around the country with Manchester bands. We felt at home there, with bands like the Fall and the Worst, journalists like Paul Morley, and the photographer

---

13. Rob Gretton went on to manage Joy Division/New Order. He was one of the mainstays of Factory Records and the key man in the Eighties Manchester scene. Alan Wise was, and still is, the most maverick gig promoter in Manchester.

14. Minor Californian popsters of the mid-Seventies, whose self-titled debut LP appeared in 1977.

Kevin Cummins. There was loads of people around. For some reason Manchester seemed to fall in love with us.

There was no scene in Birmingham, only pub rock bands who had taken their trousers in and cut their hair and played their repertoire a bit faster. We decided it was time to experiment and wind people up. Manchester was on the same sort of vibe as that, I suppose. There were no Richard Boons or Howard Devotos or Paul Morleys in Birmingham, no semi-intellectual thinkers, there were no spunky Kay Carrolls, so we were just making it up as we went along.[15] The Buzzcocks were really helpful, and Magazine – people gave us a guitar or something. I don't know how we ended up being the only non-Manchester band who played on the last night at the Electric Circus.[16] We just seemed to be adopted. We had this attitude that we didn't really want to make a record – so much so that when we were asked onto the album we refused to be on it.

The Prefects never went into a studio apart from the two Peel sessions – that was the height of our ambition in terms of recording. No one had ever wanted to make a record with us. Paul had left the band. He was not enjoying the more experimental stuff we wanted to do – he was more into the Ramones. The bass player got his girlfriend up the stick, someone was getting a proper job. Even though we were only eighteen, we thought we were not getting younger! It all fell apart. And then I got a telegram from Geoff Travis and Mayo Thompson at Rough Trade, saying they wanted to sign us – but it was too late.

Marco Pirroni

Subway Sect I liked. The Heartbreakers, they were like a real band, a bit older, and they could play properly – that was a bit of an eye-

---

15. Kay Carroll was the manager of the Fall.

16. The last night at the Electric Circus was the gig on 1 October 1977 featuring Steel Pulse, Warsaw (shortly to become Joy Division), the Worst, the Fall, the Negatives, Magazine, John the Postman, John Cooper Clarke and the Buzzcocks. It would come out as a ten-inch album documenting the closure of the classic Manchester punk venue, which was demolished.

opener. That pushed people into rehearsing more. They could really play guitar solos, drum intros – all the songs were structured. Great band. The Banshees were interesting. And I loved the Buzzcocks – they were brilliant. I still think 'Spiral Scratch' is a brilliant record.

Apart from that there was no one else. That was it. I didn't like the other ones, like Slaughter and the Dogs. All those bands missed that bit of mystery, that bit of thought that went into the early bands, the artiness – that's my background. Punk became this thing anyone can do, and actually not everyone can do this. If you want to do it, fine, but it doesn't mean you are any good!

Marc Riley

Everyone got bored of the punk thing pretty quickly. It became predictable and transparent and the Fall were something else. Looking back, the bands with the real punk spirit were the Fall, the Prefects, Subway Sect and ATV. I never got involved in the punk circus with the bin bags and all that kind of stuff.

Mark E. Smith starting talking to me and one night I ended up loading the van for the Fall and being the roadie – and then joining the band. The guy in the band before me went on to join the Invisible Girls.[17] He had a pretty volatile relationship with Mark. There were two incidents that led to him leaving the band: one, he wouldn't do a Peel session, and two, when he was playing the squat Mark threw a chair at him – that was, in effect, his P45. I know at the time they wanted to get Steve Garvey in, but I got in sharpish. These days it's quite telling that Mark would rather go for a malleable sixteen-year-old that could barely play than a better-known bass player, in case the band's power base shifted towards the musicians.

---

17. The band formed by Pauline Murray after Penetration disbanded in 1979.

THE ORIGINAL RIOT GRRRLS
Punk Rock and Women

The Sixties may have been the decade of the sexual revolution but it was mainly soundtracked by men. Punk, although still a very bloke-driven scene, had plenty of women musicians and a big female audience. And it was the first time in pop culture that girls were not expected to dress in a traditional, demure, sexy way. Ugly could be beautiful. Dress codes were getting shattered. And the women in the bands were making some of the most groundbreaking music.

Ari Up

Punk was very supportive. It was a great thing that the window opened for women – Gaye Advert, Poly Styrene, Siouxsie or Chrissie Hynde, people coming through that window of punk. It's sad it's gone away, that. Now it's forgotten. When punk died, the female energy died as well. That's why it never happens now. The Slits never get written about in general. It's the Rolling Stones who get the credit! The female chapter is missing completely from the history of rock and that's not the reality of what punk was. There was that open window for women to be themselves.

T. V. Smith

You'd never seen a female pop star like Gaye before. Maybe Suzi Quatro, but she was much more contrived. Gaye stood there with chewing gum and with a T shirt with 'Fuck Off' written on it. She was much fiercer than that, but she would always talk to the fans after the gigs.

Beki Bondage (Vice Squad: vocals)

What was great about punk was that you didn't have to be a virtuoso to get up and sing. I joined Vice Squad when I saw an advert in Revolver record shop. They weren't very together but the other girl who had turned up couldn't sing at all and I could sing a little bit so

I was in. We did our first gig after two or three rehearsals in the bass player's mum's garage. I went down to Bristol University to see Crisis, and when I got there, there was a little picture of us saying that we were playing. I didn't know till I got there that we were playing! [laughs] No one had told me, and that was our first gig. I got drunk, went onstage, did a Siouxsie Sioux impression and that was it. People liked it and all the guys who had previously ignored me were all looking at me, so I thought, 'Wow! this is the job for me.' I did notice that you were imbued with sexual power that you previously didn't have, but I didn't make any use of it because they were all old guys of 21 and I was still a schoolgirl!

For some reason I was a punk rock pin-up. I wasn't particularly comfortable with that. It's one of those things expected for a woman. I always thought I looked terrible. Posing for photographs is a bit like singing: it's something you have to be confident with when you're doing it, and I never looked right. You learn as you go on. When you're a teenager you're very self-conscious. That was a trouble with punk: it didn't have much in the manner of sex appeal. If anyone tried to come on a bit pouty, it was always considered pop, which is a bit strange as rock'n'roll has always been inherently sexual – it means 'fucking'. Punk had a lot of aggression, and maybe punk was more of a raper than a seducer. The pin-up thing was a bit crass, it was all a bit silly. I can't say it enriched me in any way.

Pauline Murray

People used to say, 'What's it like to be a woman in rock?' I never considered myself to be a woman in rock. I just thought I was part of the band. But when you look back it seems quite revolutionary, the way that the women were behaving. Females in the bands were breaking down stereotypes. Lots of these things get overlooked.

Chrissie Hynde

What punk was about was non-discrimination. And that's why I started trying to get a band together, because I knew that it wouldn't

Good times on the road! Dressing to kill, Siouxsie and Jordan suffer the touring blues

be a novelty that I was a chick. It was like, 'Oh, you can play the guitar, let's get together.'

And it wasn't about sex either, which was really refreshing and interesting. I mean, people *had* sex, but it was referred to as a 'squelching session'. It was impersonal. You weren't really having relationships. John Rotten would come over to my squat and he would spend the night, but there was never anything sexual going on. It probably wouldn't have been very hard to convince me! But he wasn't into it, you know?

Ari Up

I was a virgin when I was fourteen. I had teenage pressure. Everyone had already had sex and I hadn't. Palmolive would take the piss out of me, but I was glad I stuck to it. I was a virgin till I was eighteen, which is a pretty long time.

Nils Stevenson

In my experience punk was very sexual, fuelled by speed. Lots of girls who wanted to get a piece of a rock band made getting girls simple and quick. Sex was often sordid, not particularly good, just lots of it. In club toilets in London, Birmingham, Manchester. We weren't getting into the pervy, interesting sex like in the shop – the masks and that sort of stuff. There wasn't time. It was a biological function. Glam people were very conscious of sex and sexuality. With punk you weren't conscious of anything – you just did things without thinking.

John Lydon

Very ugly girls at last had a look-in. You didn't have to be beautiful. You could go out of your way to uglify yourself and that would be beautiful in itself, and that would be interesting and open and free-minded, and that helped women in music no end. The unfortunate tragedy is that they focussed on the word 'music', and we all ended up with the Go Gos... and Madonna.

It was nothing to do with music, and anything that means anything to anyone has very little to do with music. Music is Pink Floyd and pitter-patter pandering to mass consumption taste. The sounds of anger are not melodic. I'm not into music. I will not call it music and I will not call what I do art. I don't have a closed mind.

I don't like most of the categorisations that go on in the music industry. I don't like the label punk rock anyway. That came from Caroline Coon – she called me the king of punk. I was not amused to find out that that meant some Mr Big's little bum bandit in an American prison. That's not quite how I saw myself when I was shouting, 'Anarchy!' Not as a rear gunner.

AND THE FIRST PUNK BAND TO SPLIT UP...
The Damned are Doomed

In August 1977, the second Mont de Marsan punk festival took place, this time featuring the Clash and the Damned. By September, the new five-piece Damned (Brian James had added an extra guitarist, Robert 'Lu' Edmonds, to fatten the sound) were already recording their second album, which was released in November, mere months after their fire-brand debut. Whilst lacking the debut's brilliant songwriting and crazed energy, Music For Pleasure *still packs some good tunes like 'Problem Child' and 'Don't Cry Wolf', and has the bonus of great sleeve artwork. The album flopped, though, and the band would soon fall apart – the first band to do everything in punk, including splitting up, were in disarray.*

Captain Sensible

I got thrown onto a spiky fence by the Clash at Mont de Marsan. [laughs] That was because I was taking the piss out of the Clash. I thought that they were a bit po-faced so I decided to go onstage when they were playing. I managed to get a few stink bombs and I let them off and then I pulled all their jackplugs out and kicked their amps over. It didn't go down terribly well with the security people, who chucked me off, and I landed on a scaffolding pole, which wasn't that great. I think I passed out.

Good luck to 'em, the Clash. We weren't that close at the time. We didn't like that Bernie Rhodes that much. He was a bit of a plonker. I always got on well with Mick and that, but Bernie, Malcolm and Jake Riviera were always at each other's throats for pre-eminence. It was pretty daft really. It had come to a head on the Anarchy tour. It was all about who was Number One and all that, and just because the Pistols swore on TV I suppose that made them.

When we were recording the second album, Brian had a lot of songwriting to do. He did a valiant job. It was Brian's band and quite right as well. I'd go along with that. I was interested in writing, because it's what you do if you're in a band. Nowadays everyone is a performer, not a writer. But I knew it was Brian's thing. We were now a five-piece – Brian had got Lu Edmonds in. He played his first gig at Mont de Marsan. I don't think it worked in the slightest! No disrespect to Lu, who was a lovely bloke, but the Damned only needed one guitar. You crank it up loud and go for it! I think Brian was still thinking about the MC5 – the two-guitar thing can work, but Lu and Brian were not like the MC5 blokes. It just didn't work for me.

Brian James

I wanted to get another guitar player in. I wanted to get more energy, make everything a bit more vibey – the MC5 prototype. I made a big mistake, I guess. I just wanted to give it a shot. I'm like that. If I've got a bee in my bonnet I've just got to do it. So we got in Lu Edmonds and he wasn't that popular.

Rat Scabies

Getting Lu in was a mistake. I mean, I love Lu, I like him in every respect, but we didn't need another guitar player. We had Brian. I couldn't see the point. It devalued Brian then we had to do the album. It takes a lifetime to write the first album and three months to write the second. I realised we had a shortage of material and it wasn't a record I really wanted to make. I had tried to leave the band before. I had had enough of it. It was not what I wanted to be any more. I asked Jake what to do and he said, 'As your manager, leave. As the Damned's manager, stay and make the album and then go.'

So we went to record the second album, which didn't go to plan. The Captain always said we were expecting Syd Barrett to be the producer, but when we turned up at the studio we got Nick Mason instead. That's not strictly true![18] What we wanted to do was make a psychedelic record. We wanted it to be more Electric Prunes than anything else. Nick Mason did a good job of presenting us as what we were – but what we needed was a bigger production.

Captain Sensible

There was an idea that Jimmy Page would come down and produce

---

18. Syd Barrett had long since disappeared to a semi-reclusive existence back in Cambridge and was hardly in a fit state to produce anyone, let alone the Damned.

the second album, which I think would have been a marvellous idea instead of that plonker from Pink Floyd. The original idea was to get Syd Barrett – he was the top choice. Jimmy Page was the second choice. The reason Syd Barrett's people were so keen on it was that there was still a kind of hope that they could get him back into music again, because he was a recluse. They thought it might help, but he didn't turn up – and the door opened and Nick Mason walked through, and everyone was astonished.

We were all skint and were bunking the Tube everyday and saying, 'Fucking hell Nick, I nearly got caught by the ticket collector and I had to swing at him,' [laughs] and all he could say was, 'I came in my Ferrari.'

The thing was, we couldn't get anyone else in because Pink Floyd's people were so interested in Syd Barrett doing it and it was their studio. We couldn't throw Nick Mason out because they would have said, 'Fuck off out of the studio.' Not that he was an unpleasant bloke, mind you. There just wasn't a meeting of minds. Brian James' dream is still to go in a studio and remix the thing and do it like the first album was done, keep it really rock'n'roll and raw, because it's all clinical. They had load of compressors and gates, all the fancy toys all over the place to clean it up so much – it's not a rock'n'roll album. This is why I won't have it in the house. If anyone knows where the tapes are, please give them to Brian! Do us all a favour. There's a good album in there waiting to come out.

Brian James

I think there are definitely moments on the album that we were not given credit for at the time, but the whole album doesn't work for me. When all is said and done, the production was crappy. Mind you, when I listen back now it's not as crappy as it I remember it.

It was great having Lol Coxhill play all that sax on it. I love his playing. It was a nod to the Stooges' 'Funhouse', where Steve Mackay played all that great stuff. Nick Mason was a big fan of Lol.

There was just the three of us in the studio at the time. We'd tape everything that he did, and everything he put down sounded great.

Rat Scabies

We never made any money. I was signing on for £19 a week most of the time. If things had been going better and I could afford a train ticket, I would have been happier. When we were in the studio making the second album I was still skint and there was tension in the air. Brian was the dictator. No one else was allowed to write. I suppose when it came to the second album he didn't have any songs.

My heart had left it by then. You join a band when you're eighteen or nineteen and then you grow up. Suddenly you realise the group of people are not what you think they are. We hadn't got the songs. I had no plan. I thought it was time for me to go. It had turned into something different. I thought it was sincere. The one thing we couldn't afford to be was fake, the audience would see through that.

After the Damned I thought something might turn up. I did a few things. That's the trouble when you go from a band as great as the Damned – nothing comes close. I put together a band called the White Cats with ex-London SS vocalist Kevin Colney and ex-Clash audition man Eddie Cox for a while.

Captain Sensible

We gave it a go after Rat. We got my old mate Dave Berk in from Johnny Moped to drum, and then Jon Moss.[19] The album came out in November and we slogged on till Christmas and then Stiff dropped us. Brian could see it was going nowhere and he called a meeting in the pub in early '78. I was still shocked when he said, 'I'm moving on to other things.' He made some speech. Brian's got a good heart, he's a real gentleman. He said, 'It's been fantas-

---

19. Jon Moss was later better known as the drummer in Culture Club.

tic working with you guys and I'm really sorry but I'm moving on.' And that was it. I was so shocked. After the meeting – I must have had a few – I walked out of the pub and I realised it was all over, and I got all weepy and blubby! [laughs] I thought, 'I can't walk down the road as emotional as this,' so I went to the cinema – to *Abba The Movie*. I remember it distinctly. I was sat with all these fucking Abba fans in my rancid leather jacket and my punk haircut, and I was all blubby and weepy. I must have looked bizarre. When I recovered I walked out of there. I went off to see XTC who were having a party, an album launch. They had this huge cake with 'XTC' on it, which I must admit went all over the place. [laughs] I was pretty emotional and thought, 'Fuck their cake!' and it went flying.

A REAL RIOT
The Clash in Belfast

Guy Trelford

'White riot, I wanna riot, white riot, a riot of my own.' This is what the Clash called for and that's what they got when they visited downtown Belfast! I was a huge Clash fan. I remember how excited my mate Dutchie and myself were. This was the first major punk event to take place in Northern Ireland. So on the night of 20 October hundreds of punks (Dutchie and myself included) converged on Belfast city centre and made their way to the Ulster Hall. But the gig was cancelled, the punks were angry, some windows were smashed in the venue, the punks lay down across the road and stopped the traffic, the riot police arrived, busted a few heads, scooped a couple of kids, confiscated cameras and destroyed film.

This incident subsequently became known as the Riot of Bedford Street. Admittedly, compared to the vicious riots we were used to seeing in Northern Ireland, this one was pretty minor. But, there was one huge difference – here we had kids from the two opposing traditions, Protestant kids and Catholic kids, standing side by side, taking on the authorities out of sheer frustration at not being allowed to see their favourite band! At that time if Protestant and Catholic kids came into contact, it was usually to throw bricks and bottles at (and kick the shit out of) each other.

Whilst waiting to see what was happening, the punk kids got chatting about the Clash, punk, other bands, etc.; politics and religion weren't mentioned and a kind of blueprint was set for the local punk scene. Barriers were being broken down and friendships formed. In the end the Clash never got to play, but the whole event became the catalyst for igniting the Ulster punk scene. Joe Strummer promised that the band would be back soon as the crowds began to drift away.

Some fans' frustration got the better of them and they (wrongly) blamed the band for the gig cancellation. Some were also rather annoyed when it was found that the 'people's band' was staying in the plushest hotel in Belfast, the Europa. Of course when the events of that night appeared in the music papers all the stories had the Clash staying at 'the most bombed hotel in Europe'! The mighty Clash publicity machine even managed to turn disaster into triumph as the headlines screamed, 'The Clash Unite Protestant And Catholic Youth With Punk Rock Despite Cancelled Gigs And Repression', and photos of the band posing up the Falls Road, at police and army checkpoints, were plastered all over the music papers. Some saw this as a cynical manipulation of the situation, but at least they had the balls to come here in the first place (unlike the Pistols, Jam, Sham 69 and countless others) and all was soon forgotten and forgiven when the band kept their promise to return to Belfast, which they did in December for a gig at Queens University. They were given a heroes' welcome, and for a lot of us present that night it still ranks as the most exciting and inspiring gig ever.

Jake Burns

It's a popular mistake that we formed the band after seeing the Clash. We had already formed the band before, but we decided once we heard the Clash where we were going. Henry Cluney came up to my parents' house with every punk record at the time. I'd bought a couple of things, and some of them were not worth buying. [laughs] A lot of it was fantastic, though. Henry sat me down and we had an evening saying, 'Now we are a punk band, let's learn some songs.' At the end of the evening I was completely convinced by punk rock and thought, 'Let's do something completely original instead of just copying.'

We had already booked our first gig and we told the guy that that we were changing our name, but he says, 'Fuck off, I'm booking the ads now. I can't just leave a big blank.' I was sat beside Henry and I just happened to have an album cover, which was the Vibrators' *Pure Mania*. I ran my finger down the song list and I said, 'Tell him we are called the Stiff Little Fingers – we can fucking change it!' The thing is, we got a really good review in the local paper after the gig so we were stuck with the name then. At the time we hated the name. I was much happier when I saw it written on someone's leather jacket. It's a bit long for a band name. This was in the days before Orchestral Manoeuvres in the Dark. [laughs]

We wrote a couple of songs about boredom and being stuck in dead-end jobs, and we kind of hit a brick wall. And then Gordon said, 'You haven't by any stretch of the imagination covered what you guys lived through.'[20] Until then I always adopted the Undertones' attitude: people don't want to be lectured to. He said, 'You don't have to lecture to people, just tell them what you feel.' That was really like someone unlocking the door because you had to keep your mouth shut, you couldn't complain about the Troubles. I then realised you're standing on the stage with a guitar and people will actually listen. Gordon presented me with the full lyrics of 'Suspect Device' and said, 'This is the sort of thing I'm talking about. I don't know if they are any use to you but it might get you started.' I thought the

---

20. Gordon Ogilvie was a local journalist who managed the band and helped with some of their songs.

lyrics were fantastic. The minute I saw them it burst the door wide open and that week I wrote the music for 'Suspect Device' and 'Wasted Life', and from that point on all the frustration and anger that we all had felt for years and couldn't express came pouring out. Even today I still get people who misunderstand the lyrics: they write to me and say, 'Whose side were you on?' and the whole point was that we were not on anyone's fucking side. I was saying, 'They are making our life hell and we are sick of it.' The vast majority of people in Northern Ireland feel exactly the same way.

ANARCHY IN THE UK, ONLY THIS TIME IT'S FOR REAL
Crass, Anarchists and Squatters

In the political confusion that came after punk everyone was fighting for the movement's soul. One of the strands was the anarchist movement, seeds of which in pop-culture terms go back to the late Sixties and the hippie movement. The key band on the scene were Crass, who in a series of brilliant records and artwork stated the case for peace and anarchy, explaining the Sex Pistols' anarchy rhetoric to the punk kids and inspiring far more people than they are given credit for. Crass introduced vegetarianism and other concepts into the wild and fertile post-punk battlefield; they were enormous and became the totem band for the younger kids emerging out of the tail end of punk. They were seen as the band who actually lived by their ideals, the band that actually took the punk politic to its ultimate conclusion. The records now sound fantastic, really having stood the test of time as avant-garde art pieces hidden inside some of the angriest-sounding songs ever written. And the artwork from Gee Vaucher is astounding.

Penny Rimbaud

At that time everyone had moved away. Gee had gone to live in America for a while. I was living here at Dial House on my own.

Steve Ignorant turned up one day, and making music was our way of amusing ourselves in the evening.[21] I'd still got my drum kit. Steve had been turning up at the house for years. He was a little kid the first time I met him. He came down when we scattered Wally's ashes on the stones. Then he disappeared when I was finishing the book on Wally. Everyone was slowly leaving the house, partly because I was becoming so totally involved in the pursuit of Wally's killer – it had become very maudlin and the place had became very uncomfortable. The house emptied! Gee was the last to leave. I was actually on my own for some time, along with one goat, the chickens and cats and Gee's dog – those were my mates! By then I was spending quite a bit of time at another house about a mile away, where Eve lived.[22] I was getting to know her, partly because she was nearby, and partly because she's a beautiful woman.

I became so frightened that I burned the book. I thought that if I burned it, if they came to get me they wouldn't have anything to prove what I was up to. And partly it was burning the ghosts. It was a terrible, horrible and sad occasion, and took a lot of courage to do it. I never did entirely burn it though. When I wrote *Shibboleth*, it was a huge relief to finally get parts of it out in the public domain.

So Steve started turning up again. I was a lot older than him, from a different background – the fact that we both seemed a bit lost meant we really hit it off. We didn't ever envision going out and doing something with it. In the summer of '77 we rehearsed about five songs. We were just fucking about, and other people started turning up and mucking about, and with loads of booze to get us through it we started playing all sorts of gigs and benefits; it was all very chaotic. We got a very mixed reaction. We got banned from the Roxy; as we later sang, 'They said they only wanted well-behaved boys, do they think guitars and microphones are just fucking toys?'

---

21. Steve Ignorant was Crass' charismatic frontman, although Crass didn't really have a frontman as such. Steve was the bloke who shouted the songs in a very angry voice, the working-class Yin to Penny's middle-class Yan.

22. Eve Libertine, future Crass co-vocalist.

One day some guy who used to do window displays for record stores heard what we we were doing and said, 'I want a copy of that,' and he took it to Small Wonder Records. Pete Small Wonder got in touch and put our single out – it wasn't ever really planned.

The most important element of Crass was that it didn't patronise or talk down. We were a broad range of age groups and class backgrounds. I never changed my accent. Eve would start singing, and she is the most plummy-voiced person you could ever come across! We were not ashamed of what we are. We never pretended to be anything else and I think that made a connection. And there were an awful lot of punks who did pretend to be something else.

The hippie and punks are one and the same. I don't think there was any real difference. The Pistols came up with 'Kill all hippies', and if there was ever a hippie McLaren was one. Quite honestly, there was not a great deal of difference in the clothing either. Crass' clothing came out of Oxfam. We bunged all the stuff we bought into the washing machine and dyed it black. That was a reaction to what we felt was happening with punk, the DIY glam rock sort of thing. Westwood and people like that were making their statements, and we thought that the kids were going to get ripped off again. You saw punk clothing turning up in all the local clothes stores, a pale reflection at too big a cost. For us it was an attempt to say, 'Fuck that!'

I was into early rock'n'roll – that was my punk. Gene Vincent, Little Richard, Big Bopper, early Elvis – to me that was so revolutionary. The Pistols came close to it: for a while they were a superb rock'n'roll band, but they just quickly went up their own arses. The 'no future' bit was like a battle cry to me. The negativity was all wrong. Just like with the hippie thing: I didn't want people to think that everyone living in a commune trying to grow their own food was bloody Charles Manson. It was the same with punk: I thought these were good people – I don't want to be demonised like this. I watched the Pistols being demonised and the effect it had on them as personalities. They were probably nice young kids. No one needs to suffer like that because of rock'n'roll.

Gee Vaucher's amazing hand-painted sleeves for Crass underline the group's righteous polemic

My first punk experience came through Patti Smith and I must say I heard it far more in a jazz context than in any other, and that made sense. The Clash were a fantastic rock'n'roll band but I didn't think they were coming from anywhere different. I understood that if you were sixteen it was your Elvis. I saw punk more as the inevitable and positive outcome of the hippie thing. We're learning bit by bit. There was people like this throughout history, trying to find ways of making the world a better place. The punks, hippies, bohemians, beatniks and all the other movements before them all tried to do that, and we are just extensions of each other.

Terrie

We saw the Clash in 1977 in the Paradiso in Amsterdam. It was very, very loud! It had such an impact. The first punk converts appeared, like Jos.[23] He heard punk on the radio. It's so funny how quickly punk bands in Amsterdam started. It wasn't just the Clash and the Stranglers, but all these small punk bands in small clubs, and that fascinated me.

Also the good thing about that time in Amsterdam was that there was a lot of squats and you could do stuff right away – you didn't have to find practice rooms or venues, you could do it all in the squats. We were always involved in the squat scene. You can hardly imagine it now, thousands of squats in Amsterdam. It was so normal at the time. England was a bit narrow-minded. The squats in Amsterdam were setting up bicycle-repair shops, restuarants, venues, bars, even radio stations. It was optimistic in a way that is amazing to look back on now. A new squat would open and everyone would help set it up, building the stage if it had a venue – all this practical stuff – as well as playing benefits. That's what you did as a band: you cooked, you built, you made a noise and played benefits with bands like BGK and the Nitwits.

And there was an international exchange. We had an international outlook. The whole of Amsterdam is very international. I never see myself as really Dutch – that's not interesting for me. We had a lot in common with England. Our favourite bands came from there.

Crass were a bit too black and white for us. We liked them; they were a really inspiring example of doing your own records and being original. We were also into the Mekons and the Membranes – more into that kind of music.[24] Crass were very inspiring but one-dimensional, though I was also a big fan. I remember visiting them at their farm: they were so serious, as if you had to explain yourself before going in, whether you were right on or not. I remember Crass talking to the CIA and Russian secret agents in one meeting! It was really high-up stuff. Weird!

23. Vocalist from the Ex, the Dutch squat anarchist band with their roots in punk and anarcho-punk, who moved quickly onto their own idiosyncratic path of discordant, dislocated rhythmic jazz punk – their inventive music is still getting made today. Well worth checking out.

24. The Mekons initially took punk DIY to its logical extreme with simplistic, hardly-any-chord anthems; the Leeds student band are still going today, cutting country-flavoured and punk-spirited ramshackle songs that are the toast of American critics. The Membranes were a noisy post-punk crew from Blackpool featuring Yours Truly on vocals.

I went to all the punk bands that came over. I also went to London to see bands. You could still go to London and stay cheap – later that became impossible. In Holland the scene very quickly became very Dutch. This DIY, go-and-play thing was possible in Holland because of the squat scene, and punk was easily translatable in Holland. It looked so easy we thought we should try it as well. [laughs] It was very naive to start with. We got an offer from a Dutch punk festival at the Paradiso; I signed a contract to play, and we didn't even have guitars! We quickly had to buy guitars and decide who was playing what. We practised like hell. The drummer had no idea drumming was to do with counting! [laughs] When you look back it's fantastic. I really like that idea: just play. The Ex started as a punk band. We went to Switzerland and Italy because of all these squat connections.

Tony D

Small Wonder record shop gave me a tape of Crass over Christmas. I hated it to begin with. The tape had this stencil formation on the artwork and some writing Penny had done. It was all didactic revolutionary talk. They also gave me *International Times* and I realised there was a whole world out there. I thought everything was great about them apart from the music, but over Christmas I got it. They sounded great as well! I went into Small Wonder and told them, 'Thanks.'

I then saw Crass live and it was fantastic. Patrik Fitzgerald was on the bill as well.[25] Crass made you realise how decadent everyone was getting – they had this angriness. It was almost avant-garde. I had seen Japan the night before and how glam they were. Crass was what I needed, what I wanted. I also saw a lot of the UK Subs that summer. Charlie Harper would be at all the gigs.

I moved to London to a Willesden bed-sit. There was three of us in a room. Some friends were squatting in Latimer Road and invited me to stay there. I was plugged straight away into the squat scene – I landed on my feet. These were not punk rock squats. The

25. One of the 'punk poets' who were a feature of the era.

houses had been compulsory purchased to widen the Westway and then the whole area was squatted. It was very organised, all back gardens knocked through into community spaces, hippie buses parked outside. It was a cool place.

Kevin Hunter

I have a tape of our first rehearsal. We did an AC/DC thing called 'Livewire'. We were trying to rough it up, speed it up, trying to get anything together. It's really embarrassing, but the name of the band we had was Antichrist because it was the first line of 'Anarchy'! Now it sounds like a death metal band; at the time it seemed really right.

We didn't play till November 1977. I was out in the sticks in Hertfordshire. We couldn't find anyone else into punk to form a band – our first drummer was into the Moody Blues! It was people making do.

We had to go into London a few times. The funny thing is in November 1977 at our local club they had a punk night in a rock-'n'roll club called Hound Dogs. It was a bit iffy being a punk then – there were loads of Teds in that town – but that club welcomed everyone in and the Teds accepted us. But in December 1977 Skrewdriver came down and fucked it all up. They beat some of the Teds up and knackered it for us.[26]

I remember hearing John Peel play punk rock. I was an avid listener – God rest his soul. The stuff he was playing in 1976, he was certainly backing the wrong horse. I remember him playing loads of this really awful folk stuff, real finger-in-your-ear traditional, but then punk started creeping in. I remember the first session by the Banshees in late '77, and the same night there was a broadcast of Jethro Tull live from Madison Square Gardens, so there was no overnight transition. I do remember him playing Ramones stuff at the time. I thought the Ramones were more commercial than I was expecting.

---

26. Initially an r'n'b band from Blackpool, Skrewdriver then released one solid punk album, *All Skrewed Up*, on Chiswick Records, split up, and then reformed as a Nazi skinhead band.

A year on from 'New Rose', the Damned were already imploding, whilst the Clash were under pressure to make their second album. Meanwhile the Pistols, under the cosh for most of the year, released their debut LP Never Mind The Bollocks on 28 October. The profane title was enough to get a couple of record shops taken to court for selling the album. Defending barrister John Mortimer tore the prosecution's arguments apart. The multi day-glo sleeve perfectly captures the band's 3D rock'n'roll swagger.

Glen Matlock

I play on 'Anarchy', 'No Fun' and 'I Wanna Be Me'. Sid didn't play on *Bollocks*. They are my songs. You should listen to the difference in bass playing in 'Anachy' and 'Bodies'. I would say this: the bass playing is a bit boring on *Bollocks*. Proper bass playing has a different kind of groove, it adds something to the song, not just playing along with the chords. What I was doing added a bit of colour to it.

I remember talking to John Grey, Rotten's big mate. He said, 'The thing is, Glen, if John had the band sounding the way he wanted, it would have been unlistenable. Great lyrics, but no one would have wanted to listen to it because it would have been such a horrible row.' It was the rough and the smooth added together that made it work.

I know that we could play. To a certain extent, compared to Yes, we couldn't play, but we didn't have to play like that.

Everyone on the Pistols did their bit: Malcolm, Bernic, Sophie in the office. When Sid was in the band it became a cartoon strip. Halfway through the Anarchy tour it was a circus. I don't regret anything but I would like to have done more albums.

Noel Martin

Being able to play a little, we knew that *Bollocks* was a well-produced album. They broke it for a lot of people. I wish the Grundy thing hadn't happened, and they had their own legacy and made another album.

On 25 December, the Sex Pistols played at Huddersfield Ivanhoe's. The first of two shows was put on for the children of local firemen. These were the last UK shows the band ever played.

CHAPTER 10
1978: NO MAP OR ADDRESS

EX-PISTOL!
John Lydon Leaves the Sex Pistols

The Sex Pistols' tour of the USA in January 1978 tore the band apart. From day one it was dogged by problems, from getting visas to the constantly shifting itinerary that left the group touring in the Deep South instead of the more expected hipper Northern cities. The band were abandoned to an unlikely schedule of Bible Belt towns that didn't take too kindly to the cut of their jib. The resulting shows were packed full of thrill-seekers and freak-haters who had come to throw rubbish and abuse the band. By the time they reached San Francisco a weary John Lydon, stuck on the tour bus watching an increasingly out-of-control Sid self-destruct with drugs and booze, quit the band after their last show of the tour at Winterland. Lydon's final words sung on stage, as he finished the Iggy Pop classic 'No Fun', were, 'It's... no fun... at all...' Hunched down on the stage, surrounded by rubbish thrown at him by the audience and Sid Vicious flailing away pointlessly on his bass alongside – with his slashed chest looking every inch the rock'n'roll star, but sounding totally useless – Lydon added the ironic statement, 'Ever get the feeling that you've been cheated?'

There could be no more appropriate exit from the band by its key talisman. The end of the Pistols marked the end of an era for the increasingly frustrated Lydon. Within months, however, he would be back doing music his own way with the groundbreaking Public Image Limited.

Meanwhile Glen Matlock, who had exited the Sex Pistols nearly a year before Lydon, wasn't hanging around. He put together the Rich Kids with one-time Slik frontman Midge Ure – earlier considered as a vocalist for the Pistols in the band's pre-Rotten days. Also in the band were scenester Rusty Egan and guitarist Steve New, who had been on the fringes of several key punk bands. The group arrived with considerable fanfare but never really broke though – a shame as their power pop was well executed.

John Lydon

Punk was clichéd at that point. It was a joke on itself. Endless arseholes reading the *Sun* and the *Daily Mirror* and running out thinking that's what you needed to do: put some egg in your hair, wear a leather jacket, brothel creepers – I wore them myself, I have no problem with that, but they were not intended to be a uniform, a rigid rigmarole. I hate that. A straitjacket mentality. It's just about the worst thing for me, and I imagine for most people, to walk out and see the first thirty rows in identical uniforms to you – how Siouxsie and the Banshees ever tolerated it, I don't know.

Don Letts

The Pistols broke up during that period. The minute they broke up, I get a phone call from John: 'Do you want to go to Jamaica?' You are talking to a man who's never left this country! Next day I'm at John's, and the next day I'm in Jamaica. John asked me to go, I guess, because I was black and, like I say, I'd never been. The closest I'd ever been to Jamaica was watching *The Harder They Come* at the Classic Cinema in Brixton.

I was moving with this crazy white man and they didn't know who he was. Punk rock didn't mean shit there. This was to escape the paparazzi. John had gone with Richard Branson to start the Frontline label, which was a direct response to the new interest in reggae music which was helped by punk rock. John is there in the capacity of an advisor with Branson, to sign up reggae artists.

We land in Jamaica and take over the whole first floor of the Sheraton. There's me, John, and Dennis Morris is there as well for a month. The word gets about – there's a rich white man signing reggae artists. So I'm sitting by the pool at the Sheraton: 'All right, Big Youth! All right, U Roy! All right, Abyssinians! Tapper Zukie! Gladiators! Prince Far I! How you doing?' Everyone is there, apart from Bob Marley and Peter Tosh. Six or seven of these guys in rotation. It was a trip. These guys were legends in our minds, and here they were hustling us down, all looking for a deal.

We became really friendly with U Roy. We'd go round and smoke these big joints. Me and John – the Irish are the white Jamaicans, I don't care what anybody says! U Roy had a giant sound system: you put it on the back of a lorry, drive up into the hills and string it up and play some sounds. One day we go with U Roy to do this. We're up in the hills, John and Don and this big ganja pipe. We sit down and light up. The next thing me and John know, it's tap, tap on the shoulder: 'Wake up, Don!' They had set up the sound, played the sounds, and broken down the sound system – the whole fucking set! – and we were spark out.

Some genius has the idea to get Lee Perry to do versions of two Pistols songs, 'God Save the Queen' and 'Holidays in the Sun'. It has to be said they were really cheesy reggae versions, cod reggae versions – it was bread at the control, rather than dread at the control. Everyone got paid. I remember spending a lot of time with Prince Far I, with John as well. People come over to pay respect to John and I'd be filming them round town.

While I'm in Jamaica with John, Malcolm's trying to get *Rock'n'Roll Swindle* together and they were in the Sheraton Hotel by the swimming pool filming us through the bushes – because Malcolm was trying to get some footage of John to put in the film.

I come back from Jamaica with John, and Vivienne had painted the front of Seditionaries white and painted all this stuff on it in fluorescent orange: 'John has gone to get turned black in Jamaica'. Basically putting John down – he's a traitor and all this. I go to film it with my Super 8 camera, maybe as an ending to my *Punk Rock Movie*. Vivienne, I love the woman dearly, still do, but she attacks me in the street. She's a tiny lady, and there's this white woman and this black man fighting in the street. I don't know what this looks like! I have to pin her against the wall and tell her to chill out. She hasn't spoken to me since – not that we have occasion to. She stopped speaking to me a lot before that, the minute I started working for John Krivine, because she saw Acme as some sort of competition. I was banned from Sex, and the people that went to Sex couldn't tell her that they had been to our shop! When I look back on that time, I love all the drama.

With Malcolm, I've retained some sort of relationship. I still think he has a really entertaining spin on things, the dude.

Roots Radicals! Don and John in Jamaica looking for reggae artists to sign to Virgin just after the Pistols split

Howard Devoto

The next movement along that was given a name was 'power pop' in 1978.[1] I think the Buzzcocks got that term applied to them, and the Rich Kids got called that as well.

Budgie

I decided I'd head down to London, and initially I got a call from Glen Matlock. He was writing songs for Warner Chappell's in their writing room. I remember him doing 'Ghosts of Princes in Towers' with Steve New. I met all these guys while they were putting the Rich Kids together. Glen had come to Liverpool and hung out with Jayne Casey and the crowd – I knew him from there.

I remember doing drums for a couple of other things with Clive Langer. I was in the unusual position of being a drummer without a band.

Glen Matlock

The whole thing with the Rich Kids was it would have been very easy after the Pistols to form another punk band and do it all over again, but I didn't want to do that. After the Pistols there was all these second division punk bands. The Clash, the Damned and the Jam, they were around anyway, but after the Bill Grundy show there was all these other bands and I didn't want to be a part of that – I wanted to do something different. I tried out loads of singers, and I remembered Midge Ure. It was fairly successful: Midge had a good voice and I thought I'd give him a chance to do something a bit tougher, but I guess he wasn't that kind of bloke.[2]

With the Rich Kids, we had moved the wheel of music on another turn.

---

1. Power pop was a press invention in early 1978, an attempt to turn punk rock into some sort of Merseybeat. Groups like the Pleasers turned up dressed as the Beatles and were given short shrift by the punters, who screeched, 'Why do they always want to turn everything back into the Beatles?'

2. Midge Ure would go on to front Ultravox and co-write Band Aid's 1984 multi-million-selling charity record 'Do They Know It's Christmas?' with Bob Geldof.

PUNK'S NOT DEAD
Same Old My Generation

Never can a pop culture have been so quickly discredited as punk rock. As soon as it appeared it seemed like the main players were trying to dissociate themselves from it. For many of the instigators of the movement, it was now time to move on or maybe revert to the musics they were into before punk. For others it was a chance to indulge their prog fantasies, or a chance to ponce around as New Romantics – another day, another fashion! For a handful it was a chance to create some truly original music, sowing the seeds for the post-punk scene.

Post-punk has become a bit of a hip term, with certain bands like the Gang of Four being pulled out as key groups and having their influence greatly exaggerated. There were plenty of other bands starting in 1978 who were also changing music into new shapes. New scenes were forming from the splinters of punk, from early goth to psychobilly, from the mod revival to the new wave of British heavy metal.

There was also a whole new generation of kids whose first music was punk, and if the first wave of bands was going to retreat from three-chord punk rock then they were not! Whilst the media screamed, 'Punk is dead!' the new punk generation started to set their own agenda. It was about here that punk began to go more underground, whilst conversely becoming more popular as a whole new mob of kids picked up on the rebel spirit. Meanwhile the older bands were off somewhere else...

Captain Sensible
Punk became more of a homogenised thing in 1978/79. All the original bands were quite diverse.

T. V. Smith
Punk started to become conservative. From something that was very liberating at first, there comes a point when it's not your little secret any more. The media takes it on and they create their impression of it, and that's what feeds back for people who were not there at the

core when it started. People derive their ideas of what it is from people who don't really have an idea of what it is themselves. I pointed that out in 'Safety in Numbers'.

I was hoping it was going to be a creative movement with people who were able to express themselves, bands not tied down to anything other than their own kind of creativity. I didn't want to see bands who felt they had to be what their record company told them. We had already had years of that. The great joy of bands like Iggy, the Dolls or Bowie was they always had their own individual thing, regardless of what was going on around them, and that's what I felt about punk. Great bands like the Clash and Buzzcocks all had their own thing, expressing themselves in their own way, not following anything from the outside. A whole bunch of bands ignored the pop scene as it was, ignored the record companies. There was great music and great lyrics.

Six months later, it was a bunch of bands wearing leather jackets pretending to be the Ramones, being aggressive and playing everything at 100 miles an hour. That's not creative to me – that's just copying.

Mick Hucknall (Simply Red and solo: vocals)

A friend of mine went to the very early Sex Pistols gigs. He came back raving about it. The excitement, the energy – it was my generation. It was a perfect time for me. For a year it was incredible, but I got very disillusioned with it very quickly. By the time it came round to spring 1978 it was all about leather and spiky hair. It was too rock. What I liked about it in the first place was that it was about being original, and as that ended I kind of drifted away from it. People always talk about me being a punk and suddenly moving to soul, but it was a very gradual process. I'd been a soulboy before punk. I was actually a little bit too young for when Northern Soul peaked at Wigan. I went to some soul dances in my area of Manchester.

John Lydon

Looking back on it, people are calling the Stooges punk rock. Iggy Pop was not punk rock. The Stooges were not punk rock. The Ramones were not punk. The term is an absurdity at best. Bob Marley put out 'Punky Reggae Party' – nonsense. They were all jumping on a bandwagon, all desperate to cling to this ridiculous word. It's meaningless! Once you accept a title like that you are a slave to the system. The very thing you think you are rebelling against you are replacing. You're just a different structure with the same moronic mentality. I have to go for being an individual, and I'm sorry but a category like punk is not about individuals. I don't need the company of arseholes. I'm quite happy on my own. I sink or swim by my own merits and I don't need to be justified by 100 imitators.

Individuality? You don't buy it in shops. It's something you're brought up with. It's in your culture. It might possibly be genetic but it's most definitely important. Also a sense of values, fair play. Don't cheat or lie or swindle each other – we have an entire political system to do that.

I might as well come from Timbuktu as Ireland. It's not about geography. It's about mentality. The Irish have a thing of being able to laugh at themselves like the English used to.

Colin Newman

The important thing in 1978 was how different it was from 1976. I mean what was John Lydon doing in 1978? He didn't want to be identified with one style of music or one thing or one moment in time. If you think about where I was coming from, why would I want to stay with one style? It wouldn't make any sense. When you buy soap you don't want it to be sausage flavour! In music, if every record is the same it gets a bit boring.

Budgie

The initial thrust had moved somewhere else. Whatever had happened had already gone. It was a weird time. Till I met up with the Banshees, there was definitely a kind of scene where you had to know people: there was a Clash camp, a Pistols camp, probably a Damned camp too. Then there was a lot of other London bands around. The Vortex was still going. It was still a happening vibe down there, but it was more about your own survival when you got down there, very different from Liverpool. In Liverpool you knew everybody in Liverpool city centre.

Eric Debris

Punk sort of failed in a way. We did kick the door open but we forgot to close it back afterwards! All this new wave stuff came right through after us and swallowed the whole thing – the idea anybody could form a band was good in a sense but there were soon too many bands!

Punk made little impact on French society. Some indie labels started, and lots of bands started, but it's much harder to do anything here. It's really difficult for a band to tour – there are not many clubs to play in. In France there are still lots of people talking about punk, but they don't know what they are talking about. It was easier to tour in England. We were with Rough Trade Records, but we ended up with not enough money to continue. It was frustrating.

ACTION TIME VISION
Punk Rock Moves On

The Saints' album Eternally Yours *is one of the classic hidden gems of the punk canon. The band married the ever-melodic rush of Ed Kuepper's wall-of-sound guitars and Chris Bailey's fantastic sneering vocals with the fattest, baddest horn section and made it work. It was a whole new template for punk rock and one that has been revisited by several bands since its release. Worth the purchase for 'Know Your Product' alone, a horn-driven, pile-driving surge of raw soul power and one of the greatest singles from the punk rock period.*

Other punk bands were pushing on too. Great singles and albums appeared from the likes of the Vibrators, 999, Penetration and X-Ray Spex, whose debut album is one of the overlooked classics from the period – featuring Poly Styrene's clever wordplay and idiosyncratic take on consumer society in a series of great songs with the added bonus of Laura Logic's off-kilter sax. And punk pioneers the Damned, already the first band to split up, were now the first re-form. Punk was now starting to splinter into several different directions as everyone was starting to put their own interpretation on it.

Chris Bailey

The first couple of years in the UK were quite pleasant. After that it wasn't so good – we were on EMI and we had short-sighted management. The band were quite young and had to grow up pretty fast. The band wanted to move back to Australia – there were some hard times.

Our second album, *Eternally Yours*, came out in 1978. For me, it's our first proper release because *(I'm) Stranded* was just a load of demos, and also by that stage we had a budget – we'd go in and use a multitrack and have fun in the studio. Subtleties is not the correct word to use in this context, but there was a nod in that direction!

'Know Your Product', which was my sardonic look at consumer culture, came out and nothing happened. Tony Blackburn didn't like it, which was highest compliment you could have at the time.[3] Thank Sam and Dave for the brass section! And Stax's horns. That was our inspiration. The great thing we learned was how to electrify the audience with the marriage of the instruments to the kind of loud Marshall guitars. That's something I had always been fascinated by, the putting-together of the wrong kind of instruments. I've always considered the Saints to be a rock'n'roll band but I like the way we can jumble things around – even in a horn section we use different horns. Same when

---

3. Tony Blackburn, a rather cuddly media presence these days, was the veritable Antichrist in the punk era, symptomatic of daytime radio which ignored most punk rock singles in 1977 as the mainstream tried to kill the scene dead – ironic nowadays when you can hear punk rock everywhere.

I've used string sections, even if that sounds a bit dadaist. Blues and r'n'b are the cornerstones of what rock'n'roll is built on.

Punk rock very rapidly became marketing, and we didn't have the nous to use that. Given that the notion was to be experimental and to try not to make the same record over and over again, we were moving away. Although we still had the same energy as the first album, the added horn section seemed to confuse people and the record sort of disappeared. We didn't have that much influence over EMI and I've heard stories about how they didn't want us. Our management didn't have any clout and our image, I guess, didn't work. The music business actually hates bands.

Very quickly after that we recorded our third album, *Prehistoric Sounds*, Ed left and went back to Australia to do the Laughing Clowns.[4] I think there are a few good songs on the album. But it feels stilted in places, it sounds like a record made by a band falling apart, and sure enough soon after recording the album the line-up of the band changed quite drastically.

I was a born into that generation where beat music was very important, like poetry. I kind of like being outside the mould, and I'm very grateful that we've been able to make these records at our own pace. The Saints' name gets dropped by lots of people, like Rocket from the Crypt.

Punk rock was meant to be liberating youth and a great step forward. It was bizarre that it became so closed-rank, and stylised bands became influential.

Gavin Friday

1978 to '82 has been very ignored. We were more related to that era. You can actually trace a lot of that to Bowie fans who got into punk. Bands like Joy Division. Public Image went that way. The Slits, the Pop Group, Cabaret Voltaire, geezers from the suburbs of Manchester and Sheffield – the grey coat brigade, eyeliner. That was going on here and we attracted that crowd.

---

4. *Prehistoric Sounds* was released in October 1978.

The radio stations were freaked out by us. The whole retro thing going on at the moment about the '78/82 scene, the Gang of Four, Joy Division, the Banshees – some of our stuff could have been made in New York in 2003. I suppose that's always gone on.

Knox

We recorded our new album, *V2*. John Ellis left and was replaced by Dave Birch, then we had a five-piece line-up at one time. We were just touring a lot. We would play a brilliant gig, then a not-so-good one. People kept coming and going – we never had the right people in the band. Next we had Greg Van Cook in the band from Electric Chairs, and Ben Brierly who was married to Marianne Faithfull.

I wasn't sure if I could face all the touring. I spoke to someone from CBS about it – I thought it was off the record, but she went and told Muff Winwood who pulled all the money out of the band. The net result was we didn't make a third album at that time, and I left the band because it deteriorated. It wasn't my intention at all, and I was naive enough not to realise that it wasn't off the record. There was a gap for a few years. Eddie kept the band going and had some success with it.[5]

Nick Cash

'Homicide' charted and we were going to go on *Top of the Pops*, but there was a strike the first week and the second week we couldn't do it. I don't care – as long as I play a few gigs I'm happy. We were a bit on our own. I didn't give a fuck, really – we did what we did. We went to America. We had our own style. I never fought anybody about it.

Pauline Murray

Penetration's records sold well but never budged into the charts, whether because they were not good enough or there was not enough promotion. I don't think Virgin supported it as they should

---

5. Knox re-joined the Vibrators in 1982 when the original line-up reformed.

have. It was frustrating – we were doing well, we just didn't get into the charts – which wasn't the main reason we were doing it but it would have helped. With more promotion we would have done.

We signed to City Management, which was Status Quo's and Rory Gallagher's management offices on Wardour Street. Gary Chaplin left at this point. He got a bit frightened maybe. We didn't get anything looked at, we just signed. We said, 'If we are going to get ripped off, we may as well get ripped off professionally.' But without them we might not have got so far.

Poly Styrene

When I was doing the old hippie trail in Devon and Somerset we were living on the land, doing the complete back-to-nature thing. After that, coming back into London there was a lot of tacky things that hit me. It wasn't as consumer-orientated as today, and everything was covered in cheap, tacky plastic consumer goods – it hit me in the face, so I started writing about it, commentating on everything I'd grown up with my youth: Weetabix, Kleenex and so on.[6] I got into trouble with TV stations about advertising, but I wasn't – I was creating a diary of the times. Why should I pretend I'm living in another age? Why pretend to be neo-classical when everything I see is modern? Maybe I was being a bit more futuristic, but it's probably more true now – songs like 'Artificial'. I'd be reading about genetic engineering and it was just new then. Nazi Germany had started it, experimenting with the women.

Most people think 'The Day The World Turned Day-Glo' was about tripping, but I always said it wasn't. I grew up in a generation where we had brown paper bags in the local store. Gradually everything become more colourful. Day-glo symbolised the shift from natural to more synthetic. Like clothes: not buying cotton any more, you're buying bri-nylon, British nylon: you could wear it to school and your mum didn't have to iron it – it was

---

6. Both brands were name-checked in the X-Ray Spex song 'Plastic Bag'.

about making lives easier for housewives. I was writing about this whole thing.

We played small venues regularly. We started out with a residency at the Man in the Moon, and then we got asked to play all over the place. We got signed to EMI International, then we were asked to do a lot abroad: Sweden, Germany and on Japanese TV, and we played CBGBs in New York. All this was pre-video. It's a shame we just missed it – the band would have been perfect for videos. After our album came out, the band folded.

I went into a solo project quite quickly. It was a chill pill for me. At the time I did see a flying saucer.[7] I went to see the BBC's leading hypnotist, and his wife was the expert on UFOs in this country. They both said I had heightened sensory perception; I had all the symptoms of someone who had seen one.

I was familiar with Hare Krishna because of George Harrison.[8] I met Hare Krishnas in Bath – they stayed at our commune in Bath before punk. When I saw the UFO, they were the only ones who could tell me what I saw. They have lots of mentions of celestial travel – people from other planets used to visit here.

After punk I did a lot of searching into Hare Krishna. It is a spiritual path. I don't dress like that, I don't feel that big need to. I have a guru, follow principles, and I chant my mantras to purify my spiritual being. It's part of my philosophy.

Colin Newman

We released our second album, *Chairs Missing*, in September 1978. By the time you come to the end of the Seventies, being experimental was not to our advantage. A major label, EMI, were not going to

---

7. In August 1979 the band split through musical differences. BP and Jak left to become Classix Nouveaux. Poly disappeared off the scene after seeing a flying saucer. She re-emerged as a Hare Krishna and then made a jazz-tinged solo album.

8. Eastern mysticism was one of the philosophies popularised by the Sixties revolution. George Harrison had been instrumental in bringing these ideas to the mainstream. Even so, by the late Seventies it was still very underground, not like nowadays when plastic Buddhas sit in every yuppic flat in the world and dumb celebrities clutch their yoga mats for press shots.

get it and Wire had no facility for dealing with the culture of EMI. We sold the same amount of records for *Chairs Missing* as *Pink Flag*, but there was no pop crossover. That was partly the band's fault and partly EMI's fault – they didn't understand what Wire was. Things went wrong. Our 'Outdoor Miner' single went in the charts and they cancelled the scheduled *Top of the Pops* – that was our big moment gone, where we could have been weird and pop at the same time![9] Years later it was kind of ironic that Elastica and Blur put our sound into the charts. You know that the experimental music of one generation becomes the pop music of the next, and that works the other way round as well.

With *Chairs Missing* the sound changed. The speed at which the band was travelling was mighty fast. When 'Practice Makes Perfect' came along, we knew it was so unlike anything else that was out there, it set the tone for the album.

It's a dark album, but for me it's also very summery – it was made in the summer. *Pink Flag* had been very difficult to make, in that we had been right on the edge of our ability, especially putting down backing tracks. Robert was not an accomplished drummer and him and Graham would just fight all the time. When we did *Chairs Missing* we had been on the road and we could play a bit better. It was less of a struggle doing the backing tracks, plus it was much more interesting because there was a whole new set of toys to play with: guitar effects, sequencers, synths – and there was a real interest in making the arrangements interesting and doing weird stuff. That, I think, was the only time the band was engaged en masse in an activity and really enjoying it.

'I Am The Fly' was just the most absurd thing.[10] We did it with a distortion box and a flanger set on complete feedback, and it

---

9. The British Market Research Bureau had pulled the single from the provisional charts because 'officials became aware of the possibility that inducements had been offered for the sales of the single to be exaggerated in chart return shops.' Although EMI denied any suggestion of hyping, it didn't help. This was a song that deserved to be a hit.

10. Another great Wire single, 'I Am The Fly' was a bizarre slice of psychedelic punk pop with a great fly-like guitar lead.

sounded funny. 'I Am The Fly' is actually a complete and utter fucked-up twelve-bar. It starts in E and goes up in exactly the wrong chords. It was playing with that whole kind of thing, the absurdity, with the words just repeating 'I Am The Fly'. We thought it was very tongue-in-cheek.

Captain Sensible

When the Damned split in 1978, I joined the Softies in Holland. I was living on a houseboat by the Ajax stadium with the drummer Joe Thumper and with Big Mick who was singer and guitarist – he used to be our roadie in the Damned. He'd got us out of few unpleasant situations when punk wasn't so popular in the provinces. I remember at the Drill Hall, Lincoln a lot of people bust into our gig to beat the audience up and were trying to get on the stage to beat the band up – he sorted them out. He was big. He'd been in the army, though he was actually a gentle bloke. He never whacked any of the band, even if we was asking for it. Because he had been in the army, he knew a few gigs on the bases. I really enjoyed that for a month – it was so easy. I got in trouble a couple of times for drawing Hitler moustaches on paintings in the army bases.[11]

I got back to England, and of all people Rat Scabies phoned and said, 'How's yer fucking band then?' At the time I was trying get this band together with Henry Badowski, called King. I said, 'Not too bad. Henry is a genius. Like most geniuses, a little difficult to work with. How's your lot doing?' 'Not too bad. Not making a lot of dosh. Any chance of getting the Damned back together again? You can play guitar and we'll get some bass player in.' And it seemed to make sense. The any-old-bass-player we got in turned out to be Lemmy! He helped us out for a bit. Rat was thrashing away at the back, with me and Lemmy in the middle and Vanian at the front. It was inspiring. I thought, 'Sod King. Let's get the Damned back together.' Or the Doomed, as we called it.

---

11. It was during these sessions that Captain Sensible and the Softies recorded 'Jet Boy Jet Girl', which was later released.

Rat Scabies

We hadn't fallen out, me and the Captain. The White Cats were not doing much, to be honest. I didn't enjoy playing the material – not much excitement. The Captain was hitting a rocky patch with King. We thought perhaps we should get together again. We needed a singer and Vanian was the only choice – he was the best out there. We both realised if we got Vanian back in it would have to be the Damned. Brian was doing Tanz Der Youth.[12]

Captain Sensible

Then we thought we might as well put an album of material together. I had to go home and try and write some tunes, as did the rest of band – you had to put your money where your mouth was. Brian had let us write a couple of songs before. I wrote a couple, and I thought, 'This is quite hard work.' I had a four-track reel-to-reel tape recorder, and I recorded a few TV ads, turned the tapes back and stole the melodies: 'Do the Shake and Vac, bring the freshness back' – there you go, that was 'Machine Gun Etiquette' for you! Obviously Dave came into his own as a songwriter as well. I really like 'Melody Lee', which he wrote. I always thought that Dave was goth before his time.

Rat Scabies

It was bizarre: the White Cats played to 30 people, and so when we put out 'Love Song' I didn't realise there was that kind of interest in the Damned.[13]

Captain Sensible

We were in the studio, not concerned about what anyone thought

---

12. Tanz Der Youth were Brian's psychedelic outfit who released a great lost single, 'I'm Sorry, I'm Sorry', before putting together Lords of the New Church with former Dead Boys vocalist Stiv Bators.

13. 'Love Song' was a Top 30 hit, and the rejuvenated Damned were welcomed with open arms by the second wave punks.

we should be doing. I really wanted to work with Syd Barrett. I liked the punk thing, and I thought punk with a tinge of psychedelia and lunacy to it would be perfect – chuck away the rule book and do anything you ever dreamt of doing. We ended up doing that on *Machine Gun Etiquette*. I did think it actually worked.

We were working with Chiswick, another small label, and they seemed to know where we were coming from. Roger, the bloke that ran the company, was there to make sure we didn't get too drunk, and to go out and get the odd Cornish pasty.[14] Chiswick is a great label. They were all music fanatics that worked there.

By now the debate over whether the Stranglers were punk or not was irrelevant. If anyone else at the time made a record as hard-hitting and as innovative as the 1978 album Black and White, *then I've not heard it. For the sheer depth of the band's dark, twisted imagination, check out the black side of the record; for the melodic inventiveness go to the white side. This record was the pinnacle of the early Stranglers' aesthetic, their dark malevolence and their twisted punk psychedelia was represented at its heaviest and best here. It's worth buying for the bass sound alone.*

J. J. Burnel

Black and White was the first time we had to sit down and come up with new material, and so we were put somewhere in the wilds near Peterborough – Bearshank Lodge, it was called. Billy Bragg was around and I remember being stuck there for three months – everyone else had family at Christmas and I didn't. A couple of the Finchley Boys came over and I started collecting material, loads of bits and pieces of songs. Dennis from the Finchley Boys played the drums. I said, 'Keep that drumming going,' and we had 'Toiler On

---

14. Roger Armstrong ran Chiswick – a proto-independent label – with Ted Carroll releasing the wilder end of the pub scene along with the Damned, the 101ers, Motörhead, and Skrewdriver before they turned into a Nazi band.

The Sea'. Those cinematic ones were my forte. In those sessions I also demo'd my solo album *Euroman Cometh*.[15]

Billy Bragg

Our group Riff Raff broke up because they failed to change the world by doing gigs in Northamptonshire, where we had gone to live on account of being too poor to live anywhere else. We worked at the studio where the Stranglers were working on their new album, and lived a hand-to-mouth existence.

DONT WALK AWAY IN SILENCE
Post-Punk from Manchester

In 1976 Manchester had been second only to London as a cradle of punk. By 1978 it was emerging as a key centre of the diverse movements that get grouped together as post-punk. Even as the Buzzcocks were hitting the big time – they had two Top 20 albums and four hit singles in 1978, including the timeless 'What Do I Get' and 'Ever Fallen in Love' – more key bands were emerging. There was Howard Devoto's new band Magazine, Mark Smith's spiteful Fall with their twisted, catchy, bass-driven invective, and there was Joy Division, who had originally met at the Pistols' 1976 gig at the Lesser Free Trade Hall. Fronted by their extraordinary singer Ian Curtis, Joy Division led post-punk into darker inner spaces.

Henry Rollins (Black Flag, the Henry Rollins Band: vocals)

All these great bands from Manchester like Joy Division, Buzzcocks, the Fall – what an interesting history there! I'm one of those guys who will argue that there is no bad Fall album. Mark Smith is the

---

15. Sinister-sounding neo-electropop collection concerning the unification of Europe – years ahead of its time.

Arguably the first group to move away from the punk template, Joy Division changed everything

man. I'm a Fall fanatic! I have every record. I've hung out with him and he was cool with me, actually. I was lucky. He walked up to me and said [impersonates voice quite accurately], 'Hello Henry.'

John Lydon

The Fall – I like some of their stuff but there's too much of it and it all sounds exactly the same. I can't tell where they begin and where they are going to end. There's too much repetition. The Fall, in particular, to me are a band that's permanently writing one song and they haven't finished it yet and there are 8,000 versions. It's a good song – get a new one.

Tony Wilson

Joy Division were the first ones to experiment. They were a pure punk band who moved away. Look at early Joy Division chords: before that you had to learn loads of chords to write a song, but now you could just go up and down the fretboard.[16] Punk destroyed all

---

16. Mmm...! Maybe the Ramones, amongst others, had already taught everyone this trick!

the rules. It broke it all down. You had twelve frets, you could play a song on those frets.

Barney Sumner (Joy Division: guitar. New Order: vocals and guitar)

I think it's very hard to capture an accurate portrayal of Ian. He was quite an odd character, really. I think at some point in Macclesfield there must have been a leak of aluminium oxide into the drinking water. Everyone is a little bit strange from there! Ian was quite intellectual. He read William Burroughs, Nietzsche, stuff like that. Me and Hooky didn't know what the fuck he was going on about half the time!

But he also had a good sense of humour. He could take a jolly jape. We played a few tricks on him. Like when he wanted a piss in the car on a really busy road. He's stood there having a piss behind the car so that no one can see him, and we said, 'Steve, put your foot on it now,' and Ian went mad because he had a pair of winkle-pickers on and the car drove over his feet.

In the early days we played the Hope and Anchor in London. I was very ill and didn't want to go down to London and play to fifteen people, so I was really shivering in the back of the car in my sleeping bag. Ian was in a very bad mood – he could be babyish, really arsey. All day on the way down I'd never seen him like that before, and when we were driving back later, somewhere near Luton he grabs the sleeping bag off me. I said, 'Don't be so fucking stupid.' He grabbed it again and just covered himself with it, growling. I yanked it and he started punching out, punching Stephen who was driving. We thought, 'There's something wrong. Pull up, Stephen! Pull up!' He was pretty upset. Me, Hooky and Rob Gretton got out of the car on the hard shoulder and grabbed Ian, and realised he was having a fit. I pinned one arm down, Hooky another, and Rob his legs. Stephen went inside his pockets and got his cigarettes off him and had one! [laughs]

Howard Devoto

The first concrete thing I did musically after the Buzzcocks was to meet John McGeoch and rehearse two or three songs with him at Lower Broughton Road.[17] He was doing fine art at Manchester Poly. I actually didn't know what I was going to do. There was a point at which I was mulling over whether to manage the Buzzcocks or continue with making music. Then I stuck up a notice in Virgin record shop in Manchester. I think it said I was looking for people who were into playing fast and slow music. That's how I met Martin Jackson and Barry Adamson and Robert Dickinson.[18] We rehearsed once and then I got John involved again. I could tell he was pretty good already. I thought everyone else sounded good as well – Barry told me he had started playing bass only a few weeks before I met him. Martin Jackson had been in one or two bands before.

After I left the Buzzcocks I was still writing songs a bit with Pete: 'The Light Pours Out of Me', 'Shot by Both Sides'. 'Light Pours Out Of Me' was one of the earliest songs. It was the first one to try and do something different. I was trying to finish that college course as well. I got my degree.

We didn't have that big an advance when Magazine signed. I had plumped for artistic freedom over money, and there were an awful lot of paragraphs in the contract saying that if I wanted to stop making records I could do, no problem. I was aware of how much over the years I'd read about musicians whingeing about being ripped off by the terrible music industry, so I was going in with every radar bit of me thinking, 'You're all crooks.' We only signed for one record. I wasn't even sure if we were going to make an album – remember, I'd never done an album. That seemed quite a daunting idea. This is why we had all these get-out clauses. I only wanted to get 'Shot By Both Sides' out – it was such a good song.

Pete showed me 'Shot By Both Sides' at Lower Broughton

---

17. McGeoch was one of the key innovative guitar players who would shape the post-punk sound with Magazine and later the Banshees.

18. A different Dickinson, not the journalist who is a contributor to this book.

Road – the chords and guitar line that gave it the. basic feel. 'Lipstick' was Pete's version of it later on in the Buzzcocks – whether he had all lyrics at the time, I don't know. I'm sure he had the vocal melody. I was given the guitar and played the chords whilst he played the lead line. I really liked it and he said, 'You can have that.' It was definitely mine to take away and do something with – all I kept was the guitar phrase. I wrote the rest of the song round that. I was slightly miffed when the Buzzcocks did 'Lipstick'. [laughs] Pete's version is much more melodic. He tucked that guitar riff more behind the song than I did.

I felt a lot about that song when we recorded it. I know when I recorded the vocals it felt like one of the biggest moments of my life. I almost wanted to keep the bit of carpet I was stood on! Lyrically, political commitment was something I struggled with for many years – I always had the tendency to try and argue the other case, and I guess I was trying to sing about what that felt like. Feeling that, you don't have a lot of certainty about anything. It's not always an easy place to be.

Linder Sterling

I did the album sleeve for Magazine's debut album, *Real Life*. Howard and I were looking at the Symbolist painters together and in my sketchbook from 1977 is the Odilon Redon quote: 'Beauty and God are in Heaven. Science is on Earth, crawling on the ground.' It seemed like such a salve then. I worked in monoprint, which was quite a labour intensive method, using four inks. I made hundreds of heads and Howard made the final selection.

Howard Devoto

Linder was important in a lot of ways. Especially for me – she gave me all kinds of support, and having her visual sense and brilliance around was of great value. Her sartorial advice – what looked good to wear was important. She was at Lower Broughton Road for a year. We all left at the end of 1977. Malcolm Garrett shared a house

Where have all the bootboys gone? The underrated Slaughter and the Dogs' brief flicker of fame was powered by some great street-bovver glam anthems

with John McGeoch. It was through Malcolm that I met John. Pete lived in the house a little. Mark Roberts, who shot the Super 8 footage of the Buzzcocks playing with the Sex Pistols at the Free Trade Hall, was there, and Richard Boon. It became a student house, then full of politically radical people, and then it became the music house for a year and a half.

Mick Rossi

When Slaughter and the Dogs did the album *Do It Dog Style*, we got Mick Ronson in to play on it.[19] I bought this Marshall amp and Mick came in and used the same amp and settings and it sounded amazing! The wah-wah pedal left half-on and half-off – that was his trick to get that tone that sounds so like Mick.

The album came out and we played the Lyceum – that was great. Then we toured Europe, and Wayne met this girl in France and moved out there. *Do It Dog Style* didn't really happen the way

---

19. Ronson was the legendary guitarist on David Bowie's *Hunky Dory* and *Ziggy Stardust* albums. His solo album *Slaughter on Tenth Avenue* had part-inspired the name of Rossi's band, along with Bowie's *Diamond Dogs* – work it out!

we wanted, so the band fell apart. Wayne left, so we were on the lookout for a new singer and Morrissey came down. This was a long time before he was famous.

I've got four demo tracks that I recorded with Morrissey on vocals round at my mam's house, songs that have never come out. He was very shy, very introverted, not like he is now. He was singing more conventionally than he would do later on in the Smiths, when he tended to sing and flow into the chorus, not like in a typical song where there are separate bits. You could tell then that he was very talented. It didn't really work out although we were in the same sort of area musically.

We got Eddie Garrity from Ed Banger and the Nosebleeds in to do the vocals. He had roadied a bit for us and was an old mate, but looking back on it I wish I had waited and Wayne had come back. The album was not quite right, but egos got in the way so we carried on without Wayne, which was a mistake. Dale Griffin, who used to be Mott the Hoople's drummer, produced the second album. We got Mott's keyboard player in, Morgan Fisher, and he was great – with his moustache he looked like Terry-Thomas.

BULLSHIT DETECTOR
The Continued Rise of Anarcho-Punk

Kevin Hunter

In May '78 my first band fell apart. We used to hang around the Triad in Bishops Stortford. Motörhead, Wayne County and the Banshees all played there. There was quite a nice scene going. I met Colin from the Epileptics and joined them in mid-'78.

We first saw Crass supporting a fairly ordinary band in Bishops Stortford, and when we saw them in the hall with their big banner up and all dressed in black we thought they must be a fascist band! Well, you would, wouldn't you? I thought they only did one number, and we were shouting, 'Fuck off fascists!' and then a couple of songs later we thought, 'Actually this is really good,' and afterwards we got talking to them. They were really good people and after that they gave the Epileptics our first gig at the Basement in Covent Garden, where it was literally each band playing to the other band! It's hard to see what Crass saw in Epileptics, why they gave us the gigs – perhaps they liked the attitude.

We were so naive. Colin at the time was sixteen or seventeen.[20] ᵀ was older than them but I used to lie about my age. It's amazing how quickly the whole Crass thing touched us. From November 1978 to February '79 Colin and Derek got really into it much more quickly than me. There were two distinct sides in the band – they were into every aspect of it, while me and the drummer were more into just being in a band.

When we bought Crass' *The Feeding of the 5000*, it was difficult finding anything else like it. The nearest thing was the Unwanted's single 'Withdrawal' – musically that was quite close, it has that rush. After *5000*, a lot of stuff sounded really tame.

Deko

ᵀ had a mad angry attitude – I wrecked and robbed things. Straight out of reform school into the world – it made me hate everyone, smash things up and alienate people. Bands like Crass put a direction on my attitude. I asked questions about myself, put a direction on my nger. Before there had been no outlet for it, just beating people up.

Billy Bragg

Crass were too far out for me. I respected them for what they were doing. They were anarchists and by their nature they don't relate with the mainstream. I suppose they took the principles that punk had been founded on and pushed it as far as they could go.

Tony D

Squatting was becoming a big thing for all these people. Our squat

---

20. Colin Birkett was the vocalist in Flux. His brother Derek played bass in the band, and Martin Wilson played drums.

applied to the European Union to become a free state! There were a lot more squats appearing. You'd see these people at gigs every night. People from all over Europe were coming, people hitch-hiking in from France with a pound. People now started writing on their clothing at every gig. The graffiti on the walls would be Crass and the Ants.

I saw the Killjoys – they were great.[21] I followed The Lurkers and Generation X. The Psychedelic Furs were huge. PiL I was disappointed with – I thought they would be the next big band. The early Banshees were not released for so long. It was the same with the Ants – you've no idea what power they had in the early days.

NAZI PUNKS FUCK OFF
Punk Deals with the Far Right

The National Front was getting big in the Seventies. The far-right party had attempted to hitch its wagon to the punk movement and had been roundly rebuffed. The big anti-racist rally was the Rock Against Racism gig in Victoria Park on 30 April 1978 – a powerful statement of solidarity. Some punks and skins fell for the right-wing rhetoric but it was a small minority and the anti-Nazi argument was a strong one that would resound around pubs, clubs and gigs. This was all part of the landscape of the late Seventies – the bleakness of the UK and the reaction to it. Punk was coming up with some tough solutions to tough problems. There were a lot of political ideas in the ether and some of them were not good.

Pauline Murray

There was a time when the skinhead movement reared its ugly head – we had a few episodes with that type of thing. They started to spoil gigs, cause trouble in the crowd. You'd shout stuff from the stage and they would be waiting for you after the gig and you'd have to lock yourself in the dressing room.

---

21. Short-lived punk band from Birmingham featuring vocals by Kevin Rowland, later to front Dexy's Midnight Runners.

Garry Bushell

There was a strange wave of racism at the time. The National Front march through Lewisham – things like that were going on.[22] We went down there to oppose it. I got hit by a brick thrown by my own side! [laughs] There was a lot of politics in the air back then. It felt very unstable.

The Front had been growing for some time before punk. It all seemed to coincide with a racist wave that year, that saw Rock Against Racism appear as a reaction against people like Eric Clapton doing his speech. Then you had David Bowie at Victoria Station.[23] Rock Against Racism promoted loads of punk gigs.

There was an article in *Socialist Worker* saying that punk was really right wing, so I wrote an article defending punk saying that it wasn't.

Billy Bragg

I listened to political music like Bob Dylan. I was listening to personal politics. But the thing about the Clash was instead of saying lame things in interviews they said, 'We are doing this Rock Against Racism gig.' We thought this was the greatest thing ever. We were knocked back by the power of the National Front, but here was bands prepared to do something about it.

It's telling that the most revolutionary track on the first Clash album is their version of 'Police and Thieves'. How incendiary it is! What it does with the song compared to the lame versions of reggae that the Police did later, it really did just blow me away, and I suppose it allowed us white kids to finally meet the black culture that we had admired for so long with reggae on a common ground – in

---

22. A famous violent confrontation in south-east London on 13 August 1977, when the Anti-Nazi League confronted the NF racists and successfully prevented them from marching down their chosen route into Lewisham.

23. Rock Against Racism was formed in direct response to a speech that Clapton gave in support of Enoch Powell during one of his gigs in August 1976. Bowie was reported to have given a Hitler salute on arrival at London's Victoria train station the same year; he has denied doing it and strongly condemns racism.

the same way that the Stones, the Beatles and the Who had taken black music in the Sixties. They truly assimilated not just the music but the power of what the lyrics would be saying. You had the Clash mixing the two things together.

On top of that was Rock Against Racism, going on that march to stand up against the National Front – I had never done anything political in my life. I had never even voted up till this point, but that was the first thing I ever did. When I went to Victoria Park – which is an experience on which I base everything that I aspire to in my art – the Clash were not top of the bill. They played in the afternoon. That was pretty empowering, and after them Tom Robinson played. When they sang their key song, 'Glad To Be Gay', all the geezers around me were snogging each other on the lips! And we suddenly realised we were stood under this banner that said, 'Sing if you're glad to be gay'. I will make no bones about it: I was eighteen years old from Barking in Essex, and I'd never met an out gay man. I'll have to say we were a bit taken aback by it, but it didn't take long for me to grasp something really important here. My initial feeling was, 'Why are these gays at this anti-racist thing? It's about black people.' But the penny dropped. The fascist raving xenophobes were against anybody who was different. It didn't matter whether it was colour, gender or attitude. I made a promise to myself to be as different as possible and annoy those people if I could. It really changed my politics. I didn't hear any speeches, but it was Tom's song, not the Clash, that changed my perspective on the world and what pop culture can do. It can't change the world per se, but it can change your perspective on it. Thanks to the Clash for bringing me there, thanks for the gay men brave enough to express their sexuality in a field full of Clash fans – that gave me the politics I have today.

Jimmy Pursey

My audience was suddenly deluged by these right-wing fascists trying to punch each other. I didn't want a load of fucking Nazi idiots at gigs! Who would? They came because Sham were the most working-class band there has ever been in this country. Those people could scare people into joining them. They were saying, 'Come and join us and imagine what a force we could be.' My other mob were saying, 'No, fuck off!' Imagine how many people would have gone to Sham concerts if that wasn't going on, if they were not there scaring people away. Imagine how big the band would have been. 'Angels with Dirty Faces' was a hit, 'If the Kids Are United' was a hit, and our album *Tell Us the Truth* was doing well. We'd made it but it was all going crazy. I was confused. What do I want to be? An entertainer? A politician? A fucking comedy act? What the fuck was I meant to be doing? A few years ago Morrissey came to see me once and he said he understood what I went through, because a lot of what he was going through at the time was similar.

Punk was like we didn't have a map and we didn't have an address. It was like someone nicking a car and saying, 'Who's coming?' We're driving along the road and the car is getting faster and faster and someone asks the driver where they are going and the driver says that he doesn't know. I never asked to be a spokesman. It was ridiculous. Johnny Rotten could get away with it because he always made those sour comments. He talks very sour. My problem was that I tried to play more sentimentalist, tried to understand the problems and talk about them rather than shy away from them and make a sour remark. Johnny was a strong character. I was bit more emotional.

Aki Qureshi

The main base for punk in Bradford at the time was a pub called the Manville Arms and it was buzzing like mad – there weren't thousands of punks initially, but the tribalism was important. The many characters and weirdos attracted a lot of punks from outside of town, and madness to the maximum made it a great and healthy scene. Hippies, satan's slaves, hell's angels, skinheads and drop-outs were all hanging out in the same scene, which created a vibrancy but also a lot of violence between different groups. The only safe place for the punks was the gay scene and the gay pubs.

At the time being a Muslim did not figure, and really there was only me and my brother initially from the communities. But as time went along more Asians were coming in. The Muslim aspect did however play out in terms of drinking alcohol or taking drugs – we never got into it, which was bizarre as there was a lot of hedonism going on, but a lot of punks respected our position. When they asked questions I was not informed enough to give answers – it was just something instinctively I did not want to do and saw no need. I can say that many years after, when I *had* to learn more about my religion to answer many ignorant views, I actually saw a great connection between the ideals of punk and Islam. A quote, 'blessed are those that rebel', was enough for me not to distance myself from the religion.

Andy Kanonik (Demob: vocals)

Demob formed in 1978. Gloucester was to get its first punk band after the band's two founder members, Terry Elcock (guitar) and John Melfah (ex-drummer), decided that Gloucester needed a voice for the kids on the street. John and Terry started rehearsals in Terry's bedroom, and with the deafening racket that was being made soon got the attention of Mike Howe and he muscled his way in on vocals followed by Tony Wakefield (bass). Then more constructive, or I should say destructive, rehearsals started to take place, and Mike asked me to join as joint vocalist. So I jumped on board, soon to be followed by Chris Rush on lead guitar. Yes, a six-piece punk band!

The punk scene was very buoyant when it kicked off. Everywhere you looked you'd see punks on every corner of the city. Liberation was welcomed by the masses of teenagers of the day.

What made Demob a bit unique was the fact that we were a multi-racial band. We were soon to discover the ignorance of a few morons, but in true Demob style our answer to the ignorant was,

'You want some, come get some!' Not many did, and for those who did the Demob Riot Squad were on hand to execute their justice. Gloucester was fortunate when it came to the racial problem – the fact that most of the blacks and whites grew up together and integrated well. There was few problems and any that did occur was usually down to outsiders and the police.

POLICE OPPRESSION
The Angelic Upstarts Take On the Cops!

Demob were not the only ones who felt the police were opposing them. With 'Murder of Liddle Towers', the Angelic Upstarts issued one of the first-class punk rock singles, combining imaginative musical backing with the kind of upfront sociopolitical lyric that punk was made for, championing the cause of local boxer Liddle Towers who had died from injuries sustained overnight in the police cells. The band's relationship with the police in the area deteriorated after this. In the Socialist Workers Party's youth magazine Mensi accused the police of being National Front sympathisers and they had their gigs infiltrated by plain-clothes cops. This really was the punk rockers speaking out!

Mensi

We put out our first single, 'Liddle Towers' with 'Police Oppression', on our own label. We pressed 500 copies. It sold out in a couple of days. South Shields Museum bought two! [laughs] They must have sensed something was going to happen. Small Wonder took some and then Rough Trade re-released it and it went to number one in the independent charts, sold 30,000 copies. If you sold that many these days you'd be Number One for ten weeks. [laughs]

I never wrote a love song in my life. I don't know how to. I wrote about what was happening to us in the streets, like on 'Police Oppression'. The police were straight on us. We used to get loads of stick. It was one of the main reasons we had to move to London. It was the 'Liddle Towers' song that done it. We got T-shirts made and kids got nicked for wearing them. The whole North East police had it in for us. I got attacked at a Sunderland/Notts Forest match by the police.

We moved down to London and we signed to this label Jimmy Pursey had set up called JP Records, through Polydor. I was so taken with Jimmy. I thought the sun shone out of his arse! [laughs] I wanted to be like him. The more time I spent with him the more time I didn't understand him. Very shortly I was at odds with him, arguing all the time.

Before all that we were on Polydor and we had trouble there. We were just coming out of their building, it had been snowing and we were larking about. I wasn't even throwing the snowballs – it was the little drummer. Some secretaries came out with three blokes and he threw one at the secretary. It was miles over her head. This bloke stopped and said, 'Who done that?' There were four or five of us stood there, and I said, 'Look, I don't want nae trouble.' He said, 'You're the one with the fucking mouth,' and I said, 'Look mate, the snowball was nowhere near you.' He said, 'You threw the fucking snowball at me,' and he started taking his rings and coat off and he came towards me, so I nutted him. I slipped in the snow and went on my arse, and he got on top of me and started punching me. I heard my ear go *boiiing*, and I thought my head was going to come off. He was a big fella, so I started biting the fuck out of his leg. He went into shock, screaming. Eventually I let go. Jimmy Pursey came down and got between us and the bloke said, 'I want to shake the bloke's hand,' and he took a swing at us when I was trying to shake his hand. So I nutted him again.

I went to Tony Gordon's office ten minutes' walk away.[24] When I got there he looked at me – my hands were bleeding and I had a lump on my head – and he goes, 'You've been sacked.' I said,

---

24. Tony Gordon was manager of the Angelic Upstarts and also, at one time or another, Sham 69, the Cockney Rejects and Boy George.

'Does that mean we will get loads of money like the Pistols?' [laughs] and he said, 'No, we won't get a shilling. Don't worry about it.' I said, 'Don't worry?' I nearly started crying – it meant everything to us to get a record deal. I thought it meant you were rich and famous, go and tour the world, be set up for life – and I'd blown it with one fight.

I nearly broke down! But we went and signed to Warner Brothers the next day. Tony Gordon said, 'I got something to show you.' He had four or five telegrams, all from major record companies saying, 'We want this band, tell us your price,' and he said, 'Which one do you want to sign with?' I said, 'I don't know. You're the manager.' [laughs]

TEENAGE KICKS
Irish Punk Continued...

Punk may have started out as an elitist art school movement but it swiftly made sense on the rawer streets of the UK. The original talk of dole queue rock was coming home to roost in the beat-up cities of the late Seventies. In Belfast the added political tensions continued to give the movement another dimension and an extra edge.

Guy Trelford

By 1978 Terri Hooley's Good Vibrations record shop in Belfast's Great Victoria Street had taken over from Caroline Music as the Saturday meeting place, with fans and bands alike hanging out there. 1978 also saw the release of the first Good Vibrations single, 'Big Time,' by Rudi, and I still rate 'Big Time' as the greatest single released by any Northern Irish band, ever.

Terri Hooley was a man with a big heart and an even bigger ego! Love him or loathe him, you can't deny Terri his place in punk history. Like most small label bosses Terri was a fan of the new bands first and foremost, and he was enthusiastic enough to put his money where his mouth was. His Good Vibrations emporium became central to the whole Ulster punk scene through the shop, the record label and the gig promotion.

Brian Young

We knocked out 'Big Time' in a couple of hours, recording the backing tracks live as we thought that's how you did it! In fact, we had made three records before I realised you could do overdubs.

Terri Hooley tales are legendary. He had a thousand colourful stories about how he got his glass eye, and many an unwary visitor would be chatting away to him in the pub only to find his eye in the bottom of their glass after they'd finished their pint.

Jake Burns

There were three bands in Belfast at this point. There were ourselves, Rudi and the Outcasts. We had heard of this band from Derry called the Undertones, but no one else had ever heard them.

John O'Neill

As far as people in Belfast were concerned there was nothing outside Belfast. We were looked on as these country bumpkins from out of town. It kind of helped us in a way. It gave us an inner strength. Stiff Little Fingers were from Belfast and they were seen as our main rivals. We were never that nice about them, which seems a bit unfair now. When you're sixteen you're so purist about everything, and we thought the fact that they had this journalist who wrote the lyrics on the first record wasn't true to the punk spirit.

I had no time for the Boomtown Rats, but their early songs were decent pop records. They were like the split between punk and new wave. And we hated new wave! We were into the Ramones and the Buzzcocks. New wave to us was like a watered-down version of punk and we were definitely a punk band.

By the end of 1977 we had to make a record to show that we had made our mark and that we had existed during the punk era. We were getting a bit stale at that point. We had to just get a record out and pack it in – there was no chance of getting anywhere.

Damian O'Neill

We made a demo of 'Teenage Kicks' at Easter 1978 in Derry and our friend Bernie gave it to Terri Hooley. Terri was not sure about it because to be honest it was shite, but he gave in and said, 'All right, let them do a single.' Once we heard that we were overjoyed because we were about to break up for the twentieth time.

John O'Neill

We went to record the 'Teenage Kicks' EP in Belfast one night after a punk concert at Queens University Hall – that's where we met all the other bands like Rudi. I liked Rudi a lot – they had a New York Dolls influence. The rest of the bands, it struck us, were copying English bands. By that time we were getting into Television, Talking Heads.

We definitely didn't think that 'Teenage Kicks' was a big song. The words are pretty cliched and the chords are obvious. The chords are nowhere on the same level as 'Anarchy in the UK' and '(White Man) In Hammersmith Palais'. But it captured the way the band played live really well. We had an hour to record it and we just set up and recorded live.

The idea was to make a four-track EP like the Buzzcocks had done. We'd got on Good Vibrations label and that was brilliant. The next step was to get on a proper record label.

It was all down to John Peel. In those days you could actually ring John Peel and John Walters up during the day and make a request and Billy, whose nickname was Billy Brassneck, always had the balls to ring up and talk to people.[25] John Peel mentioned us at the time and we sent him a demo as well. He had vaguely heard of

---

25. The late John Walters was Peel's ebullient producer, who was responsible for booking many of the sessions for the show.

us. Another testament to what an amazing person he was – he was the only one vaguely interested in anything. He was trying broaden people's horizons.

Damian O'Neill

All the labels who had turned down our demo were ringing us like mad when John Peel started playing 'Teenage Kicks'. They were ringing my mum's house because we didn't have a manager. None of us had a clue how to talk to these people. Sire were the obvious choice for us because they had the Ramones, and the Rezillos who we also loved. We had no idea about contracts. We just saw these numbers and we thought we would not have to work for the rest of our lives! We were like lambs to the slaughter! But we were lucky with Sire.

The first time we came over to England was to tour with the Rezillos. We did four or five shows and they broke up, which was a good job for us because I don't think we would have lasted much longer on the road! We never played more than two gigs ever. The rest of them were fucked off and homesick. I was the young and unattached one. I stayed on in London for a week and I got to see Wire and that was amazing. Wire were the best by then. I saw Generation X as well, and it was a shock how professional these bands were.

It didn't phase us. We weren't taken over by the glamour. I know for a fact if we had moved to London we would have broken up, so it kept our feet on the ground. We spent all our money on British Airways and taxis, flying in for *Top of the Pops*!

John O'Neill

Even though we were on *Top of the Pops* we thought it wasn't that great a deal. It was great to play in a band and not have a job, and it was great having our name on the record label like Lennon and McCartney – that was more exciting to us than being on *Top of the Pops*.

I was always really aware of not being a good musician like Damian or Mickey, and writing songs was pure chance. I never thought I had a gift for it. Lyrically I think they are embarrassing. I had this thing that if you had thought too long and hard about the lyrics then it wasn't right; now I wish I had spent more time on the lyrics! [laughs] Mickey was good at words, like 'My Perfect Cousin' and 'Mars Bar'. He wrote clever lyrics, very original.

Jake Burns

We released our first single 'Suspect Device' on our own Rigid Digits label. It was picked up by John Peel straight away. I honestly believe that John Peel was the single most important person in British rock music. When you're based outside London you don't have a chance of getting a record company to see you, and Peel was crucial. We were promised a deal with Island and that fell through at that stage. We were thinking nothing was going to happen. We didn't know what to do and then John Peel championed us.

At the time we thought we were the bee's knees. We were definitely the best band in Northern Ireland, very much a big fish in a small pond, and we really had a big idea of our importance until we got to London. One of the bands we were always being mentioned with were the Skids and we were in London for a day or so and we noticed that they were playing the Nashville. We went in and after one song we are looking at each other thinking, 'These guys are miles better than us!' [laughs]

Stiff Little Fingers played Dublin after we released the first single, then we went down there as part of a seven-date package tour modelled on the Stiff tours.[26] If you played outside Belfast and Dublin you tended to get blank stares. I remember one venue bang in the middle of Ireland and the guy who ran the pub was furious:

---

26. The classic Stiff package tour was headlined by Elvis Costello and Ian Dury.

'You will never play here again,' he said. And he was right, we never did play there again! [laughs]

Dublin had a scene. We had heard of the Radiators From Space, and the Boomtown Rats played in Belfast just before they left. People forget what a good band the Boomtown Rats were. That first album is great. Then they went more poppy, and they had three Number Ones. Tough luck, lads. [laughs] Geldof is a very clever guy. His whole confrontational Bob the Gob thing was perfect. Live they were a really good band. People forget that and write them off.

It was also on our first visit down to Dublin that I met Bono. We were doing this exchange gig. I walked in before we played and this apparition in leopardskin walks up to me and sticks his hand out and says, 'Hi, I'm in a band as well. I really like your single. Come and see us play tomorrow night.' So I turned up just in time to see them get thrown off stage because they were so bad. [laughs] Whatever happened to them?

Gavin Friday

The Virgin Prunes had a big following in London. People thought Irish music was all about the Boomtown Rats. Then U2 went over to the UK. They were never punk – they were more power pop. I remember raving about Public Image, and Bono would be raving about the Jam album *All Mod Cons* that he much preferred. I'd be going much more into darker music. Then they went to England and took off.

Jake Burns

Gavin Martin, who ran *Alternative Ulster* fanzine, wanted a give-away for the cover. I said, 'I'll write you a song.' He came along to the next gig and we played 'Alternative Ulster'. I went up to him and said, 'What did you think of the song?' and he said, 'Nah, it's fucking shite.' Gavin went on to be the editor of the *NME* which just shows you what he fucking knows! [laughs]

Rough Trade put it out and it took off. We got a major deal on the back of doing the Tom Robinson Band tour, but we stayed on Rough Trade and did the album *Inflammable Material* with them. We were the first independent album to crack the Top 20. Musically we were very lucky being on Rough Trade. I don't think it would have been the same record if we had been signed by a major label. They would have knocked all the edges off the band. When I hear it now I realise how raw it was and how raw it needed to be. It was a big record both for ourselves and for Rough Trade.

Moving to London was easy. We had done as much as we could in Ireland and the next step was to try and break the mainland. The trouble was that we didn't realise that there was the rest of the world apart from Britain. That was why we stayed on the level that we stayed on.

YOU NEVER LISTENED TO A WORD THAT I SAID
Public Image Limited

In 1978, where could John Lydon go? Virgin had wanted him to carry on the Pistols. To a certain extent the band continued to exist with him, with the patchy Rock'n'Roll Swindle *film and soundtrack album that saw all manner of odd Lydon-less singles getting released under the Sex Pistols' banner: some of them were great, like Steve Jones' song for Sid, 'Silly Thing', and some of them were rubbish.*

From the wreckage of punk's standard-bearers, Lydon put together his anti-rock vision with Public Image Limited. Their debut single 'Public Image', released in October 1978, wrong-footed everyone, being a rush of great, albeit very warped, rock'n'roll with Jah Wobble's brilliant dub bass and Keith Levene's astonishing guitar screech. The band's debut album, released in December, was the sound of someone tearing up his myth, a primal scream therapy of an album, and a powerful and thrilling continuation of the musical themes on the debut single. This

was an escape route for punk – part of the 'post-punk' musical argument
that emerged as rock'n'roll was deconstructed in a thousand different
ways by the likes of the Fall, Gang of Four and Joy Division.

John Lydon

There was plenty of new bands that I liked. I loved the Raincoats,
Psychic TV – all kinds of very odd things. Vic Godard, whatever he
got up to was always very deeply strange. The boy's disturbed!
[laughs] All very thrilling. Quite a few things from up North, but
then there was an attitude that crept in. It was just, you know, like
in the football days, that Northerners-hate-Southerners thing, and
they would bring this thing into the punk world: Southern softies
and Northern bastards. What the fuck are you fighting about?
Parliament is over there – go there and fight.

Don Letts

While in Jamaica, John had the idea for something and when we get
back Public Image comes together. Sid was around but that was
never going to work out.

I used to flip between the two camps, Clash and Pistols. I always
had a foot in both camps. When John was doing his shit, I spent a
lot of time in Gunter Grove where he lived. We were genuinely
friends. At Gunter Grove there was a bit of a scene: speed was
around, spliff, booze and heavy, heavy dub sounds, and certain
people passing through paying their respects or being humiliated by
John and the rest of us. Our lives were so intertwined between being
there and me and Jeanette Lee, our relationship – I remember she
started hanging out with them as well.

Poly Styrene

John lived round the corner from me in Gunter Grove. There was a
lot of venom in the country directed towards him then, and I had this
empathy for him. I went round a few times. He didn't need much
sympathy – he's a bit of an oddball. I did run into Sid Vicious, and he
was a bit of an oddball as well – he came at me with a great big knife!

John Lydon was playing up to his image, being this person that everybody hated. He had his crucifixes upside down on the wall. He was an anarchic character, a strange person. At the time we saw this person being criticised by the mainstream press. I don't think that he was as bad himself as the people he surrounded himself with. He always had an entourage, people like Jah Wobble who was weird, Sid who was weird, Keith Levene. I can't say I was best friends with them. I was coming from a different space altogether. I went round because they were my neighbours. Don Letts as well.

With Sid, it killed him in the end, playing up to the persona. He was a bit of a moron, the court jester. He would do bad things to make everyone laugh. He'd keep everyone entertained, but in a negative way really.

Keith Levene

This guy Paul, who was John's minder, found me and said, 'John's looking for you everywhere. What about that thing – "If the Pistols broke up, we're going to put a band together"?'

I went around to John's one night and that was it. 'Are we doing it?' 'Yeah.' 'Are we going to call it Public Image?' I said. 'Limited.' So we had it. Three days later, he said, 'Wobble's coming over,' and he was in the band. John Grey, John's best friend, said, 'Don't you think we should call him Jah Wobble? Ha ha!'[27] We thought that was very cool. He couldn't play bass, but he knew about reggae and music in general. We particularly loved dub at the time.

Jah Wobble

My first bass was nicked for me by my mate Ronnie in the late Seventies. I did have a natural gift for it. There have been only two things I've had a knack for in my life: the bass and clay pigeon shooting!

---

27. Sid also gets credit for Wobble's nickname, through mispronouncing his real name John Wardle.

Keith Levene came from squats. He definitely knew more about playing guitar than everyone else. He was quite a character. Keith had seen me play bass in a squat, so I was in – I don't think there was a plan. The photographer Dennis Morris was around a lot at the time so he was on the firm, in the gang. He had a lot of views on how things would be packaged.[28]

Keith Levene

Jim came from Canada to audition for us, like it was a dream.[29] We had all these drummers in a hallway and we tried one and another. We sat Jim down and he was so fucking perfect. He played for 45 seconds and I said, 'Stop! Everyone go home – this is the guy.'

Dub was the big thing then. It happened to me individually, and it just turned out that what I felt were the *crème de la crème* of the punk scene were into it. There were some A&R guys that were so into dub reggae, more than anything. We knew the Jamaican bands as heads. We helped them get signed to Virgin. I'd been involved in the early days of the Slits, helping them get their sound together.

With PiL I thought we were going to go slower. In the Clash, everything was really fast. We were going to go really far, but in a new vocabulary. The Damned were going really fast but with a known vocabulary. I had a completely different idea in mind. The PiL manifesto was no managers, no producers, lawyers when we need them. We're not a band, we're a company. Think up your own ideas. Total control. I guess we thought we were a bit important and all that.

John's got this way of blinding people. He's got amazing charisma. At the time, he was really on. He was on in the Pistols and it pissed him off that it fell apart. As much as you slag John off for various sorts of excessive ways of entertaining himself, he's got this basic togetherness.

---

28. Dennis Morris was a key photographer from the punk period, with some great shots of the Pistols' secret 1977 tour and other frontline moments.
29. Jim Walker, the drummer in PiL. He went on to form Theatre of Hate with Kirk Brandon.

But he's such an annoying git because he doesn't do anything to help. He knows what the picture should be. When it doesn't work out, he just blames people. He likes to pretend that other people are weak and it's never him. The reason that things don't work out the way that John wants them to is because he doesn't do his bit. But at the time, he was *really* doing his bit.

Jah Wobble added spontaneity. I didn't show him a thing on bass, like we used to with Paul Simonon. By doing that, Paul got to learn how to play bass proficiently, and after a while he could make up his own thing. Wobble couldn't play, but he made up his own bass lines pretty much from scratch. He wouldn't mind me editing them, making suggestions, but he'd always make up his own bass line.

Jah Wobble

The first album cover was a piss-take of *Time* magazine. It was done very well, done as fashion photos. When the album came out the critics didn't like it – they wanted rock music. They were very middle-class rock people and they didn't trust it at all. Working-class people doing this kind of thing got slagged off by them.

Keith Levene

We made 'Public Image', the single, and that came off OK. We were getting away with being very audacious – 'We can do whatever the fuck we want. We're PiL, fuck you.' People never knew if we were serious or playing a joke on them. But we were serious.

In 'Fodderstompf', where Wobble says, 'We are now trying to finish the album with a minimum amount of effort which we are now doing very suc-cess-ful-ly,' it's what we were doing. We had this thing where we only gave the record company exactly the 30 minutes prescribed in the contract because those bastards ripped us off. Those guys played fucking hardball. We did what we did and it was a fine first record. The thing that went wrong with that record was the game logistics. Virgin imported it to America so we never had an official American release. It really fucked up our momentum. It sucked.

Brian X

I remember hearing 'Public Image', the first single from PiL, and I was totally blown away. It was like the Sex Pistols but totally different, and it had that amazing bass in it and that mind-blowing guitar line.

Keith Levene

We wanted to use John's voice instrumentally, which we thought was a very far-out idea. It didn't have to be the main thing right out front. But I do find his voice to be very, very out front and not as instrumental as I remember thinking it was.

A lot of times I'd take his lyrics, and even though we didn't have samplers then, I would put them on different places that they weren't, by putting them into a two-track and flying them in. Or if he hadn't made up enough verses, I'd just repeat a verse. But I'm making it sound like he didn't come up with anything half the time. He came up with a lot of stuff just perfectly. Like what he did with 'Theme', he did it the first time and it was perfect. We definitely produced the end product together.

John Lydon

In PiL it was shared. I had no total control. PiL was more like the real world. These were people that I knew and grew up with. And we just went out of our way to do exactly what we wanted, without consideration to commercial value. And gosh, you know what, you *do* achieve financial success that way because, oddly enough, there is a respect for honesty and integrity. We were all equal in the band. You got to stop the nonsense of 'I wrote this' and 'I wrote that' – share the money and you stay well with each other.

Keith Levene

When we formed, as soon as we had enough tunes to do a gig, which seemed to be bloody quick, we played Christmas at the Rainbow Theatre and had all the seats taken out. We were testing out sound systems. It was a wonderful time. We booked a place in

Brixton which was just an empty hall, just to test this three-bass sound system. That was a turbo rig that I wanted to use at the Rainbow. Because we were in sound system situations, we were making up new tunes. That's when 'Death Disco' was emerging.

John Lydon

The influence in PiL's music doesn't happen on purpose. It happens quite naturally. I mean, I listen to swingtime music and I'm not going to run off to do the 'Chattanooga Choo Choo'. I don't imitate. I've always been a reggae fan but you can't say, 'There's Johnny's reggae album.' It isn't like that. Reggae is done very nice and done well by Jamaicans – that's their culture and their voice, and done with their political opinion, and it ain't for Whitey to think he can move in on it and just steal it.

Don Letts

Those first three albums, they still sound brilliant. It still sounds like tomorrow. They were produced under some really bizarre circumstances, mostly fuelled by the fact that some people were going up and some people were going down and some people were going sideways chemically. It was very dark and weird round there. Funnily enough, I followed them around Europe filming them on Super 8 again, and could never see anything because John would always play with his back to the audience. But it was dark and intense. The gigs were weird and strained. You always felt the tension in the air, you always felt a hair's breadth away from erupting into a fight, a calamity – it was like the final scenes of that movie *The Day of the Locust*, that vibe. Every show Public Image played was always like that. Lydon was the head of it.

I did Public Image's first video. That was in the safety of the studio. Instead of turning to some up-and-coming video director, they looked for someone in their own ranks and I was first in the queue. I didn't know how to make a video, but the point is they gave me a chance. When someone got through the door, they held the door open for everyone else to get through. It didn't last long though.

CHAPTER 11
1979: THE SECOND WAVE PEAKS

The fallout from punk was in full effect. The creative energy unleashed was diversifying into a myriad directions. This was a fascinating and chaotic period of creativity as people followed their own agendas using the DIY ethic of punk and the fierce individualism encouraged by the movement. By 1979 there was a whole mass of established mini-scenes, including the 'death to trad rock' post-rockers; the quite brilliant 2 Tone movement spearheaded by the Specials; the mod revival inspired by the Jam (who from 1979 to 1982 achieved massive chart success) featuring the Chords, Secret Affair, the Purple Hearts; and a psychobilly scene of Fifties rockabilly cranked up with punk energy featuring the Meteors and the Cramps.

There were also various precursors to the goth, a scene that had no name at the time but was already wearing black and listening to the Banshees, the emerging Killing Joke and John Peel/student post-punkers such as Gang of Four and Echo and the Bunnymen. It began to embrace its own bands, emerging in the Batcave in London and in the Phonographic and the Warehouse in Leeds, where most of the key goth bands to come were hanging out.

There were very idiosyncratic scenes in Liverpool and Manchester, and smaller scenes like the electronic pop of Sheffield built around

Human League and Cabaret Voltaire. Parallel with this was the second wave of punk bands, taking punk rock from the art schools onto the streets; the skinheads who were re-emerging post-Sham 69; and other newly-arrived street punk bands.

It seemed like every youth cult that had ever existed was out on the prowl and sometimes it would kick off between rival gangs and scenes. This was a time of evolutionary chaos and endless arguments amongst the shrapnel of the punk scene.

In the middle of all this there was the Clash's classic London Calling *album, a record sniffed at back then despite reaching the Top 10, but one that has become an all-time classic, loved more and more as the years go by.* London Calling *seemed to capture all the loose strands at the time. Now dressed in sharp suits and fedoras, the Clash were a band at the peak of their powers, pin-striped gangsters hustling the revolution beat. There was rockabilly, soul, reggae, jazz, punk rock, guttersnipe poetry and tales of street life, backropped by an astonishing variety of sounds. Punk rock was just the start; the Clash wanted to fire up the whole world with all the rebel musics they could master.*

Meanwhile tragedy struck when Sid Vicious overdosed on heroin in New York in February.

I DID IT MY WAY
Farce Turns to Tragedy for Sid and Nancy

It had been unravelling for Sid. Fast. The Pistols' implosion had left him floundering around. There had been hits, like the excellent bubblegum reworkings of Eddie Cochrane's rock'n'roll standards 'C'mon Everybody' and 'Something Else', finally featuring Sid as the frontman. There was enough there to launch himself as a solo act – with a sneer, battered good looks and the punk rock cred to give the required bubblegum an instant edge, he could have made it huge like Billy Idol would do a a few years later – but Sid was lost in the shit world of heroin and ended up in living in New York in a narcotic hell.

On 12 October 1978 Nancy Spungen was found murdered in the room they rented at the Chelsea Hotel. It's never been clear whether Sid murdered her, whether it was a suicide pact or a drug deal gone wrong. Sid was arrested and put into Rikers Island Prison. He got bailed out by Malcolm McLaren and Virgin and was then sent back in for bottling Patti Smith's brother Todd in a bar fight in December. The last few months of Sid's life were played out as a tragi-comedy and eventually, at a party thrown by his mother on 2 February 1979 in New York to celebrate his coming out of jail again, he overdosed. Apparently, a couple of days later he would have been in the recording studio with Cook and Jones to record an album of covers under the Sex Pistols' banner, including songs like 'Mack The Knife'.

Rat Scabies

I did a gig with Sid Vicious. That was a book in itself, bizarre. The first day he arrived he was late because someone had died in his apartment, and Sid was limping because he had run out of veins apart from in his foot![1]

Don Letts

When we went to New York during the whole Sid and Nancy thing, I asked him to come to the office to sign something so I could use him in the movie. He's sitting there and he's got this knife which is about *this long*, and he's prodding Nancy with it. I was saying, 'Sid, chill with that. Someone is going to get hurt.' Nancy was saying, 'That hurt.' He signs this thing and two weeks later she's dead. I always maintained that Sid did it. He was the only one that didn't know it. He was a casualty. He wasn't a success, he was a failure, and seeing people walking around with the Sid T-shirt, I dunno. He was the punk poster boy and he couldn't play bass for shit – it shows you.

---

1. This was a one-off gig, 'Sid Sods Off', in London on 15 August 1978. Sid needed to raise money to pay the airfares for him and Nancy to fly to New York. The band, which he called the Vicious White Kids, also featured Glen Matlock and Steve New of the Rich Kids.

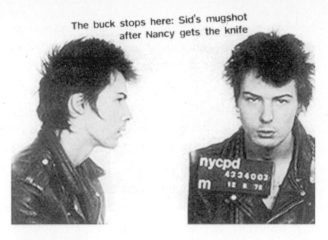

The buck stops here: Sid's mugshot after Nancy gets the knife

Marco Pirroni

Sid wasn't really useless all the time. He was quite sharp, but it was all a bit too much for him. He didn't have a strong personality. He had a self-deprecating humour. It wasn't 'I'm the great Sid Vicious', it was a piss-take. It was a stupid name. I didn't know about his background. No one knew what his real name was. He didn't know himself! No wonder he was screwed up, when the only thing you got was the character you invented, and he clung on for fear.

When Lydon joined the Pistols that didn't help. Sid thought it should have been him, really. He would have made them a completely different band. With Sid it would have become an art-school joke kind of glam rock band. Lydon was much darker, more substantial. With Sid it was a lot of style over content, which is great as well, but I don't think Sid could have written those lyrics like John did. Sid had lyrics like his song, 'Kamikaze Pilot'. I don't think it would have worked at all. Sid also didn't have that kind of confidence to really get on stage and say 'Fuck off!' which no one ever did before John. That was absolutely unheard of. I think Sid would have wanted to be Bowie – but without the talent to pull it all off.

Jah Wobble

He died very young and all that, but there just wasn't much to say about him. He used to say he wanted to be dead, but that wasn't him – he had a natural kind of intelligence and it came out stupid. If he had survived he'd probably be in the rag trade or something, some fashion thing, a New Romantic, that kind of lark.

Sid really wasn't a tough guy. He was a fucking nuisance. It's apparently come out now that he was a mugger and if I had known that, well, I'm from the East End and in the particular community I'm from, that's the line that you do not cross. Sometimes they would keep stuff like that away from me.

The axe story? It was not me! I didn't attack Sid with an axe. If it was, I'd tell you. I was there when it happened. I was upstairs at the time. I was really on one at John's house. John wasn't there at the time, and the phone went. I picked it up and it was Sid. I think he wanted to come round, he wanted to be in the PiL gang – he felt rejected by John or whatever, he thought he should have been in the band – I think it fucked him off. He came round and kicked in the door and this geezer went down with an axe. Now if you get hit by an axe you tend to die! I think the geezer prodded him a bit and Sid's completely off his head and he falls down backwards. He rolled over and cracked his head on the back of a boot scraper!

When people talk about Sid, I remember it was all such a piss-take. We gave each other names. He changed my name from John Wardle to Jah Wobble, and because he was so forlorn-looking we called him Sid Vicious.

Chrissie Hynde

Sid was very sweet and very honest. He really told you what he thought. He was so non-discriminating. If you were standing there talking to a girl and she had a big nose, he'd say 'Cor, you've got a really big nose!' But he'd be the same if she had big tits. He'd say 'Cor, you've got really big tits!' He was just pointing out what he was looking at.

I nearly got married to Sid! Only so that I could stay in the country. We went down to the Registry Office, with a fake birth certificate because he was underage, but it was closed for a holiday.

And he had to be in court the next day for taking someone's eye out with a glass, so we didn't do it in the end.[2] In fact, John offered first! But he had that Bill Grundy thing, and he was all, 'Oh my God!' And I said, 'Hey John, remember that thing we were gonna do so that I could stay in the country?' and he goes 'Wot? Wot? Wot's going on? There's got to be something in it for me!' And I said '£2, and I'll give it to you at the Registry Office.' He'd been in my bed all night, but he was with some other girl, keeping me awake. I had to keep watching him the whole time to make sure he didn't escape!

I was a couple of years older than them. Strummer and some of those guys were a couple of years older too, and those two years meant a lot. I was about 27. I'd been around the world and I'd seen and done it all. So I bridged the gap. I could hang out with Sid's mum or with him! Just like I hung out with Linda McCartney and now I hang out with her kids.

As soon as he realised how much everyone hated Nancy, man, he stuck to her like a stamp to a letter. That's why he was called Sid: he hated the name Sid, so everyone called him Sid. But when he got fucked up, he got very violent. He was shooting speed before he met Nancy, and when she got him into dope it was a very easy switch to make. Then it was all over for him. He'd never been with a woman before where she had that kind of control over him. They were in love, I guess.

John Lydon

The drugs, the heroin and the influence of New York and that Patti Smith/New York Dolls bollocks wore its way into him and he started believing the Lou Reed mythology of what an excellent lifestyle it is to walk around looking like a vampire smacked up to the eyeballs. Total self-delusion. Sid's self-destruction was depressing. It's pathetic, but you can't help those that can't help themselves. It was very sad and disappointing.

---

2. This court appearance followed the 100 Club incident of 1976. See chapter 5.

DON'T CALL ME SCARFACE
2 Tone and the Ska Revival

Reggae and punk had been bedfellows since day one. Ska, with its chop-ping rhythm and danceability, had already been big in the late Sixties with the skinheads, and it was only a matter of time before it would surface in the punk scene. In Coventry the Specials were crossing punk and ska and coming up with a whole new hybrid which they released on their own 2 Tone label. They had been on the punk scene fairly early when, as the Coventry Automatics, they were signed to Bernie Rhodes' stable of bands (cool stable as well – Dexy's Midnight Runners, Subway Sect and the Clash – Rhodes had some good ears on him). They rehearsed at the Clash's Rehearsal Rehearsals, and also toured with them.

By the time they had become the Specials they were the perfect synthe-sis of punk and ska, with a cool look in tight two-tone tonic suits and pork-pie hats, an incendiary live show, a black-and-white stage presence (common now, revolutionary then), a strong black-and-white-unite message, a political suss and some great songs that would make them briefly the key band in the country. Their debut album was off-kilter punk ska and their second was purely off-kilter, mixing muzak into the fray, but both were stuffed with great singles that signposted a genera-tion. To this day key musicians will quote the Specials as an influence – they are one of the classic British bands.

In their wake came Madness, the Beat, the Selecter and Bad Manners, a mini-youthquake. For eighteen months this was one of biggest scenes in the UK. The influence of 2 Tone has continued through the decades.

Ranking Roger (The Beat: vocals)

The first punk thing that really affected me properly was '(White Man) In Hammersmith Palais', which I thought was wicked. The Clash were mentioning people like Dillinger and Leroy Smart – these were reggae stars I had grown up with and I thought, 'Whoa, that's cool!' I didn't totally get the Clash at first, but like everyone

The Special's brew of punk and ska created the 2 Tone phenomenon that swept the UK in a brilliant rush of multiracial pop that reflected the dynamic new UK emerging despite Thatcherism

else I got hooked. There was love and unity and then I heard 'Police And Thieves' and I thought, 'They are doing Lee Perry – that's cool.'

I think Johnny Rotten was the person who turned everything around with punk and reggae. What he was saying was inspiration for me. He said people should listen a lot more to reggae, because the reggae people were saying the same things as the punk people. So I got involved and became a punk. At first I was in a band called the Dum Dum Boys, which was kind of a bit like David Bowie punk. I soon went off and joined the Beat and that was the punky reggae thing that was my dream.

Neville Staple

I was in a youth club doing my DJ stuff, playing reggae at the time, and the Specials used to rehearse in a room next door – Jerry, Horace and Lynval.[3] They asked if I could go out on the road and help them as a roadie. The punk scene hadn't really started at the time. That was just coming up. We were called the Automatics, playing reggae/ska.

---

3. Jerry Dammers, Horace Panter and Lynval Golding – three members of the Specials.

I used to see the punk bands when they came through Coventry. We saw the Clash a lot. When the Specials got going we did the Clash's Out On Parole tour – that was fucking brilliant.[4] That was the first time I had seen so many kids jumping and spitting. You should have seen the fucking spitting – it was like fireworks, man! What the fuck is going on here?

Punk made us speed our music up. Playing in front of those kids made it more energetic. I used to really like the Buzzcocks, but it was the Clash who we were very close to – they were a great band. The Bernie Rhodes connection came through Jerry Dammers. We were living in Coventry and Jerry had all the contacts and knew where to go. We used to rehearse at Rehearsal Rehearsals – it was a fucking pit, man! We used to sleep there in sleeping bags and there was rats all over the place.

The Specials was the best time of my life. 2 Tone Records was all Jerry Dammers' concept. Our first single, 'Gangsters', was about a gig in Paris that never happened. Basically we got sent to this gig that Bernie Rhodes had set up. We went there in three cars to find it ourselves – a total shambles. We had to pay the hotel bills and they said, 'You can't leave the hotel until you pay up.'

The 2 Tone thing got big. It was good but weird to deal with. I was doing the same things and went to same places, but everyone was being different to me.

The gigs got violent because some people didn't want black and white people to get on. That's why they came. What we were saying must have got to people. We sang about what we saw was happening, what was happening to us. People round us called it political, but there was enough people singing about love'n'stuff.

Ranking Roger

From what I remember there were three black punks in Birmingham in 1978, when I came on the punk scene. Walking through town, the majority of black people were scorning you. I was being snarled

---

4. The Out On Parole tour took place in June and July 1978.

at for having a ripped Union Jack T-shirt and a handkerchief hanging from my bondage trousers. I will never forget that, people staring: 'Why are you dressed like that? Why are you trying to be a white man? You are a disgrace to your race and your colour,' and me standing up firm and saying, 'I believe in love and unity and carrying on.' And a year later, and 20 years later, I'm still delivering that message to the people. I want to show somewhere in all this there is love and unity – that is always my goal.

So I carried on with my ambition and got through to a lot of people, and them same people a year later were praising me because I was on *Top of the Pops*! I'm thinking, 'What kind of hypocritical thinking is this? All I did was put a pork-pie hat on my head, changed my image a bit, but I still had the same mentality that I had a year ago.' It all started getting a bit weird when half of the punks became racist skinheads, not normal skinheads. Obviously they were just following fashion and didn't know why they were racist skinheads – they were still listening to punk music and certain reggae musics and some of them became racists, and I never understood that.

If you talk to the original racists now, they are as good as gold. They used to come to you at gigs shouting, 'Sieg heil! Sieg heil!' and the very same ones were the first to be the anti-racist skinheads. They understood how nasty all that was, and they had grown up now and they had kids, but they came back to the music. It's great: a six-foot-four skinhead, he's massive, and I would be thinking, 'I wouldn't want to meet him down a dark alley!' – but he's coming up to me saying, 'Nice one, Rog, you made my day. Great music over all the years. You been a great inspiration!' It's a great thing you could reach over and touch them on a level.

IF THE KIDS ARE UNITED
The Second Wave Peaks

Perhaps the greatest band to come out of punk's second wave were the Ruts, who in 1979 were pushing punk rock in a different direction. They truly arrived with a real state-of-the-nation album, The Crack, *that saw them easily equal their peers. As good as any of the class of '77, the Ruts combined brilliant musicianship, great songwriting and intensity in a powerful package that also managed to blend punk and reggae in a way that only the Clash had managed before. This record has never dated and sounds as powerful today as when it was first released.*

Up there with the Ruts were the UK Subs (who had been around since the beginning of punk), who had a run of hits and cut some great albums (all named in alphabetical order!) and were the band that seemed to be held in respect by almost every differing scene on the punk rock front. Regulars on Top of the Pops, *the second wave bands were a mini-boom after the initial explosion. Groups like the Cockney Rejects, the Exploited, Angelic Upstarts, the Ruts and the UK Subs caught the wave with a series of singles. Also up there were Discharge, whose brutal anti-war anthems were hardly likely to get into the charts but who, along with fellow Midlands outfit GBH, have become massively influential on bands, not least on the likes of Metallica.*

The second wave of bands also included the poppier outfits such as punklike the Members, who came and went within the blink of an eye, releasing an inventive album and scoring a massive hit with 'Sound of the Suburbs' (which reached Number Twelve in February 1979).

Garry Bushell

I had a fanzine out at the time, *Napalm*. I then got onto *Sounds*. I had a piece of luck – I wrote to them and they said, 'Show us what you can do.' They liked the fanzine and I did about eight reviews in twelve days and stuffed them through the door, and they wrote back and offered me a staff job. By '78 Jane Suck had gone and they had Jon Savage who was more into to the arty end of it all.[5] Suddenly there was all these bands appearing everywhere. I was going out to see the Skids, the Subs, the Members – the real people were now into punk.

---

5. Jane Suck was a vociferous journalist, one of the first writers to extensively cover the punk scene.

Nicky Tesco

Our single 'Sound of the Suburbs' was a massive hit. It took everyone by surprise, not least Gallup. The charts assumed Virgin must
have hyped it and dropped us down the charts. We were outselling
'Oliver's Army' by four to one.[6] He was Number Three and so we
could have been Number One. We sold a quarter of a million. We
had done the groundwork. Our gigs were rammed. It said something: people in punk pretended to have this inner-city credibility,
but loads of them came from the suburbs like Camberley where I
came from and they have their own frustrations. There was a real
dearth of any kind of activity for teenagers. As a result soft drugs,
casual sex and binge-drinking were huge. It was an anthem for the
dispossessed and the bedroom bands. After that the Members made
every mistake possible. We should have re-released 'Solitary
Confinement' and repeated the success, but we didn't want to rip
the kids off, so we put out 'Offshore Banking Business', which
wasn't a hit, and that didn't help the *At the Chelsea Nightclub* album.

J. C. Carroll

The secret of punk was that everyone had one really good song
inside them. That's why punk compilations are so much better than
actual album releases by the bands at the time.

Henry Rollins

Britain has always rendered great music, from psychedelia through
to rock'n'roll. In the punk rock days all those early seven inches and
albums, I still listen to all that stuff – the first four UK Subs albums
to me are like desert island LPs. Records that you can't do without.

John Lydon

Punk ended up to mean that awful band with Charlie Harper, the
singer – the UK Subs. They all go fast, a thousand miles an hour,

---

6. 'Oliver's Army' was Elvis Costello's biggest hit.

duh-duh-duh...[7] It's unbearable to me, that. If you can't play, speed won't cover that up. What are you worried about? What's the problem with not being able to play? Let's face it, you're piss poor, you can't afford your instruments, everybody knows you stole them, everybody knows you haven't had aeons of time with piano lessons and vocal coaches – so tell it like is. Or join the UK Subs.

Henry Rollins

The Ruts were never around long enough to make any bad music. They were one of the bands who could really play. The rhythm section was so evolved and the production on those records was so great and Malcolm Owen was completely believable, very charismatic and amazing. I still get off on those tunes, all my Ruts bootlegs and all the singles, and the albums *The Crack* and *Grin And Bear It*. Brilliant.

Segs

'In A Rut' was our first single in 1979. It didn't come out till we could afford to put it out. Me and Ruffy were working in a garage, both on the dole, and this guy put all the money up for 'In A Rut'. We got 1,000 pressed up and then distributed through People Unite label that was run by the reggae band Misty in Roots, who we did loads of gigs with.[8] At first 1,000 singles looked like a lot under Ruffy's bed, but in the end we ended up selling 52,000. It all started when someone we knew who was plugging records put it at the bottom of his pile and gave them to John Peel, who gave us a session and kickstarted it for us. One minute nobody wanted to know about the Ruts; the next there were queues round the block.

---

7. Not strictly true. The UK Subs were exciting in their use of velocity, but they also maintained a good groove to their music. Charlie had been around too long to indulge in mindless thrash, and the Subs have released some classic records. To say that guitar player Nicky Garratt is a simplistic or dumb musician is plain wrong. The UK Subs are often unfairly criticised in this way.

8. Misty in Roots were an excellent reggae band who had the Ruts supporting them and put out the Ruts' first single.

Me and Ruffy wanted to carry on independently. We had 'Babylon's Burning' and we tried to record it ourselves on an 8-track but it didn't come out that well. Then everyone was going mad trying to sign us so we signed an awful deal with Virgin and we did 'Babylon's Burning'. The track is too clean for me. Everyone said we had sold out – that had become the doctrine of a generation.[9]

Songwriting in the Ruts was a pleasure. We would work on the 'Babylon's Burning' bass line and we'd be off – there was no pretension of who did what. 'Savage Circle' was based on Captain Beefheart. It didn't matter where the music came from. Malcolm listened to 'Mr Blue Sky' and he liked the riff in it and that became 'I Was Cold' after we messed around with it.[10] [laughs] We used to go round to Malcolm's house for some legendary sessions – before he sold his stereo for heroin. We would listen to Kraftwerk, Human League, Tapper Zukie, smoke dope, then go and play.

We were political by default. We said we were not into politics, but were in a real way. We did the Rock Against Racism tour, the Anti-Nazi League things. It was all going a bit National Front then, and we stood up against that. We had a black friend, Clarence Baker, the manager of Misty, who would come round Malcolm's house. We all loved reggae. I learned to play reggae jamming along with Misty – they would say, 'Less notes, less notes...'

Rat Scabies lived down our street. He said, 'Would you lot like to support us on tour?' During the tour 'Babylon's Burning' went to Number Seven and the Damned were well pissed off. [laughs] I've got a soft spot for the Damned, they were good mates.

Andy Kanonik

Demob played on the closing night at Gloucester's most prestigious punk venue, Witcombe Lodge, in 1979 – we supported the UK Subs,

---

9. 'Sold out' was the stick used to beat every band that got out of the gutter, a pointless accusation in most cases.

10. 'Mr Blue Sky' was a top ten hit for the distinctly un-punk Electric Light Orchestra in early 1978.

a great night all round. The bastard Tories were closing down most venues across the country, so on that night we helped by trashing the venue with our bare hands. Charlie Harper still remembers this gig, and it is often brought up in conversation when we support the UK Subs. 'No Room For You' was written about Witcombe Lodge's closure, and the song voices what most kids of the day could relate to.

Were we second wave? This is an interesting one. We, Demob, were put in the second wave of punk but I've been baffled to this day because there are various opinions of when the first wave ended and when the second began, so I decided that it didn't matter a flying fuck to me. By the early Eighties the scene started to divide into punk, Oi, hardcore, anarchic, etc. I never bought into it. Punk is punk, no matter what label you try to use. The attitude with everyone was: fuck the system, liberation brother/sister, bring it on, and back to the working class.

The second wave, if ever there was one, allowed independent record labels to get more unheard street punk bands, to have their noise released and distributed nationally. Cherry Red Records springs to mind: this was one of the fastest-growing independent record labels at that time for punk and they are still helping a lot of punk bands today.

Mensi

That year the Angelic Upstarts did our first album, *Teenage Warning*. We should have been on *Top of the Pops* with 'I'm An Upstart' but the cameraman refused to work with me because I'd filled in the bloke after the snowball incident. He was worried about the violence. We got a reputation for violence. At the time we was of the opinion that everybody had their own entitlement to their views, whether it be right or wrong, and as long they didn't 'Sieg Heil' I didn't stop them coming to the show. I thought, 'Your views are wrong but they don't matter to me.' It soon changed when they started directing *us* what to say. Little whispers like, 'You shouldn't be saying this,' and, 'That was the wrong thing to say.' You don't tell me what to say.

If someone came to a show and caused trouble I thought I was obliged to give them trouble back, and I would get off the stage and give them trouble – I thought that was what everybody did! It ended up like people saying, 'I went to a fight the other night and an Upstarts gig broke out in the middle of it!' [laughs]

We used to go round the pubs before the show to check out who the boys were. We learned very early on all the trouble came from fascists and we would hunt them out. People would say, 'Pick on the biggest one and give it to him.' Sometimes we would pick the smallest one. We were in a pub in Oldham and there was always lot of trouble at the Oddies venue. The one who did all the talking and the manouvering was the little skinny kid. We waited till he went to the toilets and I went in and said, 'It doesn't matter which one of your mates starts tonight, we are going to fuck *you* up!' – and there was no trouble that night.

The Angelic Upstarts may have a rough and ready reputation but it would be unfair if that's their only epitaph. Teenage Warning *is stuffed full of great songwriting, raucous anthems and some good musicianship during blistering songs that set the stall for Mensi's righteous working-class anger and his powerful, guttural and soulful voice. The album really stands the test of time.*

Jimmy Pursey

I produced the Angelic Upstarts album. I don't want to be radical about this, but they had absolutely nothing to do with what we did. I produced them. I signed them. I gave them every chance to be what they wanted to be, but whatever they did afterwards was up to them. What they were doing at that moment made me go, 'Wow!' but what they did afterwards was different from us. Those bands were not much to do with Sham. Bands of our ilk were the Killjoys, the Saints, the Ramones, the Stooges, the MC5 – they were more like Sham than any of the other bands. We were all one entity, that 1977 sound. That's all gone now. We are the only band that tries to hang onto it because that's our sound. That's how I like it, that powerful sound put across simply.

I was looking for something else to do and then Paul Cook and Steve Jones came along with the idea that I should sing for them in some sort of punk supergroup. I think it was more that the two of them were looking for a way out after the Pistols with Johnny leaving. Maybe they could do it with me? – 'He will fill the gap.' I was worried where it would go. There were hard drugs around and it scared the shit out of me. The Sex Pistols lived off notoriety, and Sham were one of the greatest live bands in the world.

It was different things coming together, and it never really came off properly in the end. When the Sex Pistols reformed a few years ago they had to play the same songs all the time – they are like cabaret. I don't understand why they don't go and play Las Vegas. To me that would be the most perfect place for them, their most perfect rip-off!

Mensi

By 1979 I couldn't understand Jimmy's actions towards people. I thought he was disrespectful. I didn't understand the way he went on with the press. I accused him of all sorts every time we met. We were like fire and water. I would have been more accepting of him if he hadn't been so starry with the guy in the restaurant who was only doing his job – 'He's working twelve hours a day, Jimmy, don't cunt him off. These are working-class people.' He started doing all this heavy rights and wrongs of society, doing a Crass thing – left wing and right wing are all wrong. We were at odds with each other in a short space of time.

What killed it off was when he joined Cook and Jones in 1979. I didn't understand any of it. Jimmy said, 'This is the plan. We are going to Glasgow to do these shows and festivals. Mensi, you're now the singer in Sham 69.' I went, 'What!!! Am I fuck! I got my own band. What do I want to be in Sham 69 for? Find some fucker else. If Angelic Upstarts finish, I'm finished.' From that day we never seen eye to eye again. It was such a shame. I think Sham had some fantastic songs in their early days.

Micky Geggus

Sham and Jimmy, God bless him, were obviously pretending to come from where we actually did come from! Jimmy had a massive heart. If he had hindsight now, with most of the people that bit the hand that fed, I don't think he would have done what he did for them. He did lay himself open to a lot of shit and he always did everything from the heart – it was never from a financial angle. When they started they were a great band: 'Angels with Dirty Faces' – what a great record! 'If the Kids Are United' – again a great record.[11] They got the brunt of the media spite and all the rest of it for no reason but they wrote good accessible anthems and what I like to think is that we took it that stage further with the Rejects.

Garry Bushell

I got out at Finsbury Park Tube and saw the British Movement smashing glass, 200 of them running round. This is the Sham 69 riot. Sham never discouraged the skins enough. Jimmy is one of those people who believes the last things he heard. Well-intentioned, good hearted man. Naive is the word.

Jimmy Pursey

How could you not be naive in that world? Being naive in the music business is natural. I was working in a fucking Wimpy bar and six months later I'm standing on the stage at Reading in front of 40,000 people singing along with me. Of course I was naive.

The Nazi skinheads totally ruined it for us. It was ridiculous. I would say to them, 'Where the fuck have you lot come from? You're a bit late, aren't you? The fucking bus has already gone!' I said,

---

11. Indeed they are! Two of the great punk anthems. 'Kids' seems to be covered by every punk band in America these days.

'I don't want to be your fucking leader!' Some of them thought I must be gay. I thought, 'All right then, I'll pretend I'm gay, anything to fuck you lot off! [laughs]

Beki Bondage

It was 1978/79 when we seriously got into punk. We had seen the Damned on *Marc* and other groups on his series, and I would read the music press.[12] The Clash and the Pistols were all over the papers. The UK Subs I loved from the start. I remember seeing the Slits – an absolute cacophony! They were good fun and it was great to see girls doing it. Most of the bands we'd go and see down the Bristol Mecca Ballroom. I had a slightly older boyfriend who would buy the tickets and take us down there. We would go in and pretend we were eighteen when we were thirteen or fourteen.

The punk scene was pretty good in Bristol. I missed the first wave of punk. It was more arty – it seemed to be produced by people who became famous for being famous. I was fascinated by it and I'd like to have been involved. The second wave bands like the Subs were getting big and we felt more part of it. We had our own pub where we all went in the Old Market in Bristol, a place called the Crown. The Irish couple that ran it had an Alsatian, and I remember one of the punk guys went in there trying to torment their cat, so she locked him outside with the Alsatian: 'If you want to play with animals play with the dog!' [laughs]

Colin Abrahall (GBH: vocals)

It was all mates drinking in the pub in Birmingham at the time – everyone was in a band or looking to join a band. Me and Phil, the original drummer, got Sean involved. We weren't a garage band, we were a bedroom band! Our first gig was New Year's Eve 1979 in the house we lived in.

---

12. Marc Bolan's TV series, filmed in the last months of his life, regularly featured up and coming punk bands – for many it was their only mainstream media exposure.

All the big bands were on *Top of the Pops* every week. We were more roots: we still liked the Damned and the Clash, but it wasn't quite real enough for us. Our musicianship wasn't very good and it made it rawer. We heard the Discharge single and thought that was like what we were doing.[13] A month later we got the chance to support them and got on really well with them, and they invited us to support them on a tour. Next minute Mike Stone phones up and we got a deal.[14]

LOUD, PROUD AND PUNK
Street Punk and the Oi Movement

Within the second wave a major new street punk scene emerged, the much misunderstood and maligned Oi movement. Garry Bushell provided the name, inspired by the Cockney Rejects' frontman Jeff 'Stinky' Turner, who used to holler 'Oi!' at the start of each Rejects number, thereby replacing the first punks' habitual '1, 2, 3, 4!' (Before that, 'Oi! Oi!' had been Ian Dury's catchphrase, although he'd probably nicked it from Cockney comic Jimmy Wheeler's 'Oi, oi, that's yer lot.' Even earlier, Cockney music hall entertainers Flanagan and Allen had used 'Oi!' as a catchphrase in their 1930s variety act.)

Most Oi bands were either apolitical or left wing, but misunderstandings blighted the movement – several of the groups were tarred with a far-right tag when they were nothing of the sort.

Steve Kent

The original idea for the Oi scene was Garry Bushell's. He was working at *Sounds* and he felt that the *NME* and a lot of *Sounds* writers were trendy university people using long words, trying to be artistic

---

13. Hailing from Stoke, and armed with the angriest anti-nuclear-war lyrics, Discharge compressed punk down into fierce rushes of sound that seem to have influenced half of the metal bands in the world today.
14. Mike Stone's label was Clay Records, based in Stoke.

in their writing and losing touch. Bushell was not from that school, even though he's got an amazingly high IQ. I think he wanted to be different from all the other writers, so he came up with this idea for a more real, on-the-street type of music.

Garry Bushell

Punk was meant to be the voice of the tower block and the voice of the dole queue and in reality most of them were not. The Bromley Contingent came from nice middle-class Bromley. Joe Strummer's dad was a diplomat and he sang about 'White Riot' and lived in a big house. There is nothing wrong with that. But Oi was the reality of the punk mythology. Bands like the Upstarts from South Shields – everywhere was closing down and there were no jobs. In the places where the Cockney Rejects came from, it was harder and more aggressive and it produced just as much quality music.

Micky Geggus

We thought, 'We can do this thing as well as anyone else and better than some bands.' There was a hell of a lot of crap out there. 'Jesus, if this is the way punk is going we can top this.'

I never played a lead guitar break in my life till we were in the studio. It all happened really fast. We got our residency at the Bridge House, played there about three or four gigs before we signed to EMI – that's what punk is all about! [laughs] Our first single, 'Flares'n'Slippers', came out on Small Wonder in 1979 and we just took off.

Garry Bushell was very important. He was right onto the scene very quickly. Gal comes from the same stock as we do, total work- ing-class. He comes off that Ferrier Estate in Kidbrooke, south London, one of the biggest shitholes you've ever seen. Gal walked it like he talked it. We went up and met him, and I guess dealing with the middle-class pseuds in the music biz like he had to every day, when we strolled in the office it was like a breath of fresh air. We had an instant rapport. Gal deserves top marks for it: he brought it kicking and screaming from the working classes and transformed the scene. The in-crowd hated him for what he stood for, and us too, but I could never understand why.

Garry Bushell

I managed the Cockney Rejects up until they got the EMI deal. I thought I could be a proper writer or a rock'n'roll manager, and I preferred being a writer. They needed someone really tough who could steer them, and Tony Gordon was the right man for the job.

Micky Geggus

It was a big crack. We couldn't believe our luck: we signed to EMI and got £25 a week. That was a fortune! Jeff was only fourteen at the time and still at school.[15] He had to get his dad in to sign the deal. We got £500 each signing-on bonus – Jeff went walking back to the school (that he never went to anyway) and bought the whole school crisps! [laughs]

Steve Kent

I can't stress enough the elation of being youthful, the anarchy! It wasn't so much political, but you were against the government. Groups like Crass gave us a different slant – seeing them it was always an event. Steve Ignorant used to go to shows with me with a hat on. Already punk was very much split into factions: there was street punk, where we were, I suppose, the Crass way was the squatting type of punk scene, there was the Fall scene, the very early Cure types, the New Romantics, rockabilly, mods and ska scenes.

Our band got together with Mark Brennan.[16] We were called the Blackouts and we had a local following. The songs were really good. Consequently the manager of the Business got in touch. They

---

15. Jeff 'Stinky' Turner, frontman of the Cockney Rejects. Read his excellent autobiography.
16. Bass player in the Business. Now boss man of the great label Captain Oi, where you can buy most of the punk records written about in this book.

had a record deal and their label said, 'You need a songwriting team for the next album.' We were drafted in to work with Mickey Fitz and make a new Business.

The whole concept of the Business was to have a skinhead fronting a band of punks. I later found out the whole thing was a clever ploy to sell more records to the skinhead and the punk market – that was called 'skunk'. Blitz were pretty much set up on that same basis.[17] It went down really well. The idea was not to fight amongst yourselves, but fight the real enemy. The punks and skins were together on the stage – that was the message. Sometimes the message got through. Later on in our career we would play with lots of hardcore bands and there was big division but we showed it could be joined together again.[18]

Micky Fitz (The Business: vocals)

It was Sham that got us started. When I first heard the very early Sham stuff that's what made me think, 'I like this, I can do this.' We just went on from there. They were carrying the standard for skins. We had all turned skin by then, more bootboy-hooligan skinhead. The audience was more skins than casuals. The skins and punks were fighting – God knows why, but they were. That's why we had songs like 'Loud, Proud and Punk', to try and unify the two crews.

Noel Martin

Garry Bushell said that we were like the precursors to Oi. I can't see it, apart from we are more working-class. We might at the time have been criticised for being apolitical but punk wasn't about politics in the first place. It was about music. We were brought up around

---

17. Blitz were a northern punk/skin band who cut an excellent debut album.
18. Hardcore was the American development of Oi, mixing it with metal and ending up with something even faster and more brutal! It would generate the no-drinking, no-smoking Straight Edge movement, and form the basis for most good American rock in the Nineties post-Nirvana period.

King's Cross and Holloway and we were very much working-class. We sung songs about what we knew about. There was a little bit of politics but we tried to keep it out. Unlike some of the Oi bands who wanted to beat you over the head. We tried to be a bit more subtle. The meaning is there if you want to see it, but it's not blatantly obvious.

Mensi

I didn't understand this second wave thing. There was some good bands. I didn't understand what it is. To me it seemed like a bit of a right-wing movement in parts. I didn't like the exclusive white working-class thing – I would rather it was just a working-class thing. The right wing would latch onto every band, and it's not the band's fault. Sometimes they can be very intimidating so bands won't speak out against them. I wrote this song 'England' and it's always very misunderstood. Sometimes I get such emotion about the song it makes the hair stand up on the back of my neck, or sometimes it make my flesh crawl – it's one of the strangest songs I ever wrote. It was really misinterpreted by the press, who slaughtered it. I don't think I deserved what I got.[19]

Ian Brown

I did some shows with the Angelic Upstarts, hanging out with them. I saw them kicking the pig's head around with a copper's hat on it for 'Liddle Towers' at a gig and thought that was great.[20] My mate worked with them – this guy called Brummie Rob – and I saw them play in Bolton and went on the road with them for five or six shows. People always went on about them being an Oi band, but there's no way they were an Oi band.

---

19. The song was misconstrued as some sort of right-wing lament, in the way that any English patriotism seems to get mixed up with being right wing – not always the case.

20. Just to underline their hardline stance on the cop front, the Angelic Upstarts had taken to kicking a severed pig's head around during their gigs.

MEANWHILE BACK IN BELFAST
The Undertones and the Clash

John O'Neill

The first and the second Undertones albums are the two that I really like. They definitely capture the time. I still think the songs are better live. We allowed ourselves to be bullied in the studio – I would love to have the chance to re-record it. On the second album we were more confident as songwriters. We were getting into r'n'b and writing these pop songs like 'My Perfect Cousin'.

Damian O'Neill

We toured with the Clash in 1979 – that was amazing. The Clash were doing a lot of *London Calling* songs before it came out. It was the first time we'd heard 'London Calling', 'Armagideon Time', 'Wrong 'Em Boyo' and 'Guns Of Brixton' – and in America as well. Brilliant! And they treated us really well. They offered us the full tour, five or six weeks, but the rest of the band turned it down because they didn't want to be away that long. [laughs] What can I say?

We went down OK, but America wasn't ready for other punk bands. The first show we did was a 10,000 arena. They sealed half of it off, but it still seemed amazing. We didn't hang out with the Clash because we were very shy. The Clash had their big tour bus and we went in a small truck. It was tough – we didn't sleep much. And it was all too quick. Near the end we started talking to them and then we had to leave – that was a pity.

Guy Trelford

We loved the Clash, but for some fans things turned a little bit sour in 1979 when Joe was seen sporting an 'H-Block' T-shirt and started calling for the troops to be pulled out of Northern Ireland. Getting involved in Northern Irish politics is a dodgy business, as Joe found to his cost when he received death threats from Loyalist paramilitaries, which resulted in a planned Clash gig in Derry being cancelled.

Understandably a lot of young punks (especially those from the Protestant community) were quite disturbed and angry at their hero's apparent support for Irish Republicanism and the IRA. Just over a year before Joe had basked in the glory of 'uniting Protestant and Catholic kids with punk rock' and now our hero was seen to be taking sides in the conflict.

Statements like Joe's made life even more difficult for punks who lived in the Protestant/Unionist community when some Loyalists (mistakenly) began to suspect all punks of being left-wing, Republican sympathisers. This suspicion was exacerbated a couple of years later when the Undertones appeared on *Top of the Pops* and Damian was seen wearing a black armband as a show of respect for IRA hunger striker Bobby Sands. Both Joe and Damian had their reasons for doing what they did and I respect that. But fuck, they didn't half make life difficult for some of us.

I didn't agree with Joe on these points but I still had a lot of respect for the man. He still had the balls to bring the Clash back to Belfast, after the death threats, a couple more times over the years. Whilst some of my mates completely disowned the Clash, I went back to see them in Belfast because despite their flaws and contradictions (which only served to make them more human, like the rest of us – hell, we all make mistakes) they were undoubtedly one of the greatest rock'n'roll bands of our generation.

AND THE CASSETTE PLAYED POPTONES
Public Image Limited: Metal Box

No matter how much John Lydon winds people up, all he has to do is hold up two albums: one, of course, is the Sex Pistols' debut which sound-tracked 1977; and then there was PiL's Metal Box, *which proved that along with his cohorts, Levene and Wobble, he was also a visionary. Rarely in rock music can a bunch of musicians have moved so quickly.*

From the white heat of anthemic punk rock, to three twelve-inch singles encased in a metal tin that managed to squeeze dub, funk, disco, avant-garde, Can and Captain Beefheart into stunning soundscapes that sounded like none of their influences. Wobble's dub-heavy bass and Levene's hypnotic, shrill, shrapnel guitar squall were astonishing, whilst Lydon's sardonic poetry was at its best and his singing style by now like nothing you'd ever heard before. It wasn't a major international best-seller, but its influence percolates on. This was a special moment and one that tied up all the loose ends that hung around punk rock into a sprawling masterpiece and yet somehow still fitted in the punk context. Most of the post-punk bands would get nowhere near this in terms of originality.

Tony Wilson

Post-punk would not have happened without the energy of punk, because that was the essential moment. The energy of rock was taken from a simple form and turned into more complex things. Lydon, the father of all the post-punk scene, made the best album of the time – *Metal Box*. An incredible album.

Jah Wobble

John was a massive Beefheart fan. *Metal Box* was a very dense, deep, dark record, very static. The tracks stay in one uncomfortable place. It's lasted very well. We were all nuts in our way. It was genuine. Lots of bands market themselves as wayward with all the drugs and things and it's used as marketing, but it's as threatening as Christina Aguilera and Britney Spears being on the Mickey Mouse Club. But we were the real deal. PiL really was that kind of way and you can hear it in the music.

Keith Levene

Metal Box was really more what we wanted to do. That's when we were getting more freedom in the studio. And we went out of our way to make the bass as loud and as deep as possible.

Jim wasn't in the band any more because on a personal level Wobble would torture him and he had no idea of what the cockney East End sense of humour was. He couldn't take it any more and he just left. I really loved Jim. We didn't know who was actually going to play drums, though we eventually wound up with Richard Dudanski, who played on most of *Metal Box*.

We weren't under any pressure where we had to get a record out in a certain amount of time. We just booked two weeks at the Manor. Loads of people have recorded there – it's a big mansion in Oxford that Branson bought. I think 'Poptones' was one of the first things we recorded.

One tune we definitely had was 'Death Disco', because we worked that with Jim but we didn't record him. The reason it was called 'Death Disco' was because it was about John's mum. The person he was singing about, 'Seeing in your eyes,' was his mother, who was going through the process of dying from cancer. That's what John was singing about – very passionately, I might add. From my point of view, I was just trying to do something with the music. I didn't know what he was singing about at the time. He was just, 'It's "Death Disco", Keith, that's what it is!'

We'd just learned the recording process from the first album. So we're on this second album and we're in this really plush studio. We'd been through a few permutations and we'd found some comfortable way of working where we could plug in and have the engineer record. I told him to record *everything*. Sometimes we might have played something and it sounded like we were fucking around and it turns out to be something very serious – that's how we ended up with 'Albatross'.

More often than not with PiL, especially in the beginning, I always endeavoured to try and do everything with one guitar. Because the band consists of one guitar. It wasn't a rule, it was a mode. It's almost like I had all these strict rules but my biggest rule was to break the rules. Sometimes I'd set up my own rules to kick 'em down. You could draw an analogy with Brian Eno. It was like having my own set of *Oblique Strategy* cards. If it worked, use it. If it didn't, question it.

I had a very magical sort of telepathy with John because we never worked things out – it worked out better that way. We thought we were doing something quite radical by making the songs up literally as they went along. It was quite daring.

When I think about it, though, I never really spoke to Wobble much about the music or the process or anything. That's what caused the next rift in the band indirectly. With *Metal Box*, we became experimental very quickly. The way I saw it, the desk became an instrument. It was such a major part of the process. The whole studio was becoming a big synthesizer. I was having to play a lot of other instruments. The whole scope for me was really opening up. I was having to try these things because there was no one else there to do it.

Jah Wobble

I've come to like *Metal Box* more and more, but that first album is still my favourite. Stuff like 'Low Life' is great. It's very underrated. It seemed like it was a quantum leap to *Metal Box* – something very magical happened. But the first album is more of a favourite of mine. It's got a great pop sensibility as well.

Keith Levene

We didn't have the artwork in place but we knew what we were trying to do. We were looking for this weird packaging – which didn't end up so weird but it was still pretty cool. We were thinking, 'How can we put the record in a can and make it hard to open it?' It never occurred to me how much like a film canister it looked, but we came up with the metal box with three 45 rpm twelve-inches. That was supposed to be a double album in essence. It ran at 45 so you could get the best response on your sound system.

It cost us £30,000 of our advance back to get the 'official limited edition' out. *Second Edition* was the name for the Warner release. They said, 'Forget any metal box, don't even go there.' [laughs] 'You're lucky you're getting a cardboard box.'

Jah Wobble

The second album ended up with a shitty vibe round PiL. The first album was very optimistic, all lads together in a rock band kind of vibe. Then it went dark and down. There was lots of drugs being used. Not fun at all.

MALICIOUS DAMAGE
Killing Joke and Other Experimental Sounds

Underlining the diversity of what was coming out of punk, Killing Joke twisted punk into an utterly unexpected space. Post-Metal Box, anything was possible, and Killing Joke, with their heavy grinding grooves, were intense and primal, creating a dark and feral music that has become massively influential (just ask Nirvana). Post-punk has been narrowed down over the years to the point where it just seems to refer to Gang Of Four and the Fall, who both had their part to play, but at the time it had a much wider definition that easily embraced the much more experimental Killing Joke, Joy Division and the often-overlooked quirkiness of Adam and the Ants' debut album (a genuinely off-kilter record that has been used as a template by the likes of Blur and Elastica). There were also masses of small bands propped up by John Peel sessions and the burgeoning independent record labels – bands playing back rooms of pubs to a dozen diehards up and down the country, staying true to their own vision and not budging for the record industry.

Jaz Coleman

I knew I was going to make different music. I knew it would be fiery. I felt very angry as a person. When I was about sixteen the punk thing happened. I had a massive collection of punk records. Then I was looking for something that little bit more imaginative. When I met up with Geordie it all happened very fast.

I moved to London to make music. I played sessions with keyboard-reggae bands, then I joined the Matt Stagger Band playing keyboards with Paul Ferguson and we soon realised that we wanted to do something quite different. We listened to lots of music and we made a decision: we wanted to be in a band that sounded like fire.

At the time of punk's death we were seriously into different rhythm sections, black rhythm sections from reggae to funk. The idea of that very white '1, 2, 3, 4!' thrash thing that punk had become didn't interest us. We liked the guitar noise but that was about it.

Just after punk was an experimental phase with Joy Division and PiL and ourselves. We all started branching away from the conventional. None of our recordings are punk at all. You won't find a guitar solo on a Killing Joke track. There are certain things we took from the whole period: I think it's still possible for an artist to be gifted and talented and a great performer without the limo and the ego trip, and I liked that with punk, poking fun at the idea of heroes and rock stars. I'm glad that I started when I did. It was a very exciting time: the music I thought I would make when I came to London didn't end up sounding anything like it.

My first flat was a three-bedroom flat for £7 a week in Notting Hill. That's where the carnival started. There was the Moroccan community, the West Indian community, the Portuguese community – it was where multiculturalism started. That was the beautiful thing about it: a British band influenced by all the repercussions of our colonial system.

We had a contempt for the punk uniform. Apart from Youth, who was like a punk, the rest of us were misfits. They couldn't put us into a pigeonhole because we didn't conform to how a band should collectively look and we have always been hard to pigeonhole.

I don't look back to that period nostalgically, although there are some really good times – there was times we were formulating our musical ideas, philosophical ideas. London was depressing. You had that feeling that nuclear war was going to break out any second. We went to Berlin to record the first two albums and got into that Cold War vibe and I kind of enjoyed it. It was a dark kind of gloomy time. I remember playing a gig with Joy Division – we did a tour with them and we co-headlined – and the press called us Southern Stomp and they were Northern Gloom! [laughs]

We did six or seven gigs with Joy Division. No one ever moved at a Joy Division gig. There was no physical response whatever. Everyone just watched Ian Curtis. There was this kind of weird atmosphere.

Geordie

I remember the gig at High Wycombe. Our dressing room was full of fucking people and there were party tunes playing. I remember walking up the corridor looking at the party in our dressing room and walking past their dressing room and it was a very gloomy heads-in-hands sort of thing. [laughs]

Jaz Coleman

We were just as much influenced by Public Image as the Sex Pistols. Youth was good friends with John Lydon. There were actual links between the two bands. Lydon gave us our first break. When he heard a tape of ours he said it was the only band that he liked, and that sort of coincides with our John Peel session and when Peel played our three-track EP on the radio.[21]

Rob Lloyd

The Prefects had split up, and I still wanted to do music. I'd always wanted the band to be called the Nightingales. I don't know why it was

---

21. Youth was Killing Joke's charismatic bass player, a Sid Vicious lookalike who ended up being one of the world's biggest producers, working with the likes of Crowded House. The Killing Joke EP that Peel played was titled *Almost Red*; the band issued it in 1979.

called the Prefects – that was a shit name, a bit conformist. Most people would be something like the Exploited, that kind of vibe. The Prefects is like calling yourself the 'Crimefighters' or something like that!

We started getting the Nightingales together, which ironically was four ex-Prefects. I got this telegram from Geoff Travis and I went down to see him in London and said, 'Look, we haven't done any recordings, just eight songs for John Peel.' He said, 'Is that the Peel session we heard? We want to release those,' and I said, 'You can do if you give us the money to make a record,' and they said yes, and that starts another story.

I felt like we were on our own earlier. It didn't take the mohicans, leather jackets and spray-on trousers brigade to show me that punk had gone wrong. Earlier on, the thing was musically what I wanted to do.

When the Nightingales first formed, we were more or less an improvisation group – we really wanted to experiment more than the Prefects had done. We didn't want to be on the same bill as Sham 69 any more and be spat at. It was tedious. But we didn't start the Nightingales thinking we would have a new agenda – we just carried on. I'm not pretending that we are majorly experimental. Over the period of our records, we do what we want to do.

When the Nightingales started, there was a new surge of punk bands like the Exploited, and some really damn good ones like the Violators and Vice Squad – there was a whole wave of them.

Colin Newman

154 came out in late 1979. The jump between *Pink Flag* and *Chairs Missing* is bigger than the jump between *Chairs Missing* and *154*. We were refining the sound. Some of the album is fantastic and some is awful. It was the first Wire album that I cannot listen to all the way through. It was a painful record to make. What happened was that EMI brought us onto this tour with Roxy Music, the latter-day Bryan Ferry band – it cost a fortune. We were offered so little by their crew and sound people, it seemed like the most horrible waste of time, and in the end we thought, 'Is that all there is? Are we trying to be like them? I don't want to be that.'

If Wire in 1979 had became purely experimental, EMI would not have released the records. We would have had nowhere left to go. We needed pop tunes on it and for me that was a really interesting thing to do. The others wanted it to be one thing – you look at what was really developing with the really underground labels distributed by Rough Trade, and you could see that Wire could be part of that. On EMI we were getting £40 a week. We were broke! And there wasn't a culture in the band to try and address that, to do things in an independent way.

Mick Crudge (The Fits: vocals)

Adam and the Ants came to play the Norbreck Castle, Blackpool.[22] I had no idea who they were really – we just went to all punk gigs that came to town. I can recall even their roadies were weird-looking. From the moment they came on, the place just went absolutely nuts. When I'd heard the Pistols I knew that was what I wanted to be like, but when I saw the Ants *that* was what I wanted to *be*. I was not even through the first song of a virtually unknown band and I was already buried on the floor at the front of the stage. I recall looking up and seeing Adam Ant in the air – leather, make-up – a weird, dangerous-looking band who came at us. Matthew Ashman, the guitarist, was just so amazingly cool. I think 'Young Parisians' had just come out. Man, they were so different to that record – for some reason their sound at the time never made it onto vinyl. It still gives me a buzz when I think about it now. We were so lucky to have seen them in their prime.

---

22. 25 January 1979...The Ants were touring endlessly up and down the country. Punk rock pariahs, they were on the outside of the main scene but were building a huge live following through Adam's wiry charisma and the band's off-kilter music.

TYPICAL GIRLS
The Continuing Story of the Slits

The Slits had made a name for themselves in 1977 by being the ramshackle, in-your-face, inspirational all-girl punk rock gang. A year later they were starting to make some utterly startling music as well.

Budgie

The big thing for me was getting the call from the Slits. I would go and see them. The band would almost be fighting onstage – it was unlike anything else. Palmolive was a brilliant drummer. She kept her own way of making time, shifting tempos in the same verse – it was a unique way of playing. I'd seen a lot of female bands in the Seventies always trying to sound like a male rock band. Palmolive could hit really hard – but it was totally self-taught, untutored, not trying to be a rock drummer. More like Mo Tucker of the Velvet Underground.[23]

I got the call to go and help them demo some new songs when they got the Island deal. The first song we did was 'Typical Girls'. I had some experience with different types of music and this was the first time I felt I could pull all this together.

What the girls wanted was a more disciplined reggae dance beat, and through Roger Eagle at Eric's I had been listening to a lot of reggae and it felt very natural to slip in. It kind of worked and we got on. They were very loyal and protective of people – in London there were small camps of people loyal to each other, who didn't trust anyone till they knew them. We went through a couple of producers because they were very music biz. They thought the Slits were another bunch of girls in the music biz to be used and abused, so these blokes were unceremoniously shown the door.

We went on tour with the Clash, on the *Give 'Em Enough Rope*

---

23. Mo Tucker played simplistic beats in a very effective style for the Velvet Underground. She was also one of the first women operating in the most traditionally male of all rock preserves – the drummer.

tour. That was really amazing, when the Clash came into their own with a massive following. It was full-on, non-stop. I never experienced anything like it. We travelled in our car following the Clash's bigger van [laughs] – it was a proper production, proper rock.

We started to gel and everything came together playing-wise. I knew some of their older songs and they were rewriting them as we were going, and it culminated in the studio sessions for *Cut*. That was really my first album. I still listen to it and marvel at it. It was a labour of love. It took a long time to get it right. It was great working with Dennis Bovell – he certainly pulled a lot out, made me think about things differently as well. Viv and Tessa worked hard to get their parts down. They knew what they wanted in their heads – it took them a little while longer to learn how they could do it. Ari was like a musical prodigy – she was just precocious! [laughs] She could drive you crazy. She was really young. That was the charm: she was untamed, wild youth. We were all pretty mad, but with Ari there

Not so typical girls: the Slits' timeless mix of feminine rhythms, dub and punk was a potent brew

was no rules at all, the way she was brought up. She had a mad passion for music. She was a lot of fun.

Ari Up

We had been together for a while. Punk was dying a bit. By the time we got a record deal, we had already developed our sound. I listened to the Slits' stuff recently and it made me realise that I am a fan. It could have come out last week. What I find amazing is that we hadn't put out records already. At the time everyone was under the impression that we couldn't play. Now a lot of boys try and make this music and it's really very hard for people to play. Then you realise how good we really were. It amazes me when I hear them on the John Peel sessions how good they sound, and people said we couldn't play. If anything we made it too complex!

Budgie

The Slits was certainly trying by the end. There were a lot of arguments, but friction is good – that gave them an edge. A lot of good tension makes a spiky album. They treated the instruments with irreverence as well, winding all the bass out, and the kit sounded like little biscuit tins. It made an aural thing that you certainly had not heard before – it wasn't trying to be like other girl bands, like the Au Pairs or Kleenex.[24] Somehow those bands were female versions of the Gang of Four. There's something a bit political something about the fact they were women. With the Slits it was far more about music – that was Ari's bag really.

I wasn't in the photo on the cover of *Cut* as I'd left the studio before Pennie Smith came down.[25] Anyway I don't think I look good covered in mud [laughs] – it was like *One Million Years*

---

24. The Au Pairs were a British post-punk band from Birmingham, fronted by Lesley Woods. Kleenex were a four-piece all-female band formed in Switzerland in 1978, perhaps better known as Liliput, a name change forced on them in 1980. Both had limited success but were influential.

25. Pennie Smith's legendary sleeve photo featured the three semi-naked Slits covered in mud.

BC! At that point I didn't know what was going on. Maybe I thought it was time to move on. I didn't leave to join anything else – it didn't feel right going down the studio any longer. Bruce Smith came down to do some percussion stuff afterwards, then Bruce went on to play some stuff live – he was the Pop Group's drummer.

METAL WON'T RUST WHEN OILED AND CLEANED
Siouxsie and the Banshees Hit the Top Ten and Survive a Line-up Crisis

The Banshees, complete with a hit single 'Hong Kong Garden', were out on the circuit. The last of the class of '76 to get a deal and a hit, the band were big news and Siouxsie with her striking looks and fierce individuality was fast-track on the way to being an icon, the premier pin-up of the punk and then the goth scenes, without ever paying any lip service to either scene. The first big tour, though, was about to fall apart...

Steve Severin

Nils Stevenson was very, very cautious with who the Banshees signed to. He didn't want to sign for one or two albums – he wanted to sign something much more long-term. So we held out. Some labels were scared of us! When they heard 'Hong Kong Garden' that made a difference. The labels heard a hit and that was what got us our deal with Polydor. To be honest they probably thought that they would get their one hit and that would be it. There had been a couple of months just before we signed when Nils was getting very depressed. He was on the point of giving up till Polydor came in. We had complete control. As long as you're having hits they are happy, they don't mind what your songs are about.

The first album came out and we toured a lot. We toured with the Cure supporting. The band was pretty much in two camps: there was me and Siouxsie, and then the others. We met them on a business level only. Kenny ended up being on the end of my fist a couple of months after they left. They quit the band all of a sudden in the middle of the tour in Aberdeen. It was a bit of a nightmare! We had to cancel a few dates, and Robert Smith from the Cure had to learn the parts so we could continue. We then got Budgie in from the Slits to drum for us.

Paul Research

The Scars toured with the Banshees. We actually played at the gig in Aberdeen when Jon McKay left. When we got to the gig they were there waiting for us – there were just two Banshees sound-checking. The promoter came up to me and said, 'If you don't go on now, the whole gig is going to get pulled and it's your fault,' so we went on and played a blinding gig. Then the Cure played a very long set, and then the Banshees came on with Robert Smith on guitar. It was the first time he had played with them and it was just a racket, to be honest. I could have done it! It was one of those 'Should I or shouldn't I?' moments, because I knew a few of their songs. I think if I had barged on stage with my guitar they would have let me play.

I was totally gutted. It was the first night of the tour. Jon McKay at that time was my guitar hero and I couldn't believe he had left before we had actually done a gig with them.[26]

Budgie

After the Slits I went back to my bed-sit. There was not much happening. I played with Glen Matlock, Steve New and Danny Kustow, did a few gigs round London pubs playing Glen's songs – he was writing loads and wanted to see what they sounded like live.[27]

---

26. McKay's guitar style was certainly innovative: his high, shrieking style would become a motif for several other guitar players.

27. Danny Kustow had been the guitarist in the Tom Robinson Band but had recently left the group.

It didn't seem to go anywhere. I think I had a call from the Psychedelic Furs as well – I thought they were another girl band and I turned that one down, if I remember rightly![28] Then I got the phone call that changed everything, from the Banshees' management. I didn't believe a band could split in the middle of a tour, just before going to America.

I don't know why they left. Only Siouxsie would know. Having met John and Kenny afterwards on different occasions, they feel a sense of loss. They might have felt it was the right decision at the time, but even shortly afterwards they realised it was the wrong decision. Their pride would not let them go back after hurting the original members. It was cowardly. I suppose. At the time it was unfortunate because it was a very strong band, and it had to change. It blossomed into something else. How flexible was that original unit? Would they have changed? We'll never know.

It didn't leave much time to do anything. I think Paul Cook, who had heard the Slits' album, had mentioned to Nils that he should check and see if I was about because he liked that album. They had asked Paul at first, but he thought it wasn't very him at that point.

I sat in the rehearsal room with Marco who was helping them out on guitar at this point. They were looking for a drummer and Marco was the only one who knew any of the songs! Marco started making his noise and I had no idea what I was doing really [laughs] but it sort of clicked. I'd never met Siouxsie. I'd seen her at Fulham Greyhound where I went down without the Slits. I knew a bit of her sound, but not the songs. It was an initiation of fire, very much in at the deep end. 'If you want to stick around you can be the drummer,' I was told. The next thing they were auditioning guitarists and it was very odd – I already felt I was part of the team! Whilst I was learning the songs we were trying to find a guitarist: everyone came

---

28. In fact they were a very male, drone-rock band who put out some cool music in the period.

down, they were all sounding horrible, and that was when Robert Smith came in. The Cure were the support band on the tour and someone said, 'Robert knows these songs.' Time was running out and it was figured that Robert could do two separate sets, so we went back out on tour and I started learning the songs onstage. Nowadays they would pull the whole tour, but we lost a week and went back on tour. It was quite a quick turnaround but it cost the band financially and it cost them in terms of going to America – it slowed everything down by a few years.

Steve Severin

When we did the second album, *Join Hands*, John McGeoch left Magazine to play for us. Even then we still had Steve Jones playing guitar for us on a few tracks.

For me, what I wanted to achieve with the Banshees was to be immersed, to 'leave yourself' – the dervish whirl I spoke of in the song 'Ikon' on our second album. And quite simply the worst experiences for me with the group were when – for whatever reason – we were unable to achieve that sense of levitation.

INTO THE VALLEY
Punk in Scotland

There was a vibrant punk scene in Scotland, from the Skids' futuristic take on the form, to the Rezillos' comic-book flavoured sci-fi punk rock. Then there was the razor-sharp post-punk of Edinburgh's Scars, and in Glasgow there was Postcard Records releasing Scottish bands like Orange Juice's jangly pop, Josef K's wiry guitar rushes and the genius of the Fire Engines' quirky guitar riffing. There was also the Exploited, the long-running kings of the second wave.

Paul Research

There wasn't that many extreme hairstyles in Edinburgh or dyed hair. It was more school blazers and safety pins. The leather-clad element was more like the metal kind of thing, like the Exploited. We would hang out with the Fire Engines and Josef K – they were our contemporaries. We had a look, quite sharp. We were sort of before these bands. We started off as a punk band and when our single 'Horrorshow' came out we got a big record deal.

We didn't hear much about Glasgow scene. In Edinburgh people were very passionate about punk. I think it was always about moving on: what shall we do next? Do something different. Even during punk we never went for the power pop thing. We were always trying to be scratchy, even funky – take it somewhere else. The Buzzcocks, Banshees, Gang of Four – we were at that arty end of punk.

Eugene Reynolds (The Rezillos: vocals)

Before punk in Edinburgh we stuck out like a sore thumb. There was nothing remotely like us, which boded well for us. Mostly it was tired prog rock and pseudo-funk bands. Yeuch! Our reason to exist was to kick up dust in the music scene in our locale. We were sick of the clichés, disinterested in other local and national bands. We truly

The Rezillos' sci-fi pop punk injected some much needed fun in the middle of the punk wars

did not give a shit if anyone liked what we did or not. This was a musical war to us. And we were determined to win.

We had heard about this punk thing through whatever media. We figured it was a kind of validation of our attitude. When we tuned into it we realised we had in our own disjointed way been seminal in that movement. Of course, coming from Scotland ensured that we did not get the type of hype and push that many London area bands got, and so were never (at the time) given the kind of media acceptance that the southerners managed to get. Our attitude was 'Fuck London! We're gonna make our scene where we are and not follow the bandwagon.' Suddenly there were a hell of a lot of 'real punk' bands that tried to ride the wave.

I really think the trash/fun thing is overstated with us – I know that the band can draw that kind of comment. We were just honest enough to admit it. Many bands have such a brittle view of their own self-importance that they avoid the simple truth, but I thought the whole idea of being in a band was to have a riot, i.e. *fun*. But we probably take our music more seriously than the majority of bands.

The ridiculous thing was that once the public (and this included some of our audiences and promoters) read all the bull-shit headlines in the ragtag newspapers, we would often end up facing very hostile elements in the audience who had had their attitudes and opinions tainted by the gutter press. Often the same folk who had shouted us back onstage for encores when they first saw us had decided they wanted to pick a fight with us when we next appeared. We were supposed to be the *danger* and they were the ones feeling violent.

At the time we tried to distance ourselves from the punk scene because it quickly turned into a circus and everyone was suddenly a punk. One thing that really sickened us was being gobbed on. It first happened in Glasgow in a nightclub called Shuffles. We just could not believe it, and I still can't. We'd just stop playing and tell the idiots, 'Either you stop gobbing or we stop playing.' It's impossible to say if punk became an advantage or not at the time. Judging by the way our audiences had been growing in our early days I'd hazard that we would have made inroads without a punk scene, but the existence of punk certainly galvanised us and focused our direction.

Once we started having hits I think we all felt cheapened by association with the methods of major record labels in the chart arena. The hits seemed normal at the time, believe it or not. Dealing with the distortion of our lives became the difficult thing. We were kids, and used to working in a tight environment with no outside vested interests to accommodate. With chart success came pressures we had not anticipated.

We split the Rezillos and went on to form the Revillos, which was myself and Fay going off on our pungent tangent. We managed to polarise our audiences. The Revillos are a different story, to be told somewhere else.

Richard Jobson (The Skids: vocals)

In my teenage years in the early Seventies I was a member of a gang. It was pretty violent but it was also pretty cool – there was cool clothes, music, a pretty rip-roaring time. You would get beaten badly and you beat people up badly, and these things start to add up in the end. When you are a kid you are arrogant and fearless; when you get older you become more cautious.

Punk rock was the thing that saved my life. It changed me. Being in a group was like being in a gang, but the music was the violence this time. I wasn't out fighting people – it was the music itself that was the saving grace.

MY SUICIDE NOTE TO PUNK
End of the Decade: The Adverts
and Alternative TV

As the Seventies drew to a close, a couple of the pacesetters of first wave punk sensed it was the end of the road. In October 1979 the Adverts split up. Meanwhile Mark Perry, who after Sniffin' Glue *had decided to put his money where his mouth was and form his own group, Alternative TV, seemed to have run out of enthusiasm for the movement.*

T. V. Smith

Crossing The Red Sea was the first Adverts album and that had been done. No point in repeating yourself. We could have gone out with the same album again with different songs but the idea didn't attract me. Lyrically I was moving on to different things, getting more adventurous. I wrote what I felt. A lot of that was to do with the impending break-up of the band. I was growing up a lot.

Gaye Advert

I didn't like this pop star thing. I got all shy. I hated having my picture taken so I always looked *aaaargh* at the camera! Our drummer resented me getting the attention. It caused problems within the band. I just wanted to be one of the others, but that didn't happen with the press.

The line-up changed. We got Rod Latter in on drums. We were still touring. In Germany the audience was fine, but I don't like touring that much, and I didn't like the cold – I was freezing, sat in venues waiting for the PA to arrive, and it was boring. We were always supposed to go to America. I'd always wanted to go there. I'd been reading Marvel comics, and Iggy and the New York Dolls came from there, all this good stuff. I only went a couple of years ago.

We recorded the second album. It went well, pretty much like the first one. When the label was sold to RCA it was the beginning of the end. They put a really crap cover on the album. We wanted to put the burning Buddhist on there, the one that Rage Against the Machine used, but they insisted on a crap picture of the band instead.[29]

---

29. The image of the burning Buddhist protesting against the Vietnam War was used on Rage Against the Machine's superlative, eponymous early Nineties album that combined political anger with great riffs and lead guitar breaks that sounded like DJ scratching – a revolutionary record in every sense of the word.

Henry Rollins

The Adverts, what an amazing band! And T.V. is still doing great stuff. He has that long-range thinking about music. Whenever I write lyrics he's one of those people I always think about – can I write a song as good as an Adverts song? He and Gaye are completely intact – they are cool people.

Mark Perry

Because I had built up a lot of respect through the fanzine, I had a lot of people looking forward to see what we were going to sound like. We did well with the first few records. We put out an album *The Image Has Cracked*. We had some really good reviews. Paul Morley called it a 'milestone in rock' – not just punk, but in rock. But after six months I completely went off the rails. I got fed up with punk. I was having a lot of problems in my personal life. I just thought, 'I don't like the record business any more.' Then I did the second album, *Vibing Up The Senile Man*, in 1979. It was a complete freak-out. Someone described it as an album of people banging things, and that's about right. We pressed about 10,000 of them. They all got sent out to the shops and people started bringing them back saying they hated it. I think it was like my suicide note to punk. By that time, the end of 1979, I was just fed up with the whole thing.

CHAPTER 12
1980/84: PROTEST AND SURVIVE

A pair of tragic, self-inflicted deaths in 1980 robbed the punk and post-punk scene of two of its most mesmerising frontmen: Ian Curtis and Malcolm Owen. There was an air of doom and gloom about 1980. Apocalyptic nuclear war scenarios combined with the non-arrival of the counterculture revolution. Again! The deaths of Owen and Curtis seemed like a sad bookend to the punk revolution. The pop headlines were now dominated by New Romantics. The revolution was over, the Tories were in power and the greedy Eighties were kicking off.

For many people this was the end of the punk era, but the next few years were a fascinating period when there was a battle for the very soul of punk itself. If the mainstream was now boring, the underground was anything but – a fierce hive of activity raged just below the surface. Now split into very different factions, as every aspect of the punk rock culture was getting explored, the plethora of scenes were very much set on their own paths: from the rigorous street polemic of Oi and the nascent goth scene to the anti-war stance of Crass and the mega-success of the Jam and the mod revival. The energy of punk was still manifesting itself everywhere. Culturally this was an absorbing period, with a lot of great music and extreme counterculture action, easily fulfilling the promise of the original punk revolution, but musically it was all jammed below the radar.

The political backdrop, though, was anything but. The early Eighties were a political battlefield as attitudes informed by the extremes of the punk years were bursting out everywhere. There were the 1981 riots, the 1982 Falklands War, the anti-Thatcher rearguard action – a political backdrop that the punk generation had to react to. It all culminated in the miners' strike and the arrival of the iconic Orwellian dread year, 1984.

Barney Sumner

We really didn't have a clue that Ian was that low. He had tried it a couple of months before, but we still didn't expect anything else. The first time we realised that there was something up was when he turned up at rehearsals covered in knife marks from where he had slashed himself. He had woken up and didn't know what had happened. He showed us his chest and there was these horizontal knife marks, cuts to his chest. He had slashed the Bible and ripped out all the pages as well.

He used to do some pretty mad things, like when we played afters[1] once and he got pretty carried away, pretty kinetic. He started ripping the stage apart, ripping the floorboards up and throwing them at the audience. I did think that was fairly unusual! People started throwing bottles back which smashed onstage. He lived in there, rolling around in it, kind of like Iggy.

There was also the gig when he had a bit of a row with the manager of the club and to ram his point home he put a bucket on his head and started ranting like Quasimodo. Ian obviously had issues, which are obvious just by his lyrics, but to be honest with you we never really listened to his lyrics till he died.

Most of the time he was all right. There were just odd moments when he would have a bit of a rant and a rave. But everyone loses their temper, don't they? He was the most polite person. Very, very interesting to talk to, very opinionated but not in a negative way.

---

1. Manchester city centre venue.

Not judgmental. He didn't go round putting people down. He was pretty positive. I guess the illness took over. Things change. It's very well known that he had epilepsy.

Everyone has got this picture of him as a depressed person, and he was – but only at the end of his career, when most photos you see of him have his head in his hands and he's unshaven. I suppose because of that, and his lyrics, that's become his image. But he wasn't like that.

The Ruts had been a revelation. Their short series of big hit singles were not only great, razorsharp punk anthems but they also came packed with street poetry sung with one of the great guttural punk voices by Malcolm Owen. By 1980 they were certainly the biggest band on the scene. Their sad demise was not only a personal tragedy for their charismatic frontman, who died in July 1980, but a calamity for the British punk scene – if they had survived, it would have had the flagship band it so desperately needed in the Eighties.

Andy Kanonik

The Ruts were in my opinion musically streets ahead of the rest. I saw them play.[2] Awesome night. The place was rammed and the sound was superb. Two weeks after the gig Malcolm Owen died of a heroin overdose – what a waste.

Segs

Malcolm's death was a slow demise. It was a really sad one at that. None of us were into heroin. We had coke, but that was it for us. Smack was a drug that no one would do. One guy hanging round us used to do a bit and Malcolm would dabble. 'Sad velvet claw drug' we called it. Nowadays it's a very common thing – everyone knows someone on smack or on the rocks. In those days it was a rock star thing to do. Malcolm was hanging round with Phil Lynott. Phil was

---

2. At the Village Bowl, Newport, Shropshire with Gloucester band the Vox Phantoms.

The Ruts' charismatic frontman, the late Malcolm Owen

in a terrible state.[3] Malcolm started doing little lines, chasing the dragon: 'I know what I'm doing.' I used to look up to Malcolm, but then he was jacking up. We would confront him about it over that year, and he would stand there and front you out. He was prepared to fight you over it. On the last tour he got nodules on his throat and he went into hospital. They said to our manager that they couldn't operate on his nodules whilst he's under the influence. Malcolm stayed in hospital and kicked it. He wrote 'Shine On Me' in hospital.

We went to see him. We split up at that point. I made a phone call where we split up. Malcolm was upset. We were a close band, we loved each other. It was a horrible phone call to make. We carried on playing as a three piece until he came out of hospital. He had the old sparkle back and said, 'Let's do a farewell gig.' We said yes. Malcolm

---

3. Phil Lynott was the charismatic, Dublin-born, bass-playing frontman of Thin Lizzy, the key lads' band of the pre-punk era. Lynott was a street-smart poet whose distinctive swagger made him a huge international rock star. Long troubled by hard drugs, he died prematurely in 1986.

was made up and had all these plans for the future of the Ruts which we were prepared to go along with if he stayed clean. Me and Ruffy went back to south London, thinking, 'Maybe we will get back together after all. This is great! We can continue.' We stayed up, me and Ruffy, and had a good night.

The next morning we got a call and found out that Malcolm was dead. Someone had given him some smack and he went and jacked it up. He used the same amount as he used to. He did it in the bath and conked out. It was devastating.

We didn't know what to do. The grief didn't hit me till five years later. We carried on (footnote as the Ruts DC – musically great but missing the spark and focus of Owen), and when I look back at what I was doing and writing I was completely infused with grief. I was happy-go-lucky till then. Malcolm was a great mate. We had a great time together. We shared many a hotel room – get pissed, had a laugh. He was great on stage.

The band was moving in an interesting direction towards the end with 'Staring at the Rude Boys', 'Secret Soldiers' – that was where we were going. It was fucking happening really: great lyrics over the top of stripped-back music. The next album would have been really interesting.

Mick Crudge

I loved the Ruts. That first album of theirs – absolutely spine-tingling attitude. The singles 'In A Rut', 'Babylon's Burning' and the masterpiece 'Shine On Me' – I would listen to that over and over and over. Such a pity Malcolm Owen died.

SURVIVAL
The Punk Giants in the Early Eighties

In the early Eighties, the initial wave of punk bands were going through changes, adapting and developing. The Stranglers' classic first three albums had taken their bass-driven angular sound as far as possible. Their fourth album, 1979's The Raven, *was both more prog and more pop and has remained the fans' favourite for years. 1981's* Meninblack *was a very different proposition, a strange lyrical investigation into aliens and UFOs containing the weirdest music they ever came up with. It didn't sell as well but has stood the test of time. Later that year the Stranglers returned with their biggest ever hit, the mellower 'Golden Brown', from their sixth album* La Folie *and the band would remain a commercial force thoughout the Eighties and beyond.*

It was nearly time's up for the Buzzcocks. Their great run of hits was drawing to an end, and after their third album A Different Kind of Tension *in 1979 they reconvened to record a fourth. But a series of three singles in 1980 where they twisted the buzzsaw format, 'Are Everything', 'Strange Thing' and 'Running Free', were flops, and Pete Shelley, whilst recording demos with producer Martin Rushent, opted for a solo career instead. His first single was one of his oldest songs, re-recorded as contemporary electro pop – 'Homosapien'. His solo career never came to much commercially and today a reformed Buzzcocks still play brilliant live gigs and release occasional albums where the old magic is still very intact.*

The Clash, despite many haphazard, chaotic, instinctive decisions, were one of the biggest bands in the world. The triple set that followed London Calling, *1981's* Sandinista, *was slated for being too long and overblown but contains many hidden gems. Relentless road work in the States and an innate understanding of American culture, though, saw them make serious inroads across the Atlantic, which paid off with their next album, 1982's* Combat Rock, *which became their biggest seller and produced a bona fide US hit single, 'Rock the Casbah', written by drummer Topper Headon. Just when they seemed to have cracked ...merica, Mick Jones parted ways with the band. They reconvened with a new line-up – which, although great live, delivered the disappointing final album* Cut the Crap *in 1985. Only Joe Strummer from the band appeared on the album, which was cronked by its bizarre production, turning the latterday Clash's rabble rousers into electronic pop waffle.*

The single 'This Is England' stood out, and that was because of Joe's great lyrics and impassioned vocal raising the game at the final post; the rest of the songs, though, sound great on live bootlegs from the time. Meanwhile Mick Jones hit paydirt and kept moving forward with Big Audio Dynamite (with old buddy Don Letts joining him in the band) fusing electro and the emerging flavours of the hip hop scene to cinematic samples and futuristic Westway rock'n'roll.

Jah Wobble left Public Image Limited, whereupon John Lydon made another album with Keith Levene, the percussion-dominated Flowers of Romance *in 1981, before Levene left too. PiL continued throughout the Eighties, but despite having their biggest hits with 'This Is Not A Love Song' and 'Rise' they gradually drifted away from the cutting edge they had occupied at the end of the Seventies.*

The Damned continued on their ever-chaotic route. After their comeback third album, Machine Gun Etiquette, *which actually gave them a run of hit singles, they followed up with* The Black Album *in 1980 and* Strawberries *two years later, while the Captain had a surprise Number One hit the same year with the typically lunatic reworking of Rodgers and Hammerstein's 'Happy Talk'. Belatedly they went on to have big commercial success with hit singles in the mid-Eighties, including 'Grimly Fiendish' and especially their 1986 cover of 'Eloise'. By then, with Dave Vanian in control of the band, they were riding high on the goth scene that Dave's vampiric look had pioneered a decade before.*

The much-maligned goth scene was in full swing indeed. Taking its cue more from the northern goth clubs, it expanded on the darker themes set out by punk, and a whole host of black-clad youth created a dark glamour in the beat-up mill towns of Yorkshire and Lancashire. Bands like Sisters of Mercy from Leeds, Northampton's Bauhaus, and London's Sex Gang Children and UK Decay, and even a darker-sounding Cure, were the soundtrack to the scene which has remained huge but ignored by the indie-loving media.

No one would ever admit to being a goth. It was the scene that never existed, and many of its icons like the Birthday Party's Nick Cave and Siouxsie were always keen to disassociate themselves from it. But

Siouxsie's stunning image, her gothic haughty sexiness and eye for a good look made her the scene's premier icon and catapulted the Banshees into the big league. They enjoyed continued commercial success up until their eventual split in 1996.

Black was the key colour of the time. Apocalypse was the key word. Everyone firmly believd that it was the countdown to nuclear war. There was a post-punk depression. Anyway, black is the coolest colour. And none came more black than the meninblack themselves, the Stranglers.

J. J. Burnel

We developed a drug reputation in the Stranglers. In our generation we were one of the first ones to get heavily into heroin. It became an obsession with us. Originally it came from an idea that we would take it every day to see what record would come out of it. In the end we came out with *Meninblack* which was quite different. I think of *Meninblack* as my deformed child that I love. It's a dangerous period I don't want to think about too much. We went up a cul-de-sac and fortunately we came back down again and onto the main road. Now I'm so pleased we were fortunate to get out of it in one piece. It's the worst drug in the world. I had a few years out from karate at that time, but fortunately I had that to fall back on, something to focus on. I never used needles; I smoked it and got high enough. I don't recommend it at all. I don't want to glamourise it. We helped each other out of it.

We were involved in all kinds of stuff like the occult as well. I remember, one night when we were in Chiddingfold, Dave summoning up deities – he was involved with this guy who was supposed to be a warlock, and this guy who had come over – his hair went white overnight. Dave might tell you that he summoned up some kind of demon. I don't know if it's true or not. There are things beyond our vision; there are dimensions which might be beyond our perception.

There is an interesting world out there, loads to explore, discuss and write about. I can't think of a straight song that we wrote.

[laughs] Between the four of us we were interested in so many things, and still are. You wrote about them, and if some people got into them via your music you have done them a service. Life is so short. You can study your own belly button, but there are so many other things out there.

Steve Diggle

Pete Shelley wrote love songs, but I wanted to sing about other things – Ray Davies of the Kinks inspired me, growing up in a terraced street with guys with no money. Things were very natural, the way our two styles fitted together. If I had been at school with him, Pete would not have been one of the kids I hung around with. I would have thought he was a right fucking wanker! [laughs] But there are similarities. We have sat in a lot of pubs over the years – one thing Pete Shelley can do is drink!

We'd done the first Buzzcocks album and *Love Bites*, and on the third one, *A Different Kind of Tension*, it was time to do something different.[4] We went to darker areas. We had always done things like 'Moving Away From The Pulsebeat', 'Fiction Romance' and 'Autonomy' which were not like orthodox Buzzcocks songs – 'Pulsebeat' was quite experimental at the time – and the B-sides like 'Why Can't I Touch It', which was a groove thing. By the time of the third album we had been around the world a few times, and it felt natural to move on. It was getting crazy then. We'd been on the road a lot, with a lot of partying going on – we were all cracking up at that period! It was hard to hold it together.

EMI took over United Artists and the A&R men kept changing all the time. Who's dealing with us? No one seemed to be interested – we had to keep explaining what we were up to over and over. We did these three songs and we thought we would put them out as singles. We went and recorded them as demos. Martin Rushent was away somewhere, so we did them with Martin

---

4. The first two albums had been released in 1978. The third appeared in 1979.

Hannett and they came out in America on a twelve-inch. All the songs came out as singles here, great songs but not commercial. Punk was waning a bit and the songs were a bit darker. People preferred the other stuff.

After those singles we went back to do an album and we put a couple of things down. We were waiting for our producer Martin Rushent to turn up, and it felt like the end. We could feel dark clouds over it, and me and Pete were hanging around with lots of different people, different tensions there. He went away with Rushent to sort out his songs, using electronic gear at Rushent's place, and he made *Homosapien*.[5] He sent a letter saying, 'I've finished with the group,' and everybody was a bit pissed off with him. He really should have phoned up – we would have understood that after five years of being in each other's pockets! We didn't speak for a long time – there was bad feeling. Oddly enough I'm the only one who has never left this group!

It was a relief in a way as well. We were touring for months at a time in America – drugs, women, no sleep, all around the world. We were only 26 when we split up but we'd done so much in a short space of time. We were always on tour – we did 32 dates of the UK when everyone else would do fifteen. We never stopped, and eventually it caught up.

Ian Brown

We stumbled in on the Clash recording 'Bankrobber' in Manchester. Me and Pete Garner and Si Walsoncroft were at Granby Row in Manchester city centre.[6] We were just mooching. We didn't even know that they were in there, and we just heard these drums. Then the drums stopped and someone said, 'What you doing in here? Come in, come in!' Strummer was writing lyrics by the grandfather clock with a fedora hat on, and he was clicking his fingers along with

---

5. Shelley's solo album, released in 1981.

6. Pete Garner was the original bass player in the Stone Roses. Si Walsoncroft was the original drummer for the Stone Roses and drummer for the Fall.

the clock. Paul Simonon asked us, 'What's your favourite film?' Mikey Dread was there as well – that was a pure accident – we met their roadie, Johnny Green, and he went off to get the LP and he got us one LP to share and we were arguing over who was going to have the LP between the three of us. I think I got the record and Pete got the sleeve. [laughs]

I went off the Clash after *Give 'Em Enough Rope*. I loved the first LP but I didn't like the second. I was too young then but I understand now that they were going for that American market. The Clash got me into reggae – in the punk rock days it went hand in hand, didn't it? That was so important for me.

Don Letts

The whole thing with the Clash – longevity was never the point. Most of the bands I like had a natural organic life of seven or eight years: the Smiths, Led Zep. When people go on too long, they destroy their own myth. There are a few exceptions. Everyone else would have been better stopping earlier. There is a window of opportunity – you use that moment and fuck off out of the way.

After the Clash split, Mick was moping around. I went round saying, 'Mick, what the fuck are you going to do? You're not going to be a milkman!' Leo Williams was a bass player, so you're two-thirds of the way there – if you're the White Stripes, all the way there! He gets Leo, he gets Topper involved for a little while, but that didn't pan out for obvious reasons.[7] We were all at a club one night, me, Mick and Leo. Mick looks to the left and it's Leo; and he looks to his right and it's me. 'Well, this feels like a band,' he says, and the next thing I know he asks me to join the band, and I said, 'Mick, I can't play anything.' He said, 'Don, it's punk. C'mon.' And I said, 'I've got a few ideas up my sleeve.' I was thrust into the whole sample thing from watching movies and things. We were probably the first band to have a hit with major sampling with '$e=mc^2$'. I

---

7. Topper Headon hadn't resolved his health problems.

couldn't play an instrument – it was the punk rock way to create or recreate sound. I didn't write a lot of the lyrics. I wrote most of the songs with Mick. I had a filmic approach, more Nic Roeg, more abstract. It's the people who know the least about an art who come up with the best ideas. They don't know the restrictions. I was always surrounded by people who could play instruments but their ideas sucked.

. I'd be onstage with BAD with these keyboards that had coloured stickers on them and I didn't care! I'd lift up the keybaord and show the audience, basically saying, 'If you've got the balls, fucking come here and do it!'

Keith Levene

Public Image's first tour was because Warner put out *Metal Box* as *Second Edition*.[8] They said, 'Hey guys, you gotta promote this.' The next thing we know, we got a tour manager and a fucking tour. What we did was, we'd end up in New York and do the gig at the Palladium – then we'd arrange another gig and another gig and that really pissed them off! After the Palladium, we did Gildersleeves, this Hell's Angels joint on the Bowery. It was bad, a killer gig.

Jah Wobble

It got really boring. We did fifteen gigs in two years during the *Metal Box* time and I don't think we played Britain at all! We had no management, the business was disastrous, shitty deals, money going walkabout – it was a bad scene. A lot of people round the band should have not been there. It was time to get off.

I'd been using gear and powders, uppers and pills from before PiL days. I was a heavy drinker as well – you can't live this life when you are on the road. I never made a big deal about it. I can't stand it when these celebs go on about it like it's one of the basic chess moves of this game, having a problem. It's being immature, to be

---

8. Same album but packaged conventionally, not in the metal case. See pages 478–479.

honest, not dealing with things in a responsible way. That problem was moving fast – I'd been using the gear, drinking a lot, somehow functioning, and suddenly it reached a point where it was counter-productive and ended up in a bit of a mess.

I pretty much stopped drinking and drugging, and that's when I ended up on the Underground driving a train. Get a fucking job! It was one of the greatest things that ever happened to me.

Keith Levene

We had to make another record, *Flowers of Romance*. We hadn't replaced Wobble, who had left the band. It was now me, John and Jeanette Lee – I was now the only one in the band that could really play anything. I did have this habit of going around and finding these weird instruments, like these acoustic violins that have got these big horns as amplifiers, and soprano saxophones. And there was this weird bamboo instrument that I used on 'Hymie's Hymn' – Richard Branson had gotten some in Bali and gave me one of these things. We went to the Manor Studio and we had three weeks of blocked-out studio time, which was a fucking fortune.

The record is very, very sparse. The single 'Flowers of Romance' has no guitar on it – it's just a cello'd bass, all drums. We'd put the backing track together and we were getting into computer mixes, which was keeping John interested. He did a sax solo on it – he didn't know how to play but that's what came out. I said, 'It's OK, we can use it.' It was very experimental like that. It's almost like a documen-tation of me finding out about other instruments and having someone who can't play any instruments being recorded – in a state-of-the-art situation. My outlook was that a child's painting can be as far-out as a Van Gogh. I could use John's total ineptitude to an artistic advantage. At the same time, I realised that I was really branching out.

I always felt the album was not quite enough, but I think it really stands the test of time. I always felt that I should have played more guitar on it. There was stuff on it that I could have done but I didn't do.

Rat Scabies

We were very conscious of our critics. With *Machine Gun Etiquette* people were saying we were a one-dimensional punk band and that's why we had put 'Just Can't Be Happy Today' and the long introduction to 'Smash It Up' on there. We realised that stuff was very well received, so when it came to *The Black Album* we were again in the studio being very creative. We went to Rockfield and bashed it out and came out with a very interesting-sounding album.

Captain Sensible

The Black Album was Dave really coming into his own. There was once again a lot of experimenting, and we found ourselves at the front of another movement, the goth thing. The birds are so nice in that goth gear. What's wrong with goth? It's fucking great!

The idea for *Strawberries* was to make a garage album. We'd seen the Chocolate Watch Band and all this stuff we loved. Once again Dave was really into that stuff. He's a guru of garage – when garage meant garage, not J-Lo! [laughs]

In defence of my solo career [laughs insanely], the thing was I had accumulated about fifteen songs that were rejected by the Damned – they were too sugary. So I thought, 'You either throw them away or record them yourself.' And if you're a bog cleaner and you've never had any fucking cash you take whatever you can get!

My girlfriend at the time, Kirsty, was listening to New Musik, this band who did 'Living By Numbers'. She said, 'Come and see them at Fairfield Halls.' I said, 'I know the back way in. We'll get in for nothing.' So we sneaked in and we were watching the band. 'This guy is a genius,' she said. I said, 'OK, whatever you say.' She was really good at blagging and we got in backstage. She dragged me in with her and introduced me to the singer, Tony Mansfield, who ended up producing me.

I worked really hard promoting 'Happy Talk' and 'Wot', flying all over Europe, and I couldn't do the Damned as well as 'Happy Talk', which was only added onto the album because they needed one more song – I got it off my parents' *South Pacific* album. I didn't want it released as a single, but it ended up Number One in the charts. John Peel thought it was brilliant – he was the first DJ to play it.

Budgie

When I joined the Banshees, the vision for what they wanted to do was still intact, which they showed when they wrote the next album.[9] The original demos for 'Christine' and other songs were very different in approach. I had to bring in a whole bunch of things I'd been listening to. Unlike John and Kenny I'd been in a lot of bands. I had a lot of other ideas from outside the Banshees and that was their first band. Robert Smith and I had different source references anyway, and we were playing loosely off each other. When John McGeoch came along, he joined the *Kaleidoscope* sessions. First of all Steve Jones came down. I saw him recently and he couldn't remember anything about the sessions, and I was saying, 'You were great!' He played on the album on 'Paradise Place' and 'Skin' – he came in with this tremendous sustained Gibson guitar sound and it was great. That added a new dimension in the way we were recording as well. Siouxsie and Steve put their ideas down and I'd add the drums half-way through the tracks.

Then we went off and did some some demos of 'Happy House' and the B-side 'Drop Dead' and 'Celebration' – that was with McGeoch, and that's where we found a new voice with John. He had been pushing things with Magazine. Severin had seem them play and we made a real concerted effort to tempt him away from that. People like Keith Levene and John McGeogh were definitely listening to each other, though I'm not sure who was listening to who. John's way of playing took it somewhere else again. Suddenly I was playing with seasoned musicians, not regurgitating well-known chops. We wrote a lot of that album in the studio and when we started playing it live we really began to gel. When we wrote songs

---

9. The album was *Kaleidoscope*.

for the next album, *Ju Ju*, we peaked and hit a real pinnacle of telepathy. [laughs] Those moments you can only dream about, and you're lucky to find them.

INNOCENT VICTIMS OF RUMOUR
Oi and the 1981 Southall Riot

The Oi scene was moving fast in 1980–81. Fronted by the likes of the Cockney Rejects and the Business, it was looking to become as big as the initial punk explosion. Its street-tough stance struck a chord in the brutal reality of the early days of Thatcher's Britain. But it could never last and one gig would be the turning point.

On 4 July 1981 the Business, 4-Skins and Last Resort played the Hamborough Tavern in Southall. The gig was right in the middle of the Asian area and the local Asian youth were jumpy after a series of falsified rumours started spreading about the right-wing nature of the event. None of the bands were remotely right wing, and they were innocent victims of rumour-mongering and far darker forces. The tragedy of Oi has been this tarring of the movement with the Nazi brush. The rumours aggravated the local youth, who attacked the venue and the bands. It sparked a riot and within days a series of national conflagrations erupted across the UK in the tinderbox inner cities. Ever since the Tories had got back into power there had been simmering discontent, and all through 1981 there had been several incidents, but the Southall riot was the final catalyst. The next night it was Toxteth in Liverpool, and the next weekend masses of towns across the UK. Now the riots on the streets that so many punk bands had sung about were a reality. The only results were increased police power, smashed windows and the price of heroin dropping through the floor as it flooded the streets of Britain. The Southall riot crushed the burgeoning Oi movement, which was instantly and mistakenly tarred with a right-wing brush. It took a few years for the key bands to be able to play gigs without all the Nazi baggage that they were lumbered with.

Watford John (Argy Bargy: vocals)

Bands like Cock Sparrer, Cockney Rejects and Menace were all into the football thing and none of them were into the punk imagery of the Kings Road type punks.

A lot of the early punk bands had a big skinhead following and I think the connection probably stems from then. Some might say that these bands were what you might call 'real punk', bands who came from the tower blocks and back streets of the nation and therefore were latched onto by the early (revival) skinheads, because they saw them as the same people as themselves – which, of course, they were.

Micky Fitz

Southall was so long ago. I've got so many bad memories, none of us want to talk about it. We were stitched up and that's it. I'm lucky to be alive. All the old pictures of the Hamborough Tavern burnt down – that van parked outside the front door was mine. We got out of the van ten seconds before two petrol bombs were put through the front windows. It was very scary and it was a shame that it had to happen.

Steve Kent

I came to the group a little bit late, so I missed Southall. I don't think the people involved were proud of what went on at the time. The country was verging on anarchy anyway, and I'm not surprised something like that happened – the government at the time caused a lot of trouble, and it was a by-product of what they were doing. It pretty well killed the Oi scene in the media.

I think Oi had quite socialist principles. I personally think it's a good thing for working-class people to have a say, and that was the most important message that came across in street punk. It's a real simple, good, positive music. I'm so proud of bands now like Rancid and Dropkick Murphys who acknowledge their Oi roots. So many kids like it. Generally the punk rock message is very positive: it's about animal rights, things like that. The whole scene was positive, not negative.

Garry Bushell

I'm quite hardline about this. The reason these bands had bad press was because they were working-class. There is an inbuilt snobbery in the music press: although most people were left wing there was still a sort of snootiness about bands. Because the gigs they played were in Canning Town people like me and Garry Johnson were the only ones who would go and see them. When the whole Southall thing happened it was very easy for people to say it was a terrible scene but they had never been to any of these gigs. There was never any racism at the Bridge House. That just not would have been allowed. The whole idea that the bands had gone into Middlesex to provoke a race riot was absurd. We'd been talking strike benefits, not NF marches. No Oi band had sported swastikas, like the Sex Pistols had done.

Micky Geggus

I never wanted to be associated with Oi because I thought at the time it was just a genie waiting to get out of its bottle. It caused a lot of problems and I was proved right with the Southall thing.

I think Southall was an accident waiting to happen. I didn't like the idea from the start – a lot of them bands were set up for that, I honestly believe that. There was a lot that didn't add up with that thing. The bands had no political connotations – that was the last thing those blokes would mention over a beer. After Southall the press butchered their reputations. Most are respectable family men now, and it stigmatised them for years. I felt sorry for Garry too: he took huge knocks over it and he didn't have any ulterior motive. It was a sad day for everyone.

We didn't have Nazis at our gigs. If we saw any Nazi skinheads we used to lump them out the back and batter them. They are awful people: what are they doing in the country that vanquished Nazism? Sieg-heiling as a piece of entertainment? It's unforgivable. Also what angers me is the fact that they would go home and play reggae even though they were racists! They are the most ignorant people. They ruined it for everyone and they are the most godawful bullies as well.

You'd see a lot of bullying going on, which we wouldn't like – six of the arseholes picking on two little punks. Well, try us for size! I used to be a boxer and so did Jeff. Vince is six foot four and could handle himself, and the rest of the road crew were mad as march hares.

Garry Bushell

Strength Through Oi, the album title, was an innocent mistake.[10] We already had *Oi, The Album* and I was thinking of calling it *The Oi of Sex*. The Skids had an EP and one of the tracks on there was called 'Strength Through Joy' and I thought I'd do a pun on that. When I asked Richard Jobson about using it later, he said he got it from a Dirk Bogarde autobiography! The idea that we were shrewdly using a Nazi slogan was a joke – we didn't even know that 'Strength Through Joy' was a Nazi slogan!

The biggest argument they had was the picture of the aggressive skin on the front cover. This turned out to be Nicky Crane, a gay Nazi who later died of AIDS. Here's the truth: the original model had been West Ham personality and then body-builder Carlton Leach. Carlton had turned up for one photo session at Bridge House that didn't work. He never turned up for the second one. Under looming deadline pressure I suggested using a shot from a skinhead Christmas card which I believed was a still from the *Wanderers* movie.[11] In fact it had been taken by English skinhead photographer Martin Dean. It wasn't until the very last minute, when Decca had mocked up the sleeve, that the photo was sufficiently clear to reveal Nazi tattoos. We had the option of either airbrushing the tattoos out or putting the LP back a month while we put a new sleeve together. I hold my hands up. My mistake. Sorry.

Lots of the bands in Oi were political to the *left*. But after Southall even the *Socialist Worker* repeated the *Daily Mail*'s version

---

10. *Strength Through Oi* was the second compilation album of the Oi movement put together by Bushell.

11. *The Wanderers* was a cult 1979 film about gang fights in New York which struck a chord in early Eighties Britain, where inter-youth cult gang fights were commonplace.

of events. There was a tiny proportion of skinheads who were Nazis. Far more were anti-Nazis. The only people who gave us a fair hearing were the *Guardian*, who wrote a really good piece on it. They came down and interviewed all the right people.

My understanding of what went on was that the local Asian youth had been wound up about the gig and had stocked up on Molotov cocktails beforehand. They were expecting a pretty heavy mob to come down and were ready. The fans were being attacked before they had got there. It wasn't like the bands were going there to provoke the local community. The locals had been told that they were going to get invaded by all these Nazis, which they never were. So you can understand their position. There was the petrol bombs thrown into the pub.

After Southall you had people turning up at gigs expecting a right-wing rally, and it wasn't like that at all. A lot of people were getting attacked *by* the far right. I was attacked at the 100 Club. Oi never broke through because of all the stigma that became attached to it.

Micky Geggus

We got on *Top of the Pops* about three times and each one was a disaster. We always thought it a great big joke. We'd gone and got really pissed, and while filming the actual band we would be taking the piss. There was a few nasty incidents that took place and we had to clump a few people. I remember saying to Steve Wright, 'Is there any chance of standing by you while you introduce the bands?' and he said, 'Yeah, no problem.' So we stood next to him and he shoved my mate out of the camera! And he threatened to kill Steve Wright! [laughs] It was probably a good job we never did get invited back.

I always found it a bit faceless, the Eighties punk. There was never any anthems like the original stuff had. The bands, no disrespect to them, but I never listen to any of it now. People ask me about them but I couldn't tell you anything about them.

Garry Bushell

With the right management and production, the Cockney Rejects could have gone a lot further than they did. They had a big buzz about them in '79 and Micky is a great guitarist. The great thing about them was how diverse their sound was. People thought Oi was all '1, 2, 3, 4!' but then you had bands as diverse as the Business with very melodic songs. These bands were blackballed and lost out really.

POSITIVE PUNK
The Early Days of the Goth Scene

A confusion of ideas was running around the squats and bedsits. The bizarre sexpeople world of Adam and the Ants and the anarcho ideals of Crass were all mixing up in the melting pot along with black-clad groups. Talk was of dark rock'n'roll, Crass anarchism, and the nuclear holocaust; frustration at the implosion of the punk movement and the right-wing government of the vile Thatcher; and the escapism of magick, paganism, anarchism, cheap drugs and lager snakebites. All this was mixed in with classic punk and post-punk, and black clothes which were both sexy and convenient. An NME front cover termed the loosely-affiliated scene 'positive punk' as a riposte to the negativity of the rest of the punk scene. Simultaneously there was also a post-Bowie/Roxy club scene that was moving into darker areas and added to the melting pot of ideas that would forge goth.

'Positive punk' was a term coined by journalist and Brigandage guitarist Richard North in an NME front-cover feature on the upcoming scene that would soon be sneeringly tagged 'goth'. It was built around groups like the early Ants, Southern Death Cult, Siouxsie and the Banshees, Sex Gang Children, UK Decay (whose frontman Abbo is credited with coining the phrase 'gothic'), Bauhaus and even the Birthday Party and Joy Division – who even if they were not strictly goth bands (then again, no band ever admitted it was) – were listened to initially by the emerging goth audience. These bands would have people travelling up

and down the country and turning up at the gigs on the guest list armed with sleeping bags. This was a 24/7 culture. A culture covered brilliantly in Vague, Panache *and* Kill Your Pet Puppy *fanzines.*

Whilst this scene was rumbling into life, Adam Ant went mainstream with a new line-up of the Ants. Frustrated at his failure to break through into the big time, Adam had paid Malcolm McLaren £1,000 for management advice. McLaren told Adam to go for the pirate look but then proceeded to sack Adam himself from the band! Instead McLaren used the Ants to back Annabella Lwin in Bow Wow Wow, his great new hope. Adam then bounced back to brilliant effect, deciding to follow McLaren's advice about pirates and Burundi drummers. To do this he recruited Marco Pirroni and a backing band. (Since the demise of the Models, Marco had been in a new band, Rema Rema, whose one single, 'The Feedback Song', is an awesome slab of Marco's distortion over a drum beat.) The new Ants were a combination of glam rock, Burundi drumming, twanging guitars and 3D pop, all dressed up in theatrical costumes (pirates, highwaymen and all). With the album Kings of the Wild Frontier, *a brilliant record of technicolour pop, they stormed the charts, making Adam the biggest pop star of 1980–81.*

In contrast, the rest of the bands on the positive punk scene took the underground route, and the early goth scene continued to evolve in London, Leeds and elsewhere in West Yorkshire, picking up on emerging bands like Southern Death Cult.

Marco Pirroni

The Models petered out. I was fucking about after that. We had started Rema Rema in '79. That was us completely abandoning punk. In that period I was listening to *The Idiot* by Iggy Pop – I thought that was a phenomenal album, in a sense going back to Bowie, that electronic dark sound. What we were trying to do was a cross between Velvet Underground, Roxy Music and the Pistols, going back to the roots and putting it all back together again. But it became arty and up its own arse.

I left Rema Rema because we were playing gigs with these really boring bands like Cabaret Voltaire, which I thought was wank for its own sake.[12] And I left the Banshees too – they invited me back for one rehearsal. Initially I didn't like them, then we started hanging out and became mates, and all the old poses were dropped as we got older. But I thought it was too arty and dark. I didn't want to do this – I'm not arty or dark. I didn't think it was very clever. It's a pose.

A week later Adam Ant contacted me. I'd met him loads of times. I had seen the original Ants loads of times. Initially I thought they were fucking shit, absysmal. Initially Jordan was managing them and she said, 'Come and see them,' and I thought, 'If Jordan is managing them they must be really good.' They weren't, so I forgot about them really. Then I saw them supporting the Banshees and I thought they had some great songs. I didn't really want to join the Ants, even though I could play better than their guitar players.

Tom Vague

In Yorkshire the goth scene was starting out and in London Richard North wrote about 'positive punk' on the cover of the *NME*, about bands like Brigandage. It was looking for a way out, an escape, a continuation. People that don't fit in various places.

Michelle Brigandage

When Richard North was asked to report on the bands he'd been reviewing for an *NME* front cover we were so excited. All of us would get some exposure – people outside of London would hear us. He wrote with joy and in good faith and tried to mention as many bands as possible.

At first most people seemed pleased, but then the backlash came. When the other music papers realised they'd been left stand-

---

12. Cabaret Voltaire were a groundbreaking electronic outfit from Sheffield. Check out their key single 'Nag, Nag, Nag'.

Adam Ant teaming up with Marco in between being a bizzaro underground cult figure and becoming the white-stripe-painted purveyor of Burundi-drumming, native-American pirate pop

ing at the gate everyone was slagged off. I think nearly every band paid a price. Mine was to be sniped at and criticised by people who were formerly friends and allies, and then to be thrown out of my own group.

Gavin Friday

Goth. That confused us so much. We were sort of instigators in that whole movement, as a band that wore make-up. People picked up on the androgyny. There was the Cure, Bauhaus and the Banshees, and suddenly all these other bands like Sex Gang Children, the Mission. But I always had a problem with people who sing in an operatic voice!

Tony D

Bauhaus in early '79 played the Rock Garden and I was blown away with them. Pete Murphy was fantastic at the time.

Aki Qureshi

I was always passionately trying to form bands even to the extent that I would steal money from the family shop (which later went bankrupt) to buy the equipment for everyone. I had met Barry many times and after a while said, 'If you're serious then do you wanna form a band?'[13] He agreed and I then approached Buzz, who was a really pretentious, arty type. He was not interested until I actually went and dropped off a demo of the band – which he thought was crap, but he was impressed that I did what I said would do – and he agreed to join. We formed a band called Violation and, after some great coups, supporting the Clash, Killing Joke and other big bands, the lead singer left.

I had heard some Crass records but they didn't entirely inspire me at first, although I know that they were doing good things politically and in an anarchist manner. I preferred Poison Girls. As I was

---

13. Barry Jepson, bass player in Southern Death Cult.

promoting concerts I managed to get Crass and Poison Girls to play a concert at the local Italian Club. I was frightened I wouldn't make enough money to pay the band, but by the end of the night the attendance was brilliant. I think I made £150, with which I bought my first serious drum kit. I thank Crass for giving me the opportunity.

Ian Astbury was travelling around with Crass then, and it was at that gig that I saw him. After the gig Ian decided to stay in the same house where New Model Army resided (they were called Hustler Street Band at the time) and we had a rehearsal room in the basement. Buzz, the guitarist, had seen Ian at a club and liked the way he danced and invited him down to rehearse with us – and that's how it all got together. Ian eventually replaced our singer and then directed the band concept into the Southern Death Cult.

I always liked the more anarchist element of the punk movement and it seemed to have a home at the 1 in 12 club in Bradford. The '1 in 12' were the unemployed at the time. We played our first gig there in front of family and friends – it was based above the Sun pub. There was a great spirit of people working together and on the fringes of the norm, arty types and mad creative people.

My brother was putting on punk gigs in Leeds at which we supported Chelsea. Gene October loved the band and gave us a break at the Marquee club, supporting them. Suddenly by word of mouth the band was buzzing. Every gig we would do we would take almost all the punks in Bradford in the back of vans or lorries with us and a scene started to emerge and the interest built quickly. John Peel gave us many sessions and suddenly we were supporting all the right bands. The big Bauhaus tour made a massive dent and after that we were playing sell-out gigs all over the place and a massive street buzz had impacted. Record companies were bidding stupid money. Ian told all the majors to fuck off and we signed with Beggars Banquet for a small deal – nevetheless it was the best thing we did. Even my dad eventually saw us – he thought we were good but we should replace Ian with a better singer! Of course his ears were tuned to great singing voices from India.

Southern Death Cult were a continuation of the ideals of punk, absolutely no question of it, although it went into different aspects, mainly guided by Ian's depressive stance against the unjust world. Many thought us a goth band, but we were more than that. It just happened that many punks were into goth at the time. But the rebellious side of things was there for me personally throughout. It was a natural but very quick success: within months we were headlining our own gigs and no compromise was being made. Great times, and all innocent and naive.

Tom Vague

The Southern Death Cult seemed like the closest to the Ants in spirit and music. They were the hippest band on the scene. New Model Army were the least fashionable and I kind of respect them for that. Ian Astbury came from the Crass and Poison Girls scene. I put on a Crass gig in Salisbury and I ended up much more in the Crass world, in the Hackney squatting scene – Stoke Newington before it all went really crusty with dogs on a bit of string – that was when I got out.

Justin Sullivan, aka Slade the Leveller (New Model Army: vocals)

I think that goth was a further reaction to a failed revolution – a search for something different and dark and quasi-spiritual, a kind of Native American ghostdance in the face of defeat. In the Banshees, the Sisters of Mercy, Killing Joke and all, it was a genuine search for musical creativity that responded to a new reality.

New Model Army arrived in the post-punk period and raised the banner for post-punk politics – impassioned songs that struck a chord during the Thatcher years and the miners' strike. I think much of the original punk was deeply apolitical – just nihilist, a reaction to the violence and the greyness and the sense of drift in the Seventies. It was the more middle-class and educated groups (obviously Joe Strummer comes to mind) who co-opted it into being a political thing. And later this was refined into something more extreme and doctrinaire and less musical by the likes of Crass. By this point and the start of New Model Army, it is impossible to overstate how political Britain had become. Everything and everyone was political. You either bought into the new Thatcherite counter-revolution or you didn't. There were the riots in Southall, Toxteth, Brixton; there was mass unemployment, especially in the North; there was the Falklands War and finally there was the miners' strike.

AND THE SCENE KEPT FRACTURING
Including the Emergence of Indie

All over the UK the remnants of the punk scene continued unabated whilst the indie scene emerged from post-punk. Championed by John Peel, the quirky and the eccentric were imbued with an independent spirit and thrived on the new indie labels. By the time the Wedding Present emerged, the indie scene was going mainstream and the band managed to merge northern independent stubbornness with an effective ear for a pop melody.

Richie Rocker (MDM: bass)

After Eric's/Brady's, the next major punk venue in Liverpool was the Warehouse. Situated in Fleet Street, the club was home to the second generation of punks. The club played host to all the main bands of the era: the Exploited, Vice Squad, Chron Gen, Abrasive Wheels. The standout gigs for me, however, would be the So What tour featuring the ANWL, Chelsea, Chron Gen and the Defects. And also the Dead Kennedys, Test Tube Babies, MDC and Mayhem – this was the gig where the barrier collapsed at the front. How the first five rows got out alive, I'll never know.

I also saw Killing Joke play there. The place was rammed – to this day I don't think I've ever been so hot at a gig. Like all good clubs it had to end, and it did so in spectacular fashion when it burned down. This really spelt the end of the scene in Liverpool for me. A couple of clubs/promoters tried to carry the banner, but with the bést bands splitting up we were left with the dregs, and it was hard to motivate yourself to go and watch some third-division Discharge clones. But it was fun while it lasted. It may surprise people now, but at one time Liverpool was the punk place to be!

David Gedge (Wedding Present: vocals)

The bands that really influenced me were the Fall, the Membranes, the Gang of Four, Josef K – it was an exhilarating time for me, leaving home to go to university in Leeds and suddenly having the freedom to go to as many concerts as I wanted. I've seen the Fall more than any other band, although that's partly because they've been going longer than any other band. I went to see them in Wakefield with Keith Gregory and we missed the last train home.[14] But we didn't even mind walking back twelve miles because we were so excited to have seen the Fall on their fantastic 'two drummers' tour!

One of my housemates at the time was the entertainments secretary at Leeds Polytechnic. One night she said to us: 'Oi! You two are supposed to like punk. Go and see the Membranes at Becketts Park tonight.' So we went up to this little college and watched, enthralled, as the band pulled out all the stops for an audience of about a dozen people in some brightly lit common room. It was such a fantastic-sounding racket in completely inappropriate surroundings.

Beki Bondage

We had a track on a compilation. We thought that it was great and terribly glamorous, recording our first track. I think it took eighteen months till we got our first single out – when you're fourteen years old it's a long time to wait.

---

14. Gregory was the Wedding Present's first bass player.

Vice Squad's Beki Bondage relaxes between sweaty punk package tours

I liked the hardcore political, Discharge/Crass, anarcho-punk type of thing, and a couple of the band were more into the Oi football thing which I had no interest in whatsoever. People could have argued, 'What's this politics got to do with music?' but with punk it was really relevant. I was attracted to these bands because they would say things that other bands wouldn't. I remember Crass had that album dedicated to feminism with a blow-up doll on the front.[15] I wasn't so interested in Crass musically but lyrically I loved them. I was into animal rights and the rest of the band weren't – you can see the recipe for disaster already! [laughs] I went veggie and they were doing their best to see if I would slip.

Garry Bushell wasn't pro-animal rights, but I think he found me very interesting because there was not many women out there. And I can see why women wouldn't want to do it. I used to get covered in gob every time I went out there. They said it was because they liked me! It's going in your mouth and giving you diseases like hepatitis. I only did it because I was so young at the time.

We released our first album *No Cause For Concern*, which was a Top 30 album – I don't understand how, because it was a pile of shite! [laughs] We recorded it in one day. It does have a certain charm to it, a youthful naivety that is quite appealing. I was out of my head because I'd been binge-drinking the night before. The guy I was going out with at the time gave me amyl nitrate, which is not good for your voice.

At the time I would take virtually anything except heroin. I was very into speed to start with, and then I realised that it wasn't worth the come-downs. I moved onto cocaine when I wasn't buying it – my wages didn't stretch to cocaine, but if it was available I would have it. Speed was the poor man's coke. Dope and alcohol was around. Now I find drugs really, really boring.

---

15. *Penis Envy* (1981).

THE CULTURE OF RESISTANCE:
Crass & Anarcho-Punks

The Crass project was timed to end in 1984. Everything they created was in a countdown to George Orwell's iconic year. Worn out by harassment from the authorities, Crass had chosen their exit point well. They had made their statements. They had changed a lot of people's minds. They had introduced non-punk ideas like vegetarianism and made sense of them in a nihilistic period. They had offered solutions to problems and they affected people in the most unlikely places. Their influence lives on in bands that were fired by them, and in key players in the anti-globalisation protest movement. They were the starting point for a lot of political agitation. Their last stand and their key battleground was opposing the Falklands War – one of the lone voices in a suddenly patriotic post-riot UK.

Penny Rimbaud

'Die for a cause, don't die for some gesture.' The Falklands War started in April 1982 and there seemed to be no voices of opposition. Our reaction was quick. It had to be quick. The first thing we did was 'Sheep Farming In The Falklands', the flexi. We knew we were going to attack the whole war, and we were shit scared about doing it, so with the flexi, various distributors agreed to drop the flexi into other people's records with no mention that it was in there. Our defence was going to be that someone else had bootlegged it and manufactured it and it was nothing to do with us!

From then on we adopted what we called tactical responses. We decided to record an album. We had a week to make music and lyrics, to get in the studio and get it out. The album *Yes Sir* was a return to roots for me – it very much followed the tradition of free jazz and avant-garde music. It was completely what we felt at the time. The thing I love most about that album was we did it in one take. There might have been a rest between side one and side two but that was it.

The next thing we did was 'How Does It Feel?' Questions were asked in Parliament over it. When we were starting to get shit we sent it to selected MPs. Tim Eggar's brother Robin used to work for the *Mirror*, and Tim used Robin to try to denigrate 'How Does It Feel?' He started initiating a prosecution and was trying to substantiate it by running it through his brother in the press. He didn't get very far: he did a radio interview with Andy and Pete where he got absolutely slaughtered.[16] Basically he was expecting a couple of Sid Viciouses and came up against two people who could totally substantiate the arguments.

It did eventually go to the Director for Public Prosecutions. At that time Andy got hold of the DPP office phone number and rung it quite regularly as a pretend journalist following the case. We were one step ahead of them all the time – we knew what they were planning! Nowadays I don't think this could happen. They would have this surveillance going on. Anyway the net result of all this was a very strict note sent by the Tory Head Office around the Conservative Party, about Crass, saying, 'On absolutely no account should you react to these people.'

The greatest success for us was that we managed to get all the information about the war out there. Within the framework we now adopted as a band we had just about said everything we could. We then released 'Gotcha' as well. The records were coming out really quickly – rapid-fire stuff.

Jeremy Cunningham (The Levellers: bass)

I was about to leave school in the early Eighties. I was hanging round the park, and I had older friends there who introduced me to Crass. The politics of Crass were important: they politicised a generation and I was one of the people they politicised. They helped to define the movement the individual members of the Levellers came out of. Someone played them to me and said, 'This is the most punk rock record you will ever listen to,' and after a few listens and after

---

16. Crass guitarist Andy Palmer and bassist Pete Wright.

reading all their lyrics and all the information that came with the records, I got completely into that. The sleeves would fold out into multiple essays, amazing art work, and reading that got me thinking. It took me a while to get the music – at first it sounded quite extreme, properly extreme, the whole enigma of it. I was more into Discharge – they were more immediate, they sounded amazing, and they became really influential on nu-metal.

That was a really good period for punk stuff, and when I got into Crass I got into all of that scene. There was loads of interesting bands around like Rudimentary Peni, Flux, Amebix, the Mob. I was more into that Crass end of things than the Exploited, 4-Skins and Business-type bands – I didn't really get into all that scene. It got quite ugly with the Southall riots and all that. There was a split in the scene between the two sides, and any side Garry Bushell is on I'm going to be on the other one! [laughs]

By about 1984, the directions in which punk had sent different parts of the music scene were so diverse – from the politically charged worlds of Billy Bragg and the Angelic Upstarts to anarcho-pacifism, from Oi to goth to the New Pop – that it could no longer be understood as one meaningful movement. The floodwaters of the mighty River Punk which had burst its banks in 1976-77 had by now spread far and wide. Few areas were left untouched, but the very ubiquity of the inundation actually served to make punk's influence less immediately apparent. But though it may have gone back undeground, punk's energy was still there. Many lives had been changed, and many continue to be so.

Billy Bragg

My songwriting was really changed by punk. I was very influenced by the Clash, by the Jam, by the really good songwriters who came through in that period like Elvis Costello, who may not have been punk but shared the attitude. I look at those people like Elvis, and Joe Strummer till his death – they stayed true to that. They have not become Sting. I was encouraged that even Weller stayed true.[17] Subsequently I came to appreciate the Damned. I didn't get it when I first heard it – maybe it was just too radical for me. I thought they were fucking around. Once I had heard the Ramones it made more sense. I really like Ian Dury. The Hot Rods and the Feelgoods didn't really survive. In the Stalinist Year Zero the Hot Rods got elbowed out.

When Riff Raff broke up in 1980, I thought everything was fucked. In order to escape from having to go back home I joined the army. I pressed the eject button on my previous existence. While in the army I was writing more songs, and I came out of the army with a real attitude, thinking I'd got to carry on doing this. One night I saw Spandau Ballet singing 'Chant No. 1' on *Top of the Pops*, wearing kilts, and I thought, 'Fucking hell, there is not a band that's going to come along and sing the things that I want to hear, but I can do it.' So I went upstairs, picked up my guitar and everything has been a blur since then.

I wanted to be raw and in your face. I didn't want anyone else in the band. I wanted it to be all contact. The way the New Romantics had come in and covered everything in stylish considerations, rather than what you are actually saying, appalled me. I wanted to get out there and take the world on. I felt like Sgt Fury grabbing the machine gun and running off after the Jerries – it sounds a silly metaphor, and I don't mean it in a nasty way – 'C'mon you bastards, there's one of us left!' The first album is that howl of rage. Those fucking Roxy Music fans, I knew we should have got rid of them when we got the chance!

I suppose I put my flag up the mast of trying to reclaim that territory. The miners' benefit period had meaning. That experience got us to come together and do Red Wedge, to make sure the anger of the miners' strike didn't dissipate.[18] That came from the Clash.

---

17. By 1981–82 the Jam were the biggest band in Britain. Paul Weller had really struck a chord with a series of massive hit singles that managed to combine Sixties nostalgia with a razor-sharp punk rock edge. Weller split the band at their peak in 1982, possibly the only pop star to have the nerve to quit at the top.

18. Red Wedge was a 1980s campaigning movement, featuring musicians who spoke out and performed in support of the British Labour Party.

The Clash were a mass of contradictions: they wanted to change the world but they didn't want to endgame with the political mainstream and I thought that was a great failing. They should have been fighting Thatcher, not dicking around in stadiums in America. I know the Labour Party were not particularly exciting, but at least they were a vehicle and an opportunity to get rid of Thatcher. The Clash didn't push it as far as it could go. Red Wedge was as far as it could go, beyond the ceiling of previous people trying to do this. Maybe someone could go beyond Red Wedge?

Mensi

We were always thought of as being a communist band but I was a union man. I don't think to this day that I'm any more political than when I started. I think the whole place moved to the right and I stood in the same place.

The real turning point was the miners' strike when I was in a pub with a TV screen and there was a massive cheer when Orgreave came on and the police charged the miners – the whole pub cheered apart from two or three people, and I thought, 'You cunts! You bastards!' People were sitting there who said they were non-political and they were cheering. I said, 'You're all just cunts. The miners are my mates.' That was the day I became very political – although I was always a union man.

I saw suffering and wrote songs about it. When I first went to London I used to walk round and there was shop after shop after shop. I thought, 'How do all these make money?' It was so different from Sunderland. A different world.

WHAT'S ALL THIS FOR?
A Few Reflections on Punk

Punk changed the world. There could be no looking back. The debate still rolls on. The energy has not dissipated.

Henry Rollins

I was lucky I ran into the really good stuff first: the Damned, the Adverts, Sham 69, Generation X, the Lurkers – what's the downside there? You would buy album after album, single after single, and you would keep hearing these great songs. We would go to the record store and these records would come in on import, and no one would buy them and they would get down-priced and shoved into these 'punk boxes'. Everything in there would be on eBay for $50 now. It was a music nirvana.

T. V. Smith

It was disappointing the Adverts fell apart, but it would have been more disappointing if we'd stayed together. It's been hard since, especially the first fifteen years. I don't like the music business and I don't like the mainstream. I've got freedom every day. They wreck everything, they ruin creativity in music – the mainstream is bad news whether it's music, marketing, food or sport. It's ugly and it's vicious. I hope they all go bust! Then we can start all over again. We all know the real scene is out there on the live circuit. You have to go and feel it. We're surrounded by industry crap, trying to create their bands, trying to create their market – the industry has got even stronger. It's trying to proclaim itself as the music when in fact it's only the business.

You never know what's going to come out of the bands. So much has come out of that scene: Amen, Green Day, Briefs, Foo Fighters – every one of them has a little bit of punk in them.

If you had to define punk rock now, nearly 30 years after the Roxy, in my heart I know it's the same feeling of that first Sex Pistols gig. You want to know if it's for real and different, and you want to know that the band is giving you everything. That's what I do when I play a gig.

Pauline Murray

When Penetration split, I was fed up with it all. We were selling out live gigs but we had no money. I thought, 'What am I doing?

I don't want a band. I can't do with that again.' I stayed with Rob Blamire and we wrote together. I got a solo deal. I liked the stuff Martin Hannett was producing at the time, the Jilted John stuff. So I approached Martin. Rob played the bass.[19] It was different from Penetration. It was on the cusp of change, that record, a point where punk went into the Eighties – it was all a flowering. ' nd then Duran Duran came in and that was that! You always get ones who get things changed, then the other ones just come in and get the benefit.

I think none of us wanted to live in London. We were travelling about that much, it didn't really matter. But people have really short memories, and because we were not in London and hanging out at gigs we got forgotten about really.

I packed it in in the Eighties, thinking, 'I don't want to do this any more.' It was rubbish. I tried to forget about it all, but I found that I couldn't. Someone would come and say, 'I saw you at such-and-such,' and eventually I was all right with it. For a while I didn't want to do anything. The amount of interest has been amazing, and proves that you must have touched some people emotionally at the time.

To me, now the actual business people seem to be more stars than the artists. A lot of the music business has used all the punk ideas to keep its own lifeblood going without any care for the people. They now pick random people off the street. We were not interested in money. We were against it all. We were doing this because we wanted to do this. The business and the music are two separate entities.

We were lucky, our generation: we saw the world as it was. It opened our eyes. We were singing about the need to escape, to be liberated from some kind of oppression. Being able to express ourselves as well, and take inspiration from whatever – it was all interconnected with what was going on at the time.

---

19. Her new group was the Invisible Girls. See chapter 9.

Rob Lloyd

You could argue with the Nightingales that we're now in our forties releasing seven-inch vinyl records so we are probably more punky than Green Day because we do what we wanna do, outside of the establishment. Not to sound like a pretentious wanker, but what I want to do is carry on making music. I did have a period of knocking it on the head for a few years: *You've had a few bites of the cherry, you've had fun, you've now grown up and realised that you're just throwing good money after bad. The world isn't interested in Robert Lloyd as an artist – get a life...* The thing is, I really think I've still got some stuff to offer – I enjoy making music. So be it if I'm going to be a useless Peter Pan kind of character and not settle down.

Music is quite a drug. Despite the Pistols saying they were allegedly into chaos, not music, and despite going through a whole period of punk trying to wind people up, at the end of the day it's the music that has always attracted me, since I was little boy listening to Lulu, through the Ramones, Faust, Amon Düül, all the way through. I'm not going to stop.

John Lydon

I don't see myself as a punk. I'm sorry I came before that logo.

You should make your own everything! You should not copy or take from others. You can be influenced by and then progress to your own level. Stop bleating amongst the flock. Punk? What's it all panned into? Nirvana and the likes of them. Their album *Nevermind...* – how damn lazy is that! They couldn't even finish the sentence but they still needed to rip two of the words off the Pistols album. Come on, that's really poor, and if you really check out Nirvana what are they? A dismal folk band with some squalling thrown in to bump up the revenue.

Modern bands – I think, 'Why bother?' Are you really that lazy that you have to go and nick off grandad? Hilarious. I can't really physically tell them apart musically. They all are very, very similar. American radio clearly makes that obvious. Blandness is in, I suppose. It always has been. I suppose I can say this: I've never been in a bland band.

Acid house, I love techno, all of that – and then it went clichéd. The rave thing was magnificent in the very early days before the wankers caught on, before the 16,000 dumb fucks from Tring with the stupid whistles and the glow sticks turned up. Rave was enjoying yourself – dance like a raging idiot if you want! Nobody's laughing any more – freedom! They would take very bad ecstasy. That's what rave did, it ruined great drugs.

There is a connection between acid house and punk. S'Express used to come round to my house in the early PiL days. I didn't know they were going to form a band. They made very good dance records, I was quite pleased and I was surprised that they said I influenced them. For the life of me I can't see how, because there is no similarity in sound and approach at all, but that's where they are getting it right. They didn't copy. They understood that influence didn't mean note-for-note duplication. Leftfield are mates of mine I've known a long time.

I don't hate the punk scene now. I don't have the time to do that. I think it's really pissy of them to be wallowing in someone else's dreams. It's so not impressive. Like in pop with Madonna and all them. I don't need to compete with that lot. I'm not into chart positions or in fact making anything that anybody would ever remotely possibly like. I'm quite chuffed when they say that they do, but I don't do it for that reason. I suppose that makes me a true artist actually because I stick to my guns – and they're big ones.

None of these latter-day saints in punk rock have come up with anything of their own, so there is nothing left. There you go, it's all right following in my footsteps but have some of your own, leave your mark in this world.

OUTRO

Fast forward to the future.

C'mon, let's keep going! Let's see where this is going to take us. 1984 is a good place to end a book. It's got the George Orwell ring to it. Originally I wanted to carry on till today, drawing lines between all the different eras of punk, but the word count would have been insane and no one could find time to read a book that huge.

But the punk story doesn't conveniently end in 1984. In fact, by then punk had become a 24/7 lifestyle, a true outsider counter-culture. I saw it in gigantic squats in Holland, all over the UK and in America, as I toured endlessly in my original band, the Membranes, and as a journalist for the now-defunct music paper *Sounds*. Punk was still proliferating and changing. I saw its DIY ideal affect acid house. In America I saw first-hand the hardcore scene, the arty punk of the post-Sonic Youth bands, and then the rise to the top of Nirvana. I saw Green Day, Rancid and the Offspring, taking punk to the mall rats and the stadiums with multi-million-selling albums.

I see punk rock everywhere in graphics and TV adverts, in the way people talk, in the shitty footballers' watered-down take on the very punk rock spikey hairstyles they and their beer-swilling mates would have sneered at a couple of years before.

Punk didn't fuck off in 1984. It remained so much part of the culture you couldn't even see it any more.

In the Eighties the idea continued to proliferate, like a virus infecting everyone it came into contact with. The UK may have been under the austere grip of Thatcher's Tory Reich crushing the miners' strike, but just under the surface the debate raged on. Many of the original punk bands were big stars, burned out, back in the day jobs, or dead. The punk generation was even more underground, ostracised by the straight world – but was still rallying to the cause.

The smaller second-wave bands soldiered on, and a couple of decades later have the total respect of a new generation of kids fed up with the mainstream music foisted upon them by Reality Pop TV UK. Worldwide, bands like GBH and the UK Subs are held up as legends whilst getting ignored by rock historians in ever-snooty Britannia. It took the death of Joe Strummer for the mainstream to finally recognise the brilliance of the Clash and Joe's iconic status. John Lydon still crops up to agitate, annoy and amuse, the Damned continue to sell out tours round the world, the Stranglers have made their best album for years, *Norfolk Coast*, and are still a shit-hot live band, and punk festivals like Wasted raise the battered standard of punk rock worldwide.

Punk affected the Smiths, Metallica, Guns'n'Roses, the Stone Roses. It affected comedy, journalism, art, politics – so many totally different people all relating back to that big bang in late '76, the moment that an insane amount of energy was released when the establishment wasn't looking, when the suffocating grip of the music industry was shaken off.

But it wasn't just big bands. Every time the UK Subs set up and play there is punk rock in the house. Charlie Harper is still the embodiment of someone who lives his life punk rock-style.

Years later, grown men and women get sentimental talking about punk in a way that no one ever will about any groups foisted on us by the music biz, and that's because it genuinely touched people in so many different ways.

Bands like Franz Ferdinand fit very firmly in the tradition of post-punk, with their fantastic take on the twisted world of Monochrome Set and the first Adam and the Ants album, only this time they have made it mainstream pop. Wire have been rediscovered, along with the Fall and the early Ants, by the likes of Blur and Elastica – who also borrowed J. J. Burnel's ever-iconic bass sound. Meanwhile Oasis borrowed the attitude.

Punk is everywhere. It's still the soundtrack to all the best pop music, it's the meter by which everything is measured.

It never dated, it never got old. It was the ultimate in rock-'n'roll. It made its rules as it went along. Music *by* the people *for* the people, an unholy racket, a reason to live. It had the best clothes, the best music, the best drugs. It managed to make the establishment shudder. It was a design for life. It provided the groundwork for the G8 riots and the firemen's strike. It marched against the Iraq war.

And it became a worldwide culture: I get CDs from bands in Nepal, emails from mohicans in China, a downloadable MP3 from Fiji. With Goldblade, I get to play gigs in stadiums in Russia, squats in Italy, garages in California, massive clubs in LA, outdoor festivals in the middle of the Czech Republic. I hang out with freaks on the street in Havana and Rome – it's everywhere you look.

But you know that. That's why you read this book!

Vive la révolution!

ACKNOWLEDGEMENTS

Well where do you start? Obviously I'd like to thank everyone I interviewed for their unnervingly accurate reminiscences and the fact that none of them have ever burned out but still retain a creative edge. I'd like to thank Simon Price, Michael Bracewell, UKTV and perfectsoundforever.com for their interviews when I ran out of time trying track people down. I'd like to thank all the photographers. I'd like to thank Oliver Craske for the insane editing job. I'd like to thank Jake Lingwood at Ebury for commissioning the book, and Claire Kingston for all the sorting out of loose ends. I'd also like to thank Maria.

Also thanks to all the bands who in 1977 soundtracked my adolescence, stuck out there in Blackpool – which had and still has a big punk scene. The records, the artwork, the rhetoric, the debate, the clothes, the hair – everything great and extreme in pop culture rolled into one unholy extreme. I'd like to thank you for buying the book and I'd like you to go and do something with the energy of punk rock!

John Robb

PICTURE CREDITS

LYRIC CREDITS

Edgar Broughton Band, 'Aphrodite' written by R. E. Broughton and published by Essex International/Mecolico Music/BIEM/NCP. Reproduced by kind permission.

'1977': Words & Music by Mick Jones & Joe Strummer. © Copyright 1977 Nineden Limited. Universal Music Publishing Limited. Used by permission of Music Sales Limited. All Rights Reserved. International Copyright Secured.

'White Riot': Words & Music by Joe Strummer, Mick Jones, Paul Simonon & Topper Headon. © Copyright 1977 Nineden Limited. Universal Music Publishing Limited. Used by permission of Music Sales Limited. All Rights Reserved. International Copyright Secured.

Lyrics from the Crass song 'Banned From The Roxy'. Words/lyrics by Crass, from the album *The Feeding Of The 5000* on Crass Records (p) 1978. Reproduced by kind permission.

INDEX

Page numbers in *italics* refer to illustrations

ABOUT PM PRESS

PM Press was founded at the end of 2007 by a small collection of folks with decades of publishing, media, and organizing experience. PM Press co-conspirators have published and distributed hundreds of books, pamphlets, CDs, and DVDs. Members of PM have founded enduring book fairs, spearheaded victorious tenant organizing campaigns, and worked closely with bookstores, academic conferences, and even rock bands to deliver political and challenging ideas to all walks of life. We're old enough to know what we're doing and young enough to know what's at stake.

We seek to create radical and stimulating fiction and non-fiction books, pamphlets, T-shirts, visual and audio materials to entertain, educate and inspire you. We aim to distribute these through every available channel with every available technology — whether that means you are seeing anarchist classics at our bookfair stalls; reading our latest vegan cookbook at the café; downloading geeky fiction e-books; or digging new music and timely videos from our website.

PM Press is always on the lookout for talented and skilled volunteers, artists, activists and writers to work with. If you have a great idea for a project or can contribute in some way, please get in touch.

PM Press
PO Box 23912
Oakland, CA 94623
www.pmpress.org

FRIENDS OF PM PRESS

These are indisputably momentous times—the financial system is melting down globally and the Empire is stumbling. Now more than ever there is a vital need for radical ideas.

In the four years since its founding—and on a mere shoestring—PM Press has risen to the formidable challenge of publishing and distributing knowledge and entertainment for the struggles ahead. With over 175 releases to date, we have published an impressive and stimulating array of literature, art, music, politics, and culture. Using every available medium, we've succeeded in connecting those hungry for ideas and information to those putting them into practice.

Friends of PM allows you to directly help impact, amplify, and revitalize the discourse and actions of radical writers, filmmakers, and artists. It provides us with a stable foundation from which we can build upon our early successes and provides a much-needed subsidy for the materials that can't necessarily pay their own way. You can help make that happen—and receive every new title automatically delivered to your door once a month—by joining as a Friend of PM Press. And, we'll throw in a free T-shirt when you sign up.

Here are your options:

- **$25 a month** Get all books and pamphlets plus 50% discount on all webstore purchases

- **$40 a month** Get all PM Press releases (including CDs and DVDs) plus 50% discount on all webstore purchases

- **$100 a month** Superstar—Everything plus PM merchandise, free downloads, and 50% discount on all webstore purchases

For those who can't afford $25 or more a month, we're introducing **Sustainer Rates** at $15, $10 and $5. Sustainers get a free PM Press T-shirt and a 50% discount on all purchases from our website.

Your Visa or Mastercard will be billed once a month, until you tell us to stop. Or until our efforts succeed in bringing the revolution around. Or the financial meltdown of Capital makes plastic redundant. Whichever comes first.

The Story of Crass
George Berger
ISBN: 978-1-60486-037-5
$20.00   304 pages

Crass was the anarcho-punk face of a
revolutionary movement founded by radical
thinkers and artists Penny Rimbaud, Gee
Vaucher and Steve Ignorant. When punk ruled
the waves, Crass waived the rules and took it
further, putting out their own records, films and
magazines and setting up a series of situationist pranks that were dutifully
covered by the world's press. Not just another iconoclastic band, Crass was
a musical, social and political phenomenon.

Commune dwellers who were rarely photographed and remained
contemptuous of conventional pop stardom, their members explored and
finally exhausted the possibilities of punk-led anarchy. They have at last
collaborated on telling the whole Crass story, giving access to many never-
before seen photos and interviews.

*"Lucid in recounting their dealings with freaks, coppers, and punks, the band's
voices predominate, and that's for the best."*
— The Guardian UK

*"Thoroughly researched… chockful of fascinating revelations… it is,
surprisingly, the first real history of the pioneers of anarcho-punk."*
— Classic Rock

*"They (Crass) sowed the ground for the return of serious anarchism in the early
eighties."*
— Jon Savage, England's Dreaming

Spray Paint the Walls:
The Story of Black Flag

Stevie Chick

ISBN: 978-1-60486-418-2
$19.95   432 Pages

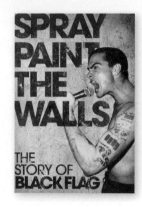

Black Flag were the pioneers of American Hardcore, and this is their blood-spattered story. Formed in Hermosa Beach, California in 1978, for eight brutal years they made and played brilliant, ugly, no-holds-barred music on a self-appointed touring circuit of America's clubs, squats and community halls. They fought with everybody: the police, the record industry and even their own fans. They toured overseas on pennies a day and did it in beat-up trucks and vans.

Spray Paint The Walls tells Black Flag's story from the inside, drawing on exclusive interviews with the group's members, their contemporaries, and the bands they inspired. It's the story of Henry Rollins, and his journey from fan to iconic frontman. And it's the story of Greg Ginn, who turned his electronics company into one of the world's most influential independent record labels while leading Black Flag from punk's three-chord frenzy into heavy metal and free-jazz. Featuring over 30 photos of the band from Glen E. Friedman, Edward Colver, and others.

"Neither Greg Ginn nor Henry Rollins sat for interviews but their voices are included from earlier interviews, and more importantly Chuck Dukowski spoke to Chick—a first I believe. The story, laid out from the band's earliest practices in 1976 to its end ten years later, makes a far more dramatic book than the usual shelf-fillers with their stretch to make the empty stories of various chart-toppers sound exciting and crucial and against the odds."
— Joe Carducci, formerly of SST Records

"Here is an exhaustive prequel to, followed by a more balanced re-telling of, Rollins' Get in the Van *journal, chronicling Flag's emergence in suburban Hermosa Beach, far from the trendy Hollywood scene (Germs, X, etc.) and how their ultra-harsh, hi-speed riffage sparked moshpit violence—initially fun, but soon aggravated by jocks and riot police. Greg Ginn, their aloof guitarist/slave-driver/ideologue dominates in absentia. Gradually, he fires everyone but Rollins, yet, his pan-American shoestring SST empire is relentlessly inspirational. A gory, gobsmacking read."*
— Andrew Perry, *MOJO*

Sober Living for the Revolution: Hardcore Punk, Straight Edge And Radical Politics

Edited by Gabriel Kuhn

ISBN: 978-1-60486-051-1
$22.95 304 pages

Straight edge has persisted as a drug-free, hardcore punk subculture for 25 years. Its political legacy, however, remains ambiguous—often associated with self-righteous macho posturing and conservative puritanism. While certain elements of straight edge culture feed into such perception, the movement's political history is far more complex. Since straight edge's origins in Washington, D.C. in the early 1980s, it has been linked to radical thought and action by countless individuals, bands, and entire scenes worldwide. *Sober Living for the Revolution* traces this history.

It includes contributions—in the form of in-depth interviews, essays, and manifestos—by numerous artists and activists connected to straight edge, from Ian MacKaye (Minor Threat/Fugazi) and Mark Andersen (Dance of Days/Positive Force DC) to Dennis Lyxzén (Refused/The (International) Noise Conspiracy) and Andy Hurley (Racetraitor/Fall Out Boy), from bands such as ManLiftingBanner and Point of No Return to feminist and queer initiatives, from radical collectives like CrimethInc. and Alpine Anarchist Productions to the Emancypunx project and many others dedicated as much to sober living as to the fight for a better world.

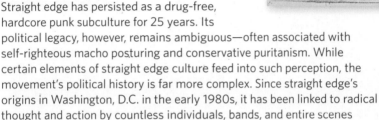

"Perhaps the greatest reason I am still committed to sXe is an unfailing belief that sXe is more than music, that it can be a force of change. I believe in the power of sXe as a bridge to social change, as an opportunity to create a more just and sustainable world."
—Ross Haenfler, Professor of Sociology at the University of Mississippi, author of *Straight Edge: Clean-Living Youth, Hardcore Punk, And Social Change*

"An 'ecstatic sobriety' which combats the dreariness of one and the bleariness of the other—false pleasure and false discretion alike—is analogous to the anarchism that confronts both the false freedom offered by capitalism and the false community offered by communism."
—CrimethInc. Ex-Workers' Collective

The Primal Screamer
Nick Blinko

ISBN: 978-1-60486-331-4
$14.95   128 pages

A Gothic Horror novel about severe mental distress and punk rock. The novel is written in the form of a diary kept by a psychiatrist, Dr. Rodney H. Dweller, concerning his patient, Nathaniel Snoxell, brought to him in 1979 because of several attempted suicides. Snoxell gets involved in the nascent UK anarcho-punk scene, recording EPs and playing gigs in squatted Anarchy Centers. In 1985, the good doctor himself "goes insane" and disappears.

This semi-autobiographical novel from Rudimentary Peni singer, guitarist, lyricist, and illustrator Nick Blinko, plunges into the worlds of madness, suicide, and anarchist punk. Lovecraft meets Crass in the squats and psychiatric institutions of early '80s England. This new edition collects Blinko's long sought after artwork from the three previous incarnations.

"Dense, haunted, shot through with black humour."
— *Raw Vision*

"Nick Blinko is a madman. That's not intended as pejorative opinion but rather a statement of plain fact."
— *Maximum RocknRoll*

"The insights it offers into the punk scene and into the unsettling landscapes of its author's mind are fascinating. The whole book has a distinct sense of coming from a mind unlike most we are used to."
— *The Big Issue*

"An intensely written and authentically Gothic look at the life of a man suffering extreme mental distress."
— *Detour*

"Fascinating and compelling."
— *Kerrang*